Resurrection
and the
Message of Easter

Xavier Léon-Dufour

Resurrection
and the
Message of Easter

translated by R. N. Wilson

HOLT, RINEHART AND WINSTON
New York

Library of Congress Cataloging in Publication Data
Léon-Dufour, Xavier.
Resurrection and the message of Easter.
Translation of Résurrection de Jésus et message pascal.
Includes bibliographical references.
1. Jesus Christ—Resurrection. I. Title.
BT481.L4513   232.9'7   73-16861
ISBN 0-03-012456-5

First published in the United States in 1975.

Printed in the United States of America

CONTENTS

Stage Three: The Easter Message according to the Evangelists

Final Stage: Hermeneutics

Preface

If Christ has not been raised, then our preaching is in vain
and your faith is in vain.

St Paul to the Corinthians

Did Jesus rise or not? This seems to be the ultimate question. It
challenges the believer to justify his faith. To speak of the resurrection of Jesus is to affirm that death has been conquered for one
man at least: and to say that this means that he lives for ever is
boldly to locate oneself at the end of time. It is a challenge to the
unbeliever to revise his idea of life: for if one man is alive for ever
after his death, why should the same not be so for all men at the
end of time? Why should there not be, after death, an existence
called heaven?

In this work, it is not my intention to reply to this series of urgent
questions. Let me say straight away that only faith can give an
adequate reply.

But I should like to clarify the terms in which the question is
posed. For faith to reply to the question of fact (did he or did he not
rise?), you have to know what you are talking about, and therefore
what language is being used used (what is the meaning of the
expression 'risen'?). My ambition, indeed, is to face up to the problem of the language in which, at the present day, we may express
and pass on the message of Easter, the Good News, that is, the event
of the resurrection and its significance.

I have come to face the problem of language at the conclusion of a
gradual evolution; and many readers, whatever stages they have
passed through or have still to face, will find that I am about to
outline a journey which is familiar to them.

Born in the Christian tradition, my faith fed by the traditional
imagery, I long confused these legendary representations with the

gospel narratives of the appearances of the risen Christ. Bowling over the astounded guards with his banner, the reanimated corpse of Jesus came alive out of his tomb. Possessing subtle qualities, it could appear and disappear at will, and even pass through closed doors.... Nothing is impossible to God!

When I began to study theology—thirty years ago—I was first of all filled with admiration for the dogmatic treasures to be found in the heritage of the church fathers, and then, under the guidance of Père de Grandmaison, compared the results of comparative religion with the narratives of the resurrection. The latter, I felt, were undoubtedly original. Then, inspired by Père Lagrange, Alfred Loisy and Maurice Goguel, I read the texts themselves with a critical eye. I then realized that it was impossible to find in them a biography of the risen Jesus, and that the evangelists were struggling to say in the form of narratives what in reality remains inexpressible. Fortunately for my life as a churchman, in 1943, two years later, Pius XII officially authorized exegetes to apply the method of 'form criticism' to the texts. The fact that at the present day there are still many who experience difficulty in the gospel narratives is largely due to the fact that they have not reached the stage of form criticism. Throughout this work, I shall refer to it constantly.

At the same time, but at another level, I ask a philosophical question. Following Edouard Le Roy, I came to resist the idea of a body which had been withdrawn from the world of phenomena. How could one suppose that Jesus's remains had been 'volatilized'? How could one imagine the existence of the reanimated corpse which like a stage magician suddenly appears within the framework of other phenomena, although it does not belong to them? A provisional reply calmed my unease: our universe must not be conceived of as a closed, predetermined world, impervious to any but a material and local presence.

Thereafter, however, the problem came to appear even more complex. Certain things became clear to me which called into question convictions which hitherto had been based on a naive faith in the resurrection. They led me to modify my understanding of the term 'resurrection', and, which may seem a paradox to some, to discover the broader and deeper meaning which our fathers in the faith gave to the term. The classical antithesis between heaven and earth, it seemed to me, depended upon a language derived from a certain cosmology: were there in fact two distinct worlds, or is there only a single reality, the universe in which we live, which is unceasingly being transformed and which one day will be fully transfigured? This is not to deny heaven, it is to ask questions about the reality in which we live. Another difficulty was that a dualist anthropology—man is composed of a soul and a body—is not biblical, but derives from one element of Hellenistic culture. Is it necessary, on this basis, to think of death as the 'separation of the soul from the body', so that the immortal soul crosses the abyss? In this case, death seems to be a 'joke' which one tries to make serious by means of the sanction of the after-life. But how consistent is this 'after-life' or these 'sanctions'? Where is the seriousness with which the supreme act of life, death itself, should be considered at the present day?

In this way, I gradually came to question the language itself. Is it possible, from then on, to maintain that the Easter message consists of repeating without variation that Christ is risen? Does not this language imply a whole series of images and representations which hold us back in a cultural world which is no longer our own?

When I began to plan this work, I affirmed that in expressing the event and the Easter message, our own language is conditioned by a particular culture, and that we have often twisted the words of the bible or eliminated scriptural expressions and images at the expense of what seemed to us to be easier to assimilate and more in conformity with our mode of thought. I also noticed that the first Christians not only used the language of 'resurrection' but also the language of 'exaltation', and that this went back to two different mental structures: the one of before and after, which enabled them to say that the resurrection of Jesus came 'after' his death; and that of height and depth, which enabled them to express the ultimate 'heavenly' glory into which Jesus entered.

If this is so, then two questions arise. Can the Easter message be uttered in any other language than that of 'resurrection'? Secondly, what would be the function of the language of 'resurrection' in working out a new way of expressing the Easter message?

This modest essay has been written slowly in the midst of many concerns, and no doubt it still requires improvement. But it is an attempt to present the central mystery of the Christian faith in a language which seeks to remain within the authentic tradition, but also to be intelligible to our contemporaries. The work seeks to confirm the believer in his faith and to face the unbeliever dormant in all of us with a question. By way of the critical elements which it is bound to contain, it also seeks to bring about a purer faith, to enable the gospel text to be read with new eyes, and to guide towards a better understanding of the Easter message.

Lyon-Fourvière, Easter 1971

Since the first impression rapidly went out of print, this book seems to have fulfilled a real need. In permitting a new impression, I have been glad to take into account a number of suggestions, particularly from Edouard Bousset, whom I take this opportunity to thank; they have enabled me to make my statements more exact in a number of places.

Lyon, 21 January 1972

Introduction

The creed contains only a scanty mention of the central event of Christian faith: 'For our sake, too, under Pontius Pilate, he was crucified, suffered death and was buried. The third day he rose from the dead, as the scriptures had foretold. He ascended to heaven, where he is seated at the right hand of the Father.' To fill it out, the believer will often turn to some life of Jesus, which is usually based on the narrative of Luke, particularly as he is the only writer to have produced two volumes, the Gospel and the Acts of the Apostles—the story of Jesus and that of the birth of the church.

A Biography of the Risen Christ?

Here is the course of events as we find it there. After Jesus had died on the cross, his body was placed in the tomb of Joseph of Arimathea, in a particular place which the holy women carefully noted. The day after the sabbath they went to the sepulchre, but did not find Jesus's body there. But two mysterious beings told them not to seek him who was living amongst the dead. The women told the apostles, who remained sceptical; but Peter went to confirm with his own eyes that the tomb was empty. Then Jesus appeared to the disciples who were going to Emmaus, and then to the apostles gathered together. He conquered their doubts by showing his hands and feet, even eating in their sight; and above all he explained to them in the light of God's plan how all this could have come about, and entrusted to them the mission of preaching the gospel to the nations. Forty days later, the apostles saw Jesus ascending to heaven, and they then remained in Jerusalem, where they received the Spirit on the day of Pentecost. They were thereby transformed into 'witnesses of the resurrection'. These witnesses, the number of whom was limited to twelve, formed the link between the earthly life of Jesus and the church. Finally, a last appearance by the risen Christ was vouchsafed to Saul, the persecutor. With the exception of the appearance to Stephen as he is dying, no other is narrated; for the era of Jesus has been succeeded by that of the church, that of the Spirit.

Reduced to its elementary structure, the text presents a narrative of Jesus after his death as a sequence of events: the discovery of the empty tomb, various appearances, the ascension, Pentecost, and, somewhat out of turn, the appearance to Paul. The life of Jesus of Nazareth is succeeded by the biography of the risen Christ portrayed in outline.

Do the gospels give grounds for the reconstruction of such a biography? It is not our purpose to indulge in the malicious pleasure of destroying the evidence, but to enable the reader to locate the statements of faith more exactly within the truth.

Every biography assumes that coordinates of place and time have been established at least in outline, for without them the narrative has no firm basis. Now an attentive reading of the text defies us to harmonize the various narratives in time or space.

If we state that the appearances took place at Jerusalem (Luke and John) and thereafter in Galilee (Matthew and John), and then in Jerusalem again (Acts) how can one explain first of all that the arrangement was made with the disciples that they should go to Galilee to see the risen Christ (Matthew 28:7; Mark 16:7), and secondly, that the same risen Christ instructed his disciples to remain in Jerusalem until they should have received the gift of the Holy Spirit (Luke 24:49)? Must we not give up the attempt to attribute any topographical value to these statements?

If we try to fix a time of the various appearances, there is a conflict between Luke and John, and indeed within Luke himself. On the one hand, Luke tells us that the time allotted to the appearances lasted many days and even, more precisely, forty days (Acts 1:3); on the other hand, he seems to place the ascension on Easter day itself (Luke 24:51). The Holy Spirit is proclaimed as a gift to come (Luke 24:49; Acts 1:4), whereas it is given (effectively) by Jesus on Easter day itself (John 20:22). How can we give due weight to all these various affirmations, except by assuming that the various gospel texts are the result of literary constructions? Thus, if the gospel narratives cannot be taken as a 'biography of the risen Christ', how should they be read?

The Gospel Narratives and the New Testament

The question becomes more complicated because it is difficult to harmonize the statements of the gospels with those of other New Testament writings. Certainly, the New Testament is in agreement that there were appearances of the risen Christ; but the list given in the First Epistle to the Corinthians (15:3-8) does not really agree with the gospel narratives: there is certainly a mention of an appearance to Cephas, that is to Peter (cf. Luke 24:34), but can the appearance to the Twelve be identified with those to the Eleven, with their companions (Luke 24: 33, 36), or without Thomas (John 20:24) or to the Seven (John 21:2)? Finally, there is no mention in the gospels of an appearance to James, nor to the 'apostles', nor to the five hundred.

Another difficult point is that the narrative of the discovery of the empty tomb, which plays so important a part in the gospels, is ignored by the rest of the New Testament. If we rightly refuse to regard the evangelists as having invented the fact, how can we explain its omission on the part of the other writers?

The reader is constantly surprised. He notices not only that Paul speaks differently from Luke when he alludes to the appearance on the Damascus road, but also that Luke himself gives three narratives of the same fact which it is difficult to harmonize.

Finally, there is some question about the portrait of the risen Christ himself. Seeing the risen Christ move about, eat, and speak with the disciples, one spontaneously comes to think of him as a reanimated body, who, restored to life, like Lazarus, can walk about amongst us. Of course by knowledge acquired from elsewhere, one then comes to recognize that the risen Christ has a particular function in relation to the church; but there remains a tendency not to recognize that the resurrection of Jesus is not simply an astonishing fact but a mystery.

For according to the New Testament the risen Jesus does not die any more. He lives for ever, and has entered the glory of the Father; he is lifted up to heaven; he is the Lord of history, present to all men and to all ages. How is this conviction expressed in the texts? The Epistles of Paul talk of the last Adam, of him who gives life to men, of the head given to the body which is the church; but these titles are not a 'portrait'. The gospels, on the other hand, give us such a portrait. But the modern reader has some difficulty in seeing it aright. With their usual calmness, the gospel writers juxtaposed two realities, one of this earth and the other coming from heaven. The disciples are locked in the upper room, and the risen Christ comes and appears in the midst of them. While they say nothing about how the appearance took place, the modern reader hastens to supply imaginary details and builds up a whole scene: the doors are closed, *therefore* Christ passed through the closed doors; Christ comes and stands in the midst of them, *therefore* he appeared suddenly. To do this is to make the risen Christ a kind of Houdini. Whereas a child does not assume that what he has been told is the whole fact, but seizes the meaning behind the narrative, modern man is repelled by the marvellous element which he himself has read into the narrative and which tends to dominate his imagination, in such a way as to lose its value as a sign of the mystery. The language of the gospels is valid, but it must be criticized if we are to grasp precisely what it means.

The Problem of Language

We now have the question which contemporary man must face: that of language. It is necessary to 'understand' what a particular language, that of the gospels or that of early Christian faith, actually means. The reader is then faced with the demands of modern critics, for whom the difficulties mentioned above are no more than the introduction to the real problem. One should ask not, 'Was Christ resurrected?' but, 'What does the term "resurrected" mean?' These are the problems with which two recent discussions of the meaning of the resurrection of Jesus have attempted to deal: those of Rudolph Bultmann and Willi Marxsen. We hope by summarizing them to show the way to a properly considered reading of the New Testament statements.

Since 1941, Bultmann has posed the radical question in this form: the resurrection 'expresses the meaning of the cross'.[1] The only historical event with which we can have contact is the death of Jesus on the cross, which marks the final point of his earthly existence. The resurrection is not a 'miraculous proof', it is itself the object of faith. To believe in the resurrection is to admit that the cross is a saving event for me. When I hear the preaching of the apostolic kerygma which is proclaimed to me at the present day, I attain to that faith; and faith according to that Word is in fact the Christian faith. Thus the resurrection is not a fact which I can apprehend in itself; it is accessible to me only through the Easter faith of the witnesses. They are not the guarantors of the fact of the resurrection, but the initiators of the Easter faith which is characteristic of a Christian.

Of course Bultmann does not identify the resurrection with a kind of recollection, as though Jesus were present amongst believers in the way that the spirit of Beethoven is present amongst those who listen to the Fifth Symphony. Bultmann simply refuses to identify the resurrection with the return of a dead man to the life of this world, for according to his terminology this would make it a mythical event. In this case, what is it? Let him speak for himself:

'It is often said, most of the time in a criticism, that according to my interpretation of the kerygma Jesus had risen in the kerygma (*dass ... Jesus ins Kerygma auferstanden sei*). I accept this proposition. It is entirely correct, assuming that it is properly understood. It presupposes that the kerygma itself is an eschatological event, and it expresses the fact that Jesus is really present in the kerygma (*im Kerygma*), that it is *his* word which involves the hearer in the kerygma. If that is the case, then all speculations concerning the modes of being of the risen Jesus, all the narratives of the empty tomb and all the Easter legends, whatever elements of historical facts they may contain, and as true as they may be in their symbolic form, are of no consequence. To believe in the Christ present in the (*im*) kerygma is the meaning of the Easter faith.'[2]

In order to understand such declarations (which of course are somewhat simplified here) we must recall some of Bultmann's presuppositions. The first concerns the relationship between nature and the supernatural: 'Nature' is a closed entity studied by science; the divine has nothing to do with the history of this world. Thus there is no longer any question of examining the relationship between the subject of theology and the natural sciences; from now on all language which represents the divine reality in human terms must be 'demythologized'.

The second presupposition concerns the relationship between reason and faith. For Bultmann, true understanding takes place only within existential life. I cannot hear the word of God except through my own personal decision with regard to it.

Finally, the third presupposition is an exegetical one. The narratives of the empty tomb or of the appearances are of late composition and were unknown to Paul: they emphasize the corporeality of the risen Christ. 'There is however one passage where St Paul tries to prove the miracle of the resurrection by adducing a list of eye witnesses.' But by this line of argument, attempting to make the resurrection credible as an objective historical fact, Paul contradicts himself, because of the anti-gnostic polemic into which he allows himself to fall.

It would be pointless to disregard Bultmann's contribution to the understanding of our subject. He is wholly right, by contrast with every kind of positivism, when he emphasizes the contemporary significance of the resurrection: it is not one fact amongst many, but an event which concerns me. Bultmann's reaction is valid against the decadence of a Protestant theology which treated the resurrection of Jesus as an appendix to the justifying death of Jesus Christ;[3] and it may also help Catholics to react against an outmoded apologetic. The resurrection is not a simple event of the past. Nor is it a 'proof' of faith. Finally, it is not one event like any other; it is the eschatological fact above all others.

Nevertheless, it is difficult for us to subscribe to Bultmann's account of it. First of all, from the exegetical point of view, the interpretation which he proposes of I Cor 15 is subordinated to his conception of revelation and 'myth'. As we shall show below, Paul was not thinking here in the same way as Bultmann. Secondly, Bultmann misunderstands what Paul says: for Paul, according to G. Bornkamm, the resurrection is 'an event *in* this time and this world, and yet at the same time an event which puts an end and a limit to this time and this world'.[4] Finally, while the resurrection must always be linked to the present day 'charisma', it must also be examined as an 'event', something which Bultmann refuses *a priori*, because of his conception of the relationship between reason and faith.

Willi Marxsen considered that he was going further than Bultmann, in his attempt to consider the event itself.[5] The formula 'Jesus is risen' is an interpretative statement (*Interpretament*) which expresses this historical reality. By interpreting this fact with the aid of the term 'resurrection', it gives a solution to the problem raised, but not the only possible solution. The formula came to be established not by chance, but because of its privileged closeness to the principal affirmation of faith: the crucified Jesus is alive. He says:

'Thus I think that in our tradition at least one cannot radically reject this way of proclaiming one's faith. But one must know what it is that one is thereby confessing and what one is not confessing. In this way one confesses that in attaining to faith one has experienced that Jesus is alive and at work; one confesses that his past is present. ... One is not thereby confessing a representation which is isolated from this confession, for it is only in faith that one can speak exactly in theological terms of the resurrection of Jesus, just as one can call Jesus Lord only in the Holy Spirit.'[6]

Thus Marxsen is attempting to find an equivalent to this *interpretative statement*. He proposes a formula: *Die Sache Jesu geht weiter*, which may be translated, 'the reality of Jesus continues'. The past is not a true past, and we continue to be challenged by Jesus. '*He* comes again today.' This 'he' is Jesus of Nazareth, though his relationship to him who is called 'the risen Christ' is not made clear.

It is not possible for us to develop here a long criticism of this enterprise. Let us note only that the exegetical basis is very narrow. Marxsen distinguishes between 'to see Jesus' (an expression which only Paul is said to have used) and 'to see the risen Christ' (which is a later interpretative statement). Moreover, he treats the narratives of the appearances as equivalent to a missionary command, refusing to admit the aspect of recognition, which as we shall see is fundamental. In consequence, although Marxsen sometimes uses the term 'encounter', we may ask whether he does not assimilate the experience (*Widerfahrnis*) to something anonymous, whereas the personal aspect of 'encounter' is essential. Finally, we are not in agreement with his presuppositions concerning the relationship between reason and faith. In our view, he radically separates these two activities, making faith consist of a pure gamble.[7] But this criticism is a denominational one.

No doubt Marxsen was right to insist on the fact that the formula 'Jesus is risen' is an interpretative statement, but he had no good grounds for failing to recognize its privileged character; if one does not take this into account in some way, one is at the mercy of successive and arbitrary interpretations.

These brief indications lead us to the view that Bultmann and Marxsen do not go far enough in their linguistic criticism. One, too rapidly abandoning the event to which the language refers, reduces it to what takes place within my present existential life, whereas the language itself imposes as the condition which makes it possible something which is its source, an 'event' which has happened, and which is not to be confused with the event which today happens to me. Marxsen wishes to go back to the primary event, but has not recognized the necessary relationship uniting language and event, and therefore does not preserve the unique role of the original language. Now we do not interpret the past event, but the language in which the event from the past is 'presented' to us. Hermeneutics is concerned only indirectly with the fact, but directly with the language in which it is communicated.

Our Method

How are we to proceed? By contrast with certain earlier works which have been concerned above all to establish what is 'historical'[8] in the strict sense, we hold that we must begin by paying attention to the texts. Faith in the God who has raised his Son from the dead is handed down in a variety of languages; and to this affirmation we shall add a study of the mutual relationship between these languages.

We have to choose between various courses. Our enquiry will always be concerned with the texts, but it may begin by considering them in their final state, or in their genesis. A structuralist analysis would concern itself solely with the text as it is at the present day, and would mistrust all history of tradition. On the other hand, an analysis which did not go on to examine the various texts as we possess them and would rest content with establishing their sources would be unhelpful, and would not enable us to get anything from reading the gospel texts. The order we have chosen is that which is the most usual in present-day exegetical criticism, and consists of first outlining the evolution of the language which is used to speak of the Easter event. This course assumes that the author has first studied the texts themselves; but this critical work, which must obviously be carried out, need not here be imposed upon the reader, whose main purpose is to profit from the theological exegesis which follows from this critical work.

Thus we shall begin by presenting the types of language and the literary categories used in the New Testament. This is an arduous task, for it must comprehend a number of texts which will be seen to be older than the gospels, and anyone who undertakes this study may find his habits of thought disturbed and feel that it is sapping his confidence in his ordinary reading of the texts. Here we must reassure the reader and advise him, if he feels discouraged, to turn immediately to the third stage, the account of the point of view of the different evangelists. We hope that this may encourage him to return to the two previous stages.

Some readers will perhaps be surprised that we do not straight away deal with the problem of the historicity of the resurrection. For them, the essential thing is to know what exactly happened. Did Jesus really rise? What did the appearances consist of? Was the tomb of Jesus really found empty on Easter morning? However important it may be, the reply to these questions cannot be given until after an exhaustive study of the narratives; and above all it must be asked in its right place, which is neither the first place nor the last, but in between: it is only one element in the search for the meaning. That is why we ask the reader to restrain his desire to reach the hard facts, the better to concentrate his attention on the problem of language.

In the course of the first stage, we shall try to work out which are the various categories of thought underlying the formulas of the Easter proclamation and to outline the developments which took place on the basis of each of these categories.

In the second stage, we shall examine the literary category of the narratives of the Easter event, and will go back to the origin of the traditions which underline them. We shall not raise here the question of the historicity of these traditions, but only their nature.

The third stage takes us into the midst of the actual texts of the gospels, showing us their various different perspectives. By this time we are no longer concerned simply with 'categories' stating the fact of the resurrection, but with points of view about the 'Easter message' itself.

The final stage will touch on the problem of hermeneutics and communication. Here we shall examine the relationship between faith and historical knowledge. Here too, in the total context of our search for meaning and interpretation, we shall deal with the problem of historicity. Finally, in order to assist the reader to transpose the message into a language which our contemporaries can understand, we shall attempt to give in an appendix a number of models of a way of speaking of the resurrection on the basis of the gospel narratives.

Let us make one final thing clear. We would not wish to give the impression that we are approaching the texts without any pre-supposition, 'objectively'. We recognize that there exists a circle linking the texts and the interpreter. I do not approach the texts without any prior understanding; before approaching it, I possess a certain idea of man, of death, of resurrection. And I tend to make the texts say what I have in my mind. Rather than recalling here the general principles of hermeneutics,[9] we shall set out as guidelines to our account the assumptions which will make clear the mental steps which the author or a possible reader may be taking.[10]

STAGE ONE

The Affirmations of the Earliest Faith

The gospel narratives are neither the only nor the first expression of the Easter mystery. Before they were put in writing, a very varied literature flourished for several decades.[1] We have some evidence of this: the Epistles of Paul, and also short and even older texts which were integrated into the various New Testament writings and have come down to us in this way. These pre-gospel testimonies show us a more immediate and almost original expression of Christian experience. In fact, whereas the gospel narratives were edited by secondary narrators (a statement which is also true of the Fourth Gospel, even if its literary origin goes back to John the Apostle), Paul is the only witness who, having been vouchsafed a resurrection appearance, spoke of it himself. The other witness speaking in the brief texts which we have mentioned is the primitive church, carrying the message of a common faith in the Easter mystery. That is why, before we described the Easter message from the point of view and according to the narrative of the gospel writers, we wish as the first stage in this work to study the way in which the Easter experience was first affirmed in sober terms.

The study of the language of Paul (chapter 3) covers a well-defined area: the letters of Paul. By contrast, our enquiry into the formulas of the primitive church (chapters 1-2) requires us first to make clear which texts contain them. One might be inclined to begin by the speeches which Luke recounts in the Acts of the Apostles, as if they reproduced in the form of a summary all the early preaching of the apostles. But this course, though many authors follow it,[2] seems uncertain. In fact, in these speeches[3], which have been thoroughly re-written and worked over by Luke, it is extremely difficult to distinguish what is primitive and what is Lucan.[4] In view of this, it is best to begin by drawing on more obvious texts. This does not mean that we have no confidence in

Luke, for his rigorousness with regard to information and his respect for his sources are well known. It is merely a matter of avoiding confusion. Moreover, in the light of formulas which critics regard as certainly primitive, it will be possible for us to give due recognition to these more complex documents.

The reader will no doubt be glad to learn the criteria which make it possible to trace within a text the presence of a stereotyped formula.[5] These principles are:

1. The formula is introduced by words such as 'hand on', 'believe', 'confess'.[6]

2. The assertion of the formula has disturbed the surrounding context, leaving a scar in the text as we possess it.[7]

3. The grammar is faulty as a result.[8]

4. The language and terminology differ from the usage of the author who quotes the passage.[9]

5. The formula occurs several times with slight modifications.[10]

6. The construction of the formula is simple, rhythmical, majestic, stanzaic even, and usually occurs without any attempt to justify it.[11]

7. Finally, the formulas show a preference for participles and relative propositions.[12]

Thus there are good reasons why critics regard themselves as entitled to treat such passages as primitive, and anterior to the writer who integrates them into his composition.

It is important not to misunderstand the purpose of this enquiry. It is not our intention to retrace the history of the formulation of faith in the resurrection, as if, starting with a formula regarded as older, one could eventually establish the exact genealogy of the texts which have come down to us. The point at which this can be done with any precision does not seem to have been reached.[13] But we shall try to distinguish the patterns of thought which underlie and condition the language of faith. How could the disciples have come to express their conviction that Jesus—he whose death they had come to know—was alive? What is the meaning of the words they used to express their experience? This is what we seek to discover in this first stage.

CHAPTER ONE

God raised Jesus from the Dead

During the forty or so years between the death of Jesus and the composition of the gospels, the infant church witnessed the circulation of numerous traditions among the faithful; above all the church created formulas in which the faith of the community was given concrete shape.[1] In working out these formulas, she reacted to some vital needs. Thus the essence of the faith was condensed, partly for the instruction of new converts,[2] partly to maintain authentic belief in time of persecution,[3] and partly to proclaim in the liturgy the unity of the participants. To that end the community used two different modes of language, depending on whether it was concerned with confessions of faith or with hymns. The former tend to assert the mere fact of the resurrection of Christ (chapter 1), while the latter mainly proclaimed the Lord's exaltation.[4]

These credal formulas had as their first object the assertion of Jesus as Messiah, and only secondly as Lord or Son of God.[5] They were rarely concerned with the one God,[6] for that was taken for granted by Jews as well as Christians. The process of formulation soon came to concentrate on the chief event of the life of Jesus, his resurrection from the dead.

The resurrection of Jesus was recalled in two different ways, one asserting the fact in a quite straightforward way, the other relating it to the death of Jesus, particularly in its redemptive significance. There is a further difference. Attention is sometimes directed towards God as the author of the resurrection, and sometimes towards the risen Christ. As a convenient way of presenting the New Testament data, we shall work backwards in time, starting with the more developed formulas and concluding with the most simple.

Numerous problems will be raised. From the point of view of literary history, is it possible to determine the original from which the other formulas probably derive? Theologically speaking, does the diversity in the formulas reflect an evolution in christology? With regard to their interpretation, what gives the formulas their unity and what is their validity when actually interpreted? Let us leave this last question for a later chapter, and try now to state precisely the meaning of these assertions of faith, to find out how they began, and to evaluate their significance.

A.   THE CREDAL FORMULAS

Amongst the credal formulas which simply state the fact of the resurrection, we can distinguish between those in which God is the active subject of the assertion, and those which, in their developed form, see Christ as the passive subject of the action. Let us begin with the latter.

I   *Christ has risen*

When the disciples from Emmaus rejoined the Eleven in Jerusalem and told them the news of their meeting with Christ, the reply they received was, 'The Lord has risen indeed, and has appeared to Simon' (Luke 24:34). In all likelihood, this is a traditional formula inserted by Luke at this point.[7] Similarly, Paul in his first letter to the Corinthians quotes a formula the character of which is clearly derived from liturgy and tradition.[8]

I delivered to you as of first importance what I also received,
That Christ died—for our sins—in accordance with the scriptures,
    that he was buried.
That he was raised—on the third day—in accordance with the
                                            scriptures,
    and that he appeared to Cephas (I Cor 15:3-5)

The rhythm of the formula can be seen at once: 3 + 1, 3 + 1. That rhythm is absent from what follows and hence is characteristic of the verses quoted. That they are ancient is guaranteed by the actual date of the letter (ca. 55/56), by the allusion to the former visit paid by the apostle to Corinth (ca. 51), and lastly by the way Paul introduces these words in the statement that he himself had received this as tradition. Two hypotheses are put forward concerning the date of this tradition: if the text is Greek in origin, it goes back to the period of his stay at Antioch (ca. 42), whereas if the formula is of Palestinian origin, it can be dated from the time of his conversion in Damascus (ca. 35).

Paul is not dealing with a controversial subject here, as he is in the rest of this epistle, which brings together his remarks 'concerning ...' (7:1; 8:1; 12:1) various topics. Here he reminds his brethren in the faith of the Good News in which they have believed and by which they will be saved, the Word which Paul had himself received and handed on in his turn as the living core of the faith (cf. 15:11). It is no concern of Paul's to prove that Jesus has risen,[9] but only to reason from a common basis of faith; the Christians of Corinth were not to let themselves be worried by opinions going about to the effect that there is no resurrection from the dead. An indissoluble link binds the resurrection of all the dead at the end of time and the resurrection of Christ which has happened within time (15:13.16). The risen Christ is 'the first-fruits of those who have fallen asleep (15:20, cf. Col 1:18). He is the last Adam, in whom all men will be made alive (15:22).

Examination of the context within which Paul quotes the traditional creed cannot be carried any further at this stage. Let us look closer at the credal formula. It contains two interrelated affirmations. The first concerns the death of Jesus, the second his resurrection. Both refer to and give an interpretation of the fact, and both underline the way in which facts are preserved in human recollection. Keeping our aim in sight, let us begin by considering the second affirmation about the resurrection.

The resurrection of Christ is affirmed by using a word which originally meant 'to wake up, to awaken' (*egeirein*). Christ has been 'woken up' (i.e. from death, which has just been mentioned). In other formulas, a different verb is used, 'to raise up, to rise, to bring back to life' (*anistēmi, anastēnai*). According to specialists in Semitic languages, the word for 'to wake up' was a rendering of the second, more primitive term 'to rise'. Both can in any case indicate the initial act of resurrection and also the result of that act. However, since this result can hardly be expressed by means of the phrase 'he who has been raised', some scholars would restrict the word 'to raise' to God's action in bringing his Son back to life, in so far as this action is in itself more open to other interpretations, i.e. as an act of exalting. In this field there are no sure answers.

It is equally difficult to define Christ's role in the act of resurrection. At first sight, one would think that since the verb (*egēgertai*) is in the passive voice, the credal formula was implying in the Semitic fashion that God himself was the agent of the resurrection: 'Christ has been raised.' But the passive form can equally well be understood as a middle voice form: 'Christ has risen.' In that case Christ would have been agent in his own resurrection as John the Evangelist was to say of him later when he represented Jesus as capable of taking his life up again (John 10:17). The middle voice sense would be required if the tense of the verb were aorist, as in Luke 24:34 for instance. 'The Lord has risen indeed (*egērthē*) and has appeared (*ōphthē*) to Simon,' or again with regard to the epileptic child whom Jesus 'lifted up' (*egeiren*): 'he arose' (*anestē*) (Mark 9:27; cf. I Thess 4:14). But this is not the case here, since the verb is in the perfect tense (*egēgertai*) and follows an aorist: 'he died (*apethanen*).' It is not possible to prove whether the formula sees God or Christ as agent of the resurrection.

On another point, by contrast, we can come to a certain conclusion by considering the tenses of the verbs. In I Cor 15 the perfect tense of the verb signifies that the interest does not lie in the past action, but in the effect which that action has for the present. Christ died once for all (aorist), he is alive today (perfect). The contrast seems deliberate, in as much as Paul uses the perfect tense in six instances in the same way in the context we are examining (I Cor 15:12-20).[11] By using the perfect tense the author proclaims that Christ is risen today: what he has in mind is the new condition of Christ. The important thing is not strictly a past action, whether on the part of God or of Christ, but Christ here and now.

Two further details given in the text make clear the meaning that the church gives to the fact of Christ's resurrection. It took place on the third day, and in accordance with the scriptures. It seems at first sight that the former information can be used for dating purposes. If so, we would have to be able to specify to which historical recollection it referred. But this is very far from easy. To what can it refer? The event itself? Nobody was there. The discovery of the empty tomb? Such a theory rests on a flimsy historical basis.[12] The first appearance?[13] But how are we to set a date on that? 'On the third day' cannot be seen simply as a historical recollection.

In contrast to that interpretation, some scholars have seen in the mention of 'the third day' a theological reflection on the Old

Testament prophecies. This suggestion is sound, in so far as the question of the fulfilment of scripture is immediately raised. But it remains fruitless, for the New Testament does not quote a single text from scripture which refers directly to the resurrection, not even Hosea 6:2. J. Dupont[14] proposes a compromise; he suggests an interaction between recollection and the searching of the scriptures, recollection having led to a search for confirmation in the bible. But here too the expression of such a 'recollection' would have to be consistent in the New Testament for it to be distinguishable; in fact in credal formulas about the resurrection we frequently find different turns of phrase such as 'in three days', 'after three days'. The terminology of the 'third day' did not impose itself as a clear recollection.[15]

The only valid and generally acceptable way of resolving the problem, a recourse to the language of the period, has recently been explored in detail.[16] On this basis the meaning of the varying turns of phrase can be defined. The formula 'on the third day' is not equivalent to the expression 'in three days', which in ordinary biblical usage means either very soon, or after some delay.[17] A possible explanation may lie in the conviction that the final resurrection was to take place on the third day after the end of the world; but the text on which this view is based is too late.[18] It seems preferable to take this phrase as a customary way of indicating a decisive event which is imminent. For instance it was on the third day that Abraham saw the place where he had to sacrifice his son (Gen 22:4).[19] The expression 'on the third day' in the primitive creed is not meant as a precise date, but suggests that the resurrection of Jesus is the principal event, which, taken in its full meaning, is tantamount to calling it an eschatological event.[20]

In the same way the resurrection is said to have taken place 'in accordance with the scriptures'. This formula may refer to a precise text, Psalm 16:10, which is quoted with one notable change by Acts 2:27; 13:35: 'Thou wilt not let thy Holy One see corruption' (see below, chapter 6). However, it is difficult to be content with this single reference. The resurrection of Jesus fulfils the long expectations of Israel. The first Christians did not seek to justify it by reference to some particular prophecy, but to place it within the economy of the divine covenant. This mode of reasoning conforms to the recognized tendency of the primitive church.[21]

Finally, the formula recalls the appearance of the risen Christ to Cephas. This is not the point to examine the significance of this (see chapter 5). We need only to point out its meaning in relation to the previous statement. The resurrection has been presented as the definitive act of God. The appearance places it within human history; it shows its concrete reality, and is without doubt one of the themes which have contributed to making Christ the subject of the sentence: he who was raised showed himself to privileged witnesses.

The mention of Christ's death comes before that of the resurrection, with the result that the latter acts as a counterpart to the statement of the crude fact of his death: the Messiah has shared the fate of mortals. He has been handed over to the merciless enemy (I Cor 15:26; 54-55) as though to a power which binds by the 'pangs of death' (cf. Acts 2:24). Thus Christ has well and truly experienced an end to his life.

But this death has scarcely been affirmed before a meaning is placed upon it. It has no meaning of itself, but only by the knowledge which comes from faith in the resurrection.

The light of Easter illuminates the scandalous event of the crucifixion of the Messiah. Jesus did not die because of his own sins, but, according to the creed, because of our sins, and with the purpose of wiping out our sins. Thus the resurrection is not simply an event in the past which continues to be effective in the present, particularly through the appearances to the disciples. It is the response of God, who proclaims that the death of Jesus is redemptive.

Confirmation of this approach is to be found in the statements of Peter related in the Acts of the Apostles: the action of God in raising Jesus is a saving action which concerns all men. 'Let all the house of Israel therefore know assuredly that God has made him both Lord and Christ, this Jesus whom you crucified' (2:36; cf. 13:33). We are to conclude that this is the stone which was rejected by you builders, but which has become the head of the corner. And there is salvation in no one else, for there is no other name under heaven given among men by which we must be saved. Salvation is a consequence of the resurrection: 'And he [God] commanded us to preach to the people, and to testify that he is the one ordained by God to be judge of the living and the dead.'

Therefore the act which raised the Christ does not just affect

Jesus of Nazareth but all men who, through him, are freed from their sins.

The redeeming death, like the resurrection, is a part of God's plan. It is fulfilled according to the scriptures. This statement is absolutely necessary, even more than in the case of the resurrection, for it is not simply a question of saying that his death occurred 'according to the definite plan and foreknowledge of God' (Acts 2:23; cf. 3:18; 4:28; 13:29). Its redeeming nature was prophesied in the poem of the Servant of God (Is 53:4-5, 6-8, 11-12). It is here that the believer finds the key to a profound understanding of the death and resurrection of the Christ.

But the formula goes on to draw our attention to the burial. Why? Certain critics have thought that the meaning here is that if Jesus is risen, then he has left the tomb. If this were so the ancient creed would in its own way be affirming the common view that Jesus came forth alive from his tomb. But the pattern of the passage (3 + 1 and 3 + 1) suggests that the mention of the burial is linked not with that of his resurrection but with that of his death. In actual fact, in Jewish thought, burial is normally referred to as a function of death, not in order to underline its reality but to describe its definitive aspect: the moment the door of the sepulchre is closed on the deceased, the descent into hell takes place: for the tomb is often identified with Sheol. According to the words of the bible Jesus 'died and was buried',[23] that is, he went down to the place of the dead.

Another purpose of burial in Jewish eyes was to maintain the identity of the deceased. The reason why tombs were the object of particular veneration[24] is because they guaranteed that the identity of the buried person would be maintained. That is why the worst fate which can befall a person is not to be buried (Jer 8:1-4; 16:4; Ezek 29:5). 'No one can say, This is Jezebel' if her bones are scattered (II Kings 9:37). In the eyes of the living the permanence of the personality of the dead person was assured not by the body which rotted but by the tomb which endured.

Conclusion

We say then, that in this extremely ancient confession of faith the mystery of the resurrection of Jesus is demonstrated on two levels. On the one hand, death and burial, resurrection and appearances follow one another and clearly show that these events take their place in the history of man. On the other hand they are unified by their inclusion in God's great plan. Thus the mystery cannot be reduced to a simple event in the past, even though this event is nothing less that the victory of God over the death of Jesus, but it gives meaning to this death and gives way to a permanent, redeeming presence. The community which expresses itself in this way is not interested in evoking past history, but rather in the present-day lives of men who continually have to go back to the witness borne to the risen, redeeming Christ.

2   God Raised Jesus from the Dead

In keeping with the previous formula there are other, shorter formulas, which are devoid of any theological interpretation but retain twofold death/resurrection pattern.

Thus we read in I Thess 4:14:

'For since we believe that *Jesus died and rose again* ...'[25]

The parallelism of death and resurrection is still significant, indicating the two aspects of the mystery of redemption. Is it as balanced as it seems in the first instance? The question arises since, unlike the creed of I Cor 15 which is unique of its kind, the brief two-part formulas lead on to other considerations. If then we examine these formulas we see that only the first part (Jesus died) is susceptible to further theological considerations, whereas the second (he rose again) remains unchanged. Thus Paul says that believers must 'live for him who for their sake died and was raised' (II Cor 5:15), or again that 'Jesus died for us' (Rom 5:8).[26] The use of the words 'for us' corresponds to the datum of I Cor 15 and is probably extremely ancient: but if the expression 'died for us' was the more primitive why then should 'for us' have been subsequently left out? It is therefore more likely that it was added later: the development is in the direction of an evolving christology, and not in the reverse direction. In the Acts of the Apostles a similar transformation is observable. '... Whom you crucified, whom God raised from the dead' (Acts 4:10, cf. 2:23-24); or again, 'But you ... killed the Author of Life, whom God raised from the dead' (Acts 3:15). The first part of the formula alters according to circumstances (cf. 2:32) or even disappears altogether (17:31). Everything seems to point to the fact that a simple formula mentioning only Jesus's resurrection existed before the double formula.

At first sight one would be led to pick out the formula 'Christ arose' (*Christos anestē*) or again 'Christ awoke' (*Christos egerthē*). As in the Antiochene creed Jesus is the subject of the sentence, though the tense of the verb is no longer the perfect but the aorist. It is a question of simply evoking the fact of Jesus's resurrection. Jesus has come back to life, he has risen from the dead. These expressions amount to a new way of confessing the Easter faith. But we cannot properly speak of a 'formula' firstly because the expressions are always to be found linked with the statement of Jesus's death (Rom 4:25; II Cor 5:15; I Thess 4:14) and secondly because they are infrequent.

On the other hand simple formulas do exist in contexts where faith is being proclaimed:

Because if you confess with your lips that *Jesus is Lord* and believe in your heart that *God raised him from the dead*, you will be saved (Rom 10:9).

In another text, where Paul is explaining what Christian conversion consists of, he uses an ancient confession of faith which repeats the same formula:

To serve a living and true God and to wait for his son from heaven, *whom he raised from the dead*, Jesus who delivers us from the wrath to come (I Thess 1:10).

There are some indications suggesting that this formula is certainly older than that of the Antiochene creed which we looked at earlier. Compared with the latter, it is markedly moderate: no theological explanation 'according to the scriptures', no specification of 'the third day', no explicit link with the death of Christ 'for our sins'. Now, we know that the less complex develops into the more complex, particularly in the case of a theological idea given expression in confessions of faith.

In order to put into focus this overall view, let us examine the different elements. The subject of the sentence is not Christ but God, and God who acts not on Christ but on Jesus of Nazareth. Of course the meaning is exactly the same and linguists would perhaps not be slow to point this out, maintaining that the agent and the object of the action are the same in both cases. In fact, however, there has been a change, and a variation between one text and another betrays a change of perspective, reflecting an evolution with which we are already familiar in the emergence of christology.

Originally, in accordance with certain Jewish ideas,[27] God is the author of Jesus's resurrection (Rom 8:11; Gal 1:1; Col 2:12; Eph 1:10). In the language of tradition it is Jesus himself who gives his life and takes it up again (John 2:19; 10:17). At an intermediate stage, it seems, Christ is the subject of the verb, but of a verb which is this time in the passive: 'Christ has been raised.'[28] It is highly probable that the New Testament tradition progressively attributed what was first of all the work of God to Christ.[29] The simple formula thus seems older than the others.

This is shown also in the tense of the verb. The aorist indicative (*ēgeiren*) looks back to an action in the past. Now, it is known through faith that this action has a significance for the present. This is recognized by the perfect tense (*egēgertai*) used in I Cor 15. In Rom 10:9, however, it is only by virtue of the parallel phrase 'Jesus is Lord' that attention is drawn to the presence of the mystery of the resurrection. These grammatical nuances need not disconcert the reader and are a reminder of the extent to which the mental outlook of those who composed these different formulas is revealed even in such details. While the choice of tense matters, the choice of word is less important. As we have said earlier, it is highly likely that the term 'to rise, to bring back to life' (*anastēnai*) is older than the term 'to awaken'.

Finally, the expression 'from the dead' (*ek nekrōn*) is unusual in that it does not appear in Greek outside the New Testament.[30] It is no doubt intended to refer to Sheol, the land of the dead, from which Jesus has been brought back. When compared with reference to the death of Jesus common to the twofold formulas, the phrase states something similar by presenting Jesus, who has come back from the kingdom of the dead, as the conqueror of death. The development therefore seems to lead from this concise expression to the more elaborate formulation of I Cor 15.

From this basic analysis, which may have been thought hasty, we therefore believe that we have reached the oldest formulation of the Easter message to make use of the language of resurrection: 'God raised Jesus from the dead.' This is the cry uttered by the Easter faith at its birth.

B.   THE ORIGIN OF THE FORMULA

Is there not a paradox in maintaining that the credal formula
originates in a simple assertion of fact? The adherents of straightforward realism, who insist that bare facts can be asserted independently of any meaning, will not of course find anything strange
in this. But if we agree with the philosophers that one cannot state
a fact without demonstrating its meaning by some interpretation,
we are bound to ask how anyone could purely and simply affirm
the fact of the resurrection. Which is to say that in this case the
statement of the fact coincides with the assertion of its meaning.
But if we accept this, we have still to show how this assertion came
into being. In other words, what is the origin of the language which
was used? In using the words they did, the early Christians were
not manufacturing an expression out of nothing, but were making
use of an already existing terminology which was at their disposal.
What was this terminology, and how was it used?

1   *Two Illusory Explanations*

The first, extremely simple answer is that the statement does no
more than translate what the apostles experienced when they saw
Jesus appear to them in the flesh. But this is an excuse for an
explanation. It is true the formula used has its origin in the experience of the apostles but it was not produced by this alone. Another
factor played a part, but the explanation ignores it. This factor was
the language which the apostles took over from their own age. To
be able to say that Jesus was raised the disciples must already have
had in their minds a given notion, or more exactly a particular
category, that of 'the resurrection of the dead'.

There is sometimes a tendency to explain the genesis of this formula
on the basis of the comment made by the chief priests and Pharisees
who came as a formal deputation before Pilate: 'We remember
how that imposter said, while he was still alive "After three days I
will rise again." Therefore order the sepulchre to be made secure
until the third day, lest his disciples go and steal him away, and tell
the people "He has risen from the dead."' (Matthew 27:63-64).
This would mean that Jesus of Nazareth had used the formula
when he told the disciples what would happen to him.

However natural it may sound, a critical reader will nevertheless find this explanation unsatisfactory. Does it not seem strange that the enemies of Jesus should remember a declaration couched in such terms, whereas the angel had to invite the women to remember what Jesus had said when he was in Galilee (Luke 24:7) and, according to John 20:9, his own friends forgot the scripture which spoke of it? Perhaps Peter and the beloved disciple were unable to remember because they were standing before the empty tomb where Jesus had been. On the other hand, as soon as Jesus appeared, his presence would have recalled the formula to their memories which had failed them. In actual fact Christ says to the assembled disciples: 'Thus it is written, that the Christ should suffer and on the third day rise from the dead ...' (Luke 24:46). We cannot deal with this difficulty until we have already set out Luke's theology of the Easter message, which we shall do in stage three (chapter 9). It is enough to say that the words of the risen Christ cannot simply be treated like those which he uttered during his public life. Scholars are firmly in agreement on this point. To sum up, then, Jesus no doubt had a presentiment of what his fate would be and expressed it in veiled terms (Luke 9:44; 13:31-33; 17:25.); but his thoughts were given clearer expression in the records set down by the evangelists. Jesus spoke of the resurrection of the dead in the ordinary language of Judaism (cf. Matthew 22:23-32).[31] But when he foretold his fate he did not use the terminology of the primitive church, which was not defined until after the events of Easter (Matthew 16:21; 17:22-23; 20:18-19).

2 The Underlying Symbolism

It is quite obvious that there exists all over the world a terminology which tries to explain what death is and what happens after death. Man has drawn an analogy between his own fate in which he is overcome by death and the apparent blindness of the forces which control life in vegetation and nature as a whole; and again, the impossibility of depicting the experience of death has lead to its transposition in the mytho-poetic imagination of our ancestors into spatial terms: the earth, or rather, that which is underneath the earth, the underworld, has become death's own domain, the dwelling place of the dead.[32] Thus the death of the nature divinities was thought of as a 'descent into the underworld' and to represent their live-giving activities they were portrayed as coming back into the light, out of the underworld where they had been imprisoned.

Thus behind the Jewish terminology there lies a human symbolism common to all civilizations. It is important to bear this fact in mind, even if we do not work out its consequences at this point. Let us simply say that if we reject the terminology of resurrection we also discard a symbolic heritage received from the whole of mankind.

Another secondary question concerns the extent of Israel's dependence on the mythical terminology of death and resurrection. Nowadays scholars are disinclined to regard the similarities as any indication of dependence.[33] Only those who know nothing of the fundamental differences between Judaeo-Christian tradition and the myths of other religions will be misled by these analogies. For example, although it is Osiris who dies, it is not he but his son, Horus, who is reborn each morning as the sun god. Moreover, it is a fundamental element of biblical tradition that God cannot die. He is life itself. Thus Hosea rounds upon an Israel which is tending to conceive of the covenant on the lines of Canaanite nature religion: 'His going forth is sure as the dawn; he will come to us as the showers, as the spring rains that water the earth' (Hosea 6:3). There is nothing in common between the recurrent cycle of nature and Yahweh, who is supremely free and alive. In short, it is a far cry from the generalization of a cosmic experience couched in symbol to the brutal fact of an act given individual expression in Jesus. Nevertheless, it is still important to retain a feeling for the symbolic meaning of the language used, and not to rest content with an abstract language without any evocative power.

3 *Jewish Belief in the Resurrection of the Dead*

Although the symbolism of rising from the dead is common to many religions, it is nevertheless through the particular influence of Jewish theology that it was present in the minds of the first disciples. At the time of Jesus the Jews as a whole believed that on the last day the dead would rise again. This is not the place for us to trace the complex history of this belief.[34] We must simply keep in mind the two principal factors which influenced contemporary terminology: Semitic thought, properly so called, such as is to be found in biblical texts which are earlier than 250 B.C., and Hellenistic thought, which appears in the works of Palestinian Judaism in Aramaic or Hebrew.[35] Let us pursue our study by passing rapidly over the data furnished first by the Hebrew bible, and then by the major witnesses of Graeco-Palestinian literature between 170 B.C. and A.D. 100.[36] This will enable us to show what the formula 'God raised Jesus from the dead' would have meant to the first Christians.

For this purpose we must be aware of the two assumptions which dominate the biblical understanding of resurrection. 'The Lord kills and brings to life' (I Sam 2:6). Faith in the living God, author and master of all life, prevents him from being confused with the cycle of nature, since, by contrast with the divinities of other religions, he cannot die in order to live again. The second assumption is that the body is not a 'component part' of man: it is man himself in his outward appearance. For man is manifested in full in soul, flesh, mind and body.[37] 'The Hebrew conceived man as an animated body and not as an incarnate soul.'[38] Also, when he dies, the whole of him goes down to the underground place which is Sheol, to lead an existence which is still corporeal, but so diminished that it no longer deserves the name of life: man still exists, but he no longer lives. From this abyss (Ps 63:10; 86:13), which lies at the opposite pole to the height of heaven (Is 7:11), from this hole with its ever-open mouth (Is 5:14) and insatiable appetite (Hab 2:5), from this 'eternal home' (Eccles 12:5), from the 'chambers of death' (Prov 7:27), from this place full of darkness (Job 17:13), where one cannot praise God (Is 38:18), from this land of forgetfulness (Ps 88:13), no one ever returns (II Sam 12:23). And yet, according to the song of Hannah, already quoted, in which God is celebrated as he who takes life and gives it, 'The Lord . . . brings down to Sheol and raises up' (I Sam 2:6).

For many centuries Israel did not dare to give real adherence to this profound intuition of faith. Let us for the moment leave on one side two other factors which might have altered this view: the assumption into heaven of Enoch (Gen 5:24) and Elijah (II Kings 2:11), and the restoration of the dead to life by Elijah and Elisha (I Kings 17:17-24; II Kings 4:31-7; 13:21). Their exceptional character serves only to throw into relief the omnipotence of God. These traditions have survived in Jewish literature, but to a marginal extent:[40] one allusion is still to be found in the psalmist's prayer. 'But God will ransom my soul from the power of Sheol, for he will receive me' (Ps 49:15; cf. 73:24). Instead, the language of resurrection which, in contrast to assumption into heaven, supposes that death has taken place, was to be formed by a concentrating first of all metaphorically on sickness, which is death already at work. The sick man or nation can be compared with those who have gone down to the pit (Ps 88: 4-8). That which we call 'resurrection' is therefore only the return to life of a man who, through illness, has fallen into the hands of death, or of a nation fallen from grace, which in its lamentable state can only be compared with a corpse.[41] Thus the prophet repeats a liturgy of penitence: 'He has stricken, and he will bind us up; after two days he will revive us; on the third day he will raise us up, that we may live before him' (Hosea 6: 1-2). Let us not misunderstand this. The same is true of the famous prophecy of Ezekiel, in which he describes the dead who have life breathed into them by God, arise and live again (Ezek 37: 1-14). In this way the vocabulary of resurrection was gradually formed: 'to bring back to life', 'to call forth', 'to raise up', 'to awaken' (Is 51: 17) from the sleep of death which happens when God forsakes men (Ps 13: 7). It is true that all this is meant to be understood eschatologically (cf. Is 25: 7-8; 26: 14-19) but these are often all only metaphors: death really and truly is the end of life.

Then one day resurrection was suddenly no longer used to refer simply to the symbols of death, but was directly linked to the reality, to death itself. 'At that time ... many of those who sleep in the dust of the earth shall awake; some to everlasting life, and some to shame and everlasting contempt' (Dan 12: 1-13). What enabled this faith to be so positive? It is not impossible that influences originating in neighbouring cultures (Egypt, Persia) played a part, but it is certain that the determining factor was the experience of the death of the martyrs during the persecution of Antiochus Epiphanes about 167 B.C. From this event came the conviction that the all-righteous God could not allow those who had borne witness to his covenant to remain in Sheol.[42] Alternatively, it would have seemed obvious that the eschatological hope of a national resurrection could apply individually and concretely to the just here on earth. Anyway, the fact is there. With regard to the form to be taken by life after death, it is not surprising that speculations regularly occur, not in the Hebrew bible, but in the apocryphal works which appear at intervals between the second century B.C. and the first century A.D. To cast a little further light on this area let us now examine the second dominating assumption in the language of resurrection, the conception of man.

Our task is made more difficult by the fact that Hellenistic thought and vocabulary have influenced Jewish terminology. In this instance, we need only recall the popular anthropological concepts of the time, and need not get involved in the labyrinth of philosophical systems.[43] At the risk of somewhat simplifying the data, though not the radical opposition of Hellenistic and Semitic thought, we can describe the situation as follows. In Greek thought, man is made up of soul and body. The soul is immortal, while the body is a material entity placed at his disposal temporarily and in which he is held prisoner. At death, the soul is set free from its prison, the body.[44] According to this view of man, resurrection would involve the restoration of the soul to the body—whether as in Pythagorism, to a new body through the transmigration of souls, or as in hellenized Christianity, to one's own body, which had become a corpse.

According to Jewish anthropology, this cannot be the case. In the writings of the period, a typical reaction is found. One might call it emulsion rather than fusion. The word 'soul' becomes increasingly frequent, but it never stands for some spiritual or immortal substance as opposed to a body which is material and mortal.[45] Death is still referred to in terms of a man's being 're-united with his fathers'; although it is occasionally spoken of as a separation of soul and body, this does not involve the liberation of the soul,[46] which thus does not become 'spiritual' in the Greek sense of the word. The souls of the dead, still 'corporal' in an attenuated way, go, if not to a dark Sheol, at any rate into the repositories[47] where they wait inertly for the last day. So the resurrection consists in the dead man entering into fullness of life, in a new kind of existence and form (II Macc 7:9). According to liturgical texts, it is God who brings back to life: in apocalyptic texts, there is also a mention of the earth, or Sheol, restoring the dead.[48]

Such are the basic ideas which in all probability inspired the first Christians when they became aware that Jesus had passed through the gates of death. We must be careful about reading the dualistic concept of man with which we are familiar into the word 'resurrection' when it is used to express the event itself. It must be understood according to the conventional Jewish anthropology of the period. It means the complete restoration to life of Jesus of Nazareth at every level of his being.

If we begin with these two postulates of Jewish thought, we realize that the formula 'God has raised Jesus from the dead' is of some complexity. But an urgent question remains unanswered, for the Christian tradition, like the Jewish, was not content simply to assert the fact, but asked what kind of existence was enjoyed by those who were raised from the dead. In Jewish apocryphas, two tendencies are found which also occur in Christian writings: a tendency towards the use of imagery, and a tendency to spiritualize the new life.

How, then, are the resurrected to enter into contact with the living? We know how the gospel accounts present the encounter of Christ with his disciples. It is worth while to recall here the way in which the 'world to come' is dealt with. The Apocalypse of Baruch, a Jewish apocalyptic text dating from the first century A.D., and hence contemporary with the composition of the gospels, puts the following question: 'What kind of life will be given to those who are to see Thy Day? What kind of glory will they possess after such happenings? Will they re-assume their present appearance?' This question is similar to that put to Paul by the Corinthians: 'How are the dead raised? With what kind of body do they come?' (I Cor 15:35). This is the reply heard by the visionary Baruch: 'The earth will give back the dead ... just as it has received them, and as I give them back to it, so it will bring them back to life again. For it will then be needful to show to those who are alive that the dead live ... and when those who now know each other recognize each other, then the judgement will take place. Then the appearance of the damned and the glory of the justified will be changed.... Their splendour will be changed into glory.'[49] The resemblance to the New Testament is striking. For Paul too the transformation is distinguished from the resurrection, at least at the parousia. We shall not all sleep, but we shall all be changed (I Cor 15:51). In the gospels, too, the aim amongst other things is to convince us that the risen Christ is truly Jesus of Nazareth. Thus a similar structure leads to the same sequence of events: resurrection followed by appearances, then by ultimate glory.

This apocryphal work is sober. Not all the others are in representing the world to come. The procedure involved a risk: that of an 'objectivizing' reading which, in process of 'historicizing', took literally elements which are used symbolically, as if they concerned realistic analogies to elements from the 'present world'. Theology has not always avoided this danger.[50] That is the least one can say.

Once this has been recognized, we must note that the same visionary writer ends his description of the elect by saying: 'They will be like angels, and made equal to the stars' (Apx Bar 51:10). Similarly, Jesus replied to the Sadducees, who sought to ridicule the resurrection and the world to come, in the same terms as the *Similitudes of Enoch* (this passage dates from the first century A.D.) 'In those days, all the just will become angels in heaven' (Enoch 51:4; cf. Mark 12:25).

One cannot say that materialistic pictures have been imposed on concepts which were 'spiritual' (and this does not mean 'non-corporeal'). The language of 'resurrection' is not fated to make the mystery it seeks to express materialistic.

Conclusion

From the very first, Christians with one accord expressed their faith by means of the formula 'God raised Jesus from the dead'. They thereby affirmed that an act had taken place at a particular moment in the past and to a particular person. Above all, they sought to proclaim in this way that Jesus is alive for ever and that he is Lord. Of the two ways of expressing it—God makes the dead rise and God makes the dead live—they chose the former to articulate their totally new experience. They took the Jewish terminology developed to describe the end of time and to apply to all the righteous, and applied it to one individual and to a time in the recent past. This demonstrates both the origin and, at the same time, the novelty of the formula 'God raised Jesus from the dead'.

In assigning to a precise moment of time a term applicable to the last days, the Christians were moving from the eschatological into the historical. An event prophesied for the end of time had taken place in the midst of time. By virtue of this anticipation, the resurrection of Jesus became an event which could be inserted into a sequence of other events. His death was followed by sepulchre, and then by the resurrection. Then followed the appearances of the risen Christ, and finally, to end the sequence, the ascension. Such is evidently the structure of the gospel narratives. Luke brought it to its final point by describing the ascension of Jesus to heaven. Thus the reader is faced with a sequence of mysteries which is accessible to reason, in that it immediately establishes an analogy between this sequence of facts and our ordinary historical knowledge. But does this do justice to faith?

It is here that the language used proves unable to speak adequately about the mystery to which it refers. In arranging the events into a structure of before and after, the evangelists, particularly Luke, did not in the least desire to reduce to a simple earthly level facts which they knew belonged primarily to the heavenly realm. They expressed this vital contrast either by talking explicitly of the cessation of contact with the risen Christ, or by appealing to another structure, complementary to the first, that of 'above' as opposed to 'here below'. In this way they showed that they were the heirs of the biblical tradition: after their message had been conveyed, the heavenly apparitions disappeared (Judg 13:20) and even 'vanished from sight' (Judg 6:21). The text from Baruch previously quoted says the same: the risen are transformed into glory when they have made themselves known to the living. The sequence of before and after is brought to an end by the disappearance or ascension to heaven. Does it therefore cease to be important? In fact, the latter structure only apparently affects the former. It has the simple role of a corrective. The ascension to heaven is only a parenthesis in the sequence of events which goes on until the return of Jesus, which is the end of history. When it is fitted into the before and after sequence, the pattern of 'above' and 'here below' lacks the coherence which we shall observe when we discuss it in the next chapter.

Thus we must stick strictly to terminology of the 'historical' type, of which Luke is the clearest example. To understand his presentation of the history of salvation correctly, we must be aware of the heavenly dimension in his history, otherwise we risk being presented only with an impoverished and reduced gospel message. The resurrection in effect becomes an event which, though doubtless extraordinary in its relation to the history of salvation, comes to be viewed within the sequence of other historical events, and this tends to limit the dimension of the mystery. The risen Christ is shown in the form of an earthly person; in this way, of course, he can never be mistaken for a phantom, but the danger is that the time nature of his new existence is obscured by such a view. As far as the ascension is concerned, the intention is no doubt to refer to Christ's enthronement in glory, but the descriptive style can hide the mystery, as is the case when Jesus is thought of as taking possession of the universe by making a spatial journey through heaven after having gone down to hell. The danger lies in forgetting that this terminology, to the extent that we fail to recognize its symbolic dimension, ultimately reduces the mystery to the level of an unusual and prodigious event. The life of glory then becomes that of Lazarus with something extra. Where has the mystery gone?

On its own, the expression 'God has raised Jesus from the dead' shows clearly how the individual, Jesus of Nazareth, has come out of death alive. Its indubitable advantage is that it allows us to identify him who is alive. But it does not indicate or suggest anything which reveals the universal significance which Jesus acquired by his resurrection, his cosmic plenitude, or his role with regard to the whole of humanity. This is why it must be complemented by considerations which are necessary if we are to portray Jesus in his new existence.

With many reservations, we have succeeded in outlining a degree of development in the usage of the primitive formula which presented the Easter mystery in the language of resurrection. It is first and foremost God who 'awakens' Jesus, who raises him. Little by little, the point of view changes and Christ is seen as he who has risen. While God remains the subject of the sentence, the event remains a beginning, an opening to a state of existence: the 'awakening' leads on to the enthronement at God's right hand. With the change of subject, the state of Christ's life is described as being that of the risen one, the resurrected one; his existence is defined and limited by what in itself would only be the beginning of a different phase.

The attempt to satisfy the natural desire to give the event a christological significance, leads to putting into two compartments what is intrinsically one thing, namely the rising and the exaltation. Now, the expression 'the resurrected one' ought simultaneously to evoke both the past event and the glorious state of Christ's present existence. But does it do so for the modern reader of the gospel? When we examine in the next chapter a different terminology used by the earliest Christians, we shall see that, if its real meaning is to be understood, the language of resurrection must reveal another dimension, that of exaltation into glory.

CHAPTER TWO

Jesus, Lord of Glory

In our previous pages on the credal formula 'God raised Jesus from the dead', different readers may have found their own ideas confirmed. One may have accepted and understood this language more deeply, recognizing in it the faith which he has received from his fathers. Another may have confirmed his inclination to reject a language which he regards as out of date, with no bearing upon our own age. Too often both will assume without further ado as obvious and beyond question, that the content of faith is identical to the language in which it is uttered. This is not the place to show how this identification has been the cause of loss of faith in many cases; but it is worth while showing how the language which we so readily take as absolute is always relative, relative to a given period and relative to other ways of speaking.

This relative aspect of the language of faith can be seen first of all in the fact that the primitive faith was expressed in other ways besides that of the formula which we have already analysed. This formula no doubt fulfilled one, but not all, of the profound needs of the church. Thus it cannot exhaust the object of our enquiry. In fact, the attentive historian finds the thought of the infant church displayed in other expressions which are equally vital. The liturgy expresses the faith of the congregation, but it does so in various ways: the creed proclaims it, while hymns state it. There exist, in addition to the credal formulas, hymns in which Jesus was acclaimed as the Lord glorified by God. These poetic passages can be recognized amongst the New Testament texts, both in the alleluias of the Book of Revelation and in the choruses or stanzas which Paul or Peter quote in their letters.[1]

These two types of proclamation of faith are distinct in function and content. The credal formulas essentially profess the fact of Jesus's resurrection, while the hymns do not speak of it directly, but proclaim the glorification of Jesus. The terms employed are dif-

ferent, and so is the terminology. This last point must be emphasized, for the hymns do not merely differ formally from the creeds,
but derive from a literary category which, since its function is
different, displays a different type of mental structure, or again a
different 'language'. This we can call the 'language of hymns', by
contrast to 'kerygmatic' language.

This state of affairs raises a question concerning the origin of
the language of hymns. Does it derive from the kerygmatic language, or is it independent of it? And if it is independent of it, is
it the source of it, or does it run parallel with it? Most scholars
assume that everything can be derived from the language of the
kerygma,[2] though some regard the language of hymns as the
source.[3] We shall attempt to show that from the very first both
types of christology co-existed, and that each was as solidly based as
the other.[4]

Amongst the New Testament hymns, we shall concentrate
mainly upon those which are usually regarded by critics as anterior
to the author who quotes them.[5] We shall then go on to contrast
their terminology with that described in the previous chapter.

A.   SOME NEW TESTAMENT HYMNS

1   *Philippians 2:6-11*

The view generally held by scholars is that this passage was inserted
by Paul into his letter for the purpose of moral exhortation. On the
other hand, there is no agreement about the modifications which
Paul may have introduced into it, nor upon its division into stanzas.
All who discuss the matter draw upon our knowledge of Semitic or
Greek prosody, but none are wholly convincing. The following
translation shows the lay-out which we regard as most likely.[6]

[6]Who, though he was in the form of God,
   did not count equality with God a thing to be grasped,

[7]but emptied himself,
   taking the form of his servant,

being born in the likeness of men
   and being found in human form,

[8]he humbled himself
   and became obedient unto death, even death on a cross.

[9]Therefore God has highly exalted him
  and bestowed on him the name which is above every name,

[10]that at the name of Jesus every knee should bow
  (in heaven and on earth and under the earth),

[11]and every tongue confess: JESUS CHRIST IS LORD
  (to the glory of the Father).

We shall not attempt here to work out an exegesis of this famous passage, but only to draw from it a few observations concerning our subject. The hymn is not constructed on the pattern of death, burial, resurrection, appearances, ascension, but on the contrast between two conditions: humility (6-8) and exaltation (9-11). By contrast to the credal formulas, it does not mention after the death of Jesus either the resurrection, the burial or the appearances; and as for the exaltation, it is the immediate glorification of Jesus, his accession to universal dominion. If the author of the hymn had been asked, 'Did Jesus rise from the dead?' he would no doubt have replied in the affirmative. But he would no doubt have explained that this was not the essential point. What matters is that Jesus is Lord, and that he is in glory.

To what exactly does the contrast between humility and exaltation, which forms the structure of the hymn, in fact refer? The answer to this question will enable us to determine its origin and meaning. It has long been understood as a description of the incarnation, of the pre-existent Christ taking on human nature, presented here as that of a slave. But this interpretation has a consequence which is unacceptable in Paul: it would mean the temporary abandonment by Christ of his divine nature in order to take on the nature of man. It also assumes that the term *morphē* should be translated 'nature'; but in fact it means not of course only 'form' but 'condition, state'.

Some critics have tried to be more precise and speak of three states: pre-existence, earthly life and heavenly glorification. According to them, the hymn describes the descent from heaven to earth and the re-ascent into heaven, so conforming to the Hellenistic pattern of the mythical descent of the deity amongst men. Its background in this case would not be Jewish thought, but the Hellenistic world. The latter can be recognized in a number of Greek expressions in the hymn;[7] but the three-state pattern does not give an exact reflection of the present text. The expression 'being in the form of God' (*hyparchōn en morphē theou*) signifies a state which is 'possessed' and is not transitory; thus there can be no reference here to *pre*-existence in the temporal sense of the word, as though the Christ had existed *before* his incarnation. From the beginning to the end of the hymn, it refers to Christ as he manifested himself here below. The eye of faith has perceived at a profound level the *super*-existence of the Christ whom faith adores as the Lord. The hymn describes the person of Jesus Christ in his two states: his divine state veiled in the humility of his earthly condition, and then the manifestation of his glorified divine state before the eyes of all.

The antithesis is expressed by way of the Greek contrast between 'slave' and 'lord', by way of the contrast between Jesus and Adam (inherent in the theme of equality with God), and by way of the link with the fulfilment by Jesus of the prophecy of the Servant of God. These antitheses are significant, but they lie only on the surface of the terminology which is used. In order to understand what the humility consists of, it is necessary above all to apprehend the contrast between the world of the cross and the heavenly world of the deity; this contrast replaces that between death and resurrection. Here we no longer have the (horizontal) succession of two 'events' but the (vertical) drawing together of two worlds. Finally let us note that in all probability this hymn was formulated in a cultic setting, though it is no longer possible to be certain whether it was that of baptism or the eucharist.

2   I Timothy 3:16[8]

Another hymn stands out by its introduction and its rhythm:

Great indeed, we confess, is the mystery of our religion:

1 He was manifested in the flesh,
2   vindicated in the Spirit,
3   seen by angels,
4   preached among the nations,
5   believed on in the world,
6   taken up in glory.

The subject of the hymn is not the mystery (the word is neuter in Greek), but Jesus Christ (a word in the masculine gender, as is indicated by the relative *hos*, 'he who'). The rhythm is emphasized by the succession of verbs (in the passive aorist) which are constructed with the preposition *en* and the dative (except in 3). It is made even clearer by the antithetical parallelism which is obvious in the antitheses flesh-Spirit (1-2), heavenly-earthly (3-4 and 6-5): this gives it a contrasted and reversed *ab/ba/ab* pattern, in which *a* signifies the earthly and *b* the heavenly. Strictly speaking the contrast is a spatial one: everything takes place either on earth or in heaven.

The passage is often interpreted in favour of the gospel facts narrated elsewhere in the New Testament: the resurrection of Jesus and his ascension,[9] which are regarded as historical facts. But what we have in fact is the ritual pattern of an enthronement.[10] We have a description of one who in spite of appearances (the accursed one who suffered the curse of the cross), has been justified by God, when God vouchsafed to raise him up beside himself. Then Jesus was manifested as the sovereign Lord to the angelic beings who formed the celestial court;[11] and then this is proclaimed to the whole earth: messengers haste throughout the world, that is, the nations: 'Lo, your King comes to you (Zech 9:9). The world welcomes the message and responds with faith. In this way Christ is glorified: he ascends his royal throne.

In spite of the appearance of a temporal succession, the dominating logic in this hymn is that of a totality which recurs again and again. Everything is already included in the first couplet. Earth is united to heaven; then, in the second couplet, heaven and earth receive the same Good News; and once again, in the third couplet, the world which believes is raised up to heaven in Jesus. Everything is present at once, and heaven and earth are reconciled.

Now in this hymn, as in that in the Epistle to the Philippians, the subject is not the resurrection of Jesus, nor his appearances, nor even his death, but his manifestation in the humility of the flesh and his manifestation in the glory of the Spirit. It seems obvious that this hymn, which is liturgical in origin, reflects a mentality different from that which inspired the confessions of faith: the understanding is not that of a series of historical events, but an apprehension of the heart of the mystery of Jesus Christ, which is presented to the religious devotion of the believer.

3   Some Other Texts (Eph 4:7-10; Rom 10:5-8; I Peter 3:18-22; 4:6)

Elsewhere in the New Testament there are passages which corroborate or complete the indications already given. These passages too

derive from hymns, either in their present form, or if not, at least
in the material of which they are composed; or else they derive from
ancient Jewish oral tradition (Eph 4:8; Rom 10:6; I Peter 3:18;
4:6). In any case, the material which we are now to examine is
earlier than the writers who used it, and enables us to go back with
certainty to the primitive church.

In these texts we find various elements of the approach described
above: the linking of heaven and earth, the absence of any mention
of the resurrection of Jesus, and the affirmation of the exaltation of
Christ. What gives particular interest to our study, however, is the
fact that in them the whole range of cosmology appears: not only
are heaven and earth mentioned, but also the underworld, so that
'below' no longer means only the earth by contrast to heaven, but
the underworld, the Sheol from which Christ re-ascends; and this
assumes that he has descended thither. In short, what is below is
linked with what is above, and the ascent to heaven is sometimes
related to the descent into the underworld. In the Creed these
statements follow in strict succession: 'he was crucified, dead and
buried, he descended into hell; . . . he rose again from the dead, he
ascended into heaven'. But in the proclamation which we have
here, these actions which apparently follow one another do not
form a strictly historical succession: the descent into the underworld and the ascension are not historical events in the same sense
as the crucifixion and death. Thus the descent into the underworld
does not follow the death of Christ, it is identical with his death.
But our purpose is not to examine the language of the descent
into hell,[12] interesting though it may be, but simply to supplement
the terminology of 'exaltation' which the previous hymns enabled
us to define.

a.   *Ephesians 4:7-10*

[7]But grace was given to each of us according to the measure of
Christ's gift. [8]Therefore it is said, 'When he ascended on high he
led a host of captives, and he gave gifts to men.' [9](In saying,
'He ascended,' what does it mean but that he had also descended
into the lower parts of the earth? [10]He who descended is he who
also ascended far above all the heavens, that he might fill all
things.)

In order to show that every believer has received a particular
gift, Paul quotes Ps 68:18, but he alters the original text. There

we read: 'Thou didst ascend the high mount, thou didst lead captives in thy train, thou didst receive gifts among men, even among the rebellious, that the Lord God may dwell there.' The alteration of 'thou didst receive' into 'he gave' is important; it is less surprising when one reads the Aramaic Targum: 'Thou didst raise up to heaven Moses the prophet, thou didst teach the words of the law, thou didst give gifts to men.' Here, as in the Epistle to the Ephesians, it is not God who ascended, but Moses whom God raised up and through whom God gave his law. The Christian, accustomed to seeing in Jesus the new Moses, would unhesitatingly attribute the ascension and the giving of good gifts to Jesus. The allusion is obvious: Jesus has ascended to heaven, and distributes the marvellous gifts of the spirit. The novelty, however, does not lie there, but in the fact that the exaltation assumes a descent to the lower regions of the earth. What are these lower regions? Some scholars identify them with the earth itself, seeing an allusion to the kenosis of Christ, as in the hymn in Philippians; and in fact the contrast between heaven and earth is that of higher and lower (Ps 139:15). Here, however, since in this text too there is no question of pre-existence, it seems preferable to regard the lower regions as Sheol itself (cf. Ps 55:16).

b. Romans 10:5-8

In another passage, Paul once again alludes tacitly to Ps 68, and explicitly to Deuteronomy. S. Lyonnet has demonstrated the connection between the text and Aramaic Targum.[13]

> [5]Moses writes that the man who practises the righteousness which is based on the law shall live by it. [6]But the righteousness based on faith says, Do not say in your heart, 'Who will ascend into heaven?' (that is, to bring Christ down) [7]or 'Who will descend into the abyss?' (that is, to bring Christ up from the dead). [8]But what does it say? The word is near you, on your lips and in your heart (that is, the word of faith which we preach).

Paul is seeking to show that justification by faith is within reach of all, since Christ has been given to us. He uses the Palestinian Targum, which gives a paraphrase of Deut 30:11-14:

> The law is not in heaven, that you should say: 'If only we had someone like Moses the prophet to go up to heaven and bring it for us' ... Nor is the law beyond the Great Sea, that you should say: 'If only we had someone like Jonah the prophet to go down

into the depths of the sea to bring it back up for us and tell
us its precepts, so that we might do them.'
In the eyes of a Christian believer, Jesus is the new Moses, and the
new Jonah, and therefore he is within reach of all who will believe
in him.

For our purpose, we must note that Christ is represented as
having journeyed through the secret places of the universe, the
world above and the world below. He has ascended, but he has
also re-ascended from the abyss into which he had descended. What
is meant is clear: the death of Christ is equivalent to the descent
into the underworld, and therefore his ascent corresponds to this
descent.

The text forms a parallel with that in Ephesians, and casts light
for us on the meaning which was given to the event of Easter.
This event was not described by the term 'resurrection', but as the
triumph which demonstrates the dominion of Christ over every part
of the cosmos. The passage is concerned not with the act by which
God raised his Son from death, but with the part played by the
risen Christ.

c. I Peter 3:18-22; 4:6

The statements in the texts which we have just read are confirmed
by other passages, such as I Peter 3:18-22; 4:6. Let us briefly discuss this fragment. It is composed of a variety of material of liturgical origin, either hymns or confessions of faith. The resurrection
from the dead is mentioned, but texts are also quoted, in parallel
and concurrently, which speak only of the sitting down of Christ
at the right hand of God and his restoration to life, as well as the
descent into the underworld.

> [18]Being put to death in the flesh
>   but made alive in the spirit ...

> [22]who has gone into heaven and is at the right hand of God,
>   with angels authorities and powers subject to him.

We recognize here elements which reoccur in the hymns in Philippians 2 and I Timothy 3. But here are statements which recall the
texts above:

> [19]In the spirit he went and preached to the spirits in prison,
> [20]who formerly did not obey, when God's patience waited in
> the days of Noah, during the building of the ark.

This adds a further detail to the activity of Jesus amongst the dead. It has long been supposed that Jesus did this during the three days which preceded his resurrection, preaching the Good News to the 'separated souls'.[14] Today, it is thought that there is no need to distinguish successive stages here: it was at his death that Christ went to celebrate his triumph amongst the angelic powers. His death was his triumph. Here again, we must take care not to reduce to distinct concrete events, in the form of successive acts in time (death, followed by the descent to the underworld) what is a unity in the mystery of the redeeming death of Christ: 'The gospel was preached even to the dead' (I Peter 4:6).

These different texts show that one New Testament tradition describes the passage from death to life as being that of glorification, the preaching of salvation throughout the universe, and of dominion over every part of the universe. The ascension, often linked to some descent, signifies the resurrection, in the strict sense, of Jesus the Christ.

B.   THE ORIGIN OF THE PATTERN

If we attempt to express in a single phrase the pattern which, as we have seen, is used in various very ancient texts, we might say, 'God has lifted Jesus up to heaven into glory', or, to use less imagery, 'God has made Jesus Lord of the universe'. The same reality recurs in expressive terms in the following form: 'I am ascending to my Father and your Father' (John 20:17), or again in the imagery of the blessing given by Jesus at the moment of his departure (Luke 24:50). The emphasis here is not so much on the original event of the resurrection of Jesus as on his new state of life. The terminology is usually that of the pattern of exaltation, and we must look for its origin.

1   *Exaltation and Ascension*

The reader will at once have thought of the apostolic experience of the ascension as the source of this new form of expression, for while Jesus did not distinctly foretell this mystery, the fact remains that Luke has described how it was realized in the Acts of the Apostles:

⁹And when he had said this, as they were looking on, he was lifted up, and a cloud took him out of their sight.

¹⁰And while they were gazing into heaven as he went, behold, two men stood by them in white robes, ¹¹and said, 'Men of Galilee, why do you stand looking into heaven? This Jesus, who was taken up from you into heaven, will come in the same way as you saw him go into Heaven' (Acts 1:9-11).

This took place at the end of the 'forty days' during which Christ appeared to them (Acts 1:2-3). Scholars now agree in placing this narrative not in the category of history, but in that of theophany.[15] In fact there are a number of speeches in it which make it impossible to attribute a strictly historical value, not to the experience of the disciples, which is beyond doubt, but to the details of the narrative. In the first place, the number forty signifies a significant length of time, a generation for example, like the years in the wilderness, or of a major revelation, as to Moses (Exod 24:18), to Elijah (I Kings 19:8), or to Baruch (Apoc Bar 76:1-4). The number also signifies a fixed period, an archetypal time, here that of the appearances which remain the normal pattern of the revelation of Christ. But it does not exactly define a period of time. Moreover, Paul seems to include the appearance to himself amongst the authentic appearances of the risen Christ (see chapter 3) while certain later traditions were to fix the length of time the risen Christ stayed on earth at about eighteen months, or even more precisely from 545 to 550 days.[16]

Another traditional element in theophany narratives is the cloud, which plays a varying part. It may manifest the presence of God or the glory of the Son (Matthew 17:1-8 para.); it may also form a celestial chariot (Matthew 24:30 para. 26:64 para.); or, as here, it may veil Jesus from sight now that he has become a heavenly being.[17]

The men dressed in white correspond to the angelic messengers who normally accompany theophanies both in the bible and in post-biblical Judaism.[18]

But none of these themes appear in the texts which we have studied above. It might be that they have been eliminated because of the intended purpose: the language of hymns derives from the experience of the apostles and was satisfied with retaining the fact that Jesus was lifted up to heaven, abandoning the details. But before accepting this interpretation, we must ask what is meant by 'experience'. As we have said in the previous chapter, no experience is handed on except in some language. Here again, the question is not that of establishing the relationship between experience and expression, but between two languages: the statements of the hymns and the description by Luke.

At this level of study, it is impossible to determine which language is derived from the other. It is possible that the hymns were derived from the description, and it may also be the case that the description embellishes the faith of the hymns. It is nevertheless difficult to suppose that either is the result of a process of abstraction or imagination; the themes which we have just discussed are profoundly biblical, and so out of place in the Lucan writings that they cannot be attributed to Luke's invention. Thus it is best to suppose that both forms of expression derive from a common mythical language which is widespread in the bible and in general religious symbolism. Both ascension and exaltation derive from the symbolism of the lifting of the righteous men up to heaven. Thus the way in which Luke proceeded to describe the ascension cannot be explained by saying that he put into visual terms the theological theme of the exaltation of the risen Christ; from the very first, faith was expressed in a 'mythical' language, or again in symbolic language, in order to describe the existential realities which, experienced at a profound level, were beyond the scope of ordinary rational language.[19]

2 *Biblical Symbolism*

The faith that Jesus was exalted at his death makes use of symbols which are universal amongst men. The first is that of height and depth.[20] In every age, men have described as 'high' and 'low' what is better and what is worse. Thus God is located in the heights, and the evil forces are relegated to the lower regions. This representation was no doubt encouraged by ancient cosmology, which located heaven above our head and hell beneath; according to specialists in the history of religion and symbols, this symbolism, or rather 'immediate notion of the whole consciousness'[21] is based upon the basic experience of falling and rising again. When they spoke in this way, the first Christians showed that they were the heirs of this ancient human symbolism.

Various groups of symbols developed this way, and came together to evolve into the language of exaltation. From the starting point in the existence of heaven and earth, one above and the other below, the encounter of God and man was represented by the image of a journey to be made between heaven and earth. In order to visit men, God 'comes down' from heaven (Gen 11:5; Exod 19:11-13; Ps 144:5) and 'goes up' again (Gen 17:22); similarly the Word of God comes down from heaven and reascends (Is 55:10-11); and the angels do the same (Gen 28:12; John 1:51). On the other hand, it is impossible for men to undertake the journey: heaven is inaccessible (Deut 30:12; Prov 30:4), as Paul said when he quoted Deuteronomy in the passage from the Epistle to the Romans which we discussed above.

From this starting point, it is understandable that in certain cases God should come in his justice and faithfulness to lift up and carry off the righteous whom he will not abandon to the common lot of mankind. Independently of any connection with Sheol, but as though it were important not to abandon a righteous man to such a lot, this leads to a new representation of death which was worked out at a very early stage in the biblical texts. The death of the righteous is a 'lifting up' to heaven. Thus Enoch was taken up (Ecclus 49:14) or 'translated' (Ecclus 44:16; cf. Gen 5:24 LXX; Enoch 11:5), and Elijah was carried up into heaven in a whirlwind of fire (Ecclus 48:9; I Macc 2:58; cf. II Kings 2:9-11). Thus before the evolution of belief in the resurrection of the dead there already existed the hope that the righteous man would be lifted up to heaven. The psalmist praised, 'God will ransom my soul from the power of Sheol, for he will receive me' (Ps 49:15), and, 'Thou dost hold my right hand. Thou dost guide me with thy counsel, and afterward thou wilt receive me to glory' (Ps 73:23-24). The verb 'receive, lift up' constantly recurs, and expresses the profound desire never to be separated from God, as one is when one dies and goes down to Sheol.

This profound desire is reflected in the way in which Jewish tradition found some way of avoiding the death of Moses, in spite of the formal statements of Deuteronomy (34:5-6): he 'vanished' (*aphanizetai*: cf. Luke 24:31), he 'went away' (*anachōrēsai*: cf. Luke 9:33) back to God; and the same is true of Adam, of Phineas etc.[22] Moreover, a linguistic phenomenon reinforced this identification between lifting up and death: in Aramaic, the same root *ṣlq* signifies both 'die' and 'be lifted up';[23] and the same Greek word *analēmpsis* can have both meanings, as is confirmed by Luke

9:51: 'When the days drew near for him to be received up'; does this mean his death or his 'ascension'? Both, for in short, they are seen as complementary. The same can be said of the verb used by the evangelist John to describe the death which Jesus was to die, 'to be lifted up' (*hypsōthēnai*: John 12:32-33; cf. 8:28; 3:14), which also has the meaning 'be crucified'.[24] The phenomenon is so tangible that in some late Jewish writings, 'die' no longer means 'go beneath the earth', but 'ascend to the third heaven', that is, paradise (II Enoch 8:1-4; Apoc Mos 37:5). From this point of view, death did not take place, but was to some extent absorbed into the lifting up into heaven. If it is permissible to make what at first sight may seem a surprising comparison, we would venture to suggest that this is the image underlying Paul's thought when he states, 'We shall not all die, but we shall all be changed' (I Cor 15:51). It is clear that from this point of view there is no room for a resurrection, since death has not taken place, in the sense that it is a descent to Sheol.

Now the symbolism of exaltation is found in a more complex form in association with the descent to Sheol, or at least with some descent. Here it is closer to the terminology of the resurrection, because it is a rising out of Sheol. But the link with Sheol is not always obvious, whereas the image of exaltation can always be observed. After the exile, in particular, a tradition grew up which stated that the righteous sufferer would be exalted. According to the law of opposites which operates in the bible (I Sam 2:7-8; cf. Job 5:11; Ps 75:7-8; Luke 1:52) the Servant of God, after voluntarily accepting suffering, was glorified and exalted (Is 52:13; 53:12). This pattern dominates the description of the fate of the righteous man: 'The righteous man will stand with great confidence, in the presence of those who have afflicted him ... why is his lot amongst the saints?' (Wis 5:1-5).[25] There are many comparable passages from Jewish tradition, either that of Qumran or the rabbis, which promise exaltation to those who accept suffering; thus Hillel (ca. 20 B.C.) declared: 'My humiliation is my exaltation, and my exaltation is my humiliation.'[26]

Conclusion

Thus the fact of Easter has been expressed here in different terms from those of resurrection, in language which emphasizes the heavenly aspect of the event. Did this language take form because of the contact between Christian faith and the Hellenistic world? There are many critics who would say that this is the case.[27] There are no doubt many similarities to Greek literature which can be adduced in favour of this view: the theme of the hero who comes down from heaven and re-ascends thither after having triumphed upon earth is very widespread. But one must not be deceived by these similarities. As we shall see below, while it is possible to suspect some influence from the Hellenistic pattern of descent and re-ascent on the Johannine presentation of incarnation and exaltation, we must not forget that the descent—re-ascent pattern also applies to Sheol, that the lifting up into heaven is independent of this, and that the derivation from biblical and Jewish tradition is at least as clear as that from Hellenistic thought.

In this connection, we must also note that the confession of Jesus as Lord (_Kyrios_) did not simply develop in the Hellenistic setting, and in particular as a reaction against emperor worship. For the title _Marana_ is typically Palestinian. It can be accepted that the 'exaltation' pattern of thought is also rooted in the Palestinian world, and may be as old as the 'resurrection' pattern. The question that now arises is that of the way in which the two patterns are interdependent.

C. THE TWO THOUGHT PATTERNS COMPARED

1   _The Events Seen from Different Points of View_

It should first be said that the two patterns assume similar anthropological and cosmological conceptions, those of the bible. Both affirm that Jesus has not remained in the power of death, but is alive with God. Their emphasis, however, is different. To express the same continuance of existence after death, the resurrection pattern (let us call it pattern R) states that Jesus was 'wakened' from the sleep of death, was 'raised' from the tomb and from Sheol, in order to return once again to this world. In the exaltation pattern (which we shall call pattern E), Jesus was 'lifted up' was 'exalted', 'ascended' to heaven, and left this world below for the world above.

Since the direction envisaged by the images is not the same (either to this world or to the world above), it follows that a different account will be given of the new condition of Jesus. In R, the focus of attention is on the bodily likeness which enables him to be identified; in E, the main concern is with the transformation which makes Jesus the Lord of the universe. In the Easter event, which is both fact and mystery, one emphasizes the fact and the other the mystery. Here we observe the advantage and disadvantage of each form of representation. In R, the identity of the risen Christ with Jesus of Nazareth is more obvious than in E, while in the latter, his lifting up into glory means that he is carried away from the earth and breaks with men and their history, so that there is no longer any room for 'recognition appearances' but only for the proclamation of the Lord who is glorified in heaven. On the other hand, pattern E makes more immediately obvious the fact that Jesus is Lord after his death, and his dominion over the universe.

It is nevertheless pattern R which clearly won the day against pattern E. In fact apart from the few liturgical passages mentioned in this chapter, all that has survived of the second pattern are the fragments or theological allusions which we have discussed (Col, Eph, Heb, John). We have the impression that pattern R completely took over pattern E. Thus it seems that there was difficulty in the two patterns co-existing without competing. Pattern R was better adapted to making the new existence of Jesus to some extent tangible and providing a basis for Christian faith.

Let us therefore attempt to show how the two patterns came to be combined in the course of time, the second continuing to exist within that which took it over, pattern R.

The address by Peter in Acts (Acts 2:2-36) is important here. 'This Jesus ... you crucified and killed ... But God raised him up' (pattern R). This is taken up in the same way after the development of the address: 'This Jesus God raised up, and of that we are all witnesses' (pattern R once again). But immediately afterwards Peter continues: 'Being therefore exalted at the right hand of God (pattern E), and having received ... the promise of the Holy Spirit, he has poured out this which you see and hear. For David did not ascend into the heavens; but he himself says, "The Lord said to my Lord, Sit at my right hand, till I make thy enemies a stool for thy feet" (E). Let all the house of Israel therefore know assuredly that God has made him both Lord and Christ' (E). There are apparently a certain number of events occurring in succession: death (23), resurrection (24-32), ascension (33), triumphal enthronement (34-36). A similar harmonization is found in 5:30-31: 'God ... raised

Jesus (R) ... God exalted him at his right hand' (E). But when we find there a temporal succession of events, we must take care not to project upon it our customary pattern of thought, which corresponds to pattern R. If we look closely, we can see that the harmonization is artificial. In the texts quoted (2:32), the new mention of the resurrection does not lead on to another act following and complementing it, but to an explanation: 'being therefore exalted at the right hand of God'. The exaltation does not follow the resurrection, but makes its true significance clear. Behind the spontaneous outlook which sees successive events here, an outlook which is probably in accordance with what Luke intended, there is a tendency to identify the exaltation and the ascension, the latter being an event which Luke seems to have set on the fortieth day after Easter (Acts 1:3, 9-11). Now according to the exaltation pattern, there is no succession of events in time, but a manifestation and unfolding of a single mystery, the glorification of Jesus. One may say that from this point of view, the exaltation is identical with the resurrection. These are not two events, but the unveiling of two aspects of a single mystery. H. Schlier has well expressed the intrinsic relationship which unites the two aspects, when he shows how the resurrection is fitted into the movement which lifts Jesus up into the glory of God: these two mysteries, he tells us, 'were perhaps originally independent interpretations of the same event' [29] When we re-read the gospel narratives of the appearances (chapter 5) we shall find that the exaltation pattern has also left its traces in the present redaction.

If pattern R is so clearly dominant, does it follow that pattern E is secondary? Or alternatively, that pattern E is anterior? These questions are difficult to answer, and yet an answer would take us back to the origins of christology. The present state of scholarship does not provide sufficient basis for reconstructing what took place. [30] Nevertheless, we should like to put forward several suggestions, with the aim of avoiding hasty solutions.

There are many who even do not suspect that the problem exists, for they deny that pattern E is of any value on its own. For them, the solution is simple: pattern E is an interpretation of pattern R. Others, like E. Schweizer, [31] have closely examined the problem, and regard the christological hymns as reflecting a Hellenistic type of thought; since the Greek areas were the scene of the second advance of Christianity, it follows that pattern E is later than pattern R. But we consider that Schweizer does not sufficiently distinguish between the Hellenistic pattern of 'descent—re-ascent,' which may have contributed to the Johannine christology with respect to the incarnation, and the 'exaltation' pattern which may follow a humiliation, but does not necessarily do so. In the latter case, there is sufficient biblical evidence for it to be unnecessary to have recourse to a Hellenistic origin.

Other scholars[32] assume that a belief in the imminence of the parousia preceded the elaboration of christology of type E. It would then follow that resurrection and exaltation were both ways of reacting to the disappointment caused by the delay of the parousia. In this case, a parousia type of christology would have been original, and patterns R and E would have been secondary derivations from it. But this reasoning assumes that there exists a single type of presence of the Lord in glory, that of the judge who is to come; whereas according to certain texts, and particularly in cultic celebrations, Jesus is described as him who from now on exercises his dominion over the congregation of believers. Thus this theory does not seem to cover all the facts. From the very first, Jesus was proclaimed Lord (*marana*) and this could be rendered either by pattern R or by pattern E. Thus the question which of the two came first remains open.[33]

In our view it is not possible to show that pattern E is later than pattern R. At the very beginning, the first Christians seemed to have telescoped together the Easter event and the parousia; dazzled by the living light of Easter, they were not concerned to recount in detail the very precise recollections of what had just happened. It was sufficient for them to affirm the pascal event itself, and this could be done in several ways: by affirming the initial fact (God has raised him from the dead) or by proclaiming Jesus as Lord in glory (God has exalted him). The need to place the 'events' which as a matter of history were experienced by the disciples in chronological order only gradually came to be felt. These remarks suggest that the sequence resurrection-appearances-ascension may be regarded as later than pattern E, but not the brief proclamation of the fact of the resurrection which we have recognized in the credal formula.

Other scholars have emphasized that pattern R was a refutation of Jewish attacks upon faith in Jesus, and have sought to show how

R was derived from E. But this is possible only at the cost of correct-
ing the texts, and this is to go beyond the rights of an exegete. The
affirmation of the exaltation is no doubt more full of meaning than
that of the resurrection, but it does not follow that the former preceded the latter.

Our conclusion may seem unsatisfactory to a reader who is concerned to establish the history of the texts and of the formulation of
Christian faith. But it is better to admit that the best one can do is
to state that the two patterns co-existed. But to state this is valuable,
for it is then no longer necessary to treat pattern R as exclusive, as
though the term 'resurrection' was the only way of expressing the
mystery. To accept this risk is important for the understanding of
the gospel texts, and especially for hermeneutics and the communication of the Easter message.

2   *A Point of Convergence: 'The Lord Showed Himself'*

We have just emphasized two different points of view, but common to both languages is an affirmation of the primitive faith
which concerns the way in which Jesus made known the fact that
he had returned alive from the dead and that from now on he was
in glory. The same verb *ōphthē* serves in I Cor 15[34)] to state that
Christ 'appeared' to Cephas, to James and to Paul, and to say in the
liturgical hymn in I Tim 3:16 that the glorified Lord 'appeared' to
the angel. This agreement in the use of one and the same term is
surprising, for it occurs in two different patterns and refers to two
realities which are not of the same order—an earthly reality in the
case of Cephas and a heavenly in the case of the angels.

Must we here treat as similar two types of manifestation, the
'tangible' vision described in the gospels and the 'spiritual' vision
which the angels had? Most scholars have not answered this question, and have thought it sufficient to look for a better term than
'appearance' for what took place and, for example, to substitute that
of 'vision', which is considered closer in its etymological sense to
the verb 'see'. Then, since the term 'vision' is ambiguous, there is
a tendency to treat the disciples as 'visionaries' and consequently a
corrective epithet has been added: *objective* vision (an apparently
contradictory phrase) or *pneumatic* vision (an attempt, which does
not succeed, to avoid the adjective 'spiritual' in the meaning 'not
tangible').[35)] In spite of these corrections, the result is to place the
phenomena within the category 'vision', because of the emphasis on

the simple word 'see'. Others have therefore preferred to emphasize other aspects of the event and talk of *experience*.[36] But while this term succeeds in stating that the whole being was renewed by contact with Christ, is it not too vague and too remote from the imaginative strength of the word 'see'? The principal objection which we would have to these interpretations is that they describe the phenomenon on the basis of the subject who sees or experiences, whereas the biblical writers are seeking to emphasize the intervention of Christ himself. For the moment, then, let us retain the classical word *appearance*. What does it mean?

Grammatically, the verb *ōphthē* is a passive aorist. It has therefore often been translated by 'He was seen'. Since the Greek language demands after the passage an indirect complement preceded not by 'to' but by 'by', this departure from practice is explained by appealing to a favourite usage of the Jews: the function of the passive is to disguise the true agent of an action produced by him whom one does not wish to name, God: 'Hallowed be thy name' means 'May God hallow his name'. An equivalent is said to be found in Acts 10:40: 'God made him manifest ... to us who were chosen ...' though there with another Greek verb. In our view there is an insurmountable objection to this interpretation: the constant usage of the Greek translation of the bible, which uses *ōphthē* to translate the niphal of the verb 'see', that is, the passive of the causative (hiphil): 'make to see'. Thus in the phrase which describes the appearance of Yahweh to Abraham, 'God appeared to Abraham' (Gen 12:7), there is a nuance which Philo brings out well: 'God went to meet him and showed (*edeixe*) to him that of his nature which he who looked at him was capable of seeing. That is why we do not read that the wise man saw God, but that God showed himself to the wise man.'[37] Thus the correct translation of the verb *ōphthē* is 'he showed himself to Cephas ...' These remarks confirm our reservation with regard to the suggestions mentioned above, vision or experience, both of which exclude any allusion to divine action.

A brief study of the Greek bible will supply some details about the manifestation to which this word refers. Something which has been hidden becomes visible. Thus by gathering together the liquid element into one place or in reducing the amount of water, God shows the dry land (Gen 1:9) or the tops of the mountains (8:5). In addition to this simple transition from invisible to visible, there is also the nuance of a step taken voluntarily, in particular in sacrificial terminology, to indicate the way in which one should go to encounter the Lord with offerings: 'one goes off to show oneself', that is, 'to present oneself before Yahweh'.[38] Finally, when God himself is the subject, the two previous elements—making visible and taking action—are reinforced in a particular way. For by nature God is invisible, so that if he himself, his glory or his angel appear, this is the unmerited result of his own decision: he wishes to enter into contact with man, for example with Abraham (Gen 12:7) or with Moses (Exod 3:2). Thus we have here not the simple unveiling of something hidden, but a presence which shows itself and enters into a dialogue. For if he shows himself it is in order to speak or to act, to call or to send on a mission.[39] When we note that this usage is also found, for example, in Josephus and in rabbinic literature, we may conclude that this is the essence of what the gospel description of the 'appearance' is telling us: that the risen Jesus takes on the role of God himself; that of initiative and sending on a mission.

How about the 'visible' character of the appearance? If we keep to the Old Testament view, God clearly does not show himself in a 'tangible' vision.[40] It is not sufficient to say of the appearances of the risen Christ that they are tangible because Jesus has a body; it is necessary to make clear what this 'body' consists of. The expression 'to show himself' goes far beyond the 'tangible' aspect that is sometimes imposed upon it, as can be seen from the way it is used not only in the Old Testament, but also to state that Christ 'showed himself' to the angels. To demonstrate that the appearances are 'tangible' it will be necessary to use other arguments.

But our brief enquiry does not simply lead to a negative conclusion. First of all, the aspect of 'presentation' in the appearance must be retained: God presents himself to someone, imposes himself upon someone. He does not show himself as an object to be seen but becomes involved in a relationship, the hearing of a word. Again, the concern is not with him who sees, but with him who shows himself, who lets himself be seen. Thus if the subject who sees begins to speak, yet another step has taken place: it is not God who is imposing himself, but Isaiah or Paul when they say, 'My eyes have seen the King' (Is 6:5), 'Have I not seen Jesus our Lord?' (I Cor 9:1). The active form of the verb modifies the relationship: from God who imposes himself the interest moves to the

human being who bears witness to his experience. Our final conclusion is that we must take note of the efforts made in the terminology not to limit this experience to a simple visual perception and
to express its existential and universal character: many other words
are used which have a far greater scope than the verb 'to see':
meet, present oneself, appear.[41)]

Conclusion

The way the two patterns, of resurrection and exaltation, unite in
the term 'show himself' does not modify the conclusions to which
we have already come. Let us recall the most important.

In trying to penetrate more deeply into the statements in the
texts and to discover in them the existence of a different language
from that of resurrection with regard to the event of Easter, we
have no intention of giving prizes for antiquity or for greater or
less truth. It would be naive and wrong to want to replace the
resurrection language because a different terminology existed to
describe the same mystery. In chapter 11 we shall make clear the
sense in which the language of resurrection can be called the
'standard terminology'. The occurrences of the E terminology
enable us to understand more clearly the meaning and scope of the
R terminology: it is only the exaltation which gives the resurrection
of Jesus its full meaning. Moreover, we have observed that the
terms used to describe contact with the risen Christ are numerous.
When we come to examine the way in which Paul talks of the
appearance vouchsafed to him, we shall see how important it is to
break the mould into which we spontaneously fit the Easter experience.

It was the evangelist John who was most sensitive to this wide
range of meaning. In order to talk of what happened to Jesus he
did in fact retain an R terminology which we shall examine in
chapter 10; but his 'theology' shows a preference for speaking of the
'glorification' or 'exaltation' of Jesus.[42)] It is in the light of Easter
but not *after* Easter, and indeed even by the cross that the mystery
of Jesus is to be understood; and the glory of God in his Son is
manifested in an earthly event in the life of Jesus.

CHAPTER THREE

When a Witness Speaks

When the gospels give accounts of the appearances, they are not those of direct witnesses. We have the words of only one man who was a witness himself, Paul. Though his disclosures were not made until about fifteen years after the event, they are of immense value to us, for they show us the attempt, just as it took place, to describe this unique experience. They present us with a terminology of surprising freedom in the moment of its creation.

Of course Paul never described in detail the appearance which was vouchsafed to him. We cannot exclude on *a priori* grounds the possibility that he gave verbal accounts of this event, but we have no certain way of knowing what they were like. In the writings that are readily available to us—letters which were usually written for a certain audience and in particular circumstances—Paul never revealed any intention of giving a narrative account of what took place; on four occasions at least he simply refers to the event which changed the course of his existence. There are some difficulties in interpreting these texts. Do they refer to an appearance of the risen Christ identical to that seen by the Twelve? Is it Paul's intention to speak directly and exclusively of this specific event? What is the relationship between it and the 'visions and revelations' which he mentions on other occasions? If one bears in mind the Lucan narrative of Saul's conversion on the Damascus road, one cannot but be surprised by the contrast in vocabulary and expression. An explanation of these can be found in the difference between the context of a letter and that of a narrative, and also in the different points of view of each writer. But no valid comparison is possible until Paul and Luke have been considered separately. In the next chapter, we shall follow Luke's narrative. Here, in order to proceed methodically, we shall work, in their probable chronological order, through the passages which Paul addressed to the Galatians, the Philippians, and the Corinthians, in order to appreciate the way in which this exceptional witness recounted the event. We shall find that the background to Paul's thought is formed by the two kinds of terminology, that of resurrection and that of exaltation, which we have just examined: the term resurrection is found, and so too is the designation of Jesus as the Lord of glory. But his original experience also found other words to describe the event; and this leads us on to his understanding of the mystery of Easter and allows us to raise fresh questions.

A. IN THE EPISTLE TO THE GALATIANS

The context of the epistle is known.[1] Paul's authority has been questioned by those to whom he is writing, and he recalls the origin of his apostolate: men have had no part in it, he says, and it was God alone who called him to preach the gospel to the gentiles. We cannot analyse the whole of the first chapter here, and we shall restrict ourselves to verses 13-23 which tell how the 'revelation' (*apokalypsis*) of Jesus Christ (1:12), raised from the dead by God the Father (1:1), took place. Two points should be emphasized: Paul locates the event, the meaning of which he understood (1:15-16b) in the course of a history with a before (1:13-14, 23) and after (1:16c-17, 23). After describing his point of view (1:13-17) Paul reflects that of the churches of Christ in Judea (1:23):

[13]For you have heard of my former life in Judaism, how I persecuted the church of God violently and tried to destroy it; [14]and I advanced in Judaism beyond many of my own age among my people, so extremely zealous was I for the traditions of my fathers. [15]But when he who had set me apart before I was born, and had called me through his grace, [16]was pleased to reveal his Son in[2] me, in order that I might preach him among the Gentiles, I did not confer with flesh and blood, [17]nor did I go up to Jerusalem to those who were apostles before me, but I went away into Arabia; and again I returned to Damascus.... [22]And I was still not known by sight to the churches of Christ in Judea; [23]they only heard it said, 'He who once persecuted us is now preaching the faith he once tried to destroy' (Gal 1:13-17, 22-23).

1   *The Before and After*

Paul is eloquent on the subject, plunging us into a history he had experienced himself. He describes himself as not having had 'before' any relation with the Christians, except that of a persecutor. Some critics have assumed that Paul felt an inner tension concerning the Jewish law, and that this tension led him to 'be converted' from the law to Christ;[3] but we follow the majority of Christian commentators in assuming that here as elsewhere Paul is describing his past in a positive way, and not by way of a criticism of the law, such as he was to make later when he had come to have faith in Christ. Paul had kept the law faithfully, and was well acquainted with the rabbinic traditions.[4] If he persecuted 'the church of God'[5] violently, this was because he saw in Christian belief an attitude which was incompatible with the Jewish faith. In what respect? In Paul's eyes, the law in its totality was of vital importance: it was the vehicle of salvation. This conviction is difficult to explain if Paul is regarded as a disciple of the rabbis, most of whom considered the law simply as the guiding light of conduct. We therefore consider the hypothesis of U. Wilckens an interesting one: that according to apocalyptic tradition, the law possessed in reality a saving function.[6] This explains the reaction of Paul, a Jew who, when he saw Jesus denying the essential and sacred function of the law, unleashed a violent persecution. But in any case, in order to understand the transformation which we assert took place, we do not need to suppose that Paul inwardly criticized the law.

Paul tells us little about what took place 'after' the event. What he says here relates to the major concern of his letter; his purpose is not to describe his apostolic activity or his inner transformation, but to emphasize his lack of contact with the authorities in Jerusalem. Finally, at the conclusion of his exposition, in 1:23 Paul returns briefly to the contrast (once—now) between the situation before and after the episode of the Damascus road.

2   *The Event Recounted by Paul*

What exactly took place? We are not yet able to say. Paul talks about it, but in a new terminology which we must now try to describe. For while the situation before and after is set out in terms which are historical in character, relating it directly to the sphere of history, the style changes once the event of the appearance is reached. It remains an event, because it is introduced by the conjunction 'when' (*hote*; 1:15) which marks off a precise moment between before and after. But it is evoked in a secondary proposition, in terms which no longer belong to the category of history, but which, drawn from a scriptural background, relate the event to apocalyptic.

A prophetic vocation   Paul understands his encounter with Christ in the light of the song of the Servant of Yahweh, and particularly that of the missionary Servant (Is 49:1-6). In the Greek version of this passage the expression occurs: 'From my mother's womb he called my name' (49:1); there is a reference to the glory given by 'my servant' (49:3) and his mission: 'I have set you as a light to the nations, for salvation unto the ends of the earth' (49:6). Following L. Cerfaux and many other writers,[7] we consider that Paul was not directly inspired by Jer 1:5: 'Before I formed you in the womb I knew you, and before you were born I consecrated you; I appointed you a prophet to the nations.' For this text does not contain the essential word 'call' (*kaleō*) nor the positive aspect of the evangelization of the nations; Paul is referring to Is 49, which in its turn is inspired by Jeremiah.

No doubt Paul does not conceive of himself as a new Servant of God, but 'his role, as a continuation of Christ, finds its place in the fulfilment of the prophecy of the Servant. In appearing to Paul, Christ passes on his own mission to him.'[8] But this latter statement must be qualified, for one may ask how far, for Paul, the title of Servant can be applied to the Messiah; for in the tradition of Hellenistic Judaism,[9] it is Israel who is the Servant: Israel is the 'light to the nations' (cf. Rom 2:19-20). If it is to be maintained that in Paul's eyes Christ fulfilled the prophecy of the Servant, it was by bringing to reality the covenant of God with his people. Paul is the missionary servant.[10] In short, the appearance shows him that he must proclaim at the present time what according to the prophecy the Servant would have to proclaim in the future.

Through this calling Paul discovers his essential being. He uses the verb 'set apart' (*aphorizō*) and not 'choose' (*eklegomai*): the terms of predestination and election, of setting apart (alluding to Ps 22:11 and 139:11-16) show that Paul described in the story of his life a period which preceded that in which he received the law. By so doing, he is following a movement of thought similar to that which in Gal 3:6-29 enables him to place the law in the history of his people, as an intermediary period between Abraham and Christ.[11] For him, the situation before the appearance of Christ is related to what preceded that situation, the gracious favour of God.

For it is God alone who took the initiative. In 1:15, God suddenly becomes the subject of the sentence and the agent, while Paul is the object of the divine intervention. Thus what characterizes the appearance of the risen Christ to Paul is that it is a 'calling' the origin of which is due entirely to God; and this is a guarantee that it is not the outcome of a personal evolution. Paul of course does not record a single word spoken by Christ, but he interprets his vocation as a calling to fulfil a task which will take him over completely and which in some sense will define what he is in himself: a mission to the gentiles.

An apocalyptic revelation   In this passage, Paul does not only say that he has been called as a prophet, but makes clear the nature of the appearance. He does so by using not the terminology of 'vision', but that of 'revelation', literally, that of apocalypse. By contrasting this word with what comes from man, Paul has just described the origin of his gospel, which he received 'not according to man (RSV margin: 'In a human manner' or 'on a human scale'). For I did not receive it from man ... but it came through an *apocalypse* of Jesus Christ' (1:12). What does this term mean?

It seems certain that it did not originally mean a revelation with an intellectual content, but that of an eschatological event, that is, of a heavenly reality which was awaiting men at the end of time. Thus Paul uses it to refer to the coming of Christ at the parousia (II Thess 1:7; I Cor 1:7), the action of the Antichrist (II Thess 2:3, 6, 9), the eschatological glory (Rom 8:18-21), the anger of the judge (Rom 1:18; 2:5), and the purifying fire (I Cor 3:13). These events are sometimes anticipated: thus even now divine righteousness is revealed to the believer (Rom 1:17) and faith saves those whom the law kept under its tutelage (Gal 3:23). In this text too, God was pleased to reveal his Son to Paul, that is, to make him present in order to authenticate his apostle and to confer the eschatological gifts upon him.[12] Thus here Paul seems to have in mind the nature of the appearance as an event. Through this event, he is introduced into the universe of the end of time: for is this not in a word identical with the risen Christ? Perhaps there is an allusion to this conviction in II Cor 4:6: 'It is the God who said, "Let light shine out of darkness," who has shone in our hearts to give the light of the knowledge of the glory of God in the face of Christ.' This strange grandeur is given to the person of Paul, who from now on lives in the absolute of the end of time, by virtue of the Lord of glory who has come to take hold of him within time; and so he becomes the herald commissioned to proclaim 'the mystery which was kept secret for long ages' (Rom 16:25).

By describing the appearance as an 'apocalypse', Paul raises a problem. For in his letters there is frequent mention of 'apocalypses' or 'revelations'. Of course there should be no confusion between 'appearance' (*ōphthē*) and 'visions' (*optasiai*), but due value must also be given to the fact that in Gal 2:2 Paul uses the same term, *kata apokalypsin* to describe the inspiration which he had to go to 'lay before' the brethren in Jerusalem his gospel (cf. Eph 3:3, 5). He talks of 'revelations' at the same time as of visions (II Cor 12:1, 7) and this is not surprising because he is aware of the existence of a charisma of 'revelation' (I Cor 14:6, 26, 30, cf. Eph 1:17) which is itself rooted in the imparting of the wisdom of God by the Spirit (I Cor 2:10). Though Paul seems to connect the appearance or revelation at Damascus and later charismatic revelations, he nevertheless radically distinguishes the one from the others in proportion to the distance which separates the fundamental event and its consequences. What has happened is that event and revelations have eventually been united in the wisdom which gives access to the mystery.

For Paul, these are the consequences of his encounter with the Lord. As far as the appearance itself is concerned, Paul does not say that it consists of the fact of recognizing that the risen Christ is identical with Jesus of Nazareth; but the divine initiative has shown him that it gives access to the end of time; through the understanding of the scriptures, it apprehends the mystery which spreads out and develops into mission.

B. IN THE EPISTLE TO THE PHILIPPIANS

The second text in which Paul alludes to his encounter with the risen Christ is found in the Epistle to the Philippians, which, following a number of scholars, we date in approximately 55-56.[13] The passage which we shall study is related in style to the Epistle to the Galatians and consists of a violent polemic against judaizers. As before, though with the intention not of authenticating his apostolate but of presenting himself as an example, Paul recounts his own calling, for he sees in it the attitude proper to every Christian: one must cleave to Christ alone. The structure of thought here is similar to that found in the Epistle to the Galatians.

> [7]But whatever gain I had, I counted as loss for the sake of Christ. [8]Indeed I count everything as loss because of the surpassing worth of knowing Christ Jesus my Lord. For his sake I have suffered the loss of all things, and count them as refuse, in order that I may gain Christ [9]and be found in him, not having a righteousness of my own, based on law, but that which is through faith in Christ, the righteousness from God that depends on faith; [10]that I may know him and the power of his resurrection, and may share his sufferings, becoming like him in his death [11]that if possible I may attain the resurrection from the dead. [12]Not that I have already obtained this [the prize] nor that I am already perfect [i.e. have completed the race]; but I press on to make it my own [the goal], because Christ Jesus has made me his own. [13]Brethren, I do not consider that I have made it [the goal] my own; but one thing I do, forgetting what lies behind and straining forward to what lies ahead, [14]I press on towards the goal for the prize of the upward call of God in Christ Jesus (Phil 3:7-14).

The before and after are also set out in detail here, and once again in such a way as to describe the radical change which has come about. Before, Paul was an authentic Jew, a pure Israelite, of the tribe of Benjamin, and a Pharisee whose righteousness was profound; his career was the fruit of a real and admirable zeal. There is no question of any tension concerning the law, any more than in the Epistle to the Galatians.

But what is found after the change is a severe judgment upon the past, a judgment caused by the intervention of Christ who has turned established values upside down: all this is nothing more than loss, refuse. But what comes after is also indestructible confidence, thanks to the new faith in Christ which lays down a new principle of existence. Once again, the problem appears of the demarcation between the event proper and what follows it. When looking at the Epistle to the Galatians, we asked what was the link which united the fundamental event and the later 'revelations'. Here the problem is that of 'knowledge': is it knowledge of the event itself or of the consequences which it brought about?

To know Christ, to be apprehended by Christ   The event before Damascus is hinted at by a 'but' (*alla*) in v. 7. It at once demands a new judgment upon the old values: 'Whatever gain I had, I counted as loss.' But the emphasis is upon the motive for the change, that is, upon Christ. The transformation took place 'for the sake of Christ' (3:7); or again, in 3:8, 'for his sake' and 'because of the surpassing worth of knowing Christ'. Christ is the cause and is also the goal: Paul is aiming to gain Christ and to know him (3:8-10). It is certainly only the person of Christ which forms the bridge between before and after in Paul's experience. To say any more, we have to examine in turn the meaning of the verbs 'know' and 'attain'. Paul twice describes the intervention of Christ in a formula which expresses a new experience.

To know Jesus Christ is something which in Paul's view is very rare: normally, according to his epistles, the Christian is known by God and must not suppose that he knows God (I Cor 8:2-3; Gal 4:9), except in part (I Cor 13:12). Those who know that God exists no doubt 'know' God but they do not 'honour' him (Rom 1:21); the knowledge of Christ, achieved 'from a human point of view' is of no use (II Cor 5:16). Thus for Paul this is an exceptional act;[14] it is even 'an insurpassable reality' (rather than an 'insurpassable knowledge') the effects of which will be perceptible throughout his existence. This knowledge is not directly of the plan of God nor of the gifts of salvation, but actually of 'Christ Jesus *my* Lord'; and there is an equally exceptional note of intimacy (cf. Phil 1:21; Gal 2:20) which suggests a unique personal encounter. This would suggest that we should identify the appearance of the risen Christ and the existential knowledge of the Lord[15] which calls for a new judgment. This is not the place to describe in detail the transformation which leads Paul to reverse all his previous values. On the other hand it should be noted that the verb 'know' occurs shortly afterwards, and is used to describe what the initial encounter led to: 'that I may know him and the power of his resurrection, and may share his sufferings, becoming like him in his death, that if possible I may attain the resurrection from the dead' (3:10-11). By using the same word to describe the original encounter and its consequences, Paul is telling us that the appearance was not merely a past event. The shattering contact with the risen Christ did not consist simply in the imparting of knowledge as information, but was a radical remoulding of his existence, of his whole being, so that in the light of the resurrection (which is mentioned first) his sufferings and death are meaningful. From now on Paul understands himself as continually passing with Christ from death to resurrection.

The other verb with which Paul attempts to describe his experience—*to be made his own by Christ, to attain Christ*—is difficult to translate. It occurs in the context of an image which presents life as a race towards heaven, towards a prize which has to be carried off. The race began when Paul set out to persecute the Christians (the same verb *diōkein* means run, pursue and persecute); it is still continuing for him, but is entirely transformed by his contact with Christ. To translate the verb *katelēmphthēn* 'I have been seized by Christ Jesus' (3 : 12) or, with RSV, 'Christ Jesus has made me his own' is an attempt to express the personal nature of the contact. E. Deissmann interprets the fact to which it refers as a Hellenistic type of conversion. J. Lebraton saw the act of Christ as a seizure by violence. Since the word normally means[16] 'reach', 'gain the goal of the race' (as in Rom 9 : 30; I Cor 9 : 24; Phil 3 : 12-13), L. Cerfaux has proposed a translation which attempts to unify the images, as in the original texts:

'Not that I have already received (the resurrection as a prize) or that I have already arrived at my perfection (by the resurrection); I pursue (as in a race), in hope of attaining the goal (*ei kai katalabō*) because I have myself been attained (in the race: *katelēmphthēn*) by Christ Jesus. Brethren I do not consider that I have yet attained the goal (*kateilēphēnai*); but one thing I do, forgetting what lies behind, and straining forward to the goal which lies before me, I run (*dioko*) straight to the goal, to obtain the prize (*eis to brabeion*) for which God has called me from on high in Christ Jesus.'

As in the Epistle to the Galatians, Paul is groping and stammering to express his experience in terms appropriate to those receiving his letter. He succeeds in describing what precedes and what follows; but when he comes to the heart of the matter he finds himself dependent upon descriptive verbs which help him as far as possible to say something ineffable. The first person, 'I', is more obvious than in Galatians, but several times the verb is also passive: Paul has been overtaken, reached, seized in his own race; and that shows

that by intervening Christ does not stop the movement on which
man has set out, but fulfils it by transforming it radically: thus
although it appears completely new, the future possesses a continuity with the past. Finally, this passage makes clear the content
of the 'revelation' which was shown to be apocalyptic in character
in the Epistle to the Galatians. Here the verb 'know' describes in a
personal way the transformation of Paul's existence, beginning with
that which controls it, the faculty of judgment. Paul Claudel read
the French word *connaître*, 'to know' as *co-naître*, 'to share someone's birth'. Perhaps this is applicable here: for the believer in fact
shares in the resurrection of Christ by being united with his sufferings and his death. All that follows is imbued with the event itself.
The appearance does not simply give access to the end of time, it
inaugurates a new being and a new judgment, reducing to nothing
(*ezēmiōthēn*) all the past, it leads on to the perfect confidence which
brings about the new righteousness, that is, the new and authentic
relationship which unites man to God.

C. IN THE FIRST EPISTLE TO THE CORINTHIANS

In this letter[17] the appearance to Paul is mentioned twice, always
in a polemic context and with the aid of the verb 'see'. This final
sounding in Paul's letters will show the diversity and therefore the
freedom of his language.

1 I Cor 9:1-12

In the 'defence' (9:3) of which 9:1-27 consists, Paul defends his
conduct by showing that he is acting with the authority of an
apostle; and he is an apostle because he has seen Jesus our Lord. So
he introduces his plea with the essential point.

> [1]Am I not free? Am I not an apostle? Have I not seen Jesus our
> Lord? Are you not my workmanship in the Lord? [2]If to others
> I am not an apostle, at least I am to you; for you are the seal of
> my apostleship in the Lord.

It is interesting that all that is left of the before and after here is
what happens after. There is no mention of Paul's activity as a
persecutor which he was following when he heard the call of Christ.
Thus unlike the passage examined above, there is no question here
of a revelation which is astonishing because it is unmerited, nor of

any encouragement to give up Jewish practice for the sake of Christ who has overtaken the persecutor. Paul's interest here is in the personal character of his apostolic authority, as is clearly shown by the general context (cf. I Cor 9:15-23; 11:1). To set out his apostolic 'personality' against the right background, he shows the origin (*ex-ousia*) of the new being which has made him an apostle whose conduct for practical purposes derives from Christ alone.

These considerations themselves explain why the personal role of Paul at the time of the appearance is more strongly emphasized in this text. God is no longer the subject of the sentence (Gal), and the verb is no longer in the passive voice (Phil), but in the active 'I have seen'. On the basis of this verse, W. Marxsen makes a radical distinction between 'Christ appeared' and 'I have seen Jesus'; and according to him it is this latter expression which alone supplies the original character of the appearances.[13] But he is reading too much into an expression which is due to the polemic context of the passage; in fact Paul personalizes in the verb *ōphthē* in chapter 15. Another modification shows how much Paul is more free in his language than he reveals. Here he says, 'I have seen Jesus', but he immediately adds, not as in Philippians, 'My Lord', but 'Our Lord'. In this way, Paul takes up again the confession of faith in the hymn in Philippians which acclaims the Lord (Phil 2:11): he too has turned to the Lord whom he has recognized in Jesus.[19] What is new in this precise context is the possessive adjective 'our' placed before Lord, perhaps because of the traditional usage of the expression, but perhaps also (because of the contrast between *I* and *our*) in order to emphasize Paul's connection with the church of Corinth, the fruit of his apostolate. In any case, this Lord is the risen Christ, the Lord of our community.[20] Let us note the essential point in this reference: for Paul there is a constant circular movement between the appearance of the Lord by which he was once picked out and the apostolate which is now his life.

2   *I Cor 15:8-10*

The second text immediately follows the creed which was examined in chapter 1. Its purpose is to provide the basis for the kerygma of the resurrection of Jesus. To the list of those to whom a vision has been vouchsafed, and of whom he states that some are still alive (15:6), Paul adds his own witness.

[8]Last of all, as to one untimely born, he appeared also to me.

⁹For I am the least of the apostles, and fit to be called an apostle, because I persecuted the church of God. ¹⁰But by the grace of God I am what I am, and his grace towards me was not in vain. On the contrary, I worked harder than any of them, though it was not I, but the grace of God which is with me. ¹¹Whether then it was I or they, so we preach and so you believe (I Cor 15:8-11).

The before and after are indicated, especially the situation before, with the same purpose as in Galatians or Philippians: the former persecutor has now become a witness of the grace of God. Thus God's unmerited initiative in the event is emphasized.[21]

The verb *ōphthē*, used for the appearance to the witness of the risen Christ, is applied to himself by Paul in the same sense: 'He appeared also to me'. As in the other passages, Paul allows the immediate context to guide him: he applies to himself the verb which is traditionally used to describe the appearances. In this way he confirms that in his eyes the event on the Damascus road has the same value as the appearances to the Twelve or to the apostles.[22]

But there are two further details. First of all, Paul says, 'last of all' (*eschaton de pantōn*). This expression can have two meanings: 'last of the list' or 'very last'. If, as is usually the case, the second meaning is accepted, then Paul is saying that after the appearance to him, the appearances ceased. But we would not be so bold as to adopt this interpretation.

The other detail, 'as to one untimely born' (*hōsperei tō ektrōmati*) has been the subject of much dispute, since the word can mean equally well either 'abnormal birth', 'abortion', 'birth before time' or even 'outsider'. Some regard it as an allusion to the small stature (*pōlos*) of Paul (*Paulos*); others relate it to the nature of the persecution to which the rest of the text refers, supposing that this made this appearance 'abnormal'. Perhaps another interpretation can be proposed; if we take into account the article before *ektrōma*, which suggests a particular person, Paul may be alluding to a nickname which had been given to him. In any case, with regard to its content and value, the appearance to Paul must be placed on the same level as the appearances to the disciples; but it is additional to the received tradition and outside the normal framework. If this is so, Paul would be showing that Christ is the Lord of the tradition and that he is not dependent upon it; the action of the Spirit and the *Kyrios* cannot be restricted to tradition as it has taken shape in history, since it is itself a living tradition.[23]

From the four passages which we have briefly examined, we can draw a provisional conclusion about the fact of the appearance and the meaning which Paul gave to his encounter with the risen Christ. We shall return in chapter 11 to the historicity of the fact; for the moment, let us simply describe what Paul thought about it. To him it was a certainty which could not be called into question. The way in which he communicated it is an argument in favour of the authenticity of his witness; he never describes it in detail as it happened to him, as though he were imparting some historical or narrative information, and bears witness to it only when he feels obliged to do so by some polemic, defence or theological discussion.

The meaning of the event is not self-evident, but lies at the heart of a meaningful history, the history of Paul's life, which was radically changed by the encounter. This history is recounted in various ways. The persecutor becomes an adherent of the faith, the runner is overtaken in his race, he who did not know Christ 'knows' him. From now on his existence and calling are determined by the event; the mystery of the resurrection passes into him; visions and revelations make the original revelation a present reality, and the knowledge received once for all is the source of a new judgment and becomes more and more profound as he enters further into the mystery.

The event itself is described in terms which display the profound freedom which Paul exercises towards the traditional formula. The list in I Cor 15 of course includes 'He appeared also to me'; but once Paul is speaking spontaneously, he adopts another style altogether. When he uses the traditional expression, he reverses it and becomes its active subject: 'I have seen Jesus our Lord.' In other texts he uses terms of his own: sometimes 'reveal', sometimes 'be overtaken in the race' ('be seized'), or 'know'. This liberty is very significant, and invites us to break away from a slavish following of the letter, and the use of a single word—'show himself', 'appear' —to describe the appearances.

Two dimensions which are typical of the gospel narratives of the appearances can be clearly recognized in Paul's words: the divine initiative and the divine mission. The divine initiative is expressed by the use of passive verbs and is given a more profound expression in the mystery of pre-destination and prophetic vocation understood on the pattern of that of the Servant of Yahweh. Secondly, the divine mission is characteristic of the event: Paul is called to preach the gospel to the gentiles.

Where is the third dimension, that of the progressive recognition of Jesus, so strongly emphasized by the gospel narratives? It is not to be found, and this in itself is significant. At first sight, its absence may not seem unusual, seeing that Paul had no direct connection with Jesus of Nazareth. But it remains surprising when we remember that the theme of identification is developed by Luke in his narratives of the conversion of Saul of Tarsus. This raises a question: if it is true that Paul regards the appearance to him as equivalent to those to the Twelve, does the theme of recognition belong to the 'essence' of the appearance of the risen Christ?

Another question remains unanswered. If we admit that the appearance to Paul is 'abnormal', since it took place much later than that to the others, does this mean that it was the 'last'? Is the expression *eschaton de pantōn* sufficient to show this? Since the words 'revelation', 'know', 'visions' extend to later interventions on the part of Jesus, ought this not to lead us to review the outlook which makes an absolute distinction between the appearances and the other manifestations of the risen Christ? No doubt there is something unique in the appearances proper, but should the power of the appearance of the Lord be limited to what took place during a privileged period? If not, then the appearance to Paul shows the way towards another view of the official appearances of the risen Christ and the contact which he has with the world after the 'forty days' of which St Luke speaks.

The Narratives of the Encounter with the Lord Jesus

Two kinds of terminology were used by the primitive community to express the fact of the encounter of the first disciples with the living Jesus: he has risen from the dead; he is exalted in heaven, Lord and Christ. The same term *ōphthē* is found in both sets of terminology to express the content of the experience. When it is compared with other observations, we realize that its meaning has been considerably extended—it means not only to show oneself, but to manifest oneself in action—and always implies an 'experience'. This is confirmed and given greater depth by Paul, who in his epistles set forth how he understood the fact: access to the end of time: a radical transformation of his being and the entrusting to him of a mission.

By way of these various means of expression—stereotyped formulas and spontaneous expression—the Easter faith affirms the mysterious fact which we call the resurrection of Jesus. But this tells us nothing about the way in which the encounter of the Lord Jesus with his disciples took place. The gospel narratives and the Lucan narrative of the appearance to Paul give an answer to this question. We possess them in a narrative form which is peculiar to each writer. In the course of this second stage, after examining the Acts of the Apostles, we shall attempt to identify the origins of the narrative tradition underlying the gospel narratives, by relating them to the different languages identified in the first stage. We shall discuss each gospel on its own in the third stage.

CHAPTER FOUR

The Narratives of the Appearance to Paul

Paul simply alludes to this appearance in his epistles, but Luke describes it in three narratives full of life and light, at various points in his Acts of the Apostles: narrative I (9:1-19), narrative II (22:6-21), narrative III (26:12-23). To assist the reader, we give a synopsis.

I *Acts 9*	II *Acts 21*	III *Acts 26*
[3]Now as he journeyed he approached Damascus	[6]As I journeyed and approached Damascus	[12]Thus I journeyed to Damascus, with the authority and commission of the chief priests.
and suddenly,	About noon, suddenly,	[13]At midday, I saw, O king, on the way,
From heaven	From heaven	from heaven, brighter than the sun,
A light flashed about him.	A great light flashed about me.	a light shining round me and those who journeyed with me.
[4]And he fell to the ground, and heard a voice saying to him:	[7]And I fell to the ground, and heard a voice saying to me,	[14]And when he had all fallen to the ground, I heard a voice saying to me in the Hebrew language,
'Saul, Saul, why do you persecute me?'	'Saul, Saul, why do you persecute me?'	'Saul, Saul, why do you persecute me? It hurts you to kick against the goads.'
[5]And he said: 'Who are you Lord?' And he said: 'I am Jesus whom you are persecuting.	[8]And I answered, 'Who are you, Lord?' And he said to me, 'I am Jesus of Nazareth whom you are persecuting.'	[15]And I said, 'Who are, you Lord?' And the Lord said, 'I am Jesus whom you are persecuting.

I	II	III
Acts 9	*Acts 21*	*Acts 26*

I (Acts 9)	II (Acts 21)	III (Acts 26)
	9Now those who were with me saw the light but did not hear the voice of the one who was speaking to me. 10And I said, 'What shall I do, Lord?' And the Lord said to me,	
6But rise and enter the city and you will be told what you are to do.'	'Rise, and go into Damascus and there you will be told all that is appointed for you to do.'	16But rise and stand upon your feet. For I have appeared to you for this purpose, to appoint you to serve and bear witness to the things in which you have seen me and to those in which I will appear to you, 17delivering you from the people and from the Gentiles—to whom I sent you 18to open their eyes, that they may turn from darkness to light and from the power of Satan to God, that they may receive forgiveness of sins and a place among those who are sanctified by faith in me.' 19Wherefore, O King Agrippa, I was not disobedient to the heavenly vision, 20but declared first to those at Damascus, then at Jerusalem and throughout all the country of Judea, and also to the Gentiles, that they should repent and turn to God and perform deeds worthy of their repentance. 21For this reason the Jews seized me in the temple and tried to kill me.

I *Acts 9*	II *Acts 21*	III *Acts 26*
7The men who were travelling with him were speechless, hearing the voice but seeing no one.		
8Saul arose from the ground; and when his eyes were open, he could see nothing. So they led him by the hand and brought him into Damascus.	11And when I could not see because of the brightness of that light, I was led by the hand by those who were with me, and came into Damascus.	
9And for three days he was without sight, and neither ate nor drank.		
10Now there was a disciple at Damascus named Ananias. The Lord said to him in a vision: 'Ananias.' And he said, 'Here I am, Lord.' 11And the Lord said to him: 'Rise and go to the street called Straight, and enquire in the house of Judas for a man of Tarsus named Saul: for behold, he is praying, 12and he has seen a man named Ananias come in and lay his hands on him so that he may regain his sight.' 13But Ananias answered, 'Lord, I have heard from many about this man, how much evil he has done to thy saints at Jerusalem: 14and here he has authority from the chief priests to bind all who call upon thy name.'	12And one Ananias, a devout man according to the law, well spoken of by all the Jews who lived there,	
15But the Lord said to him, 'Go, for he is a chosen instrument of mine to carry my name before the Gentiles and kings and the sons of Israel.		22To this day I have had the help of God, and so I stand here testifying both to small and great, saying nothing but what the prophets and Moses said would come to pass

I *Acts 9*	II *Acts 21*	III *Acts 26*
¹⁶For I will show him how much he must suffer for the sake of my name.'		²³That the Christ must suffer, and that, by being the first to rise from the dead, he would proclaim light both to the people and to the Gentiles.
¹⁷So Ananias departed and entered the house. Laying his hands on him he said, 'Brother Saul, the Lord Jesus who appeared to you on the road by which you came, has sent me that you may regain your sight and be filled with the Holy Spirit.'	¹³came to me and standing by me said to me, 'Brother Saul, receive your sight!'	
¹⁸And immediately something like scales fell from his eyes, and he regained his sight.	And in that very hour, I received my sight and saw him.	
	¹⁴And he said, 'The God of our fathers appointed you to know his will, to see the Just One and to hear a voice from his mouth; ¹⁵for you will be a witness to him to all men of what you have seen and heard ¹⁶And now why do you wait?	
Then he rose and was baptized, ¹⁹and took food and was strengthened.	Rise and be baptized and wash away your sins, calling on his name.' ¹⁷When I had returned to Jerusalem and was praying in the temple, I fell into a trance ¹⁸and saw him saying to me, 'Make haste and get quickly out of Jerusalem, because they will not accept your testimony about me.'	

I *Acts 9*	II *Acts 21*	III *Acts 26*
	19And I said, 'Lord, they themselves know that in every synagogue I imprisoned and beat those who believed in thee. 20And when the blood of Stephen thy witness was shed, I also was standing by and approving, and keeping the garments of those who killed him.' 21And he said to me, 'Depart; for I will send you far away to the Gentiles.'	

In order to understand Luke's thought, we shall first of all compare the three narratives with each other, and then look at the result in the light of the Pauline statements which were analysed in the previous chapter.

A. THE THREE NARRATIVES COMPARED

It is not sufficient to attempt to harmonize the three narratives, which do not agree at every point. They must be subjected to a literary criticism.[1]

Context Narrative I shows a particular interest in the historical context of the event. In narrative II, where Paul is defending himself against the accusation of profaning the temple (21:28) by showing that his mission to the gentiles is willed by God, the narrative comes to a climax with the command, 'Depart; for I will send you far away to the Gentiles' (22:21). Finally, narrative III is a plea, rudely interrupted (26:24) before Festus and Agrippa. The event is always the same, but it is seen in different lights.

Divergencies A first glance reveals the following differences:
The episode of Ananias is dominant (I), short (II), absent (III).
Paul loses his sight and Ananias restores it (I and II).
The voice commands Paul to go into the city to receive from Ananias the revelation which concerns him (I) (II); a mission will

be given to him there (I, II) or during a vision in the temple (II; in III) Christ himself tells Paul everything.

In a vision in the temple (II), absent in I and III, Christ entrusts to Paul his mission to the gentiles (22:21).

The effects of the appearance on Paul's companions differ:

I: They hear without seeing (9:7);

II: They see the light, but do not hear the voice (22:9);

I: They remain standing speechless (9:7);

III: They all fall to the ground (26:14).

In III Christ says something further: kicking against the goad (26:14).

Similarities   The narratives agree in the following elements:

Saul, journeying to persecute the Christians,

is met by Jesus

who overwhelms him

and after making known to Paul who he is,

entrusts to him the mission to the gentiles.

What can be retained of all this in order to distinguish the 'event'? In the absence of reliable literary criticism, the texts must be studied in a different way, by comparing them with the statements in Paul's epistles.

B.   A COMPARISON WITH PAUL'S STATEMENTS

Agreements   Several elements are found in both:

The location at Damascus (Gal 1:17; cf. II Cor 11:32-33);

The context of persecution (Gal 1:14, 23; Phil 3:6; I Cor 15:9);

The fact of the appearance (Gal 1:15; I Cor 9:1; I Cor 15:8);

The consequence of the appearance, a radical change;

The mission to the gentiles (Gal 1:16);

The meaning of the appearance (the Servant of God; Gal 1:15-16).

Differences   The literary category is different; a narrative in Luke, and no narrative in Paul.

What did Paul see? According to himself, he saw Jesus; according to Acts, a light which flashed around him, rather than the appearance of Christ in person to him. Yet Luke seems to suggest that too when he describes Ananias as saying, 'God ... appointed you ... to see the Just One' (22:14; cf. 9:17, 27; 26:16). But he avoids pronouncing upon the form taken by the vision; he does not say that in the light Paul saw someone. Paul likens the appearance to him to that to the Twelve. Luke seems not to do so, since the description he gives is so different. For according to his gospel the risen Christ encounters his disciples not in glory, but in a familiar setting; and then they recognize Jesus of Nazareth in him. By contrast, in the appearance to Paul, the glory of the Lord who has been lifted up to heaven is manifested, and the risen Christ identifies himself with the church persecuted by Paul. Thus from the phenomenological point of view, the two kinds of appearance cannot be identified.

According to Paul himself, his vocation as an apostle was immediate, and his mission was entrusted to him directly 'through Jesus Christ and God the Father ... not according to man' (Gal 1:1, 11). For Luke, Paul's calling and mission are communicated, except in narrative III, by Ananias.

These are the principal differences between the Lucan narratives and the Pauline references. How can the apparent contradiction be removed?

C. ATTEMPTED EXPLANATIONS

Various kinds of explanation have been proposed to reconcile the Lucan narratives with each other and with Paul.[2]

Some scholars, more concerned to harmonize the texts than to respect them, put forward this kind of suggestion: Paul must have recounted his vision at Damascus 'innumerable times';[3] if there are variants, they are due to the laws of repetition which have led to the modification of details.[4] But these hypotheses break down against the fact that, as we have observed, Paul does not seem to have had any inclination to recount his visions (II Cor 12:1-4); and above all he never communicated the 'narrative' of his calling, when he would have had some interest in doing so to the Galatians or to the Philippians. Of course it is not unimaginable, and is indeed probable, that he would have 'narrated' the decisive event of his life; but while this probability leads us to suppose that a popular narrative could have derived from information given by Paul himself, nothing suggests that Luke was making use of a Pauline 'narrative'.

Other scholars, accustomed to dissecting texts in order to detect sources, have supposed that the information originally given by Paul is to be found in the third narrative in Acts, for this contains most agreement with the statements in the epistles. In I, they suppose that Luke was recording another tradition of the event which did not agree with III. II would in this case be a compromise between III and I.[5] Unfortunately it is difficult to pin down and justify the criteria which they followed to identify the sources. Thus it cannot be said that I and III are mutually exclusive: for the calling of the apostle of the gentiles (9:15) is mentioned in both. If it is supposed that the latter theme is characteristic of III and the theme of the punishment of the persecutor is characteristic of I, it must be proved that the theme of vocation has been interpolated from III in to I. But is is just as easy to imagine that the reverse has taken place, that is, that an important element from I has been repeated to provide narrative III.

That is why, following M. Dibelius and E. Haenchen,[6] we consider that the scholars discussed above were wrong in regarding Luke as a modern historian seeking to harmonize as best he could the documents at his disposal; as we shall see, his purpose is above all to edify the reader by using the narrative procedures of his time. In short, it is difficult to suppose that any Pauline account forms the source of Luke's narratives. Luke has his own manner of writing, and it is this which it is necessary to apprehend in order to find our way through his own point of view to the historical and theological value of his narratives. Only then can they rightfully be compared with Paul.

D.   LUKE'S MODE OF COMPOSITION

If Luke did not simply transcribe a narrative source going back to Paul, he must nevertheless have used a popular narrative of the event at Damascus. This *popular* narrative, it seems, contained a certain number of elements; and we can establish what they were as a minimum by first of all retaining, in what is common to the three narratives, the points confirmed in the Pauline epistles. The following points can be attributed to it:[7]

Christ appeared near Damascus,
to Saul, the persecutor of the Christians,
he caused such an upheaval in his existence that he made him the
great apostle of the gentiles.

To these almost certain elements we can probably add the mention of Ananias and that of the house of Judas; for if they were
invented, why would the names suggested have been such as to
recall Ananias the liar (Acts 5 : 1-6) and Judas the traitor (cf. Acts
1 : 16)? Moreover, there is no reason to suspect the theme of the
light, the episode of Paul's blindness and healing, and his baptism
and the gift of the Spirit.

1. *Luke's way of writing history*   By contrast to Paul, Luke presents a very lively picture of the incident. And here there is a risk
of error. The twentieth-century reader is accustomed to making a
radical distinction between scholarly history and the historical novel.
His ideal of scholarly history is a factual account, and to put words
into the heroes' mouths would be to turn it into a novel. Although
at the present day this naive conception of history is being put on
trial, our minds have an unshakable need to trace the facts as they
actually took place. Now we have just admitted that there is no
irrefutable evidence enabling us to authenticate most of the details
and even the dialogues as historical.

Does this mean that Luke invented the scenes? Before admitting
this, we must recall the way in which history was written in the
ancient world.[8] Thus Tacitus records a magnificent speech by
the emperor Claudius before the senate; but the original text of this
speech, preserved on an inscription and therefore undoubtedly
known to the historian, has little or no connection with the text of
the *Annals*. Another example is that of the historian Josephus, a
contemporary of Luke, and a Jew who was convinced of the literal
accuracy of the writings of Moses. He did not hesitate to supplement
the bible where it was silent and to put words in Abraham's mouth
when he was at the point of sacrificing his son Isaac. Summing up
at this decisive moment the very thoughts of Abraham, he is trying
to introduce his reader into the dramatic situation of the patriarch.
What Josephus does with the artlessness of a novice in theology,
Luke achieves with sovereign art. His narrative is interwoven with
speeches, and they form about a quarter of his long work. They
are obviously too short to have been uttered as they stand, and yet

they are too long and too well composed to be regarded as simple summaries. They are speeches composed to fit the proportions of the book and are addressed to the reader, rather like puppets who speak like true human beings but on a reduced scale. They are stereotyped to fit the various situations in which the reader finds himself, in order to draw his attention to some main concern. Thus in order to interpret correctly the narratives of Paul's calling, it is necessary to identify what Luke has in mind in his way of describing the event.

A writer can vary his effects by his choice of vocabulary. Thus Luke readily alters the words and phrases which he employs, no doubt with the sole purpose of making his narrative more elegant. Here are some examples: [9] 'Enter the city' (9:6) becomes 'Go into Damascus' (22:10). The letters of recommendation to the synagogues of Damascus are given to Paul either by the high priest (9:1-2), by the council of elders and the high priest (22:5), or by the chief priests (26:12; 9:14). The Christians persecuted by Paul are called in turn 'the disciples of the law' (9:1), those 'belonging to the Way' (9:2), 'this Way' (22:4), 'the saints' (26:10), 'the brethren' (9:30), 'those who call on the name' of Christ (9:14, 21). Paul's companions are 'the men who were travelling with him' (9:7), 'those who were with him' (22:9), 'those who journeyed with him' (26:13). Can these variations of style be regarded as literal faithfulness to some stereotyped narrative?

The writer Luke was a Greek; he had at his disposal ways of expressing himself and literary categories which do not all derive from biblical tradition. Thus the double vision, the vision which Paul and Ananias have simultaneously, is a redactional procedure which enables him to produce a more smoothly flowing narrative, for by embedding Paul's vision in that of Ananias, the narrative takes a fresh course and from now on centres upon Ananias (9:10-16). Is this what actually took place? It is not impossible. But it is doubtful whether this narrative could have come from a Palestinian or Jewish setting, for the procedure is one which is unknown to the Old Testament, but is used again by Luke in the narrative of the conversion of Cornelius, and belongs to Hellenistic literature.[10]

2. *The theological point of view*   As a historian who was able to make use of the procedures of his time, Luke's main inspiration was nevertheless a theological purpose. Throughout Acts he is seek-

ing to show how God is bringing about his plan for the salvation of the gentiles unto the ends of the earth.[11]

The activity of the persecutor is described in increasingly powerful terms; it is only the last narrative which shows how he himself threw Christians into prison, forced them to blaspheme, and pursued them even to foreign cities (26:10-11; cf. 8:3; 22:4). The radical judgment of God is passed upon this zeal: 'It hurts you to kick against the goads' (26:14). But did the risen Christ speak like this? It is difficult to suppose that he did, for the phrase is strictly Greek or Latin. While it is not impossible that Luke was translating a similar saying of Jesus, it is more likely that he put it in the mouth of Christ to show that all resistance to the law was in vain. Moreover, Paul expresses the equivalent of this idea: 'For if I preach the gospel, that gives me no ground for boasting. For necessity is laid upon me. Woe to me if I do not preach the gospel!' (I Cor 9:16).

Paul is a crucial figure in God's plan, and that is why his calling is recounted three times. But whereas on the one hand Luke demonstrates the irresistible hand of God, in exactly the same spirit as Paul himself, on the other hand he arranges the narrative in such a way that the true initiator of the mission to the gentiles is not Paul, but Peter, on the occasion of the conversion of Cornelius.

Luke's theological point of view becomes evident with regard to *the relationship of Paul to the church*. In the Epistle to the Galatians, Paul stresses that he received his apostolic authority directly from God and not by way of men (Gal 1:1-11). For Luke too, in narrative III, Paul's vocation is a direct calling from God. But in the first two narratives, it is only by the intermediary of Ananias that Paul learns what he has to do (9:6, 17; 22:10, 14-16); and later, Barnabas introduces Paul to the apostles (9:27) and Paul goes in and out amongst them (9:28). Here Luke's intention is to relate Paul's mission to the apostolic church, in order to legitimize it. The same intention on the part of Luke can be seen in his use of the word 'apostle'. Outside Acts 14:4 and 14:14,[12] the title of apostle is reserved for the Twelve, and is identified with that of a witness, in a sense determined by the narrative of the choice of Matthias (Acts 1:21-26). For Luke, the authenticity of the apostolate is derived from the reference to the twelve apostle-witnesses, who linked the community of believers with Jesus of Nazareth. Thus in the episode of Philip at Samaria, it is important for Peter and John to come in person to confirm the work done by Philip (Acts 8:14-17). The matter is even more clear in the address of Paul at Pisidian Antioch. Paul by his own words distinguishes himself from the witnesses, when he explains: 'He appeared to those who came up with him from Galilee to Jerusalem, who are now his witnesses to the people. And now *we* bring you the Good News ...' (13:31-32). According to Luke's categories, Paul is not included amongst the witnesses, and since he is not an 'apostle' in the same sense as the Twelve, a connection must be made between him and the unique apostolic foundation, if his work is to have any meaning. Hence the vital part played by Ananias; but his part is too closely linked with Lucan theology and too much in contradiction with what Paul says for us to retain it as pre-Lucan.

3. *The appearance itself* is therefore described from Luke's own theological point of view. According to Paul, 'Christ showed himself' to him after the other apostles (I Cor 15:8), or again, reversing subject and object, 'Have I not seen Jesus our Lord?' (I Cor 9:1). Here we have an Easter appearance of Jesus in person.

According to Luke, this appearance is of course a special case amongst the visions and apparitions which he recounts in his work (e.g. Acts 16:9; 18:9-10; 20:22-23; 22:17; 23:11; 27:23), and indeed is unique. He makes Ananias say, 'The Lord Jesus who appeared to you on the road ...' (9:17), 'the God of our Fathers appointed you ... to see the Just One' (22:14); while Barnabas (9:27) or the risen Christ himself declares, 'I have appeared to you' (26:16). But *the appearance itself is not specifically distinguished as an Easter appearance*. It could not be so distinguished in Luke's mental categories, for it was Luke who worked out the historic pattern of the forty days, during which the risen Christ showed himself alive to the disciples, and at the end of which he ascended into heaven (1:2-3). From then on, there could no longer be an Easter appearance in Luke's sense, neither for Stephen (7:56) nor for Saul.

This explains *the scene in which the appearance is set*. We do not see the risen Christ coming to converse familiarly with his disciples, so that they can recognize him as identical to Jesus of Nazareth, alive after his death. Instead, there is a luminous glory which at once blinds and enlightens. Of course the description of this light (9:3), brighter than the sun, shining at midday (26:13), so bright that it even blinded Saul's companions, works up to a climax. But we are never told that in this light Paul saw a particular figure. The variations in the description of the light add to an impression of vagueness about the way the appearance took place. The fact is that Luke, who could not proceed in the same way as for what he considered an Easter appearance, settled for the style of a theophany, and emphasizes the words of the risen Christ.

But do these words of the Lord go back to pre-Lucan tradition? If we compare them with what Paul says, we can distinguish three elements. The discourse in narrative III corresponds to expressions in the Epistle to the Galatians. Both Luke and Paul see the event in terms of the prophetic calling of the Servant of Yahweh. The same is true of the mission to the gentiles. On the other hand, the third element, the recognition, is missing in Paul. Is this not an indication that he was unaware of the three dimensions in the structure of the gospel appearance narratives?[13]

Whereas the narratives differ from each other in their total structure, there is one invariable central section, the dialogue between Christ and Paul (9:4-6; 22:7-10; 26:14-18). A superficial consideration would assume too hastily that this went back to its source. But on the one hand it is characterized by a three-fold structure: the repeated call of Christ, Saul's question, and the reply of Christ as he makes himself known, a form which reoccurs in a stereotyped way in the Old Testament, as the following tables show.

	Gen 22	*Gen 46*	*Exod 3*
A	[1]Abraham, Abraham!	[2]Jacob, Jacob!	[4]Moses, Moses!
B	Here am I.	Here am I.	Here am I.
C		[3]I am ... the God of your father.	[6]I am the God of your father.
	Take your son ... and go ...	Do not be afraid to go down to Egypt.	[7]I have seen the affliction of my people. [10]Come, I will send you forth.

Acts 9	*Acts 9*	*Acts 10*
A [4]Saul, Saul!	[10]Ananias!	[3]Cornelius
B [5]Who are you Lord?	Here I am, Lord.	[4]What is it, Lord?
C I am Jesus, whom you are persecuting.		
	[11]Go to the street called Straight.	[5]Send ...

The same form reappears in the course of Jewish tradition. On the other hand, in the New Testament only the Book of Acts possesses such a structure. Thus we are inclined to attribute it to Luke himself,[14] and not to the primitive tradition, at a stage which is difficult to decide.

There is nothing strange in this, if we grant that Luke, lacking a fixed tradition concerning the appearance, used a biblical pattern for narrating it. What could he do better than to search the sacred writers, as he did in order to tell how God, through the angel Gabriel, visited Mary?[15]

The mission entrusted to Paul is explicitly described in the third narrative. It agrees in substance with the theological interpretation given by Paul himself, especially in Gal 1:11-16. Nevertheless, if we are not to be dazzled by assuming that it is a literal recollection, we must note that the discourse in 26:16-18 is a string of biblical texts drawn from the Greek tradition of the Old Testament (Ezek 1-2; Jer 1; Is 42) and concludes with terminology related to that of the primitive church (cf. Col 1:12-14): the lot of the saints, the forgiveness of sins, the power of the realm of darkness, etc. All this shows that Luke was a writer who, with the literary means which he possessed, was capable of creating the atmosphere of Paul's calling and thereby to increase the reader's understanding of the event.

CONCLUSION

For some, the result of the analysis above would be to destroy their confidence in Luke's narrative. But at most it ought only to drive out an illusion: the assumption that one is reading a modern type of factual narrative. It is not possible to reduce to a common denominator the elements provided by the different narratives. We must give up the secret longing to watch a film of the event, and adopt the different points of view of the writer Luke. This principle is admitted nowadays: in order to avoid giving the details a value which distorts their significance, the different points of view of the narratives must be recognized.

Our critical study has been taken even further, in a comparison not only of Luke's narratives with one another, but of the different points of view of Luke and Paul. Both witness and narrator agree about the reality of the event; neither doubts that Paul was vouchsafed an appearance of the risen Christ. But the ways in which they present it, taken literally, differ so profoundly that we have attempted to draw a lesson from these differences. Instead of attempting some kind of specious harmonization, it is possible to show how the two writers agree at a profound level and to expose the various consequences that follow from this, in order to interpret correctly the appearances of the risen Christ.

The principal difference between Paul and Luke is obvious to anyone who compares the appearance to Saul and the appearances to the Twelve. We shall not discuss the latter until the next chapter; but we may assume that the pattern which characterizes them according to the gospels is already known: the triple structure of initiative, recognition and mission. On the other hand, we came to see that the period of forty days was an aspect of Luke's personal theology.

For Paul, the appearance which was vouchsafed to him was the same in nature and significance as that of the Twelve; for Luke, it does not authorize Paul to be a 'witness' (cf. Acts 13:31). Luke would even deny that the appearance to Paul was an Easter appearance in the same sense as the others in the gospels. On this point, it seems to be impossible to reconcile Luke and Paul, and we must attempt to discover to which of the two writers the modification is due. Some scholars suppose that Paul himself adapted the appearance which he received to the others; but if so, it is difficult to see why the ancient formula itself rapidly came to include the mention of James and the apostles in addition to Cephas and the Twelve, as well as that of the five hundred brethren (I Cor 15:5-7). If the various appearances were assimilated to each other, Paul was not the first to take this step. Thus we prefer to think that it was Luke who as a result of his theological conception clearly distinguished the appearance to Paul. An important consequence followed from this. The Lucan framework no longer holds: it has been broken by the information which Paul gives himself.

Another consequence concerns the duration of the appearances of the risen Christ. According to Luke, they ceased on the fortieth day; but this statement is valid only if, in reality or according to ancient tradition, the forty days are more than a convenient Lucan pattern for presenting the way in which Jesus founded his church upon the Twelve. In fact the list in I Cor 15 already goes beyond the usual framework, where it includes the appearances we have just mentioned. Luke carries one of the tendencies of the primitive church to its conclusion—that is, the tendency to concentrate the basis of Christian revelation upon the Twelve. In so doing, Luke expresses an ancient and traditional truth, that only the apostolic generation of witnesses received appearances of the risen Christ in the strict sense, that is, the appearances which founded the church. Luke uses a time structure to state this. Paul enables us to express it in terms of persons: only the apostolic generation founded the church of the risen Christ.

The divergence between Luke and Paul is important on another point, that of the language in which the appearance is recorded. In the case of Paul, we distinguish two fundamental elements: the initiative of God (or of Christ) and the mission entrusted to him. For Luke, a paradox when we remember his tendency to distinguish Paul from the Twelve, the appearance includes the three dimensions which are found in the gospel narratives. Here again, which of the two is right: Luke in introducing the dimension of 'recognition', or Paul in passing over it? It may well be, of course, that in giving his personal account, Paul had no need to stress this aspect of his encounter with the Lord. This is not improbable, but is not necessarily the case. There is no support for it in the Lucan narrative, in spite of appearances. When the risen Christ declares to Saul, 'I am Jesus whom you are persecuting,' it would be possible to deduce that on this account Paul identifies Christ and the church; but if this is the Lucan point of view, this does not mean that it can be attributed to Paul himself, for this identification does not properly appear until towards the end of his epistolary activity, with the elaborated idea of 'body of Christ'. It would be strange if such an insight had not left a trace in his teaching before that late date when the occasion of an epistle might sometimes have called for it.[16] Thus we are not very inclined to regard this latter feature as original. What should our conclusion be? It would be an over-simplification to dismiss Luke's description as of no interest; it would be no more reasonable to treat it as the only one possible. What, then, is the background to the way in which Paul speaks? Here we must remember the existence of a pattern in two dimensions, the pattern of the epiphany, where the explicit connection with Jesus of Nazareth is absent, and the whole concern is concentrated upon the breaking-in of the Lord of glory who comes to entrust a mission to a privileged person.

Further support will be given to these considerations. They show that a Christian must not confer exclusive authority on the language of Luke, if he is not to close his mind to the hermeneutics of the Easter message. The way in which Paul talks of the appearances to him leads us to review our usual way of understanding the relationship between the appearances to the apostles and Christian existence. Paul uses the same words to describe two realities which differ in respect of time and significance, although they are intimately linked; reveal, know, be apprehended, or be overtaken in a race. Here the appearances are not simply part of a privileged series of encounters, but the prototype and model of the later relationship between the risen Christ and Christian believers. This is the basis of the Easter mysticism which Paul worked out: it is the flowering of the appearance of the risen Christ.

Finally, if the appearance to Paul is substantially identical to the appearances recounted in the gospels, it follows that its essential substance is not always to be found in the images which are used to narrate it. An appearance cannot be defined by whether or not it is to a greater or lesser degree material, but by the initiative which brings it about and the mission which derives from it. In our two first chapters we have demonstrated the existence of two languages, those of resurrection and exaltation, to describe the encounter with the living Jesus after his death. The same is true of Paul. Whether it was the exalted Lord in glory who encountered Saul, or whether it was the risen Christ, who after the forty days were over, came and overwhelmed his future apostle, in both cases it was the same Jesus of Nazareth.

CHAPTER FIVE

The Origins of the Narratives of Christ's Appearances

We are now more or less ready to approach the gospel narratives of the appearances. By discovering the two major influences which govern the language of the early church, we have stepped into its thought world and are in a position to see how these influences have controlled the writing of the gospel narratives. On the other hand, we have observed the difference between Paul's testimony, when talking of his meeting with Jesus, and Luke's account of it; similarly, we shall see the transformation from a simple affirmation —'He appeared to Cephas' (and to some others)—to a description of the event. Once we recognize this difference, we can avoid approaching the texts as we would the report of a meeting or a film we have seen.

The gospels can and should be read in two stages. The first and classical method of exegesis consists in isolating the pre-gospel traditions; the aim of this method is not to determine the intentions of each gospel writer, but to establish, from several related sources, a version of the text before it was written down in its present form, reflecting an element in the primitive tradition. An examination of joins and transitions enables us to distinguish the outlines of a set of analogous texts, and a common pattern begins to emerge. A second method is that of studying the texts in this present situation in the gospels, in order to understand better their respective functions in each gospel. These two methods are equally valid for their own level of redaction. We shall try to apply them successively in this second stage and the next. We shall see at the end of our study whether it is possible to relate them to each other in an attempt to grasp the meaning of the whole gospel tradition.

Among the literary accounts of the appearances of the risen Christ we can distinguish between the list in I Cor 15, the summaries in the Acts of the Apostles and the gospel accounts. From the list in I Cor 15: 3-8 there is not much to be learned about the nature of the appearances; but its order agrees with the Gospel of Luke: the appearances to Simon (Luke 24: 34), then to the Eleven (24: 36-49), correspond to the Cephas-Twelve sequence.

From the summaries given by Luke in the Acts of the Apostles (Acts 1: 2-8; 10: 40-42; 13: 30-33), we gain some interesting indications about Luke's own point of view, as we defined it in connection with the appearance to Saul on the road to Damascus. The pattern of the forty days (1: 3) signifies the unique and privileged nature of the apostles. The risen Christ appears to them in a very familiar way, for example 'while eating with them' (1: 4); to us, says Peter, 'who ate and drank with him after he rose from the dead' (10: 41); and he gave them the task of being his witnesses (1: 8; 10: 42; 13: 31). Luke recapitulates by saying that it was by many proofs that Jesus presented himself alive to them (1: 3). Imbued with Lucan theology, the summaries seem to reproduce and adapt material which was already established, whose existence and nature is more clearly shown by the gospel accounts.

The gospels report five official appearances, i.e. to the assembled disciples. In Galilee, according to Matthew (and what Mark foretells), by the Sea of Tiberias in John 21; in Jerusalem according to Luke (and ps.-Mark[1]) and John (twice). There are three accounts of private appearances to individuals: to the holy women (Matthew) or to Mary Magdalene (John, ps.-Mark) and to the disciples on the road to Emmaus (Luke, ps.-Mark). These must be distinguished from the official appearances; although they form a related literary category, they lack a content which relates to the church as a whole, and what is more, they have been adapted to a greater extent. From our point of view then, it is preferable to consider first of all the accounts of official appearances.

Of these, three stand out most clearly: those which form the climax of the gospels of Matthew, Luke and John (Mark has no account of any appearance). Their object is to conclude the gospel, and they all contain the same message, even though they relate it in different ways. They fall into two types, one located in Galilee, in Matthew, and the other at Jerusalem, in Luke and John.[2] From these two types, looked at in turn, we shall try to reconstruct the traditions upon which they are based. In this way, the models which must have been used in the preparation of the various existing narratives will begin to appear.

A. THE JERUSALEM APPEARANCES
(Luke 24:36-53; John 20:19-29)

The traditions which locate the official appearance of the risen Christ at Jerusalem are reported by Luke and John in such a way that, ignoring the details, one is inclined to think of them as reporting the same incident.[3)] We are, then, looking at these two texts to glean from them, if possible, the pre-gospel state of the traditions. A synoptic table enables us to get a panoramic picture of the texts and their relationships.

Several facts about the structure and elements of the two texts emerge from this table.

Luke 24:34-53		*John 20:19-29*
	SITUATION	
at Jerusalem		at Jerusalem
		19(26)the doors shut for fear of the Jews
on the evening of Easter day	on the evening of Easter day	eights days later
the disciples and those who were with them	the disciples	with Thomas
	INITIATIVE	
36Unexpected presence (*estē en mesō*) 'Peace to you!'		unexpected presence (*ēlthen kai estē eis to meson*) 'Peace to you!'
	RECOGNITION	
37startled and frightened they supposed they saw a spirit		
39*Jesus calls them to see* his *hands* and feet 'It is I myself.' and *to touch him* A spirit has not flesh and bones like me	20Jesus shows his *hands* and his side	27*Jesus calls them to see* his *hands* and his side *and to touch*
41*Joy* ↓ but *unbelief* He asks for food and eats before them	Joy at seeing the Lord	Do not *be faithless* 26confession of Thomas Blessed are those who have not seen, and yet believe.

Luke 24:34-53

MISSION

44Discourse	21'Peace to you!'
44b-46fulfilment of scripture	
47preaching in his name (c)conversion *remission of sins*	(a) sending of disciples
48(a) you will be my witnesses	
49(b) I send you the promise Stay at Jerusalem	22Act: he breathes Gift of the Holy Spirit. 23(c) Power to *remit sins*

SEPARATION

50Blessing them
51he departed (*diestē*)
52they returned to Jerusalem
    full of *joy*. ↑

1   The Structure

1.   Between the indications of place and the conclusions three parts seem to have been neatly fitted together.

The risen Christ is suddenly there among the disciples. This unexpected presence is common to both texts and is simply noted by the phrase, 'He stood among them.'

Jesus is then recognized in the person who has appeared. But his recognition takes different forms. In Luke, the disciples' disbelief has to be overcome by positive proofs. In John, the idea of disbelief has been transferred to the second appearance, eight days later, to Thomas. In both accounts, then, the disciples recognize Jesus, explicitly in John (their joy and Thomas's confession), implicitly in Luke (their joy).

The two texts diverge even more over the mission which Christ entrusts to the disciples. In John, it is closely connected with the recognition of Jesus; in Luke, it is presented as a theological discourse. In John it is accompanied by an act, in Luke, by a promise. But in both cases, a mission is entrusted.

2.   These three elements, which appear in the same order in spite

of variations in the presentation, constitute a structure which governs the reduction of both accounts of the *official appearances in Jerusalem*. Is this structure the work of one or other of the gospel writers, or was it inherited by them both? This is the question facing anyone trying to identify the pre-gospel version.

The *Johannine text* appears to be a fitting together of earlier literary elements. The second appearance is prepared by a transitional passage in which Thomas states his requirements, using the same words as the risen Christ (20:25=20:27). The account of the first appearance is itself composite.[4] Jesus twice says, 'Peace be with you' (20:19-21); and this gift of peace is linked with the following gesture or word by the same expression, 'When he had said this' (20:20, 22). Furthermore, the missionary command and the gift of the Spirit seem to have been added artificially. The mission corresponds to what Jesus said in this discourse after the last supper (17:18). The verb 'breathe' (*emphysaō*), which means here the giving of the Spirit by Jesus (cf. Gen 2:7; Wis 15:11; Ezek 37:5, 6) is unique in the New Testament and presents a symbol which is unusual in John. All these facts lead us to suppose that this latter tradition is pre-Johannine. By inserting it here, John undoubtedly meant to lay the foundations for the disciples' mission, even though this raised several problems. For it to agree with Luke's account of Pentecost, John had to assume that Jesus had already gone to the Father (16:5, 10). And how could the Spirit have been given in the absence of Thomas? Everything suggests, then, that John, to obtain a tripartite structure (initiative, recognition, mission), had linked this tradition with the preceding one. Why should he have done it, unless it was a traditional structure which he felt bound to follow?

Even more clearly the Lucan redactor seems to feel obliged to adopt this structure. The transitions between the account of the pilgrims to Emmaus and the official appearance (24:36), between the appearance and the setting of the task (24:44-45) and between the setting of the task and the farewells (24:50), all suggest the division of the text into three parts. The transitional phrase, 'as they were saying this' (24:36a) is, no doubt, not specifically Lucan (except perhaps the *de*) but is there to establish a link with the preceding narrative. Finally, in the vv. 44-45, there are seven Lucan characteristics; in 24:50-52 there are nine.[5] Once again, we come to the same conclusion: behind the present text of Luke, as of

John, there are earlier traditions.

3.   A tripartite structure, earlier than Luke or John, seems, then, to have dominated the gospel arrangement of the earlier traditions. Let us make a brief examination of the accounts of *private appearances*, to confirm this.

Two narratives recount an appearance of the risen Christ near the tomb, one *to several women* (Matthew 28:9-10) and one *to Mary Magdalene* (John 20:11-18). Most critics agree that there is one tradition behind the two accounts. A synopsis shows this clearly.

Matthew 28		*John 20*
⁹And behold, Jesus met them and said, 'Hail!'		¹⁶Jesus said to her,
	INITIATIVE	'Mary'.
And they came up and took hold of his feet and worshipped him.		She turned and said to him ...,
¹⁰Then Jesus said to them,	RECOGNITION	'Rabbouni!' ...
		¹⁷Jesus said to her, 'Do not hold me ...
'Do not be afraid; go and tell my brethren	MISSION	But go to my brethren and tell them,
to go to Galilee, and there they will see me.'		I am ascending to my Father and your Father.'

In spite of the differences which are due to the private nature of the appearance, the pattern indicated is clearly seen once again.

Coming from the tomb, the women run joyfully to give the angel's message to the disciples; Mary stands before a man she takes to be the gardener. Jesus comes and meets the women; Jesus calls Mary. The risen Christ takes the initiative.

The women show that they have recognized the Master by falling down at his feet and kissing him; and (a reality implied by Jesus's retort, 'Do not hold me') Mary also kisses (the feet of) Jesus.

Then the missionary command is given for the disciples, who are here called 'brethren', a rarely-used term. The message to be conveyed to them varies according to the point of view of each writer;

the meeting place in Galilee, or the ascension of Jesus to the Father.

Obviously, these accounts conform to the Jerusalem type of appearance, as previously described.

The account of the appearance by the Sea of Tiberias (John 21 : 1-17) combines two traditions: an appearance to Peter while fishing, and an appearance to the disciples during a meal of bread and fish. In its final literary stage[6] it also presents a structure connected with the Jerusalem appearance type. The initiative is made quite clear: 'Jesus stood on the beach' (21 : 4; *estē* as in John 20 : 19, 26 and Luke 24 : 36), and he calls to the disciples. The recognition is slow (21 : 5-14). Finally, Peter is given the task of feeding Jesus's flock (21 : 15-17). The tripartite structure seems to have helped the narrator to arrange his account.

A quite different picture appears in Luke's masterpiece, which we shall examine in detail in Chapter 9: *The appearance to the disciples on the road to Emmaus* (Luke 24 : 13-35). The absence of a mission entrusted by the risen Christ stands out and upsets the preceding structure; we cannot attribute to him the fact that the disciples go and announce the news to the eleven who had remained in Jerusalem. Of the structure, only the initial stages (which are normal and necessary in any appearance) and the recognition remain. The latter is specially developed with all Luke's artistic skill.

The very existence of such an account shows that the gospel tradition is not entirely dominated by the tripartite structure. If Luke did not feel constrained to subordinate this narrative to it, it was because he could draw on another aspect of the tradition, the proliferation of all the smaller literary units which we distinguished behind the accounts of the official appearances. In any case, we are only talking about the account of a private appearance.

4.   With a high degree of probability, we can conclude that there is a dominant typical structure, at least at a certain level: initiative, recognition, mission.

The gospel narratives show unanimously that it is Jesus who appears to or among people who are not expecting him. The intention is clear; to show that the experience is not the result of pure invention on the part of those concerned, produced by an overactive faith or a fertile imagination. This presentation corresponds to the use of the verb *ōphthē*, which we have already discussed in chapter 2, 'the Lord has been seen', 'he showed himself', rather than 'I have seen the Lord'. So the passive nature of the appearance is underlined; the accounts emphasize that the initiative is that of the risen Christ.

The second characteristic of the accounts is the theme of recognition. The disciples discover the identity of the person who commands their attention: it is Jesus of Nazareth, whose life and crucifixion they have witnessed; he who died is alive. Moreover, as Luke says, the whole scripture is summed up and finds its meaning in Jesus. In him, prophecy is fulfilled. In a way, the disciples have nothing more to expect nor to 'see' in the future: everything has been given to them by the risen Christ.

The way in which the recognition takes place is progressive: in the man who comes to them, the disciples see first of all an ordinary person, a traveller (Luke 24: 15-16; John 21: 4), a gardener (John 20: 15). Then they recognize the Lord. This recognition is quite voluntary, since, according to the theme of disbelief found in most of the gospel tradition (Matthew 28: 17; ps.-Mark 16: 11, 13-14; Luke 24: 37-41; John 20: 25-29), they could have refused to believe. Often, then, the statement is collective, thus enabling the verification to be mutual, as Paul hints in his commentary on the creed of I Cor 15. It is quite likely that the description of the way the recognition takes place has been subject to some literary revision, some search for more suitable expression; we cannot, however, attribute the theme of recognition either to apologetics or to theology.

The appearances do not amount to a simple 'visual' recognition of the person they knew before; they also expose, in the 'auditory' sphere, the relationship with the future, which is from now on going to govern the life of the disciples. If, in recognizing the Lord, the disciples anticipate the vision which is the prerogative of heaven, they are also reminded of the terrestrial nature of the hearing of the word. In fact they turn towards Jesus of Nazareth, towards a past which they wonder to see fulfilled in the living Christ, but they are also encouraged to look towards the future, where the richness of the present, found in the risen Christ, will be given expression and developed.

First of all we have the appeal to continue the work of Jesus, the mission in the strict sense, which makes possible the promise of the Holy Spirit or the immediate gift of the Spirit. Thus the mission is not the simple continuance of the activity of Jesus of Nazareth before Easter, but the taking up and transfiguration of this work by the presence and activity of the Holy Spirit.

It is interesting to note how the 'seeing' fulfils the apocalyptic movement which first appears in the Old Testament, turning it back towards a fact in the past. In this way it requires a radical readjustment of the former attitude. In accordance with Jesus's teaching in the synoptic apocalypse, there will no longer be any signs to see in the future; attention must be given to the event of the past which alone gives the future its meaning. As for the 'hearing', it prolongs the religion of the prophetic word. The church is founded upon the word.

In order to demonstrate the dynamic circularity of these three aspects, let us choose a temporal pattern. By his initiative, which is that of God himself, the risen Christ unceasingly renews the *present* of the disciple who is thereby called upon to take on the *past* in the person of Jesus of Nazareth, who enables him to build the *future* which is the church.

The official appearance narratives obey this structure; and the same is true of the narratives of the appearances to the holy women and to Mary Magdalene, and that of the appearance at the lakeside. It does not apply to the narrative of the appearance to the disciples on the road to Emmaus and the very different narrative of Matthew 28:16-20. The existence of these exceptions shows the composite and consequently relatively late character of this structure. It is of course prior to the redaction of the gospels, but reveals the existence of previously existing material, belonging to an even earlier stage of the gospel tradition.

2   *The Elements*

Let us return to the two narratives of official appearances in Luke and John. They unquestionably follow a common pattern, which, as we have seen, is earlier than the gospels themselves. But the exception formed by the Emmaus episode points further back behind this structure to the contexts in life which formed the very first traditions. This will be confirmed by examining the elements of which these narratives consist.

1. *The elements of the two narratives*   If the reader turns to the synopsis on p. 82 he will see at once that the elements of the narratives are closely related. But the liberty with which they are used shows that the two accounts are independent of each other.

At a very early stage, a connection was made between them. This is shown by the textual tradition: on two occasions, the copyists introduced into the narrative in Luke words which are really Johannine. The phrase 'And he said to them, "Peace to you!"' gives the impression of being an interpolation in Luke 24:36b;[7] and similarly, in 24:40, we find another Johannine passage: 'And when he had said this, he showed them his hands and his feet.'[8] What is suggested by the witnesses to the manuscript tradition is made clear by the verbal similarities between the texts: the narratives of Luke and John are not interdependent, but derive from traditions common to both.

Let us begin with the elements which are identical, that is, the material which is presented in the same terms and has the same function. Both scenes take place on the same day and in the same place. Moreover, John contains two Lucanisms: the verb *estē*, for Jesus's sudden appearance[9] and the expression 'among them, in the midst of them' (*en tō mesō*).[10] Does John derive from Luke? This seems unlikely, for John uses a similar turn of phrase in cases where there is no parallel in Luke (John 20:14; 21:4). To suppose that Luke derived from John would be to overlook the fact that we have a term which is itself Lucan. Thus the unexpected presence of Jesus is recorded in identical terms, although there is no dependence of one narrative on the other.

Some elements have a similar function, but are expressed in different terms. By the words of the risen Christ—'It is I myself'—Luke reveals his intention: to emphasize the recognition of Jesus of Nazareth. John's purpose is indicated by the way in which Jesus at once gives his peace and shows his hands and his side. Besides this, the purpose of the invitation to see and to touch in both Luke and John is intended to demonstrate the identity of him who has appeared. Finally, although the words are very different, the mission is concerned with the same reality: the forgiveness of sins and the gift of the Spirit. These latter elements do not require mutual dependence, but assume a common dependence upon a similar tradition.

Finally, a number of identical terms have a different function. In Luke the fear of the disciples is due to the appearance itself, while in John it is caused by the Jews. The showing of the hands and feet (or side) of Jesus has the function in one case of assuring his identity (John), and in the other of demonstrating his reality (Luke). Similarly, the function of faith and joy differ: in Luke, the unbelief must be overcome, and yet is mingled with joy; in John, the recognition is immediate, the unbelief is transferred in its entirety to Thomas, and the joy is full and unblemished.

As in numerous cases in the synoptic tradition, for example in the parable of the wedding guests (Matthew 22: 1-14; Luke 14: 16-24), the resemblances and differences between the two narratives show that a common tradition underlies them. The following reconstruction can be proposed:

Before the assembled disciples, Jesus appears.

He suddenly stands in the midst of them.

He shows them his hands and his feet (or side).

They do not believe.

Finally, the disciples rejoice.

Another less clearly defined tradition, concerning the mission entrusted to the disciples, was later added to this common basis.

2. *Elements common to Luke and to other narratives* In the course of the preceding enquiry, we limited ourselves to the elements common to Luke and John. Must we then attribute the other elements to the respective evangelists? That would be a somewhat hasty step. For it is possible to show that various aspects of their work, particularly the style of an epiphany, and the distinctive theme of the meal, are traditional.

When compared with the account of the walking on the water (Matthew 14=Mark 6=John 6) the literary category of Luke's christophany shows up more clearly.[11]

Luke 24	*Matthew 14=Mark 6=John 6*
[37]They were startled and frightened.	Matthew 26 they were terrified, saying (John 19)
they supposed (*edokoun*) they saw (*theōrein*) a spirit (ghost)	Mark 49 they thought that it was John 19 they saw (*theōrousin*) Jesus.
[38]Why are you troubled (*tetaragmenoi*)?	Matthew 26 Mark 50: they were terrified (*etarachthēsan*)
[39]It is I myself.	Matthew 27 Mark 50=John 20: It is I.

Such an accumulation of similarities in the language, and in the reaction of the disciples, makes us recognize once again not the interdependence of these narratives, but the mutual influence of pre-existent themes. The whole derives from the style of an 'epiphany', according to which a being belonging to the other world shows himself to men, first reassuring them, and then making them accept the reality of the miraculous appearance.

This comparison, however, does not necessarily mean that Luke was making use of a source. A comparison between the narratives of *Emmaus and the Sea of Tiberias* will bring us nearer to the discovery of a traditional theme.

Luke 24	*John 21*
[36]Jesus himself stood (*estē*) among them.	[4]Jesus stood (*estē*) on the beach.
[41]Have you anything here to eat (*brōsimon*)?	[5]Have you anything to eat (*prosphagion*)?
[42]They gave him a piece of broiled fish.	[10]Bring some of the fish that you have just caught.
cf. 24.30 (Emmaus) he took the bread, and blessed and broke it and gave it to them.	[13]Jesus came and took the bread and gave it to them and so with the fish.

At first sight, one would say that Jesus twice shared a meal with the disciples, on one occasion in Jerusalem, on the other at the lakeside. As far as the events are concerned, this is not impossible. But a literary critic would prefer to see here, without being able to give precise details, a tradition showing the risen Christ eating with his disciples. In addition, this tradition appears elsewhere in a number of passages. Thus in the conclusion added to Mark, we read that Jesus appeared to the Eleven themselves as they sat at table (ps.-Mark 16:14); in the same way, according to Luke the last appearance of Jesus took place 'while he was eating with them' (Acts 1:4).[13] Finally, Peter summarizes the contact which the disciples had had with the risen Christ by declaring that 'God ... made him manifest ... to us who ... ate and drank with him after he rose from the dead' (Acts 10:41).

From the variety of these attestations, we can deduce the existence of a fairly firm tradition. Furthermore, apart from the appearances to the holy women, all the accounts show the community taking a meal at the moment when the risen Christ appeared. This feature enables us to define the actual setting (*Sitz im Leben*) in which they took shape.

3 *The Original Setting*

The fact that the occasion is a meal leads us to suggest, as one of the contexts in which the accounts of the appearances took shape, the liturgical setting, and more precisely the eucharistic meal. John suggests this by dating the appearances on the first day of the week, and a week later. More precisely, in Luke, we hear of the 'breaking of bread', a specialized term to indicate the eucharist (I Cor 10:16; Acts 2:42, 46; 20:7, 11)[14] In the Emmaus narrative, this scene even constitutes the final point of the appearance, since it is at this moment that 'their eyes were opened and they recognized him' (Luke 24:30-31). We shall show in chapter 9 that the Lucan account does not set out to be biographical. It is a catechetical account meant to describe how those who have not seen the risen Christ can recognize him in their turn.

In the account of the appearance beside the Sea of Tiberias, the meal has already been prepared by the mysterious traveller. 'When they got out on land, they saw a charcoal fire there with fish lying on it and bread' (John 21:9). And Jesus did not use any of the 153 fish that the disciples had just caught; 'he took the bread and gave it to them, and so with the fish' (21:13). Finally, let us note that this last action is introduced by the classic words 'Jesus came (cf. 20:19, 24, 26), indicative of the solemn 'coming' of the Lord (cf. 14:3, 18, 28; 21:23). As in the case of the episode of the multiplication of the loaves and the discourse on the bread of life (John 6: 1-66, esp. 6: 11) John offers here a narrative, which is understood by the believer in a eucharistic sense.[15]

Against this background, the frequent mentions of the meal suggest that in all probability the liturgy of the eucharist was the occasion for the meeting between the risen Christ and his disciples. Were these meals held in common already eucharistic, or did they become so because of the coming of the risen Christ? It is difficult to make a decision. It seems more likely that the original assemblies were only the result of a loyalty to the memory of Jesus of Nazareth which still survived, and that the appearances of Christ made this remembrance a paschal reality.

The details of these meals show moreover that before being adopted by the evangelists the tradition was communicated in the form of vivid *popular accounts*. Christians wanted to describe how the recognition of him who was alive after death came about. These accounts easily become apologetic, certain details being intended to prove the reality of the body of the risen Christ. This tendency was to grow, and gave rise to an apocryphal literature. Thus in a text from the beginning of the second century, the disciples are not only invited to touch the Lord's body, they actually do touch it (something the evangelists never say). 'And we touched him, that we might learn of a truth whether he were risen in the flesh.'[16] Likewise, by about A.D. 110, Ignatius of Antioch was already writing to the people of Smyrna: 'And immediately they touched him and they believed, apprehending his flesh and his spirit.' Thus we can clearly see that these narratives, away from the typical structure, were at the mercy of pious imagination.[18]

A third setting, which can be called catechetical, is concerned to demonstrate in the appearances of the risen Christ the founding of the church. The missionary commands go back to such a context. It is hardly possible to recapture the primitive sense of these words, because they come to us in very different forms. What is certain is that they reflect the faith of the infant Church. Remission of sins, baptism, scriptural proof, such are the themes which continually appear in the Acts of the Apostles and in current liturgical fragments.

We must not separate these contexts too drastically, as if they existed independently. We might equally well speak of different 'functions' in the Church. But this analytic approach gives a clearer picture of how the accounts gradually took shape. There was first a eucharistic context, with a stronger or weaker emphasis on either the apologetic aspect or the popular narrative. Then a set structural pattern (initiative-recognition-mission) enabled the different elements to be gathered together, and prepared the way for the composition of the gospels. Such are the characteristics of the Jerusalem type, as they progressively evolved. We must now turn to a third narrative with an original structure which was profoundly different from those already mentioned.

B.   THE GALILEAN TYPE

1   *The Account of Matthew 28:16-20*

From our study of the affirmations of the infant faith, and recognizing in particular the existence of a scheme of thought which differed from that of 'resurrection' and which derived from the tradition of Christ exalted into glory, we now turn to consider more closely the account of the appearance which closes the Gospel of Matthew:

> [16]Now the eleven disciples went to Galilee, to the mountain to which Jesus had directed them. [17]And when they saw him they worshipped him; but some doubted. [18]And Jesus came and said to them, 'All authority in heaven and on earth has been given to me. [19]Go therefore and make disciples of all nations, baptizing them in the name of the Father and of the Son and of the Holy Spirit, [20]teaching them to observe all that I have commanded you; and lo, I am with you always, to the close of the age.'

Compared with the Jerusalem type, the narrative seems at first sight to have been constructed according to the same plan; worship-doubt-mission. But looking at it more closely, we realize that it lacks several of the elements of the Jerusalem structure.

Certainly the initiative comes from the risen Christ who has arranged a meeting with the Eleven; but we cannot say that his presence is unforeseen and surprises the disciples; on the contrary, very naturally, 'when they saw him they worshipped him'. We are even astonished to note that they prostrate themselves before Jesus comes near them. There is no greeting, no invitation not to be afraid. If there is initiative, can we still recognize the Jerusalem pattern in it?

Is the fact of worship truly recognition? This equivalence might be established if there had not, immediately after, been a mention of doubt. The normal sequence is inverted here. The doubt follows the adoration instead of preceding it. This fact is all the more surprising in that, as opposed to the Jerusalem type, the doubt does not have the function of requiring Jesus to prove his identity or to give evidence of his corporeality. The doubt is there without any apparent function, since the text does not say that it was overcome by what followed. Everything in the narrative takes place as if it was an alien element. Finally, it is not easy to say exactly who those who doubt are. The Greek expression is very difficult to translate. It certainly refers to a present doubt and not, as it is sometimes translated, a past doubt ('they who had doubted'), for the aorist cannot be the equivalent of a pluperfect.[19] Who are those, then, who immediately start to doubt? Since it cannot be anyone other than the Eleven,[20] does it follow that they were divided into believers and unbelievers? Some scholars think that they all worshipped, but some with a hesitant and uncertain faith.[21] But the difficulty remains: Matthew does not say that these hesitations came to an end. But could the witnesses of the resurrection have less faith than that of the lowest disciple, who must 'have faith and never doubt' (21:21). A likely reconstruction of the origin of the text has been given 'Like Luke, Matthew only wants to recount an appearance to the Eleven. He knows that they began by doubting.... He therefore has to mention this doubt at the beginning of his only account.'[22] But, even after this explanation, it is difficult to see why Matthew does not mention the cessation of their doubts: we have no authority for saying that the faith of the disciples was in the end flawless. In our opinion, this verse came to be added to a tradition which contained no mention of doubt, for a good reason: it was not based on the theme of recognition in faith, the basic theme of the Jerusalem type.

If unexpected presence and recognition are missing in this account, there is, by contrast, an extraordinary emphasis on the mission, which clearly becomes the essential point of the passage. Whereas, in the Jerusalem type, the missionary command constitutes a third element added to the accounts of appearance and recognition to form the structure we have identified, here the command has attracted to itself the framework of a gospel appearance, without forming a distinctive structure. To sum up, to

appraise Matthew's narrative correctly it is necessary to look elsewhere for its literary category.

The Old Testament contains accounts of Yahweh's meetings with
men to whom he entrusts a mission. The patterns of these accounts
of vocation and mission can be set out as follows:

Exodus 3	*Jeremiah 1*	*Matthew 28*
PRESENTATION		
[6]God said: I am the God of your Father ... (Moses' reaction)	[5]Before I formed you in the womb I knew you ... (Jeremiah's reaction)	[18]All authority ...
MISSION		
[10]Come, I will send you to Pharaoh that you may bring forth my people ... out of Egypt. (Moses' reaction)	[7]To all to whom I send you you shall go (Jeremiah's reaction)	[19]Go ... !
PROMISE		
[12]I will be with you.	[8]I am with you.	[20]I am with you.

The structure of Matthew's narrative seems to be modelled on
that of the vocation stories in the Old Testament. They normally
stress the certainty of God's presence in the sight of his chosen
one, and, in this case, of Christ's presence amongst the Eleven.

The fact that there is no reaction on the part of two disciples,
may stem from the fact that the appearance is addressed to a
group: in any case, the structure is retained. Let us look at the
constituent elements.

Who appears? Not Yahweh, but Jesus. He reveals his new situation, apparently by means of words from the prophecy of Daniel:

Behold, with the clouds of heaven there came one like a son of
man. And to him was given dominion and glory and kingdom,
that all people, nations and languages should serve him (Dan
7:13-14).

But this resemblance is only superficial. The saying of the risen
Christ does not stop at fulfilling the prophecy of Daniel—in that

prophecy, there is no question of heaven and earth, or of mission. Thus to account for the saying it is necessary to seek a twofold origin. In this being who appears, we must see the Son of man proclaimed by Jesus in terms which bring together Dan 7:14 and Ps 110:1: 'I tell you, hereafter you will see the Son of man seated at the right hand of Power, and coming on the clouds of heaven' (Matthew 26:64). In addition, we have to understand the faith proclaimed by the Church in the Lord exalted to heaven. In fact we find here the language of the confessions of faith and hymns discussed in chapter 2. Jesus appears in the omnipotence of the glorified Lord. Whereas the Jerusalem type recasts the confessions of faith in the risen Christ in the form of a narrative, here the text is recasting hymns to the Lord exalted in glory. But this glory, by reason of the gospel context, is not manifested itself in the classic way of apocalyptic—as, for instance, when the Son of man appears in splendour to the seer of Patmos (Rev 1:12-18; cf. Dan 10:4, 12) and provokes the fear which such a situation demands—but only through the majesty of the discourse. In fact, these first words are intended, not to provide an identification of Jesus (the Jerusalem type), nor to manifest his glory (apocalyptic), but to authorize to the mission which is to be entrusted.

This *mission*, unlike the appearance, offers numerous points of contact with that of the Jerusalem type. Christ uses the same words as on other occasions 'Go ...' (cf. 9:13; 10:6; 11:4), then gives a command which is equivalent to the words in Luke, 'You are witnesses' or in John, 'As the Father has sent me, even so send I you.' And so we find in Matthew, 'Make disciples of all nations.' Baptism corresponds to the 'forgiveness of sins'. The mission which he entrusts is the one which the primitive Church recognizes, as its own, no longer to Jews alone, as during the earthly life of Jesus (Matthew 10:5-6; 15:24), nor even to the Gentiles (Dan 7), but to the whole of mankind (Matthew 24:9, 14; 25:32). This universalism is the result of a gradual growth of awareness on the part of the Church.

That *presence* of the Holy Spirit, promised (Luke) or given (John), which is found in the three evangelists, becomes here the presence of Jesus himself (Matthew). Emmanuel, the name of the predestined child (Matthew 1:32) is now a living reality to the end of time: he is to be not 'in the sight of' but 'with' his own.

These remarks lead us to ask whether the story in Matthew can still be called an 'appearance', at least if we are to use this term of brief encounters with the risen Christ in the course of which the Lord makes himself known in a familiar way and confers a mission. The impression there is that in order to make contact with his disciples, Jesus for a time 'survives', without any glorified appearance. In Matthew 28 : 16-20, however, there is a sudden bursting in of the Lord who imposes his presence and gives his command. There is no condescension, but the authority of the Lord who from now on has charge over the whole history of mankind. It is clear that the two traditions cannot be assimilated, and that the Galilean type is original.

2   *The Presupposition of Matthew's Narrative*

What distinguishes Matthew's narrative basically from those of the Jerusalem type is of course the difference in structure. But of a more profound level, there is a different christology, and a different conception of history.

The categories which we analysed in the first two chapters are represented in the narrative, and this reveals their meaning. A brief examination will help us to grasp the importance of the exaltation structure in understanding the appearances of Jesus, who has come out of death the victor.

The notions of history in the Old Testament vary between prophecy and apocalyptic. As a generalization, we may say that the category of 'resurrection from the dead', although apocalyptic in that it refers to the end of time, belongs to the structure of prophetic thought, while the category of 'exaltation' belongs to a non-historical view.

According to the pattern of prophecy, characterized as it is by a particular notion of time, a coming event is foretold, or a present event is a fulfilment of prophecy. By triumphing over death, Jesus is the final, 'eschatological' culmination of Israel's long expectation; at the same time he gives it a new and more vital impetus, until the parousia. In his person the destiny of the chosen people is fulfilled. Jesus shows himself alive to his disciples, and they recognize God's action upon him : from the moment of that decisive act of God, one age replaces another. Brought for an instant to a standstill, history takes up its course again, or rather begins again in a new way, by taking as its reference point the instant in the past which saw Jesus rise from the dead. History can continue, thanks to the Holy Spirit which comes from him who rose from the dead.

The lordship of Jesus and the salvation of men are the consequences of the ultimate divine act. The riches contained, but not yet brought to light, in this unique event in time are projected on to a horizontal plane, in a historical sequence. In this way the elements of mystery, which are characteristic of the Easter event are 'made good': they are booked in and come up in their place in time.

According to the non-historical view, the writer puts himself deliberately at the end of time and, confident in the all-engrossing knowledge he possesses, strives to reveal the mysterious riches of the present, no longer as the consequences of an act of God within time, but as dimensions concealed within the present. His perspective is not really temporal, nor even terrestial, but eternal and heavenly. He reveals the permanent depth of the historical, rather than showing the way to the consequences manifested in the progress of history. Thus the Revelation of John does not describe the kingdoms that are to come, and it is useless to seek to put names, dates or periods on the figures he depicts; they serve only to depict the depth of history, the categories of the history of salvation. It is a discernment and a discovery of the eternal within time. This example shows the danger that lies in confusing literary categories; the apocalyptic is not the prophetic.

A particular christology is characteristic of Matthew's narrative. Jesus had access to the higher, definitive world. In the risen Jesus, Matthew makes known the Son of man, installed in glory in the world to come, and controlling the history of mankind. He comes to reveal himself to his disciples, on a single occasion conferring on them the mission which he extends to them. From this view point, we are not waiting for the return of the Son of man: he is there with us. Could there possibly be any room here for a second book, like the Acts of the Apostles, or for an 'age of the Holy Spirit'? Jesus the Lord replaces them all. He no longer needs the ascension to express his separation from mankind: on the contrary, his exaltation demands that a new presence be intimated to men.

It follows that another pattern can exist, that of *christophany*. Luke sets us on the path, when in order to describe the appearance to Saul on the road to Damascus, he changes the classic structure. Of course he retains a short dialogue where the equivalent of the 'recognition' occurs: but this no longer relates to Jesus of Nazareth, but to the Church. The essential point is the mission, and the promise of Jesus's assistance. This is the epiphany pattern, similar to the pattern of Matthew's narrative, though in Matthew there are not even any phenomena of glory during the appearance. Paul, in the allusions he makes to his encounter with Christ, is even more categorical: he only mentions his mission, following the initiative taken by the glorified Lord.

There are other examples in the rare appearances of the Son of man, with the difference that they do not entail a mission. They are like appearances of the epiphany type, sudden interventions or encounters with the glorified Lord, who does not take on the characteristics of an earthly man. Thus the Son of man reveals himself to the dying Stephen (Acts 7:55-56). As in the prophecy of Daniel (but not in Ps 110), the Son of man is standing, perhaps to bear witness on behalf of Stephen, who has just done so for him. Again, according to John of Patmos (Rev 1:12-16), the Lord appears, as in a magnificent theophany, with the attributes of the Living One who holds the key of Sheol (1:17-18).

Is this another appearance in the classic (Jerusalem) sense? The vocabulary of 'resurrection' has disappeared. There is no trace of the familiarity which characterizes these narratives. It is the sudden irruption into the presence of the Lord in glory.

C.   CONTRAST BETWEEN THE TWO TYPES

The differences of perspective and of language which we have just outlined do not compromise the profound unity of the Easter message. In the appearances of the risen Christ, all the evangelists reveal the final culmination of the life and work of Jesus, that is to say, the inauguration, by means of his death, of the age of the church. The appearances all have as their goal the founding of the church. The narratives, however, are divided into two types which cannot be assimilated to each other without violence. It is worthwhile to compare them once again in a systematic way, for they correspond to the two thought-structures which are revealed in the affirmations of the infant faith.

Two original types of presentation of the risen Christ   The difference between Matthew and the others has not failed to intrigue scholars who have explained it in various ways. The two types are usually traced back to a single tradition.

The Jerusalem type is usually regarded as the origin of the Galilean type. So many similarities suggest as the origin of the two accounts, if not one source (the verbal similarities are too tenuous), at least a common tradition. These similarities, however, are limited to the fact that the appearance concludes the gospel and presents the content of that experience in a few solemn words of Jesus, the messianic Lord who founds the universal mission. But it must be admitted that Matthew does not define the lordship of Christ in the same way. His tradition, therefore, is thought to have consisted of: 'The appearance to the Eleven, their doubt, their conviction about the reality of the risen Christ, and a link between the appearance and the mission.'[23] But our own brief analysis suggests that Matthew, or at least the narrative on which he drew, in fact lies outside that tradition: neither the doubt, nor the assertion of reality from an integral part of his presentation. By contrast, P. Seidensticker—to whom we are greatly indebted—considers that the Galilean type is older, and that the Jerusalem type consisted of a 'translation' of the Galilean type.[24] In his view, the origin of the Jerusalem type is as follows.

The setting of Jerusalem would little by little have taken the place of Galilee. It is clear that Luke artificially locates the appearance to the Eleven in Jerusalem, as we have already said. This location is explained by the dominant role of the holy city and by that of the mother church. 'The deliverer from Zion' (Ps 137; 110:2; Is 2:3; cf. Rom 11:26); 'Behold, your salvation comes' (Is 62:11). It is at Jerusalem that the saving events are to find their fulfilment. Luke gives systematic form to this (Luke 24:47; Acts 1:8), according to a tendency which was already present in Paul (Rom 15:19) and which John brought to its ultimate conclusion.

The Galilean tradition marked the end of history with the revelation of the Son of man exalted to heaven. Now, the church had to face up to the problem of the history which went on after Easter. The Galilean presentation alone makes it impossible to resolve adequately the problem that this raised. But the category of 'resurrection from the dead' made it possible to locate the Easter event in the past, and the event of our own resurrection in the future. If this is so, the category of resurrection 'translated' that of exaltation.

From this starting point, preaching was able to present the various aspects of the Easter mystery as a succession of events. Luke followed this structure most clearly, as we shall show in the chapter devoted to him.

These reflections are valuable if we are to understand how the Jerusalem type finally came to dominate the gospel tradition. But they are not sufficient to show that the Jerusalem type is only a translation of the Galilean.

Thus, we consider that the two types, Jerusalem and Galilean, cannot be derived from each other. They correspond, moreover, to the two types of christology, which, it seems, have existed from the beginnings of the Christian faith, the christology of the risen Christ and the christology of the exalted Lord. But the relative difficulty with which we are able to re-establish the existence of the exaltation christology[25] shows clearly that the Jerusalem type has to some extent absorbed the Galilean. The narrative in Matthew is an excellent witness to this: the Jerusalem sequence monopolizes the account, and all that clearly remains of the Galilean tradition is the setting.

The Jerusalem type triumphs   While we have tried to distinguish the Galilean type, this is not because we secretly regret the fact that the tradition finally adopted the Jerusalem type exclusively. To take such an attitude would be to shut one's eyes to the gospel narratives. Before we indicate the role which the Galilean type can play, let us point out the value and the disadvantages of the Jerusalem type.

The resurrection is conceived of as rising or awakening from death, and more specifically as coming forth from the tomb. Jesus shows himself alive to his disciples. He walks on the earth like any other man, though without being restricted to the mortal condition. He is not recognized at once (Luke 24:16, 31; John 20:19, 26). He is expected to prove that he is neither a 'spirit' (Luke 24:37) nor an angel (Acts 23:8-9). His identity, or at any rate his corporeality, can be verified by his wounds. Finally Jesus takes leave of his disciples, at the appointed time, when sufficient evidence has been provided to dispel any doubts.

This biographical type of narrative has the incontestable advantage of making us feel that we are touching the risen Christ, so that we can no longer reasonably doubt the reality of the resurrection. It would be a mistake to see this as a trick of language and not as the actual expression of the apostolic experience; the details of the narratives are valid, as long as they are seen in the context of the unifying factor of the Jerusalem type, the threefold structure of initiative, recognition and mission. By virtue of this structure, the whole of Christian life can be shaped on that of Christ. By the initiative of the risen Christ, the believer is preserved from illusion; recognizing Jesus of Nazareth, he can no longer surrender himself to an activity which is isolated from all reference to past history; the mission prevents him from adhering rigidly to the past, and directs him towards the building up of the world in the faith of Christ. Properly understood, the Jerusalem type is a permanent lesson for the believer; the gospel has simply to be read correctly.

But these undeniable advantages are counterbalanced by no less certain dangers. For if the risen Christ is also seen as continuing to lead to some extent an existence which, apart from the surprising aspects which it presents, is exactly the same as our own, there is a risk of comparing the resurrection to a survival. Of course the ascension represents a breach, but this brings in the danger of making the period of the appearances an era of the past, a golden age, with respect to which our own time has hardly any meaning.

The Galilean type enables us to avoid treating the risen Christ as a man who has survived death, and reducing his presence to physical contacts. Based directly upon the lordship of Jesus, it describes the basic encounter which founded the Church in the form of a gratuitous and definitive irruption of the Lord enthroned in heaven. The corrective administered to the familiar presence of the risen Christ among his disciples is due not merely to extraordinary phenomena, but to the very being of Jesus, the Lord in glory. We do not have simply a period of forty days, but a new era which typifies a presence of a new kind: Emmanuel.

This language also has its disadvantages, and this is immediately evident from the fact that it has been replaced by biographical language. Because it does not attempt to place the appearances of Jesus within a fixed period of time, it runs the risk of doing away with the distance which in fact separates the privileged time of the resurrection from the time of the church. What difference is there between the official appearance to the Eleven and later manifestations, to Saul of Tarsus or to the mystics? The link with Jesus of Nazareth tends to be absorbed by the link with the church, to the extent that the global view which we have striven to acquire through the Jerusalem type is in danger of being truncated.

The two terminologies must be taken in their totality. At first sight, we might hesitate to combine them, as this would tend to distort them. Yet it was on this basis that the final gospel tradition was drawn up: there was no hesitation in subordinating everything to the 'Jerusalem' type of presentation. The modern reader must proceed in the same way. Aware of the Galilean type, he will be more easily capable of seeing in the traveller or the familiar companion at table something more than an individual who has come back to life on earth: he will see the Lord exalted in glory.

CHAPTER SIX

At the Tomb of Jesus

The four gospels all preface the narratives of the appearances of the risen Christ by recounting the episodes which took place at the tomb. On the first day of the week, the women went to the sepulchre and saw that it was open, and that Jesus was not in it. In view of the unanimity of the gospels, how is it that the other New Testament writings ignore these facts and that the primitive kerygma never mentions them? Some scholars have concluded that the gospel accounts were later than the other statements, and were merely legendary narratives, invented for apologetic or theological purposes. Of course we must recognize that a harmonization of the gospel texts is here again impossible. But it does not follow that they can in no way reflect ancient traditions. This is what we would like to examine in this chapter: not the historicity of the events, but the nature and antiquity of the traditions concerning them.

In so doing, we disagree with the majority of scholars in thinking that we ought not to rely primarily on the text of Mark, as if he were the oldest witness of the tradition from whom the other recensions are derived. In our opinion, the literary problem of the connections between the gospels is far from being resolved by the two source theory.[1]

On the other hand there is a fifth witness, the *Gospel of Peter*,[2] in which original features are so numerous that we cannot say that it is merely harmonizing or making a compilation from the four canonical gospels.[3] We even consider that it depends on pre-Marcan sources.[4] Thus, in the account of the resurrection, it is unaware of the angel's message about the meeting in Galilee, and yet reports an appearance in that very place (*Gospel of Peter* 58-60). A comparison of the *Gospel of Peter* with Matthew shows the real value of the Matthaean elements in it.

Various methods can be followed to account for the tradition.

In view of our decision about the literary criticism, we shall not use Mark as our sole source.[5] That would be to beg the question. In a first attempt to go back to essentials, we shall distinguish in all the narratives together the different themes of which they are composed. Then we must define the function which these different themes have in each account. Next, we shall try to describe their history. This method requires that we respect the structure of each account. Before we speak of sources and literary dependence, we have to understand the texts as texts, as whole entities within which the themes may no doubt be derived from varied sources, but where they must above all be examined in the role which they play there. Literary criticism alone cannot suffice, for it endlessly appeals to the 'purpose' of changes, which may be in the highest degree hypothetical.

We will set out the texts in three groups, the second being as it were a substitute for the first:

A. The narrative of the visit of the women to the tomb
B. The descriptions, brief (Luke 24:12) or in detail (John 20:3-10), of the visit of one (or more) of the disciples to the tomb
C. The traditions concerning the guards at the tomb.

A. THE VISIT OF THE WOMEN TO THE TOMB

These texts are of varying importance and will be dealt with individually.

As the basis of our study, we shall take the versions of the *Gospel of Peter*, Matthew and Mark, referring only to the modifications in the versions of Luke and John. Here are the fixed elements common to these three recensions:

1. The first day of the week (*Gospel of Peter*: the Lord's day)
2. the women come
3. with a fixed purpose;
4. they find the stone rolled to the side of the tomb;
5. they see an angel (or angels)
6. who gives (or give) the Easter message;
7. they react.

In common with most other scholars,[6] we consider the message entrusted to the disciples, to go to Galilee, to be a later addition. Moreover, it is absent from the *Gospel of Peter*, and Luke has completely altered it. In Matthew and Mark, it looks back to the prophecy of Mark 14:28, which was itself an addition to the text. The episode is coherent in its present form; but to get at its meaning, it is necessary to discover the interconnection between the various elements according to their respective functions. This is not a simple task, for it is necessary both to bear in mind the different recensions, and to envisage an imaginary text.

1 *The Dating*

Gospel of Peter	Matthew 28:1	Mark 16:1	John 20:1
The night when	After the Sabbath,	And when the sabbath was past,	
the Lord's day	towards the dawn of *the first*	they bought	
broke	*day of the week*		

	Luke 24:1	Mark 16:2	
At the dawn of	*On the first day of*	Very early on *the*	On *the first day*
the Lord's day,	*the week*, at	*first day of the week*	*of the week*, while
Mary Magdalene	early dawn	when the sun had risen	it was still dark

All the accounts fix the event on the first day of the week, i.e. the day after the sabbath; *The Gospel of Peter* uses a later term, 'the Lord's day' or Sunday (cf. Rev 1:10; Acts 20:7). It is not the 'third day' which dates the resurrection, but Sunday, no doubt because of liturgical practice, which fixed the commemoration of Christ's resurrection at the time of eucharistic worship. Even if the data is not firm enough for us to be certain,[7] the narrative has a liturgical flavour.

While the day is agreed, the exact moment is rather less so. Reading Mark, 'very early' means about three o'clock in the morning, a statement which is promptly corrected by 'when the sun had risen', perhaps after six o'clock.

This double statement is often interpreted as a characteristic literary trait in Mark, who with the second remark makes precise what was indeterminate in the first.[8] The conclusion would be acceptable if the duality was not also reflected in the other recensions: 'at daybreak' in the *Gospel of Peter* and for Luke, and 'while it was still dark' in John. And some scholars[9] reasonably ask whether Mark has not misinterpreted the expression used by

Matthew and the *Gospel of Peter*, 'toward the dawn' (*epiphōskousē*), which does not necessarily mean 'break of day', but the 'start' of the day. For the Jews reckoned days from what we would call the night before, from nightfall.[10] In all likelihood, Matthew thought that the women went to the tomb after the sun had gone down, at nightfall, after the sabbath had ended. This statement would correspond with the first one in Mark, 'when the sabbath was past', designating the time when the women went, not, in his account, to the tomb, but to the market to buy spices. The tradition is not unanimous, but we are inclined to think that Matthew reflects the original tradition; this choice also depends on what one makes of the intention of the women.

In the five recensions, in each case, the role of the indication of day and hour is the same: to place the episode, and equally the reader, at a point in time.

2 *The Holy Women*

The names and number of the women vary with the recensions: in Mark there are three, Matthew two, in Luke three and more; in John only one, and in the *Gospel of Peter* the same one, with anonymous companions. A somewhat elaborate study leads to the conclusion that the tradition has evolved towards the multiplication of witnesses; on the other hand, only Mary Magdalene is mentioned by all. The variations of the recensions show that the tradition is hardly concerned to be precise on this matter; it is thus pointless to look for a way of harmonizing the data.[11]

These names are not wholly in time with those mentioned at the crucifixion and burial, but are so sufficiently to indicate the intention of the narrators: to establish a link between the witnesses of the death, the burial and the visit to the tomb.

3 *The Intention of the Women*

There are two principal indications on this matter: anointing (Mark, Luke, *Gospel of Peter*) or mourning (Matthew, *Gospel of Peter*, John).

By attributing to the women the intention of going to embalm the body of Jesus, the tradition is seeking to indicate the link with previous episodes; it also shows that the women's attention is still exclusively directed towards the past, towards a dead body. Nevertheless it runs up against numerous difficulties. These do not arise from the climatic conditions, as though it would be madness in Palestine to want to anoint a corpse after three days, because its decomposition would not necessarily be far advanced at that time of year.[12] But there are other difficulties which lead even supporters of the priority of the Marcan narrative to attribute this detail to the evangelist himself. In particular, if this is the intention of the women, it assumes not inadvertence on their part, but the conviction that the anointing had not been carried out by Joseph or Arimathea. Now, it seems clear that the burial was carried out according to the rules.[13] We may add that the detail plays no part in the account and that it is easier to add it to a visit to mourn than the other way round.

We think, then, that the original tradition presented the women as quite simply intending to go and 'see' the tomb (Matthew) that is, to 'mourn' (*Gospel of Peter*, John) for Jesus. This more restrained tradition does not distract attention from the rest of the narrative; as clearly as the purpose of anointing, it demonstrates to whom the thoughts of the holy women were directed, by contrast with what was to occur.

4 The Theme of the Stone

All the narratives, including those of the episode of the guards, attach great importance to the stone which was placed in front of the tomb. It was big (Matthew 27:60; Mark 16:4; *Gospel of Peter* 32, 54); it had been carefully placed by the guards (Matthew 27:66); it aroused the anxiety of the women (Mark 16:3; *Gospel of Peter* 32, 53), and lastly it had rolled away itself (*Gospel of Peter* 37; Mark 4; Luke 2) or been rolled away by the angel of the Lord (Matthew 2). This stone helped to stimulate the imagination of the narrators. Not that this matters much; what is important is the role which it retains in the structure of each narrative. The stone in fact can either stop people from entering the tomb, or prevent the dead man from coming out of it.

All the narratives are concerned with the removal of the stone, since this makes it possible to look inside, or even go in. So the women who came to anoint Jesus go into the tomb (Mark 5; *Gospel of Peter* 52); and so do the 'angels' (*Gospel of Peter* 37, 44, 51), the disciples (John 5, 8) and Mary Magdalene (John 11). This makes it possible to observe the absence of the body (Luke 3) or to be invited to verify that fact (Matthew 6; Mark 6; *Gospel of Peter* 56). The removal of the stone is not intended to arouse wonder, but to make belief in the resurrection easier, while leaving open the possibility of the theft of the body (a theme stressed in Matthew and in John). Its function can be called apologetic.

The stone can have another function. By closing the sepulchre, the stone makes it impossible for the body to be removed, as the episode of the guards suggests (Matthew 27:66; *Gospel of Peter* 33). Moreover, it signifies that the dead cannot come back from Sheol; for, according to Jewish thought, the tomb was not the equivalent of our cemetery, but symbolized Sheol, to which the dead go down.[14] This is why, at the death of Jesus, the tombs opened before (and so that) the dead could rise (Matthew 27:52). Then the tomb of Christ is opened, so that the man who had gone into it can bring back the risen Jesus (*Gospel of Peter* 39). When it is set aside, the stone signifies the defeat of Sheol; it thus has a function which can be described as 'epiphanic'.

On the basis of these two traditional interpretations, it appears to us that it is the tendency of the narrative in Matthew which is closer to the original. There is of course still a trace of the 'opening' theme, permitting verification of the absence of the body (Matthew 6), but the stone is not connected with the visit of the women. It is the object of an intervention of the divine power over death: the angel of the Lord rolls it away and is sitting on it triumphantly. It is easy to conclude from this, without its being asserted, that Jesus has risen already. Everything occurs as if Matthew were using a tradition akin to the *Gospel of Peter*, and were trying to make it more 'evangelical'. It is not a question of making us see the resurrection as if we were there—that is not possible—but of showing its consequences, namely that Jesus is no longer there. To this apologetic tendency is added an epiphanic orientation. Once the stone has been rolled away, its function is to symbolize the fact that it no longer has any meaning. Sheol is no longer guarded, death has been defeated by God himself.

With this theme of the stone, the narrative begins to make sense. The previous themes are arranged with respect to it. The first day of the week is 'the day' when the eschatological omnipotence of God is revealed, his day of victory. Setting out with devotion to perform their duty for the body, the women are in the presence of an act of God: Sheol is defeated. What is missing? The response of faith.

5 *The Angel*

A heavenly being intervenes at the tomb. It is sometimes a young man (Mark 5; *Gospel of Peter* 55), sometimes the angel of the Lord (Matthew 2), who becomes simply an angel (Matthew 5); sometimes two men (Luke 4; *Gospel of Peter* 36), or young people (*Gospel of Peter* 37). Such a variety in the descriptions leaves the field open for their interpretation. In any case, they are described as heavenly figures; they come down from heaven (Matthew 2; *Gospel of Peter* 36, 44), possessing a kind of brilliance (Matthew 3; Luke 4; *Gospel of Peter* 55), and a white garment, typical of apocalyptic (Matthew 3; Mark 5). This is a way of indicating the eschatological character of the meeting of heaven and earth; we are a long way from any 'discovery of the empty tomb'. We are in the presence of God who acts.

He acts in various ways. 'The Angel of the Lord'—God in person (cf. Gen 16:7, 13; Exod 3:2)—rolls the stone away himself and triumphs over the death which it symbolizes. According to all the recensions God also sends one or two angels who have other functions: first, to show the heavenly character of the event, as in the case of God's act on Christmas night, and then to express the faith of the infant church. We are now going to make this clear.

6 *The Message of the Angel*

Gospel of Peter 56	*Matthew 28:5-6*	*Mark 16:6*	*Luke 24:5-6*
Wherefore	Do not be afraid;	Do not be amazed.	Why
are ye come?	for I know		
Whom seek ye?	that you seek	You seek	do you seek
Not him that	Jesus who	Jesus of Nazareth who	the living
was crucified	was crucified	was crucified	among the dead?
	He is not here		He is not here
He is risen	for he is risen	He has risen	but has risen
and has departed,		he is not here;	
If you do not	as		remember how he
believe it	he said		told you ...
Look in	Come,		
and see the place	see the place	See the place	
where he lay,	where he lay.	Where they laid him.	
that he is not here for he is risen and is departed thither whence he was sent.			

The first item in this message is a saying of the epiphany type, which reassures the women in the face of the heavenly intervention.

The second has two aspects. The resurrection is announced by a heavenly messenger, and is a revelation made to the community, not the community's view of the events. On the other hand, it is proclaimed in the very terms of the kerygma of the primitive church, such as we find for example in Acts 4:10, where a similar antithesis occurs: 'By the name of Jesus Christ of Nazareth, whom you crucified, whom God raised from the dead, by him this man is standing before you well' (cf. 2:22; 3:6). How can these two elements be united? A possible answer is that the church, in confessing her faith in the risen Jesus, understood that it was God himself who was revealing him to her. Though it is the word of God, the angel is at the same time the voice of the church; in response to God's act in rolling away the stone and triumphing over death, she proclaims her faith in the risen Jesus.

The third point puts the message in context. In fact, it is not simply a question, as in the first Christian confessions of faith, of affirming that Jesus is risen; here, this affirmation has to be seen in relation to death, which the tomb symbolizes, or, more exactly, to the victory over death, symbolized by the stone which has been rolled away. At this point an important difference between Matthew and Mark becomes apparent. In Mark, it is the announcement of the resurrection which comes first; in Matthew it is the pointing out of the fact that Jesus is not in the tomb. Of course, in the end, the two statements amount to the same thing, since one is the obverse of the other. But it is obvious that in Matthew it is the fact of Jesus's absence which is announced first. The narrative is given a slightly different slant. In Mark it is the announcement of the resurrection which is alluded to first, and the fact that the body is missing is added later. A comparison with Luke is illuminating on this matter. There, the stone does not concern the women at all, since they 'found the stone rolled away from the tomb; but when they went in they did not find the body; while they were perplexed about this ...' (Luke 24:2-4). It is not the angel who announces to them, as the corollary of the resurrection, that the body of Jesus is no longer there; it is an observable fact. In Matthew the shift of meaning is not as obvious, but it has begun, which means that, although the message of the resurrection is still the most important point in the three synoptic gospels, yet, more and more, the absence of the body becomes a tangible proof meant to confirm the fact of the resurrection.

Finally, we must not forget the concluding words: 'See the place where he was.' For this is not simply an announcement of the Easter event. What we have here is a community imagining itself in immediate proximity to the tomb, and the narrative must be read in this sense. This is the meaning of the surprising interest in the location. It is not a question of demonstrating the reality of the resurrection by the fact that the body is not there. A liturgical celebration immediately springs to mind, a gathering of the community to celebrate the Lord's victory over death; it is not necessary to suppose that there really was an annual gathering at the tomb of Christ—it is difficult to prove the existence of such a pilgrimage.[15] We have only to think of Sunday worship, with the purpose of calling to mind how God, in Jesus Christ, conquered Sheol and death. The open tomb is the place where the victory of God over death is apprehended.

The narrative reaches its climax with the message of the angel; the response of faith is given to the divine act by which the stone was rolled away. This narrative does not relate the 'discovery of the empty tomb'; it proclaims God's victory over death.

In conclusion, it is interesting to note how the *Gospel of Peter* formulates the angel's message. The invitation to see the place where Christ lay is preceded and followed by the same words, 'he is risen and is departed', followed in conclusion by the words 'thither whence he was sent'. These are the two aspects of the mystery, the contrast between the descent into Sheol and the re-ascent into heaven, from whence Jesus had come. Obviously this formula is reminiscent of the Johannine point of view: it may also be the vestige of a primitive conception which saw the exaltation of Christ as identical to the resurrection.

7 The Reaction of the Holy Women

We are in agreement with the majority of scholars in believing that the silence of the women (16:8c) is a Marcan detail, which relates not to the Easter proclamation, but to the message meant for the disciples (16:7). What is common to all the recensions is that 'the women fled' from the place (16:8a). This reaction is part of the traditional appearances category (cf. Gen 28:17; Exod 3:6; Judg

6:22-23; Ezek 1:28). It marks the end of the account.

Conclusion

Before suggesting a possible reconstruction of the original tradition, we must first answer a very important question, for our answer implies a particular interpretation. Briefly, some writers have thought that behind the present text we can go back to an older text, which referred neither to the angel nor the Easter message. Originally, it is thought, there was simply an account of the discovery of the empty tomb, leaving those who witnessed it in a state of astonishment and stupefaction. Such a text would be affirming the historical fact for its own sake and not through a kerygmatic or liturgical celebration of the fact. Here the interpretation which sees in the account not the discovery of the empty tomb, but the victory of God over death, is called into question.

According to A. Vögtle,[16] the intervention of the angel is the result of redaction. If we omit vv. 16:5b, 6, 7, a stumbling block is removed from the account, in which the women are naturally seized with fear when they see that the tomb is empty. This would be the first stage in the tradition. The second stage is determined by concerns of an apologetic nature: the silence is emphasized (16:8c) to show that the faith of the disciples does not derive from the experience of the women nor from the account of the empty tomb. Finally, at the third stage, vv. 56-57 were added, when the need was felt to connect the Easter kerygma with the tomb. However convincing it may be, this reconstruction deals with the data in completely the wrong order. It starts at the end, as Luke does. Moreover if we omit vv. 56-57, how could the women have known that the tomb was empty, since it is the angel that tells them so? The Lucan presentation is the result of later reflection about the tomb.

According to P. Benoit,[17] a more ancient tradition than the narrative of Mark lies behind John 20:1-2. Similar to that of Luke 24:12, it is seen as describing how Mary went to the tomb and was amazed to see that it was empty. Here the Lucan text is taken as a model, although, as we shall see, it is of a relatively late origin. Above all, this view fails to appreciate the very nature of the gospel tradition. Is it imaginable that there were ever formulated, traditional *narratives*, which were limited to the neutral statement of a material fact? Has there ever been a *single narrative* concerning the tomb of Jesus which was not in some way illuminated by faith in the resurrection?[18] We therefore continue to hold that the account of the women's visit to the tomb, from the very beginning, contained an Easter message.

From very early times, a tradition existed concerning the women's visit to the tomb. This tradition ran parallel to the kerygmatic tradition proclaiming not only the resurrection but the appearances and the exaltation of Christ. It is difficult to be sure of precise details, and we sometimes have to make a decision without being completely sure. Thus our tentative reconstruction is subject to continual revision.

First Stage   Once the sabbath was ended [probably at night] Mary Magdalene (and her companions) go to the tomb to mourn for Jesus. But when they arrive they see that the stone has been rolled away. An angel is there who says to them: 'Be not afraid. You are seeking Jesus of Nazareth who was crucified. He is risen, he is not here. (He has gone to the place from which he was sent.) See the place where he lay.' Then, overcome with fear, the women flee.

At this stage, in which we can already discern the interpretation of whatever recollection is there, we cannot talk of an apologetic development arising from the kerygmatic tradition, partly because of the way the text is presented and partly because at that time Jewish thinking would have denied that the evidence of the women was valid in law. It is the transposition into narrative style of God's victory over death in his son Jesus Christ. The whole account is constructed around the fact that the stone has been rolled away, and the response of faith proclaimed by the angel. The reader of the gospel, in his turn, does not believe because something marvellous is asserted: he too needs to recognize the mark left by Jesus in coming back to life. This leads him to celebrate God's victory over death.

Starting from this very simple account, the rolling back of the obstacle represented by the stone took an increasingly important place.

Second Stage   The addition of the meeting in Galilee linking the tradition with the disciples, in order to give it authority. The message is treated differently according to the different points of view of the evangelists (particularly the interest in Peter shown by Mark).

Third Stage   The tradition is modified in Luke: it is no longer a matter of establishing the fact that the stone has been rolled away. The empty tomb, with no body, raises a question. At this point the tradition raises the discovery of the empty tomb to the status of a 'sign', though this term is hardly appropriate, and it is preferable to go on speaking of the question which is posed, and the 'amazement' of the women. In fact there is a great risk of going on from here to speak of a proof of the resurrection, something which Luke does not offer.

B.   THE VISIT OF THE DISCIPLES TO THE TOMB

According to Luke and John, the women were not the only ones to go to the sepulchre. The texts are as follows:

> But Peter rose and ran to the tomb; stooping and looking in, he saw the linen cloths by themselves; and he went home wondering at what had happened (Luke 24:12).

> Some of those who were with us (say the disciples going to Emmaus) went to the tomb, and found it just as the women had said; but him they did not see (Luke 24:24).

> ³Peter then came out with the other disciple ... and they went toward the tomb. ⁵Stooping to look in ... ⁷he saw the linen cloths lying, and the napkin which had been on his head, not lying with the linen cloths but rolled up in a place by itself. ⁸Then the other disciple, who reached the tomb first, also went in, and he saw and believed (John 20:3-8).

Even if we cannot say precisely to what extent these accounts are interdependent,[19] a tradition about the visit of the disciples to the tomb is clearly to be found here. It adds some new elements to the visit of the women. The important point is no longer the fact that the stone has been rolled away, nor the message given by the angel. When the disciples stoop down they do not simply establish that the body is no longer there; they also notice the particular way in which the linen cloths, in which the body was wrapped, are laid out.

This tradition seems to be secondary compared with that of the visit by the women. In fact, it is always mentioned after the latter, it has no substance of its own, but is always connected to what precedes it. In Luke it comes either naturally in the course of the conversation between the disciples going to Emmaus and the mysterious traveller, or abruptly between the episode of the women at the tomb and that of the road to Emmaus. Since these two references are not exactly identical—Peter alone in 24:12, several disciples in 24:24—it is usually thought that Luke prefaced his Emmaus narrative with a fragment of tradition which he had picked up, the meaning of which is only shown by the context in which it is embodied.[20] As for John, he has altered the tradition to such an extent[21] that it is difficult to take it as a straightforward report.

An obviously apologetic slant is discernible at three points in this tradition. It is trying, if not to compete with, at least to counterbalance the evidence of the women in accordance with the development of the tradition, which tended to ascribe everything to the disciples. Moreover, we note the tendency to show that the discovery that the tomb is empty does not bring about faith but simply arouses astonishment.

Finally, the presence of the linen cloths, so carefully arranged, is meant to exclude the hypothesis that the body was stolen.

In the history of the tradition concerning the tomb of Jesus, then, these verses represent the remains of an interesting but nevertheless later tradition, with a directly apologetic purpose. It must therefore be taken into consideration, but it is clearly of secondary importance.

C. THE GUARDS AT THE TOMB

The first gospel mentions the presence of guards in three passages which the *Gospel of Peter* also gives in the same order, as is shown in the following table:

Gospel of Peter	*Matthew*

A. THE GUARD POSTED AT THE TOMB

Gospel of Peter 28-34	*Matthew 27:62-66*
[28]gathering of the Pharisees	[62]gathering of the chief priests
[29]before Pilate	[63]and Pharisees before Pilate
[30]The tomb to be guarded for three days lest the disciples steal him away and the people say, 'He is risen from the dead.'	[64]The tomb to be guarded for three days lest the disciples steal him away and tell the people: 'He has risen from the dead.'

Gospel of Peter 28:34	*Matthew 27:62-66*
[31]The guard is posted, the stone rolled,	[65]The guard is posted
[32]A seal is stuck on the monument.	[66]The stone is sealed.

B. THE THEOPHANY

Gospel of Peter 35-44	*Matthew 28:1-4*
[35]The night whereon the Lord's day dawned.	[1]toward the dawn of the first day of the week
[36]a great sound in the heaven	[2]a great earthquake
[36]two men descend thence	[2]an angel of the Lord descends from heaven
[37]the stone rolled away of itself	[2]rolls back the stone and sits on it
[38]the guards wake up the centurion	[4]The guards become like dead men

C. THE REPORT MADE BY THE GUARDS

Gospel of Peter 45-49	*Matthew 28:11-15*
[45]the guards go to Pilate	[11]the guards go to the chief priests
[45]centurion's confession of faith	(=Matthew 27:54)
[46]Pilate maintains his innocence	(=Matthew 27:24)
[47-49]Tell nothing to anyone	[12-15]Make up a story

Unlike certain critics[22)] who try to reduce vv. 2-4 to a simple transformation of Mark's text by Matthew, we consider that the three verses in B belonged to a tradition comprising A and C.[23)] The apologetic legend A and C logically presupposes the experience described in B, which is missing from Mark. Another theme suggests that B does not depend on Mark, namely the presence of elements which are at odds with the actual narrative of the visit. The guards distract the attention of the reader, which has hitherto been on the women. Moreover, here we have the angel of the Lord (not just any angel), whose function is not to speak, but to roll the stone away. The passage was thus in all probability interpolated by Matthew into the account of the visit of the women to the tomb. The final reason is that the elements A, B and C are in the same order in the *Gospel of Peter* (28-49) and in another apocryphal work, the *Ascension of Isaiah* (3;14b-17). Matthew, it seems, drew the two traditions together.

Let us attempt to define the form and function of the narrative in Matthew. It clearly has an apologetic function, that of showing that the body had not been removed. Still, this apologetic slant is grafted, without radical alteration, on to a previous account of the theophany type. This is revealed by a comparison with the *Gospel of Peter*.

1. *The stationing of the guards* (Matthew 27:62-66; *Gospel of Peter* 28-34) In the two recensions, the Jewish leaders take the initiative, there is an allusion to the later preaching of the disciples, the guard is justified by the possible theft of the body, and finally the tomb is sealed. The difference is only in the kind of guard: a Roman cohort in the *Gospel of Peter*, the guard at the disposal of the Jewish leaders in Matthew. The *Gospel of Peter* insists on the presence of the scribes and Pharisees, the stone and the seven seals. The essential point is nevertheless the same in both. Thus we cannot determine which text was prior to the other, or even if there was some literary interdependence.

2. *The event itself* (Matthew 28:2-4; *Gospel of Peter* 28-34) Matthew has a few elements in common with Mark alone: the women at the tomb, and a single heavenly figure, seated and dressed in white. Like the *Gospel of Peter*, Matthew places the resurrection itself at the dead of night, and describes a cosmic sign (earthquake or thunder), the descent of the angel, the sudden light and the open tomb. This epiphany is not to the women, but to the guards. But here the difference between Matthew and the *Gospel of Peter* is revealed. While the episode in the *Gospel of Peter* is an account of the resurrection itself,[24] intended to make it credible and even obvious, in Matthew the resurrection is only perceptible through its consequences: the stone rolled away by the angel of the Lord, the guards thrown to the ground 'like dead men'. To the theme of the stone that has been rolled away, which symbolizes the triumph of the omnipotence of God over death, there is added the effect on the unbelievers who, when faced with life, are dead men. The duel between life and death takes shape. At this level, we cannot say that the account is simply apologetic; it has a theological function.

3. *The Report of the Guards* (Matthew 28:11-15; *Gospel of Peter* 45-49) But apologetic reclaims its rights; Matthew shows the deceit of the Jewish leaders, and explains how the story of the theft of the body still came to be told up to that time. The *Gospel of Peter* adds the testimony of the guard, 'Truly he was the Son of God', a proclamation already made by the centurion and the soldiers in Mat-

thew 27:54. Pilate then says that he is innocent of the blood of the Son of God, a confession which Matthew had located much earlier (27:24). The effect of these two references is to acquit Pilate, and to present the reality of Jesus's resurrection as proclaimed by gentiles, i.e. by witnesses assumed to be 'objective'. These apologetic details derive from a level of redaction later than the one we are trying to elucidate, which is typified by the epiphanic and theological viewpoint described above.

Thus it seems that in addition to the tradition of the visit of the women to the tomb, there was another version, that of the guards at the tomb. Its original setting must have been less central than that of the former, for it is reflected only in Matthew and the *Gospel of Peter*. When is it to be dated? It is difficult to be precise. Nevertheless, if we admit that the *Gospel of Peter* is independent of the synoptic tradition (cf. especially of the lack of any message to the disciples, and the different nature of the epiphany), and if we recognize that the *Gospel of Peter* on some points offers a tradition that is less developed than that of Mark (e.g. no interest in the disciples), we can agree that very early in the history of the church a story about guards at the tomb was in circulation. What was its content?

The apologetic orientation of this tradition is clear. There was a desire to use a narrative which described the resurrection of Jesus in such a way as to convince unbelievers, and also to put paid to a current legend about the theft of Jesus's body.

But behind this apologetic, a theological tendency can be seen, which under the form of a theophany seeks to narrate the Easter event. It seems that Matthew cut short a story which he thought was not in conformity with the authentic tradition, using its excellent material not for a positive proof of faith, but in order to set forth God's act in raising his son, by means of the images of the stone that was rolled away and the guards falling like dead men. In this respect, the tradition of the guards at the tomb provides some interesting elements which are additional to those of the visit of the women.

D.   LOCATION OF THE TRADITION

There was clearly an ancient tradition concerning the events which occurred at the tomb of Jesus. This tradition is not central by comparison with that of the appearances. We have tried to indicate this by dealing with the gospel narrative in reverse order. Instead of dealing with the visit to the tomb, followed by the appearances, we have dealt with these different traditions in order of importance.

If the essence of the matter lies in the appearances, why were the episodes which revolve round the tomb of Jesus retained? We shall try to answer this question by briefly looking at the way in which these traditions were presented or retained in the New Testament tradition.

In the beginning, to judge by the texts which we consider primitive, the narratives did not imply that the tomb had been seen empty and that those who saw it then believed in the risen Christ. They reveal that faith in the resurrection did not arise from the discovery of the empty tomb, but from the heavenly message. Their intention was not strictly biographical, but theological. In the tomb, which symbolizes death, God, through his angel, announces to the community that he has raised Jesus from the dead; and in the words of the same angel, the community celebrates the act of God, triumphant over death.

In the course of the gospel tradition, two tendencies which seem to place genuine importance on the tomb become more prominent. First of all, a connection is established between the tomb and the actual person of the risen Christ. In Mark, the women flee from the tomb deserted by Jesus; in Matthew, they meet the Lord not far away; finally, in John, it is at the tomb itself that Mary hears her name spoken by Christ. Though in this way the risen Christ is connected with the tomb, the purpose is not to increase its importance. On the contrary, this tendency may make it easier to fit in better a tradition thought to be marginal by comparison with that of the appearances. It also tends to make the angel's saying dependent on Christ's. The episodes at the tomb of Jesus do not acquire an importance of their own, but fit better into the general tradition.

Another line of development confirms this conclusion. In Luke, the discovery of the empty tomb becomes a statement of fact which precedes the message of the angel; but the purpose here is not to give it any importance other than that of posing a question. If Luke mentions the empty tomb on a number of occasions (24:12, 23, 24), he does so in order to raise a more pressing question. At the same time, it is Luke who, like ps.-Mark, underlines most strongly the scepticism with which the news was received (24:11, 22-24). It is Christ, and in person, who can give the meaning and the answer to the question. In John, this development is brought to its conclusion. The beloved disciple 'saw and believed' (John 20:8). While it may be difficult to define what belief is intended here, since immediately afterwards we read that they were ignorant of the scriptures concerning his resurrection from the dead, it seems certain that John wishes to say that to the eyes of faith the answer is contained in the question that is asked.

Moving on from this high point of gospel interpretation, there are many who have tried to base an apologetic on this sign. It is a slippery slope, however, that leads us to use the empty tomb as proof of the resurrection of Jesus. The gospel writers were very careful to avoid this. Can we say as much of all twentieth-century apologists? Is there actually a 'proof from the empty tomb' in any passage of the New Testament? The question deserves examination, for some texts seem to permit an affirmative answer. The data, however, suggest the contrary.

Firstly, we must note that the actual fact narrated in the gospels did not at first possess great importance. Thus, in answer to the question 'How are the dead raised? With what kind of body do they come? (I Cor 15:35), Paul does not reply by recalling that Jesus was seen as a reanimated body come from its tomb. He calls to mind the way in which the germination of plants was thought of in those days. The seed and the plant are no doubt the same, but Paul does not insist on this obvious fact. He highlights the radical change: it is God who gives an appropriate body to everyone (I Cor 15:38). An earthly body is sown, a spiritual body is raised (15:44). On the other hand, when he enumerates the witnesses of the risen Christ, he does not mention any witness of the empty tomb, either women or disciples, or the Jerusalem community, who would be bound to have known of the event anyway. As to the creed of I Cor 15:3-5, we have shown above that the reference to the burial did not imply a reference to the visit to the tomb. But it by no means follows that Paul was ignorant of the fact. If he had not faced problems of decorum in the liturgical assemblies, Paul would probably not have mentioned the institution of the eucharist; and hasty critics would have been able to suppose that Paul was ignorant of the tradition of the last supper. But in fact Paul does not argue from the discovery of the empty tomb. Why not? We can give our imagination a free rein. Some have suggested that the testimony of women carried no weight in the eyes of a Jew; but that is to forget that the tradition also speaks of verification by Peter and John at the tomb (Luke 24:24, probably independent of 24:12; John 20:3-10). It matters little what explanation one thinks likely. What is of interest to us is that, in the eyes of Paul, this recollection did not appear to be either indispensable or even useful in confirming the fact of the resurrection of Jesus.

In the speeches of Peter and Paul reported by Luke in the Acts of the Apostles, we sometimes get the impression that there is a trace of an argument drawn from the empty tomb.

> [25]David says concerning him ... [27]'Thou wilt not abandon my soul to Hades, not let thy Holy One see corruption...' [29]Brethren, I may say to you confidently of the patriarch David that he both died and was buried, and his tomb is with us to this day. [30]Being therefore a prophet, and knowing that God had sworn with an oath to him that he would set one of his descendants upon his throne, he foresaw and spoke of the resurrection of the Christ, that he was not abandoned to Hades, nor did his flesh see corruption. This Jesus God raised up, and of that we all are witnesses (Acts 2:27, 29-32).

> [36]David, after he had served the counsel of God in his own generation, fell asleep, and was laid with his fathers, and saw corruption; but he whom God raised up saw no corruption (Acts 13:36-37).

Who is speaking in this way? Peter, Paul or Luke? It is noticeable that the argument is based on the Greek translation of Ps 16, which renders the Hebrew 'see the pit' (the psalmist is hoping to escape death) by 'see corruption'. A Hellenistic community, reading the text in this way, has identified 'the holy one' with Jesus: unlike David, Jesus did not experience decomposition because he had risen. This reasoning does not mean to prove the resurrection of Jesus, but to 'establish that, having truly risen, Jesus is really the Messiah of whom the psalm speaks.'[25] The expression 'not see corruption' corresponds to the formula 'be risen', whether it is concerned with the actual moment of the resurrection (as in Acts

2 : 31) or with eternal life (as in Acts 13 : 34). The argument, though a late one, does not deny, yet does not assert, that the body placed in the sepulchre had undergone any particular fate, although it was evident to the early Christians that, as we said above, the resurrection signified the full bringing to life of Jesus of Nazareth at every level of his being. The conclusion is that by itself, the occurrence of the empty tomb is unimportant.[26] A Christian does not believe in the empty tomb but in the risen Christ.

Pending our discussion from the hermeneutic point of view, let us indicate a line of possible advance. Three major symbols are apparent which indicate the meaning of the events which occurred at the tomb.

The major symbol is the stone that has been rolled away. Of itself, it expresses the fact that the power of Sheol, sealing as it does the door of the tomb and of the underworld, has been defeated. Once rolled aside, the stone symbolizes the triumph of God who has freed his Son from the bonds of death. This symbol has complete validity, in the sense that as a reality of this world, it designates a reality of the next.

The second symbol is more abstract. It is the absence of the body of Jesus. By the gap, by the empty space, by the absence, it calls upon something else, namely the hidden presence which rouses the hope of the appearances. Poets and symbolic thinkers can venture quite properly along that path. As for the believer, the pilgrim to the holy sepulchre in Jerusalem, he understands better the meaning of the inscription engraved on the tomb: NON EST HIC! 'He is not here', opening an infinite horizon for his quest for the living Jesus.

Finally, a third symbol seems to have been provided by the later traditions, the linen cloths left in the tomb. Like an abandoned garment, they are present, bearing witness in their own way to the fact that the body of Jesus has attained its fullness of existence, and must be looked for elsewhere. The evangelist John shows the meaning of the linen cloths, carefully folded and put aside, unlike those in which Lazarus was wrapped when he emerged from the tomb.

The Easter Message according to the Evangelists

As we turn to describe the different ways in which the gospel writers proclaim the Easter message, we must take care not to forget what our previous studies have contributed. The writers known to us were preceded by a considerable tradition, which has guided them in their work of presenting the Good News that Jesus, who died to save us, has been raised from the dead by God.

Thus the evangelists are not objective historians who set out simply to describe events as they took place. They were involved in a tradition, and were witnesses who sought to invite their readers to believe, or to believe more. The composition of the gospels depends in its entirety upon the affirmation of the Easter faith. The narratives of Easter day must be approached from this point of view, as a call to believe.

How shall we set about our task? We obviously do not have to supply a detailed commentary on the four gospel narratives. They were composed for the benefit of a particular Christian community; their purposes vary and a given background offsets the portrait which each paints and gives it its particular shade. It will be enough here to suggest a way of reading the texts according to the particular point of view which each adopts. The situation is in fact very complex. For it is always a tricky matter to attempt to explain, or even to put into better words, what a writer has said. It is a hazardous enterprise, and yet it is necessary, although it is something that must be constantly repeated; there is always more in the text than in its interpretation, even if one devotes several pages to a commentary on a few verses.

CHAPTER SEVEN

The Easter Message according to Mark

A first reading

The narrative of Easter morning consists of only eight verses (Mark 16:1-8). Nevertheless, in spite of the many difficulties which it raises, it is pregnant with meaning. Let us begin by working through it to show its apparent coherence.[1] The story is clearly located in time and space. As soon as evening has come on the sabbath which follows the death of Jesus, the women, whose names are given, go to buy spices to embalm Jesus's body; and they go to the tomb the next day, the first day of the week, when the sun has risen. The women have already been mentioned by the author, on the occasion of the crucifixion (15:40-41) and the burial (15:47). Thus they know where to go and understand what they are going to do there.

But as they are on their way, they ask who will roll back for them the stone placed at the end of the tomb. This seems a strange reflection on the part of persons who the previous evening had prepared for the expedition; one immediately wonders why they did not think of it earlier. But such a question arises from an error of judgment on the part of the reader, who supposes that this is a strictly biographical narrative. In fact the reflection is based upon 15:46, '[Joseph of Arimathea] rolled a stone against the door of the tomb,' and is meant to prepare for the surprise effect which follows immediately: 'And looking up, they saw that the stone was rolled back.'

The women, however, do not seem to be surprised, and go into the tomb, where they see a young man dressed in a white robe sitting on the right side. Then they are frightened, in the sense which this word has in biblical appearances; that is, they feel that they are in the presence of a heavenly intervention.[2] To understand the narrator's point of view, we must realize that not a single word has yet been said about the presence or absence of the body of Jesus: the interest lies elsewhere. These women have come to embalm a body, and find an angel. They do not ask any questions, but, as is proper in this kind of appearance, they hear the angel reassuring them, in order to proclaim the great news to them, 'You seek Jesus of Nazareth, who was crucified. He has risen.' With these words, the angel takes up and transforms the purpose that the women had in mind: behind their search for a body, the angel shows that they were searching for Jesus, but for a Jesus, who, since he is risen, is no longer here. As we have indicated in the previous chapter, the order of the narrative is deliberate. It does not give a factual statement from which a consequence is drawn; it first of all affirms a mystery, and then gives an invitation to recognize the signs of it in an astonishing fact.

This revelation makes the women's plan pointless, since there is no longer a body to embalm. The angel gives them something else to do, by entrusting a mission to them: they are to announce to the disciples not the Easter message, but the fulfilment of the prophecy which Jesus made before his passion, that of the gathering together at Galilee, under the crook of the shepherd, of the scattered flock (Mark 14:28). The narrative continues normally until suddenly nothing else happens: 'And they went out and fled from the tomb; for trembling and astonishment had come upon them; and they said nothing to anyone, for they were afraid.' Even if we do not automatically assume that every story should have a happy ending, this conclusion is surprising, and the question arises whether part of the narrative has not been lost.

This is in fact one of the most difficult questions of critical exegesis. Most manuscripts add after v. 8 brief narratives of the three appearances and of the ascension, but these twelve verses have no connection with Mark's style, nor with what one would expect, that is, a detailed narrative of an appearance of the risen Christ. How is it that the climax of the gospel contains fifteen times fewer verses than the passion narrative? Is it possible for the proclamation of the Good News to conclude with the strange disobedience of the women, to whom the heavenly messenger has entrusted a mission to the disciples?

Some writers, therefore, have supposed that in accordance with the traditional kerygma (death, burial, resurrection, appearances:

cf. I Cor 15 : 3-7) the gospel contained an appearance narrative; for did not the message to the disciples foretell this? Moreover, without undertaking a futile attempt at harmonization with the narratives in the other gospels, in which the women speak to the disciples, it may be recognized that the phrase, 'they said nothing to anyone' is typical of Mark and is not necessarily definitive. For example, the healed leper was instructed by Jesus both to say nothing to anyone and to go and show himself to the priest (1 : 44). In view of this, is it not possible to add as a conclusion, 'and immediately they told everything to the disciples'?[3] Thus it is possible to speak of the 'lost ending' of the Gospel of Mark, without its necessarily containing a narrative of the appearance to Peter.

In spite of all these arguments, the hypothesis of a lost ending can never be more than a mere possibility. Moreover, there is such a contradiction in the angel's command and the silence of the women that the narrative must stop there.[4] It is for us to look for an interpretation, but the narrative must be taken as it stands, consisting simply of vv. 1-8.

The difficulties of the narrative

Let us therefore reread the narrative, emphasizing the difficulties which it presents to anyone who tries to treat it as a biographical narrative. These very difficulties will lead us in the direction which will enable us to state what kind of narrative it is. To help the reader to be aware of these difficulties, we shall transcribe as a synopsis the present text and the tradition which we believe we succeeded in isolating in the previous chapter.

Restored Text	*Mark*
After the sabbath Mary Magdalene *and her companions*	[1]And when the sabbath was past, Mary Magdalene, *and Mary* [*the mother*] *of James and Salome* bought spices, so that they might go and anoint him. [2]*And very early on the first day of the week*
went to the tomb	they went to the tomb *when the sun had risen*
to mourn for Jesus.	

³And they were saying to one another, 'Who will roll away the stone for us from the door of the tomb?'

When they arrived, they found	*⁴And looking up they saw*
the stone rolled back	*that the stone was rolled back, for it was very large.*
	⁵And entering the tomb, they saw sitting on the right side,
An angel was there	*a young man dressed in a white robe; and they were amazed.*
who said to them,	*⁶And he said to them,*
'Do not be afraid	'Do not be amazed.
You seek Jesus	You seek Jesus
of Nazareth, who was crucified.	of Nazareth, who was crucified
He has risen, he is not here	He has risen, he is not here;
see the place where he lay.'	see the place where they laid him.
	⁷But go, tell his disciples and Peter that he is going before you to Galilee; there you will see him, as he told you.'
Then the women were afraid	*⁸And they went out*
and fled.	and fled from the tomb; for trembling and astonishment had come upon them; and they said nothing to any one, for they were afraid.

A first difficulty concerns *the number and the names of the women*. Of course they are apparently those who were present at the crucifixion and burial, but it must be noted that in 15:40-41 there are four of them, while in 15:47 there are only two; but here there are three. Moreover, their names do not exactly correspond. The purpose behind these details is not that of a historian but of an apologist, who is attempting to show that in spite of differences in detail the same witnesses were present at these three crucial moments in Jesus's existence. On the other hand, these differences show the nature of the sources which Mark used. The mention of the women at the conclusion of the burial narrative belongs to that pericope. But the mention of them following the crucifixion seems to have been added later, and has no intrinsic function with regard to the preceding narrative; it increases the number of witnesses and seems to have been composed by Mark on the basis of the two other mentions. Finally, the list of women in 16:1 cannot have been made by Mark himself (for if it had, why did he not reproduce that which he composed for the crucifixion, where there were four of them?). It cannot derive from the same source as that connected with the burial (because the two passages do not agree, and follow one another unnecessarily closely). Consequently, the narrative of the visit of the women to the tomb must have existed independently of that of the burial, and it was Mark who placed them one after the other. Thus the interpretation of the latter cannot be argued from the fact that they are in chronological sequence. Here we see the evangelist working at the process of harmonization. He wanted to conclude his gospel in this way, as a climax of the narrative of the passion and of Jesus's ministry.

A second difficulty will enable us to identify one of Mark's main concerns. This is the *moment* at which the women went to the tomb. The beginning of the sentence states that it was 'very early', about three or four in the morning; but at the end of the sentence Mark states that it was 'after the sun had risen'. As we said in the previous chapter (n. 8) these double indications are characteristic of Mark's style, and the emphasis in them is on the second. Thus for Mark the scene took place when the sun was fully risen, and this detail may have a symbolic significance.

We have already mentioned a third difficulty: *the question* asked by the women *about the stone*. This question gives an effect of suspense, and there is nothing biographical about it. Mark probably wanted to emphasize the women's main purpose: to embalm the body of Jesus. How could they get into the tomb? They could do so only if the stone was rolled back.

The final difficulty concerns the last two verses. In v. 8, it is hard to justify the *repetition* of the feeling of terror, far less the *silence* of the women. But this difficulty disappears if it is accepted that

Mark has combined two traditions. In fact all scholars are unanimous that v. 7, concerning the message to the disciples, is an addition. The women remain silent not about the Easter message, but about the errand on which the angel has sent them to the disciples. Thus the text can be read as follows:

... He has risen, he is not here; see the place where they lay him ... And they went away and fled from the tomb; for trembling and astonishment had come upon them.

[The message to the disciples.] 'Go, tell his disciples and Peter that he is going before you to Galilee; there you will see him, as he told you.'... And they said nothing to anyone, for they were afraid.

These difficulties are inherent in a text which one might be tempted to read as a biographical account or a psychological experience; but they mean that we must modify our way of approaching the narrative. We propose therefore to make three comparisons of the texts: first with the whole of the Gospel of Mark, then of its own several parts, and finally with the other versions of the narrative.

The Narrative and the Whole Gospel

The Gospel of Mark begins as follows: 'The beginning of the gospel of Jesus Christ, the Son of God.' Thus it begins with the Good News initiated by the preaching of John the Baptist. This gospel has to be carried to the ends of the world (Mark 13:10; 14:9). Now Jesus preached to Israel, without success (1:14-8:26), and then revealed the mystery of his destiny to the disciples, without any greater success (8:27-10:52). Everywhere Jesus found only a failure to understand, and closed minds. According to Mark, he wished to keep secret his identity as Messiah and Son of God, until he is at the point of being condemned to death (14:62). It is not until after his crucifixion that the pagan centurion proclaims, 'Truly this man was the Son of God!' (15:39). Thus the time now seems ripe to proclaim to the nations that God has raised his Son and to invite the flock of disciples to come together.

It is here that Mark surprises us most. As far as the Easter message is concerned, his narrative attempts no more than to reveal it in a very simple fashion to the women. But he does not give any narrative of an appearance; he simply shows the effect of the revelation upon the women: they are overcome with trembling and astonishment. Though they flee, there is of course no comparison to be made with the flight of the disciples when Jesus was arrested (14:50), except on a single point. Jesus was abandoned by his disciples; only the women accompanied him to the cross. Now that his resurrection is proclaimed, these women also abandon him. The vocabulary which Mark uses is the same as in the case of the disciples to whom Jesus foretold his destiny for the third time: 'They were amazed, and those who followed were afraid' (10:32). To the very end Mark maintains his understanding of the gospel. It is not Good News which the human mind can accept without being profoundly disturbed; and to overcome this terror, the word of an angel is not sufficient, nor is a gospel text: it is necessary to be silent and await the enlightenment of God in person.

This reservation about any human capacity to hear the Easter revelation is in a way reinforced by Mark when he says that the women did not pass on the message to the disciples. There is no point in accusing them of disobedience; this would be contrary to the intention of the narrative, which is not concerned with the human course taken by the revelation. The text does not tell us the outcome of an irrational situation, but the evangelist knows God will have the last word. For how could he have known what he is telling us, since the women did not tell anyone? Here we have a literary device which enables him to show not only how the women were faced by the unfathomable mystery of God and of death, but also how the reader himself is faced with the mystery.

The text and its internal unity

At the very beginning of our reading of the Easter message according to Mark, we pointed to the apparent coherence of the text. One might conclude that its unity is supplied by the Easter revelation. This is true from the point of view of its content, but not from the point of view of its structure, from which we now wish to examine it. This structure can be apprehended at two different levels: that of its unity and that of the contrasts.

The unity of the narrative is supplied by the women. They are named, they go buy spices, they go to the tomb, they ask questions as they are on their way, they see that the stone has been rolled back, they go into the tomb, they are afraid, (they listen), they come out, they flee, they are silent. In demonstrating the unity of the narrative, many scholars refer to the 'setting in life', the annual pilgrimage to the tomb of Jesus. This hypothesis is of some value with regard to the pre-Marcan narrative, but has little interest or meaning with regard to Mark himself, for the passage forms part of a whole which is formed by the gospel. From this point on, it is the women who replace the disciples, and whose purpose it is to suggest to the reader that he should identify himself with them, as they come face to face with revelation. Like them, the reader has been able to affirm the death of Jesus, and identify the place of his burial; like them, he is full of wonder and gratefulness for this man Jesus, and would like to pay his last respects to him; the way into the tomb is open, because the stone has been marvellously rolled back, but this brings him face to face with the overwhelming revelation of the resurrection of Jesus. After fleeing, he has to move on to another task which is not laid down in advance.

Like the counterpoint, the *contrasts* maintain even more firmly the original harmony. They fall into three categories.

The first contrast is not explicit, but is present. Darkness contrasts with light; the risen sun is contrasted with the evening of the sabbath. This contrast overflows into that between within and without: the women go into the tomb and come out of the tomb. The strange thing is that the Easter mystery is revealed in the darkness within the tomb, whereas it is in the sunlight outside that the women take fright and flee.

There is a contrast between speaking and silence. The women speak in full daylight, the angel speaks in secret, but outside they are silent. They begin to act in the night, they come, and then flee in the light, after having been paralysed with fright in the darkness.

Presence and absence. The body is present to them in thought, leading them to act by buying spices and coming early to the tomb. When they are shown that the body is absent, all their activity is brought to an end, and they flee and are silent. They still have to discover another form of presence through this absence.

These three contrasts help to sustain the narrative, as in the paintings of the masters colours and lines correspond and contrast to give form to the portrait. Analysis can go no further than this; the text must speak for itself once again.

The Text of Mark and the Other Versions

Returning a third time to the text of Mark, we shall now contrast it not with its 'sources' but with the parallel versions. For it is possible to discuss *ad nauseam* the text which Mark, more or less certainly, had at his disposal; on the other hand, the parallel texts of Matthew, Luke, John and the *Gospel of Peter* are there staring us in the face. Before we turn to the personal way in which Mark presents the elements of the narrative, let us note the 'absences', what Mark did not say, and did not consider appropriate to retain in his text; though we cannot be certain that an absence is necessarily a voluntary 'omission'.

The first thing which is obviously missing when we compare Mark with the *Gospel of Peter*, but which is similarly absent from all canonical gospels, is any description of Jesus rising or ascending to heaven. This absence is of great significance, for it leaves the moment at which God raised his Son as his own secret. The divine act is hidden for ever. The other thing missing, in Mark alone, is a narrative of the appearance of the risen Christ. This omission is voluntary, for it is hardly possible for Mark to have been unaware of the credal formulas. Since he knew of their existence, he had to have some motive for not mentioning them. The first indication is given by the instruction which the women had to carry to the disciples: '... to Galilee; there you will see him.' What does the verb 'see' mean in this context? The reply depends in part upon the meaning given to the word 'Galilee'. Some scholars consider it refers to the geographical region where Jesus exercised his ministry, while in the view of others, it is the eschatological land, Galilee of the nations, which was to see the final salvation of God. If it is the latter which Mark has in mind, then he is not thinking of any appearance in the strict sense. If he is thinking of the earthly Galilee, we must try to discern the reason why the tradition preserved this command. The intention was probably to show that this was the fulfilment of the promise made by Jesus to the disciples when they were about to be scattered: 'After I am raised up, I will go before you to Galilee' (Mark 14:28). Since Mark mentions that Peter in particular had to be reminded of this, it is likely that the message refers not directly to a special appearance to Peter, but the restoration to grace of him who denied Jesus (14:30, 66-72), and through him, the gathering together once again of the disciples. When Mark specifies the prophecy of 14:28 by adding the words, 'There you will see me', he does not seem to be thinking of a particular appearance, but is pointing the reader towards a future which he defines solely by the encounter with Christ. Why? Here we are in the field of conjecture. That of L. Schenke is as follows.[5] Mark shared with other Christians of his period a concern that they should be freed from the tutelage of Jerusalem. The appearance narratives were of course located at Jerusalem, where the disciples probably settled in the end. So he shows them having to leave as quickly as possible for Galilee, where Jesus precedes them in person. Thus it seems that Mark deliberately eliminated the appearance narratives, first of all in order to direct the Christian community beyond the Jerusalem establishment, to which it ran the risk of becoming inextricably attached. Other motives too seem to have contributed to this reserve with regard to appearance narratives, and we shall mention them in our conclusion, after examining the points which Mark has particularly emphasized.

Let us now go through the texts to stress the points which Mark emphasized or which, alternatively, he blurred.

Special attention is paid to the women. Their action in going to buy spices in described separately, whereas in Luke it is mentioned only as having taken place the previous evening (Luke 23:56). Why did Mark prefer to describe them as having done this, rather than mourning? Probably in order to link the present narrative to that of the burial, which, as he describes it, could not have been carried out in full. Moreover, this gesture perhaps shows more affection than a lamentation on its own.

The reflection about the stone which would not be rolled back leads up to the affirmation that it had been; and the stone rolled back permits their entry into the tomb. As we see, the stone does not play the part in an epiphany which it possessed in the older tradition, by symbolizing the victory of God over death; its value now is solely psychological.

On the other hand, the note that the sun had risen has probably a different function from that of mere chronology. The first day of the week is the day of the Lord, and is also the day on which the sun of righteousness rises, at least if this symbolism was known to Mark.

Finally, the silence of the women is of great importance from Mark's point of view; and we have already discussed this.

Conclusion

In spite of its brevity, the Easter narrative in Mark is of great significance in the gospel tradition of the events of Easter.

The gospel narratives of the appearances lose the absolute character which is sometimes attributed to them. They no doubt remain the foundation stone of faith in the resurrection. Nevertheless, the evangelist Mark did not feel it necessary to reproduce any of them. He preferred to place his reader in the company of women who experienced no more than the earthly presence of Jesus. They stumble upon the Easter mystery, but are not yet able to receive it. Yet it is proclaimed.

It is of course necessary and proper that some of the gospels should have recorded narratives which tell how the Lord Jesus showed himself; they enable the believer to understand better the situation with regard to the risen Jesus. But it is unquestionably vital that Mark, remaining faithful to the total purpose of his gospel, should place us in the presence of the mystery without daring to give it any kind of visible form; the reader remains face to face with the mystery as it is fulfilled. How does this come about? No one knows exactly, not even Mark.

But Mark places the reader in a specific place, that of the women who follow a certain itinerary. They have scarcely been invited to look at the place where Jesus lay, when they are asked to leave. Like a springboard which repels whoever puts his weight upon it, the tomb pushes them away from itself. It symbolizes everything that remains of the life of the earthly Jesus; we have to go to the tomb, but only in order to accept that we are taken over by a different purpose, without having first to be carried up into ecstacy, without having first to keep silence without understanding, so that we are better able to receive the word of God which is to be heard in the vacuum left by what remains unuttered. This is particularly true of Peter who denied Jesus, for the faithfulness of God is greater than the unfaithfulness of man. He waits for us in Galilee, the land of hope.

CHAPTER EIGHT

The Easter Message according to Matthew

At a first reading, especially following that of the Gospel of Mark, the sequence of Easter events according to Matthew seems to provide the continuation of Mark. Here again, the angel announces the resurrection of Jesus to the women who have gone to the tomb, and tells them to give the message to the disciples, whom the risen Christ arranges to meet in Galilee. Matthew, it seems, is completing the second gospel by not abandoning his reader at a point when the meeting is still to come. His account goes further and extends into a continuous narrative: the women tell the news to the disciples, and the risen Christ appears to the Eleven in Galilee. This is how Matthew is read by scholars who are accustomed to regard him as simply basing himself on Mark.[1]

But we have shown in chapter 6 that Matthew probably has available two traditions, and not merely a single tradition similar to that of Mark: there is also the tradition of the guards at the tomb, for which the *Gospel of Peter* is remarkable evidence. If this is accepted, it can be seen that Matthew's Easter narrative is organized in a way that can be compared to a diptych. The form of its first panel is drawn from the tradition of the guards at the tomb, and does not begin on the evening of the sabbath day (28:21), but the day after the crucifixion (27:62); it alternates between guards and women in the following way:[2]

A. The guards have to be posted at the tomb (27:62-66)
  B. The women go to the tomb (28:1)
A¹. The guards die of fright (28:2-4)
  B¹. The women receive the angel's message, which is confirmed by an appearance (28:5-10)
A². The guards go to tell the chief priests (28:11-15)

The second panel of the diptych portrays the meeting of the Lord Jesus with the disciples (28:16-20). This diptych provides the culmination of the gospel. Matthew tells how, after having had Jesus crucified, the chief priests and Pharisees persuade Pilate to order the tomb to be sealed and well guarded. But in spite of these precautions, the angel of the Lord rolls back the stone and reveals to the holy women that Jesus is no longer in the tomb, and that the disciples have to go to Galilee to see him. The risen Christ comes in person to meet the women, as they are hastening to bear the news, while the chief priests and elders buy the silence of the soldiers. Finally the disciples worship the Lord, who promises to be with them and sends them on their mission. These events form the culminating point of a sequence which began with the infancy narrative at the opening of the gospel. The purpose here is to show how the history of Jesus Christ, which began so marvellously, concludes on earth and opens up another history, that of his mysterious presence here below.

But Matthew's purpose is even more complex, and can be seen in the way in which he sets out the successive episodes. Rather than being the conclusion of a narrative, they are its epilogue. Some of the elements in this epilogue balance the prologue formed by the two first chapters of the gospel. For they present prior events, while the present passage contains facts which are subsequent to the action proper, the ministry of Jesus of Nazareth. In fact in the prologue, as in the epilogue, a long vista opens through time: in the former case back to Abraham and even to Adam,[3] and here forwards to the end of the world, a vista which goes beyond the horizon of history proper.

The content of both passages confirms this total impression. The angel of the Lord appeared, i.e. probably the Lord in person.[4] Extraordinary phenomena take place during the night, in dreams or through words from heaven: heaven communicates with earth. Sudden and surprising meetings of the Sanhedrin are called. The chief priests play their part, and Pilate supplies the equivalent of Herod. The divine child found refuge in Galilee, and there too the disciples are to go. Finally and above all the promised Emmanuel—that is, God with us—himself comes to proclaim, 'I am with you always, to the close of the age.'

Other elements, which find no parallel in the prologue, largely have their counterpart in the narrative of Jesus's public life. The authority which in the wilderness (4:8-10) Jesus would not accept from Satan is now conferred upon him, over all men; the teaching of the Sermon on the Mount, addressed to the disciples (5:1) is now to be communicated to all nations, of whom they are to 'make disciples'; Jesus was formerly transfigured upon a mountain (17:1) and now comes as Lord of glory. Thus the epilogue condenses and opens towards infinity the facts recounted previously. Let us examine the two panels of the diptych more closely, and then attempt a synthesis of the Easter message according to Matthew.

A. THE VICTORY OF GOD (27:62—28:15)

The title which we have given to the first panel of the diptych is inspired by the prologue found in the first two chapters of Matthew. The drama of the Messiah, rejected by his people but welcomed by a few, is evoked there in a skilfully arranged diptych: Jesus, the son of David, is welcomed by the righteous (1:1-25) but is persecuted by the Jews; he who was later to draw the gentiles to him is forced into exile when he first comes (2:1-23). God triumphs over Herod and the chief priests by saving his Son from death, symbolized by the massacre of the innocents. In the epilogue too, God triumphs over the plan of the Jews to lock up for ever in the darkness of Sheol.

The structure of the narrative sets out what the story itself suggests, as can be seen from the following synopsis.

27:62-66		CHIEF PRIESTS		28:11-15
	meeting		meeting	
	chief priests and Pharisees		chief priests and elders	
	before Pilate		(the governor)	
	He said: I will rise again			
	a guard		(while they were asleep)	
	against possible theft		they stole him	
	a sealed stone		some of the guard	

The women came to see the tomb	WOMEN	The women depart, kiss Jesus's feet and worship him. with joy they run. } 28:9-10
earthquake descent of the angel Stone rolled away Sitting on the stone description of angel fear of the guards *(28:1-4)*	GOD	go quickly Come, see the angel hears and says the women are not afraid } 28:5-8
	GUARDS DEAD 28:4	

This synopsis shows straight away that the women are playing the part of spectators and hearers and messengers, while the drama takes place between the chief priests (and their friends) and God himself in the person of the angel of the Lord. The guards are the emissaries of the chief priests, instructed to keep the tomb hermetically sealed by the stone. But the angel of the Lord rolls back the stone, and in triumph, sits down on it. The guards are left lying, as though they were dead. If they get up, it is so that the chief priests, in confusion, may find the worst possible solution. At that moment the wickedness of men breaks out, and God is victorious.

Matthew's narrative has often been described as apologetic. There is no doubt some trace of this point of view, which is obvious in the *Gospel of Peter*. But this approach is not sufficient to account for the purpose of the present narrative: it is theological in the strictest sense, describing the victory of God over death. An examination of the elements of the narrative will confirm our hypothesis.

1 *The enemies of God*

The 'wicked' enhance the quality of the divine intervention, particularly as their activities (27:62-66; 28:11-15) are the framework for the encounter of the women with the angel and with the Lord (28:1-10). The chief priests and the Pharisees (or the elders) are not only actors who take part in the drama, but men whose feeble and shifty behaviour provides a contrast to the sovereign freedom of the angel. They go to some trouble to avoid the body leaving the tomb. Thus they are making a prophecy without knowing it, and assist the reader to recall the prophecy made by Jesus, which the angel needs only to mention ('as he said'). In their confusion and fear they form a dark background to the picture; by their deceit, which contrasts with that which they attribute to the disciples, they make their defeat inevitable. The money itself, similar to that which was given to Judas, is their ultimate infamy.

As for the soldiers, they are neutral and powerless spectators. They are certainly not witnesses of the resurrection of Jesus itself, as they are portrayed in the *Gospel of Peter*; they are as dead, when they see the angel who has come to proclaim him who is alive. The same soldiers are to bear the news, that is, 'all that had taken place', and allow their silence to be bought. This is typical of the wicked in the face of God who comes in triumph.

2   *The Theophany*

From the tradition reflected by the *Gospel of Peter*, Matthew has excluded the elements which tended to visualize the resurrection itself. We can see this if we reread the description given in the *Gospel of Peter*.

> [35]Now in the night whereon the Lord's day dawned, as the soldiers were keeping guard two by two in every watch, there came a great sound in the heaven, [36]and they saw the heavens opened and two men descend thence, shining with a great light, and drawing near unto the sepulchre. [37]And that stone which had been set on the door rolled away of itself and went back to the side, and the sepulchre was opened and both of the young men entered in. [38]When therefore those soldiers saw that, they waked up the centurion and the elders (for they also were there keeping watch); [39]And while they were yet telling them the things which they had seen, they saw again three men come out of the sepulchre, and two of them sustaining the other, and a cross following after them. [40]And of the two they saw that their heads reached unto heaven, but of him that was led by them that it overpassed the heavens. [41]And they heard a voice out of the heavens saying: [42]Hast thou preached unto them that sleep? And an answer was heard from the cross, saying: Yea. [43]Those men therefore took counsel with one another to go and report these things unto Pilate. [44]And while they yet thought thereabout, again the heavens were opened and a man descended and entered into the tomb (tr. M. R. James).

Iconographic tradition has readily drawn upon this portrait. But we should note that until the ninth or tenth centuries in the East and until the eleventh century in the West,[5] nothing of this was ever portrayed. In accordance with the sober reserve of the gospels, this mystery was not made accessible through some experience of the unbelieving guards, but only through those to whom Jesus appeared.

But while the women who had come to 'see' the tomb are not present, any more than the guards, at the resurrection of Jesus itself, they are called to witness an extraordinary sight. To imagine it, the reader must remember that the scene takes place while it is still dark (28:1). Why? No doubt to draw a parallel with the ancient biblical tradition according to which the deliverance of the people was to take place during the night: 'For while gentle silence enveloped all things, and night in its swift course was now half gone, thy all-powerful word leaped from heaven, from the royal throne.' (Wis 18:14-15) This is a wisdom comment on the famous night of the exodus (Exod 11:4; 12:12, 29). In this way a tradition was maintained which placed the Easter event during the night[6] and not at dawn (Luke) or after sunrise (Mark). Thus there is no need for the darkness of the tomb or of a powerful contrast with the light of the supernatural being who descends from heaven. 'His appearance was like lightning, and his raiment white as snow,' according to a description borrowed from the portrait of the Son of man in Daniel (7:9; 10:6; cf. Matthew 17:2).

This supernatural being is 'the angel of the Lord' and not simply 'an angel', for according to Matthew's usage (1:20, 24; 2:13, 19) which seems to be based on the Old Testament,[7] it is the Lord in person who descends from heaven. In this case, it is natural for the earth to 'tremble at the presence of the Lord' (Ps 114:7); it trembled at Sinai (Exod 19:18; Heb 12:26) and at Horeb (I Kings 19:11), and is to tremble at the day of the Lord (Is 13:13; Joel 2:10) and at the moment when Israel will rise again (Ezek 37:7-12). And had not the earth already shaken when Jesus died (Matthew 27:51, 54)? The stone which, rolled across the entrance of the tomb, symbolized the victory of death, is now put aside by God himself. It is not the cause of any fear on the part of the visitors (Mark) nor the object of a statement that it has been rolled away (Luke, John), and its immediate function is not to permit the women to enter, but to symbolize the object of the conflict between man and God. By sitting on the stone, the angel of the Lord signifies the final triumph of God over death.

Very much in the style of the theophany, the guards are overcome by this same 'trembling' (the word itself is the same) and they are as though dead (cf. Acts 1:17). The guard is conquered. The message can be given to the women.

3   *The Message*

'Do not be afraid', says the angel to the women. In fact fear has come upon them at the moment of the splendid theophany. But they are to pay attention. The angel does not recite the kerygma of the primitive church (Mark), but talks to them in a very personal tone: 'I know' that by coming to see the tomb, you are looking for Jesus; not Jesus of Nazareth, whose name draws attention to a distant past, but Jesus 'who was crucified'. Here too, there is a contrast between crucified and resurrected, but we do not find the stereotyped formula of Mark. In a natural way, the angel continues by discouraging the women from looking for this Jesus in the tomb: 'He is not here,' and the theme returns, 'for he has risen'. A modification can be observed by contrast to Mark, who gives these two statements in the reverse order; but we cannot see why certain scholars have attributed to Mark the intention of demonstrating by the fact of the resurrection that the tomb is empty; all we have here is a dialogue setting out the event, and meant to direct the attention of the women to the essential point. The angel takes up what was positive in the behaviour of the visitors who have come to 'see' the tomb, for they no doubt sensed something extraordinary. He then alludes to what the chief priests have just said to Pilate, that is, that Jesus 'said' that he would rise again (27:63): 'He has risen, as he said.' Thus the message of the resurrection rests not upon what the angel says, but upon the word of Jesus. The women are then invited to go into the tomb, which they have not yet done, by contrast with Mark's narrative, for a glance at the open tomb is sufficient to confirm the message which they have just heard.

Finally, having entrusted to the women the task of going to tell the disciples that the risen Christ is going before them to Galilee, the angel concludes his message with a solemn 'I have told you', as though his words were those of God himself.

4   *The Holy Women*

They are the same as those who watched the burial of Jesus (27:61), and who, amongst others, watched his death from afar (27:56). Thus the chain of witnesses is solid and unbroken; the probability of the story increases. They have come not to anoint the body of Jesus (Mark, Luke), nor even explicitly to mourn him (*Gospel of Peter*), but to see the tomb, rather like Mary in John. To read the text as Matthew sets it out, one would be inclined to think that they share the disquiet of the chief priests and guards: the women want to see on the spot. This makes it easier to understand why they leave with great joy, running to tell the Good News to the disciples. The results of what they did are not mentioned, but it may be supposed that by contrast with what Luke tells us (Luke 24:11) they were listened to; for the disciples go to Galilee.

And the women too are met by the Lord who goes before them. This appearance is somewhat surprising, particularly when we remember how the text is constructed: it is a little out of place. In fact the risen Christ repeats in almost the same terms the message which the angel had entrusted to them for the disciples. There is only one new point: the disciples are called the 'brethren' of Jesus. This title recalls the Johannine tradition of the appearance to Mary Magdalene, and from now on characterizes the new relationship which unites Jesus and the disciples. If Matthew reproduced at this point the tradition of an appearance in the neighbourhood of the tomb, it was probably to emphasize once again the importance of Galilee, where the risen Christ was to find his disciples. The reader is therefore kept completely in suspense, waiting for the meeting which such a theophany has foretold and prepared.

B. THE MISSION (28:16-20)

The final scene sets the tone of the whole Easter sequence, but also of the entire gospel, as we said when we began our study. In chapter 5, we described how this narrative was constructed on the pattern of vocation narratives, in a very different way from the ordinary appearance narratives in the gospels. There is no recognition and no doubt to overcome. It is a sudden manifestation of the Lord who has been raised to heaven.

This narrative calls upon believers to have faith in the *kyrios* (cf. Ps 110:1), as we have described it in chapter 2, that is, faith in him who is Lord over heaven and earth (I Tim 3:16; Acts 2:36;

13:33; Rom 1:4; Phil 2:5-11). From now on Jesus can present himself as Yahweh in person; he possesses all power and all authority. It was appropriate for this proclamation to be made on the mountain, the point where heaven can touch earth, the stepping stone of God when he visits mankind. The fact that Jesus did not fix the meeting on one of the sacred mountains of the bible, Sinai or Zion, but on an unknown mountain in Galilee, prepares for the universal nature of his message.

Two methods are mentioned for spreading the gospel: baptism and teaching. The mention of baptism, in the name of the three persons of the holy Trinity, may be surprising on the lips of the Lord himself. Indeed it is pointless to look for the *ipsissima verba* of the risen Christ, even more than those of Jesus of Nazareth. This does not mean that these words were invented in their entirety by the church community to which Matthew belonged. For the faith of the church has done no more than make specific the way in which Jesus, in the gospel, introduced the disciples to a special relationship with the Father and the Holy Spirit. Teaching does not come after baptism, but concurrently with it, since one cannot exist without the other in the constitution of the church.

The Lord's instruction is unique: they are to 'make disciples'. In these words, Jesus commands the Eleven to continue along the lines of his own behaviour: they are first of all to teach what he taught; and this teaching itself is not just a matter of handing on a pure doctrine, but calls for a personal contact with the one and only Master. It is not simply a matter of 'proclaiming' but of bringing into being this intimate link with Jesus, without which there is no true Christian faith.

Finally, the mission of Jesus is to all nations. The time when Jesus voluntarily limited his actions and those of his disciples to the Jews and the lost sheep of Israel (Matthew 10:6; 15:24) is past. It is now the entire world which is to be taught since the Lord has all authority in heaven and on earth. Basically, the point of view is the same as that of Luke, as we shall find when we study the final appearance to the Eleven at Jerusalem.

What is new by comparison with the other traditions is the promise which the Lord Jesus makes: 'And lo, I am with you always, to the close of the age.' The mission is not only universal in space, but for an unlimited time, because Jesus declares that he will remain with his disciples until the end of time. There is no question of sending the Holy Spirit. There is no 'ascension'. In fact, Jesus is already in heaven and is guiding his disciples in the task which he is entrusting to them. When we look at the narrative as it stands, we may ask why there is any mention at all of the doubt of the disciples. Jesus does not overcome this doubt by displaying his body and demanding recognition; he by-passes it by pronouncing his sovereign and sufficient word (cf. John 20:29). The purpose of the evangelist is to indicate that Jesus, the Lord of the universe, is also the Lord of history. By his presence, the Good News which Jesus of Nazareth proclaimed continues to ring out for ever, and the world goes on being transformed.

It is possible to speak, in connection with this appearance, of the setting up of 'the church', but as has rightly been pointed out,[8] the question is not primarily one of an institution, but of a community of disciples, no doubt officially baptized, but all with a personal link to Jesus, the Lord. This is the way the church understood itself at the time of Matthew, and the churches of later times must always draw upon that understanding if they are to remain faithful to the teaching and the will of the Master, the Lord Jesus.

CONCLUSION

The triple structure which we have identified in the appearances of the risen Christ can on close examination be found in the Easter message of Matthew. There is in fact an initiative, powerfully emphasized by the sudden breaking in of the Lord into the existence of the disciples. The recognition is transformed into a reference to the commandments and the teaching which were given previously. The mission is clearly given. Nevertheless, we must taken care not to read Matthew as though we were reading Luke, and particularly not to suppose that, like Luke, there is a place in Matthew for some kind of 'history of the church'. Jesus does not take leave of the disciples, he does not 'ascend' to heaven, and does not send them the Spirit. But he remains with them, and this is Mark's original contribution: he remains 'christological' to the very end, demonstrating the enduring presence of Emmanuel. It is possible that in some cases Christians may prefer this conception to that of Luke. It is a matter of personal choice.

Matthew also set out to show in this Easter message how the Lord rose above the storm of human wickedness throught the divine power of God who rescued him from the darkness of Sheol. The majestic Lord who comes down on to the mountain is he who has come out of the darkness of the underworld, in spite of the stone which men had rolled across the way out of the tomb. The Lord to whom all authority has been given is he whom God has set free from the bonds of death.

CHAPTER NINE

The Easter Message according to Luke

The reactions of readers to the Lucan narrative of Easter day (Luke 24:1-53) will differ. Some, already familiar with Mark, will recognize in it the traditional elements such as the narrative of the visit to the tomb, and will also observe the introduction of entirely new sources, such as the Emmaus episode. Others, more sensitive to the pattern of the text as it stands, will be aware of Luke's magnificent composition. We no longer have, as in Mark, the simple opening of a way into a mystery which is no longer manifest, nor, as in Matthew, the juxtaposition of essential scenes which concludes a long narrative. The account here is self-contained, and at the same time forms an introduction to the second volume of the Lucan work, the Acts of the Apostles. This twofold reaction on the part of the readers can be explained by recalling the prologue of the gospel: Luke is both an evangelist and an original writer.

There are many scholarly studies of the sources of this chapter in Luke.[1] But this is not our purpose. Here we propose to assess the text as it stands rather than by reference to its sources. To do so, after seeing how Luke set out to compose a text which was a unity, we shall show how the recurrent themes are linked together and progress as the narrative proceeds, and we shall then relate the three main episodes to a better definition of Luke's point of view.

A Unified Narrative

In this chapter, as elsewhere in the gospel, Luke displays his skill in gathering disparate traditions together. Thus in 5:35, the Pharisees who come to criticize Jesus for eating with sinners are the same as those who ask whether the disciples fast; in this way, two narratives which in Mark and Matthew simply occur side by side are placed in the same context.[2] This skill is clearly found in the narrative of Easter day. Let us go through that narrative and briefly note the way in which the separate elements are drawn together. Who are the women who on the morning of the first day of the week (24:1) come to the tomb? Up to 24:10, we do not know that they are Mary Magdalene, Joanna and Mary the mother of James, with some others. Luke names them at this point to show who it was who came to tell the apostles. But why should so good a writer wait so long to state who was taking part in this episode? This question arises from the false impression given by the division into chapters and verses. Luke has already said that these women are those who went up with Jesus from Galilee, but that was in 23:55, where it is noted that they observed the body laid in the tomb; and the following verse (23:56) prepares for 24:2 by mentioning the preparation of spices and ointments. Thus the Lucan narrative of Easter day is intimately linked with that of the two previous days. But the reader does not come to the conclusion, on reflection, that it is the some women who watched the death of Jesus, his burial and his disappearance into the tomb; the text itself says so explicitly.

The holy women take us to the apostles (24:10), and this is referred to by the disciples going to Emmaus (24:22-23). In this way attention is directed towards those who are at Jesusalem; Peter runs to the tomb and remains astonished (24:12),[3] an incident which is recalled in a general way by the disciples on the road to Emmaus (24:24) and which creates an expectation which is satisfied by the appearance to Simon (24:34). In their turn, the disciples going to Emmaus return to Jerusalem, so that once again attention is directed towards the Eleven and their companions (24:33). Thus the first two episodes lead on to what for Luke is the essential matter: the gathering of the apostles in the holy city, where the official appearance of the risen Christ was to take place.

A transitional phrase, common in Luke, 'as they were saying this' (24:36; cf. 8:49; 22:47, 60), links this appearance with the dialogue that precedes it. Similarly, in 24:44 Luke uses the same words to link the missionary command with the recognition scene. The risen Christ at once takes leave of his disciples (24:50-51), and they return to Jerusalem and go to give thanks to God in the temple (24:52-53).

The reason why Luke arranges such transitions is in order to invite us not to consider the different episodes separately, even though critics may show that they come from different sources or from parallel narratives. Thus in Luke's composition, the one day of Easter leads in its entirety towards the mission which is entrusted to the disciples. Mark had already suggested this by the announcement of the meeting in Galilee (Mark 16:7). And Matthew had demonstrated it in the appearance to the Eleven (28:16-20). Luke introduces a nuance of his own. The mission is not strictly speaking entrusted yet, but is foretold as imminent with the coming of the Spirit. Thus this text is meaningful only in relation to the narrative of Acts, where we see the Spirit coming down upon the disciples gathered in the upper room.

Unlike Matthew (and John) Luke does not describe a church set up on Easter day, but a community waiting for what is to come about on the day of Pentecost; and this provides the structure and the unity of Luke's whole work.

A. THE RECURRENT THEMES

In this literary unity a certain number of themes or statements constantly recur, running throughout it and tying it together. These are no longer merely the transitional phrases, but elements of content which unify the narrative and carry it forward. This is more immediately obvious when the reader is familiar with Luke's work, which is characterized throughout by a unified composition.

Presuppositions

Two theological themes dominate the Lucan history (gospel and Acts) and cast light on our reading of the gospel narrative. Luke is a theologian of history, or, to use the language of faith, a theologian of God's plan. The common gospel tradition has removed the scandal of Jesus's death on the cross by placing it within the mystery of the great divine plan which secretly controls the history of men; this is what is implied by the expression 'it is necessary that . . ., it was necessary . . .'. Thus in the synoptic gospels, a threefold prophecy recurs during the ascent to Jerusalem (Matthew 16:21 para.; 17:22-23 para.; 20:18-19 para.). Luke emphasizes this by prefacing the second prophecy with a statement which in his style seems forced, 'Let these words sink into your ears' (9:44); he makes these prophecies the subject of the conversation which the transfigured Jesus has with Moses and Elijah (9:31); finally, he recalls them on Easter day (24:7, 25-26, 45-46).

When the risen Christ commands the disciples to be his 'witnesses' (24:48) Luke is using the term to sum up the attitude of the infant church. He is demonstrating a tendency which can already be perceived in the formula in I Cor 15, where the witnesses of the resurrection of Christ are listed. In this way, he is developing a genuine ecclesiology. He defines a witness on the occasion of the choice of a replacement for Judas. The lot must fall upon a man who has been seen in the company of Jesus of Nazareth during his earthly life and to whom an appearance of the risen Christ has been vouchsafed. From then on, Luke goes out of his way to restrict the title of witness to the Twelve, whom alone he calls 'apostles'; according to him, the church must be based exclusively upon this body of witnesses.[4]

According to God's Plan, the Christ is Alive

The common terminology speaks of 'him who is risen'. So too, in the third gospel, the angel tells the holy women, in accordance with the earliest expressions of faith, 'He is not here, but has risen' (24:6). This traditional kerygmatic formula may result in this text from a contamination by the text of Matthew; moreover, a new element is dominant, the previous question of the angel: 'Why do you seek the living among the dead?' (24:5). In fact Luke has a predilection for the term 'living, alive', which is peculiar to him in the Easter gospel narrative, and is found throughout the Acts of the Apostles.

Why is 'risen' transformed into 'alive'? We shall try to explain this in chapter 11, when we discuss the hermeneutics of Luke. Let us note only that it refers to the same reality as the Jewish terminology of 'resurrection'; everywhere, Luke is proclaiming that Jesus is alive. Again, a similar parallel is established further on between 'Christ should ... on the third day rise from the dead' (24:46) and 'Christ should suffer these things and enter into his glory' (24:26): the resurrection is identical with heavenly glorification.

This person who is alive has triumphed over death. Luke is not content merely to affirm the event, he explains its meaning by placing it, according to his theological point of view, within the great plan which God has revealed in scripture. The three narratives give a more and more precise interpretation of it.

In the first narrative, the angel does not suggest that the women confirm that the tomb has not held Jesus of Nazareth (Matthew 28:6; Mark 16:6), nor does he entrust to them a message for the disciples (Matthew 28:7; Mark 16:7) but asks them to remember the words of Jesus of Nazareth, which he recalls in detail. This allusion to the words of Jesus was already found in the tradition, in the form of the words, 'as he told you', either in foretelling the appearance in Galilee (Mark 16:7) or to proclaim the resurrection (Matthew 28:6). But in Luke they are extended into a lengthy comment on the understanding of the plan of God, so that the centre of gravity of the text is completely changed: 'Remember how he told you, while he was still in Galilee, that the Son of man must be delivered into the hands of sinful men, and be crucified, and on the third day rise. And they remembered his words' (Luke 24:6-8). Thus Luke systematized these prophecies, so preparing for the Easter message.

In the second narrative, that of Emmaus, the same plan of God forms the climax of the interpretation of scripture given by the risen Christ. The disciples cannot make sense of the scandal of the prophet Jesus (cf. Luke 24:19; Acts 3:23), whose crucifixion has reduced the hopes of Israel for a speedy deliverance to nothing (24:19-21; cf. 1:68; 2:38; Acts 7:35). Christ tells them, 'Was it not necessary that the Christ should suffer these things and enter into his glory? And beginning with Moses and all the prophets, he interpreted to them in all the scriptures the things concerning himself' (24:26-27). Whereas the angel did no more than recall the prophecy as it occurs in the gospel, the mysterious traveller does the same as Peter and Paul in Acts. Thus Peter appeals to all the prophets, who prophesied that the Christ would suffer (Acts 3:18), 'according to the definite plan and the foreknowledge of God' (Acts 2:23; cf. 4:28), and particularly as prophesied by Moses (3:22) and 'all the prophets who have spoken, from Samuel and those who came afterwards' (3:24; cf. 13:27). Paul too tried to convince the Jews about Jesus, 'both from the law of Moses and from the prophets' (28:23), 'testifying both to small and great, saying nothing but what the prophets and Moses said would come to pass: that the Christ must suffer, and that, by being the first to rise from the dead, he would proclaim light both to the people and to the Gentiles' (26:22-23). It is clear that Luke is making the traveller and the apostles speak in the same way, proceeding from a theological interpretation of the divine plan revealed in scripture. This is entirely in accordance with the practice of the primitive church, which achieved an understanding of itself by rereading the Old Testament.[5]

The same is true in the third narrative. In order to bring about an understanding of the plan of God, there is an allusion to what has been said previously, but the reference is to the whole of the scriptures, and there is a proclamation that repentance and forgiveness is to be preached to all nations:

> These are my words which I spoke to you, while I was still with you, that everything written about me in the law of Moses and the prophets and the psalms must be fulfilled. Then he opened their minds to understand the scriptures, and said to them, Thus it is written, that the Christ should suffer and on the third day rise from the dead, and that repentance and forgiveness of sins should be preached ... (24:44-47).

This is the climax of the revelation, as is confirmed by the presence of the word 'Christ' (24:26, 46), replacing the term 'Son of man' which is used in all other gospel prophecies in Luke up to 24:7. Outside the infancy narrative (2:11, 26) the title Christ is mentioned only in an indirect way (3:15; 4:41; 9:20; 20:41; 22:67; 23:2, 35, 39). It might be tempting in view of this to attribute to Luke the intention of demonstrating that 'Jesus is the Christ', but although Luke undoubtedly attributes this intention to Paul in Acts (Acts 17:3; 18:5, 28) it is not his own here as a gospel writer. When, in order to explain events, Luke on several occasions refers the reader to Jesus's own words and to the words of the prophets, his purpose is not to affirm that Jesus is truly the Messiah, but to make clear what is the Easter message as such. For this purpose, he does not basically appeal to the fact of the empty tomb, nor even to the appearances of the risen Christ, but to the word of Jesus of Nazareth, which itself is situated in the great context of the biblical revelation of the plan of God.

The Mission of the Witnesses

Luke does not restrict himself to presenting in this way the profound content of the Easter message, but also wishes to show how the community of witnesses of Christ came into being.

Let us first note the convergent structure of the three narratives. As we have seen, their movement ineluctably draws the persons in the narrative towards the disciples, and the latter towards Jerusalem. The women came out of the tomb, and then 'returning from the tomb' they told the disciples all that they had seen (24:9). The disciples 'returned to Jerusalem' and found there the Eleven gathered together and those who were with them (24:23). Finally, after they had seen Christ parting from them, they 'returned to Jerusalem with great joy' (24:52). It is no accident that Luke should have given this structure to his narrative. The story begins in the temple at Jerusalem (Luke 1:9) and concludes there in the gospel (24:53), but the purpose of this is for the Good News to leave there and, as though by centrifugal force, to spread to the end of the earth (Acts 1:8). These literary devices on the part of Luke are sufficiently familiar for us to do no more than recall how he omits the digression to the borders of Galilee (Mark 6:45-8:26), and gives a solemn description of the theological journey which Jesus takes to Jerusalem (Luke 9:51-19:45).[6] Thus it was appropriate for the episodes of Easter day to take place at Jerusalem.

The same movement first of all leads the holy women and the travellers on the Emmaus road to the disciples. For the narratives concentrate the reader's attention on these men, who have remained at Jerusalem. Peter goes to the tomb, but only to wonder at what he has seen, for even though there is an indirect mention of the Lord's appearing to him, he has to be with the others for the official appearance of the risen Christ. Everything moves towards the latter.

It is this appearance by which a 'witness' of what has taken place is designated (24:48). Of course the women have recounted their meeting with the angel, but their 'words seem to them an idle tale, and they did not believe them' (24:11), although the news 'amazed' them (24:22). The two travellers 'told what had happened on the road, and how he was known to them in the breaking of the bread', but their witness was preceded by that of Simon, to whom an appearance had been vouchsafed (24:24-35); for only the official disciples are the witnesses. It is once again necessary for the Lord to come to them as a group and to constitute them as his witnesses, his sole witnesses.

From then on the Easter message is based not on any appearance of an angel, nor even on a private appearance of the risen Christ, but on the formally appointed body of witnesses. In the context of the prophecy of Isaiah which it echoes (Is 43:10-12) Jesus's words make the apostolic body the inheritor of Israel, with the mission of testifying to the gentiles that God is the sole redeemer and that Jesus is the living Christ (Luke 24:46).

These brief notes have introduced us to Luke's distinctive point of view. With consummate art, he has distributed the major themes of his theology throughout the episode. Though he concentrates the long history of the gospel upon the official appearance, this is in order to send the witness out to the ends of the world. In Luke's eyes, the appearances, however essential they may be, form only one element in the Easter message.

B. THE EPISODES

Guided by these two major themes, we can attempt an interpretation of the principal episodes of Easter day according to St Luke.

The Holy Women at the Tomb

Numerous modifications have profoundly altered Luke's narrative by comparison with those of Mark and Matthew. At the beginning, we note a point of contact with Mark: at daybreak, the women bring to the tomb the spices which they have prepared the evening before. Then Luke continues the narrative in his own way: when the women go into the tomb, they do not see a young man seated on the right, but observe that the body of the Lord Jesus is absent. While they stand perplexed, they meet (as at Bethlehem: 2:9) two men (described as angels by the disciples travelling to Emmaus: 24:23), whose dazzling appearance corresponds to that of the angel of the Lord in Matthew 28:3. As in the parallel passages, according to the ordinary reaction of human beings faced with heavenly manifestations (1:12, 30; Exod 19:21ff.), the women are seized with fear. As Luke describes them, they 'bow their faces to the ground', perhaps because they are still not yet able to 'look up and raise their heads', since they do not know that their redemption is drawing near (Luke 21:28). Then, after repeating the traditional formula, 'He is not here, but has risen', he adds 'Why do you seek the living among the dead?' Galilee is mentioned. But it is no longer the place where the meeting is arranged; it is the place from the past during which Jesus proclaimed the plan of God for the Son of man. Once again following Matthew, the women go to tell what has happened to the disciples.

It does not seem very interesting to us to specify Luke's sources, particularly if this whole composition has been based on Mark alone (which is improbable), or if he drew first on Mark, and then on Matthew. The changes are so profound that they must be attributed to Luke himself, drawing upon tradition related to those underlying Matthew and Mark. It is more important to describe exactly the point of view which can be distinguished in Luke's modifications.

It is sometimes described in terms of a closer attention to the empty tomb. But in fact the contrary is true. At first sight, the process of evolution seems to have been as follows. In Mark, the women learn from the words of the angel that Jesus is no longer in the tomb, as a confirmation of the resurrection. In Matthew, a slight change can be perceived in the reversal of the two statements by the angel: 'He is not here' precedes 'He has risen'. Finally, in Luke, the women observe themselves that the body of Jesus is absent.[7] These observations are not without interest; but they must be related to a different evolution, which is equally clear and much more important. According to Mark, the formula 'as he told you' has no function other than to authenticate the message concerning the meeting in Galilee (Mark 16:7). The resurrection is attested by the angel alone. In Matthew, what Jesus said becomes the basis of the announcement of the resurrection (Matthew 28:6). Luke in his turn refers it specifically to the recollection of what Jesus said of his fate during his earthly life; and in the light of this, he does not consider it worthwhile mentioning 'the place where Jesus lay' (Matthew 28:6; Mark 16:6). This fact is not a means of verification, and its sole function is that of arousing the astonishment of the women or the perplexity of Peter, until the mystery is revealed to them in another way. Thus, contrary to appearances, the gospel tradition evolved in the direction of a growing lack of interest in the empty tomb.

The behaviour attributed to the women supports this interpretation. In Mark, they say nothing, as though to justify the fact that in its kerygma the church did not mention the discovery of the empty tomb. In Matthew, they seem to have been heard by the disciples, who accordingly go to Galilee. In Luke, their words are not believed, and their story is described as an idle tale (24:11). Peter, looking at the linen cloths by themselves, wonders, but does not understand (24:12). The disciples at Emmaus are to give an explanation: 'Him they did not see' (24:24). Here again, the tradition shows that the fact of the empty tomb is fundamentally inadequate for evoking faith. And Luke sets out the substance of the words of Jesus which are the sole basis of faith: the understanding of God's plan for the Son of man (24:6-8).

In another respect, Luke's modification is illuminating. Instead of a young man (Mark) or an angel (Matthew) there are 'two men' (24:4), who form the 'vision of angels' (24:23) which was vouchsafed to the holy women. It is normally Matthew who has a tendency to double the number of persons (those possessed of demons, the blind, false witnesses), whereas Luke tends to avoid everything which involves repetition or doubling.[8] Thus if there are two persons at the tomb, there is some deliberate purpose. What we have here is probably not a popular way of telling a story, but a desire to supply two witnesses in the legal sense. Legally acceptable witnesses had to be not youths (twenty-one to twenty-eight years), but twenty-eight to forty-nine years of age,[9] and had to be two in number.[10] This is the procedure adopted by Luke, who promised to Theophilus that he would 'know the truth concerning the things of which you have been informed' (1:4).

On the other hand, Luke does not mention 'the other women with them', besides Mary Magdalene, Joanna and Mary, 'the mother of James', when they tell the apostles what has happened (24:11) in order to increase the number of witnesses. For their words are not believed. It is more likely that in this way Luke is preparing for the mention of the 'women' in the upper room with the Eleven (Acts 1:14).

With the same purpose, to prepare for the narrative in Acts, Luke says, 'the apostles' (24:10) instead of 'the Eleven' (24:9); the women tell everything 'to the Eleven *and to all the rest*' (24:9). Again, when they returned to Jerusalem, the disciples who were going to Emmaus do not meet only the Eleven, but also 'those who were with them' (24:33) and who are therefore present at the moment of the official appearance (24:36). Thus when Judas has to be replaced to make up the numbers to twelve, it is easy for the divine lot to fall upon those who from the human point of view are capable of having been witnesses (Acts 1:22; 10:34-41).

The Appearance to the Disciples on the Road to Emmaus (24:13-35)

Luke has no appearance to the holy women (Matthew 28:9-10; John 20:11-18); but with marvellous skill he portrays the awakening of faith in the heart of the two disciples. Thus he passes from the description of a collective faith to that of a personal experience on the part of the believer, seen from within.

A considerable amount of research has been undertaken to establish the literary category to which this episode belongs: 'A divine being takes human form to have dealings with men without being recognized, and disappears the very instant his identity has been revealed.'[11] In this way Yahweh appears to Abraham and walks with him in human form (Gen 18). The angel Raphael accompanies Tobias, without being recognized by him (Tob 5:4) and then suddenly makes himself invisible (12:21). Similar narratives, even in secular literature, are too numerous for the existence of such a literary category to be rejected without further ado. In no sense do they authorize conclusions in the field of historical criticism, but they make it easier to understand the nature of the original tradition, and that of Luke.

Because of the existence of this type of narrative, we are inclined to recognize, underlying the present account, a narrative consisting of vv. 13, 15b, 16 and 28-31, describing this appearance on the recognition pattern.[12] Here is an attempt to reconstruct the underlying tradition (the references to verse numbers are approximate).

[13]Two disciples were going to a village named Emmaus, about sixty stadia from Jerusalem. [15]Jesus himself drew near and went with them. [16]But their eyes were kept from recognizing him.... [28]So they drew near to the village to which they were going. He appeared to be going further, [29]but they constrained him, saying, 'Stay with us, for it is toward evening and the day is now far spent.' So he went in to stay with them. [30]When he was at table with them, he took the bread and blessed, and broke it, and gave it to them. [31]And their eyes were opened and they recognized him; and he vanished out of their sight. [33]And they rose that same hour and returned to Jerusalem; and they found the eleven gathered together and those who were with them, [35]and they told what had happened on the road, and how he was known to them in the breaking of the bread.

According to the summary given in the conclusion of Mark, Jesus appeared 'in another form' (*en heterai morphēi*: Mark 16:12). He seemed to have been taken for a traveller, just as in John 20:15 Mary took Jesus for the gardener; or else he took on another form which made him unrecognizable.[13] Such a mistake is not possible in the Emmaus narrative. Here Luke explains how the two disciples were the object of a radical inner transformation: 'Jesus is in no way disguised',[14] and there is no room for any appeal to an 'outward' miracle, as if other eyes were needed which might be called the 'eyes of faith'; the same eyes 'were kept from recognizing him' and then 'were opened' (24:16, 31). This is the theological theme of the awakening of faith which is so delicately set forth by Luke. As A. Puech puts it, Luke's purpose is to hand on to us not historical facts in a pure form, but an 'interpretation of that history', by means of 'his instinctive understanding of human feeling'.[15] At every point on the disciples' journey there are psychological observations. The disciples are 'deeply distressed'; they stop, 'looking sad'; they are surprised at the ignorance of the fellow traveller who has just joined them; they urge him to stay with them. Why? Had a confused hope arisen within them, of which they wished to make sure, or did they want to go deeper into a recollection which was so dear to them? Luke does not say. But he shows them reliving, in a flash-back, the emotion which had seized them on the road. In this way Luke enables the reader to understand the extraordinary intimacy which united the disciples to Jesus of Nazareth; they had to descend into the depths of disappointment in order then to exult with joy. He gives a magnificent description of the experience of recognition, the characteristic element in the appearances.

To understand the significance of other elements within the narrative, and in particular the discourse of the risen Christ and the breaking of the bread, other factors must be introduced.

The literary composition of the passage presents a structure of parallel passages enclosing other similarly parallel passages, and this makes it possible to distinguish the decisive elements.[16] First of all, introduction and conclusion correspond closely:

[13]The disciples leave Jerusalem   The disciples return to Jerusalem[33]

[14]They converse   They converse[32]

| ¹⁵Jesus goes with them | Jesus vanishes out of their sight^{31b} |
| ¹⁶Their eyes are kept from recognizing him. | Their eyes are opened^{31a} They recognize him. |

17-30

DIALOGUE

| ¹⁷initiative by Jesus | initiative by the disciples²⁹ |

18-21 $\left\{\begin{array}{l} \end{array}\right.$ ¹⁸you do not know   ¹⁹prophet   ²⁰put to death   ²¹disappointed hope

you do not know²⁵   prophets^{25c} death and glory²⁶   prophets²⁷ $\left.\begin{array}{l} \end{array}\right\}$ 25-27

^{22-23b}They did not find   They did not see him²⁴

^{23c}HE IS ALIVE

Of course some of the parallels and oppositions are formal, but a good many are meaningful. At the very centre we find the statement: 'Jesus is alive' (23c). Vv. 20 and 26 provide the parallel and a contrast, the former declaring the fact of the crucifixion, a theme of sadness, and the other the mystery of glory, the breaking in of hope. The place of the breaking of the bread is also noteworthy; it shows a transition from non-recognition (16) to full recognition (30).

Another way of grasping the meaning of the passage is to determine the situation in life in which it could have arisen. We have no similar apparition narrative to assist us, but Luke himself offers a narrative in which the structure is similar: the encounter between Philip and the eunuch of Candace the queen of the Ethiopians.[17] Let us look at the significant parallels between the two narratives.

Luke 24	*Acts 8*
¹³On the road from Jerusalem to Emmaus two disciples	^{26-28a}On the road from Jerusalem to Gaza, Philip and the eunuch
¹⁴The two disciples converse	^{28b}The eunuch is reading Isaiah
¹⁵⁻¹⁷Jesus goes with the two disciples and asks them a question	²⁹⁻³⁰At the bidding of the Spirit Philip overtakes the chariot and asks the eunuch a question

[18-24]'The disciples recount the facts that concern them

[25-27]Jesus expounds the scriptures (which make clear the meaning of what has happened)

[28-29]'The disciples ask Jesus to stay with them

[30-31]Jesus breaks the bread. The disciples recognize him. Jesus disappears

[32-33]Still deeply moved, the disciples return to Jerusalem

[31-34]'The eunuch asks for an explanation of the text of Isaiah

[35]Philip tells about Jesus (which makes clear the meaning of Isaiah)

[36-(37)]'The eunuch asks for baptism

[38-39a]Philip baptizes the eunuch and at once disappears

[39b]'The eunuch continues on his way, rejoicing

The structure of these two narratives is clearly provided by the same Lucan pattern. This enables us to distinguish the situation in life which probably provided their origin. On the one hand, following the type of scriptural interpretation characteristic of Luke, the risen Christ and Philip both interpret the Old Testament in terms of Christ; the travellers and the eunuch make a similar request. Secondly, the eucharist and baptism respectively form the climax. It is clear that in these two episodes, Luke is showing the reader what the behaviour of a Christian must be: it is in baptism and the eucharist that contact with Jesus Christ takes place. In our narrative, the interpretation of the scriptures was not sufficient for the disciples to recognize Jesus, and the breaking of the bread was also necessary. Today there is general agreement that this gesture represents the eucharistic liturgy;[18] as in Acts 2:42, as well as in Acts 2:46 and 27:35, to Christian ears the expression has a eucharistic sound (Acts 20:7, 11; I Cor 10:16).

In his adaptation of the primitive narrative, Luke gave his readers a deeper understanding of the way to faith and recognition. The word and the bread are the two banquets to which man is invited in every age. Before everything else, the Lord himself must interpret scripture, which then becomes meaningful. It is no use having known the man Jesus in his earthly life; yet it seems that the two disciples were privileged in their relationship with him. But neither the history of their nation, on which their hopes were fed, nor the amazing information from the women concerning the empty tomb aroused faith in them. To overcome the obstacles which make it difficult to see clearly, it is of course necessary to listen to the scriptures interpreted in and through Christ; but though the heart may burn within (cf. Luke 12:49-50; Jer 20:9) recognition takes place only during the breaking of bread. Only a personal encounter of the risen Christ can arouse faith. This is also the reaction of the Eleven: 'The Lord has risen indeed, and has appeared to Simon' (24:34).

The Appearance to the Eleven and to Their Companions (24:36-53)

In chapter 5 we tried to distinguish the tradition which Luke and John must have used. It probably consisted of the following. Jesus appears in the midst of the assembled disciples, perhaps at the moment when they are taking a meal. They are afraid. Jesus overcomes their unbelief and enables them to recognize him. They are filled with joy. Jesus entrusts a mission to them.

Luke adapted this tradition. At the beginning of the present chapter, we showed the great importance given to teaching about the scriptures and the mission given to the witnesses. Similarly, the central part of this appearance narrative (24:44-49) is characterized by two themes; the first part (24:36-43) is subordinated to it and the third part (24:50-53) is added.

We shall now set out here the way in which Luke makes use of the first part, the recognition appearance.[19] Luke gave his own structure to the popular tradition which he had received, as the following table shows.

[36]He himself (*autos*) stood among them	ACT BY JESUS	Jesus[43] eats before them
[37-38]They were afraid and supposed that they saw a spirit		Jesus asks them[41] a question
	REACTION	They give him fish
Jesus asks them a question	OF THE DISCIPLES	Wonder and joy
		A spirit has not flesh and bones
[39a]See my hands and my feet	MANIFESTATION	Touch and see[39c]
[39b]It is I myself (*ego eimi autos*)		

Setting out the narrative in this way shows how it converges upon the identity of him who is manifested himself to the disciples, and this may help to resolve a much debated problem concerning Luke's purpose. An 'apologetic' purpose is often attributed to him. It is suggested that by emphasizing the material aspect, he is trying to demonstrate that the risen Christ was truly corporeal. In fact he concentrates the reader's attention upon the recognition of Jesus, on him whom the disciples knew previously.

What the structure of the narrative suggests, Luke's tendencies confirm. Luke, of course, likes to make scenes more lifelike,[20] with the aid of a delicate psychological understanding. Here again, he goes out of his way to describe, on the basis of traditional themes, the fear or the joy of the disciples. This is clear. But to suggest that Luke made the appearance narratives more 'material', it is necessary to show that this is his practice in his gospel. Now while two specific cases can be observed—the Spirit who comes down in bodily form like a dove (3:22) and Jesus sweating blood at Gethsemane (22:43-44), the opposite can also be found: the description of the events which took place on the occasion of the death of Jesus is much less visually striking in his narrative than in that of Mark or Matthew (Luke 23:44-49; cf. Matthew 27:45-56). One cannot take for granted that he wanted to make the appearances of the risen Christ more material.

By retaining an expression which is not Lucan, an exceptional case in the whole episode[21] (that is, that 'a spirit has not flesh and bones'), Luke shows his true purpose: the appearance is not an illusion, and Jesus is not a 'spirit' or a 'ghost'. At that period men believed in spirits; when Jesus walked on the sea, the disciples thought they were seeing a spirit. Similarly, in Acts 23:9, when Paul has finished talking of the resurrection of the dead, a dispute arises between Pharisees and Sadducees; some scribes of the Pharisees' party strongly protest: 'We find nothing wrong in this man. What if a spirit or an angel spoke to him?' Luke is well within biblical tradition. For the bible does speak of the 'spirits of the dead' (Luke 19:31; 20:6; Deut 18:11). In the episode of the witch of Endor, the witch calls up the spirit of Samuel and says to Saul: 'I see an *elōhīm* [a supernatural being; cf. Judg 13:22] coming up out of the earth. . . . An old man is coming up; and he is wrapped in a robe.' And 'Saul knew that it was Samuel' (I Sam 28:13-14). Saul does not see, and does not touch but recognizes by a distinctive sign, apparently the robe, that it was Samuel. In fact 'the dead person who dwells in the tomb and wanders about at night on earth is a spirit who lives in heaven'.[22] And the spirits of the dead can appear in human forms; they can be recognized for what they are by the fact that they have no body, that is, neither flesh nor bones.[23] These words signify 'the substance of earthly man, signifying the opposition which exists between the corporeal and the incorporeal world'.[24] Finally, let us point to the *midrash* on Ruth 3:9. To make sure that Ruth is not a spirit or demon, Boaz puts his hand on her head, for 'a spirit has no hair'. It is clear that in the biblical world, the representation in Luke's narrative is perfectly natural, and differs profoundly from what is found amongst the Greeks.[25] Yet similar representations are found amongst them too;[26] thus we learn that 'one cannot touch the blessed who have neither flesh nor bones, while at the same time one cannot be sure of their lack of corporeality except by touching them'.[27] Thus Luke's presentation is also suitable for the Hellenistic world.

It follows that it is difficult to decide whether the sentence included by Luke is of Palestinian or Hellenistic origin. Can it not be admitted that we have here a common way of representing the contact of the dead with the living, and therefore what we have is a popular tradition, with the purpose of stating that the risen Christ had truly risen in bodily form, and was not a ghost imagined by visionaries? In any case, the narrative was not simply invented by later apologetic aimed at the Greek world.

In the appearance narrative, the conclusion is at first sight surprising: it represents *Jesus eating* before the disciples. Here too, one is tempted to suppose that this tradition comes from Hellenistic circles concerned to demonstrate the material corporeality of Jesus. But there is nothing strange in the fact recorded; for it can be located in the tradition of table fellowship, which in its turn of course derives from a liturgical setting. Nevertheless, it should be seen rather as signifying the reality of the resurrection of Jesus. What exactly, in Luke's view, is taking place? Not apparent eating, like that of which the angel Raphael speaks to Tobias: 'All these days I merely appeared to you and did not eat or drink, but you were seeing a vision' (Tob 12:19). Here, on the contrary, the purpose is to show that the risen Christ is truly corporeal. By taking some food, Jesus behaves like the young girl raised from the dead: did he not tell her parents to give her something to eat (Luke 8:55)?

Eating is an act which proclaims a new life: Elijah takes bread before setting off for mount Horeb (I Kings 19:1-8), Esther calls for a feast when she learns that her people have escaped destruction (Est 8:17) and Job does the same when his trials come to an end (Job 42:11). Finally, it is a sign of great joy, as in the case of the father of the prodigal son when he is 'alive again' (Luke 15:23-24). Jesus no longer belongs to the world of the dead, but partakes of the heavenly banquet. We must not ask what this food consisted of.[28] What matters here is that when Jesus is shown eating, the sole purpose is to affirm that the appearance was real. If in Luke he eats 'before' the disciples and not simply 'with' them, this is probably in conformity with Eastern practice, where the guest eats alone before those who receive him (cf. Gen 18:8). What need is there to suppose that there was some spectacular demonstration on the part of Jesus? Let us not forget that Luke expresses his thoughts more clearly in Acts 10:41 (cf. 1:4).

By taking up this narrative of a recognition appearance from popular tradition ('It is I myself'), Luke wished to prepare the way for the concluding teaching of the risen Christ: his lesson on the meaning of the word of God set down in the scriptures, the sending out of the disciples as witnesses, and the promise of the gift of the Holy Spirit. By concluding with this promise, Luke, who is above all the evangelist of the Holy Spirit,[29] points towards the expectation of Jesus's return and therefore to the age of the church which is to begin at Pentecost.

The third part of the narrative now follows: Jesus takes leave of his disciples (24:50-53). Here Luke offers a 'doxological interpretation of the Ascension'.[30] Blessing his disciples, Christ emphasizes the link with the future gift of the Spirit, making it known that he will remain present amongst his own. Then he departs (*diestē* corresponds to the *estē* of 24:26); but joy fills their hearts,[31] for a new way in which the Lord is present is now inaugurated: that of the Holy Spirit. Has the gospel finished? Rather, it begins with the witness of the disciples, which starts in Jerusalem and goes out to the ends of the world.

CONCLUSION

Luke is not an innovator, but an interpreter of the tradition. The Easter message is set out on the threefold pattern which is characteristic of the appearances of the risen Christ according to the Jerusalem text; but Luke goes beyond the bounds of this pattern in a magnificent way.

The Easter message points first of all towards the future. The resurrection of Jesus opens the way to the witness of the disciples and the preaching of the gospel. The age of the church can begin, for the Spirit is given by him who has conquered death.

But at the same time, this Easter message is a recollection of what was said in Galilee. This reference to what Jesus did in the past is essential to keep the proclamation of the Good News on a straight line, and this past includes the plan of God which has been expressed in the holy scriptures.

Finally, this Easter message is a contact with a living person, a man who is there, present in the totality of being, wholly real and corporeal, even if not under the same conditions as before. He who is alive will be present with us, adapting himself to our feeble understanding and ready to bestow the word and the bread upon us.

CHAPTER TEN

The Easter Message according to John

Like the Gospel of Luke, the Gospel of John at first seems to form a continuity; yet it is difficult to determine its literary unity with certainty. Thus chapter 21 has been added to a text which was already complete, as is shown by the conclusion found in 20:30-31: 'Now Jesus did many other signs in the presence of the disciples, which are not written in this book, but these are written that you may believe that Jesus is the Christ, the Son of God, and that believing you may have life in his name.' For this reason, we do not discuss chapter 21.[1]

In chapter 20, the distribution of the episodes corresponds in its main outline to that found in Matthew. Following the visit to the tomb, the holy women (or Mary Magdalene) tell the disciples what has happened, and this is followed by an appearance of the risen Christ to the women. Then the official appearance takes place. Within this framework, elements occur which are related to the Lucan tradition: the disciples at the tomb, the location of the appearances at Jerusalem, the mission entrusted to the apostolic college, and the doubt of Thomas which corresponds to that of the disciples in Luke. John has linked these various episodes together in his own way by means of such transitional phrases as: 'on the evening of that day', 'eight days later', and others that we shall point out below. If there is any unity in this chapter, it can be clearly distinguished only after an attentive study of the two groups of episodes which form Easter week according to John.

A. AT THE TOMB (20:1-18)

[1]Now on the first day of the week Mary Magdalene came to the tomb early, while it was still dark, and saw that the stone had

been taken away from the tomb. [2]So she ran, and went to Simon Peter and the other disciple, the one whom Jesus loved, and said to them, 'They have taken the Lord out of the tomb, and we do not know where they have laid him.' [3]Peter then came out with the other disciple, and they went towards the tomb. [4]They both ran, but the other disciple outran Peter and reached the tomb first; [5]and stooping to look in, he saw the linen cloths lying there, but did not go in. [6]Then Simon Peter came, following him, and went into the tomb; he saw the linen cloths lying, [7]and the napkin, which had been on his head, not lying with the linen cloths but rolled up in a place by itself. [8]Then the other disciple, who reached the tomb first, also went in, and he saw and believed; [9]for as yet they did not know the scripture, that he must rise from the dead. [10]Then the disciples went back to their homes. [11]But Mary stood weeping outside the tomb, and as she wept she stooped to look into the tomb; [12]and she saw two angels in white, sitting where the body of Jesus had lain, one at the head and one at the feet. [13]They said to her, 'Woman, why are you weeping?' She said to them, 'Because they have taken away my Lord, and I do not know where they have laid him.' [14]Saying this, she turned round and saw Jesus standing, but she did not know that it was Jesus. [15]Jesus said to her, 'Woman, why are you weeping? Whom do you seek?' Supposing him to be the gardener, she said to him, 'Sir, if you have carried him away, tell me where you have laid him, and I will take him away.' Jesus said to her, 'Mary.' She turned and said to him in Hebrew, 'Rab-boni!' (which means Teacher). [17]Jesus said to her, 'Do not hold me, for I have not yet ascended to the Father; but go to my brethren and say to them, I am ascending to my Father and your Father, to my God and your God.' [18]Mary Magdalene went and said to the disciples, 'I have seen the Lord'; and she told them that he had said these things to her.

The passage seems to consist of two different traditions. For according to v. 11, Mary is at the tomb, whereas in v. 2 she has left it, and it is nowhere stated that she returned; and there is no further mention of the meeting of the disciples with Mary. Moreover, it is only on the second visit (v. 11) that Mary stoops towards the tomb; previously (v. 2), she had concluded from the fact that the stone had been taken away that the body of Jesus had also been removed. Finally, in v. 11 again, Mary sees two angels in the tomb, whereas just before the disciples found nothing there except the linen cloths carefully rolled up. Vv. 3-10, therefore, seem to derive from a different tradition, and not to have been known by whoever composed the narrative of Mary's visit to the tomb. One may even ask whether the message which Mary is to take to the disciples (20:17) retains any meaning, since the disciples (or at least the beloved disciple) have already believed (20:8).

In order to remove these difficulties, several attempts have been made to determine the source which John used in preparing the present redaction. Some scholars consider that there was a single continuous narrative. According to R. Bultmann,[2] the source consisted of the greater part of vv. 1, 6, 7, 11, 12, 13, which correspond to the synoptic elements underlying the Johannine narrative; but it is difficult to attribute all the other verses to John, particularly the narrative of the appearance to Mary. According to the more subtle reconstruction of G. Hartmann,[3] the source used by John consisted of the greater part of vv. 1-3, 5, 7-11, 14-18. But this hypothesis too raises several difficulties. It would make it necessary to attribute vv. 11b-13 to John, and in order to reconstruct the source, many transpositions and important modifications have to be made.

P. Benoit[4] has also attempted to define the nature of the material of which John made use: not a single narrative, but two traditions. One, he thinks, was of the synoptic type (basically 20:1-2), and the other peculiar to John (20:11a, 14b-18); John completed the first (20:3-10) and linked it to the second by 11b-14a, the substance of which was also drawn from a synoptic basis. But on grounds of literary criticism, we find it difficult to accept the existence of a tradition which did no more than record the bare fact of the discovery of the empty tomb.

Thus, following R. E. Brown in particular,[5] though with many qualifications, we prefer to recognize three different traditions amalgamated by John, two visits to the tomb and an appearance. We shall examine each in turn.

1   The Disciples at the Tomb

In the Lucan tradition there are two allusions to this visit: 'But Peter rose and ran to the tomb: stooping and looking in, he saw the linen cloths by themselves; and he went home wondering at what had happened' (Luke 24:12). Those journeying to Emmaus also say, 'Some of those who were with us went to the tomb, and found it just as the women had said; but him they did not see' (24:24). The account of John 20:2-10 corresponds to this latter passage. But the Johannine text presents difficulties: the preposition 'to' (*pros*) placed incorrectly not only before 'Peter' but also before 'the other disciple' (v. 2), the passage from the singular to the plural in v. 3, the repetition of the same words in two successive verses (the line cloths lying there; vv. 5 and 6), the incoherence of vv. 8 and 9 ('he believed' and then 'they did not yet know'). Thus the text seems to have been edited. Amongst the hypotheses that have been put forward, let us mention two, which attempt to overcome the difficulty of fitting in vv. 8 and 9.

Some scholars consider that v. 9 was interpolated by John. This simple solution makes the text coherent, but there is no manuscript evidence for it; and it is difficult to attribute this verse to John, for there is nothing Johannine about it, particularly as John usually avoids describing the Easter event by the word 'resurrection'. Thus it is preferable to retain v. 9 in the source used.

The attempt can also be made to separate everything concerning the beloved disciple (a profoundly Johannine theme, although in other cases it has added to the text, as in 13:23 or in 19:26). The most simple hypothesis is to suppose that it was enough for John to identify his companion. In this case, by mentioning Peter alone, Luke 24:12 would have simplified the tradition. This is probable if we remember that the mention of 'some' disciples (24:24) is probably older than 24:12. Luke, this implies, wanted to attribute everything to Peter alone, in the same way as in his gospel Simon was the first to whom a special appearance was vouchsafed. Thus there is some probability that the text which John used, and which was not very far from that of Luke, was as follows:

> ³Peter then came out with the other disciple and they went to the tomb. ⁵Stooping to look in, he saw the linen cloths lying there, ⁷and the napkin, which had been on his head, not lying with the linen cloths but rolled up in a place by itself.... ⁸He saw and [was astonished], ⁹for as yet they did not know the scripture, that he must rise from the dead. ¹⁰Then the disciples went back to their homes.

The tradition underlying John   In all probability, Luke and John represent two branches of the same tradition. This matter would take a long time to discuss, and is not of great interest for our present purpose. Thus we shall do no more than define the content of this tradition, making use from time to time of the way it is presented in Luke.

The most obvious interpretation is that the linen cloths remaining in the tomb have an apologetic purpose: by their presence, they signify that the body of Jesus had not been stolen. How could thieves have taken the trouble to undress the body? That would be most improbable. Chrysostom[6] had already observed this long ago. It was one way of dismissing the legend that the body had been stolen, a story which Matthew repeated in his own way (28:11-15).

Some writers, however, have thought that the purpose of the Johannine narrative could be deduced from the way in which Jesus is said to have come out of the linen cloths with which he was covered. It is suggested that the impression is meant to be given that he passed through the cloths and the napkin like the sun through a window pane. This would be possible because the risen Christ had passed through material objects, such as the door of the upper room (20:19). But this hypothesis raises difficulties. Would the risen Christ have folded up the linen cloths before leaving? And is it realized that the situation is not the same in the two cases? In the appearance to the Eleven, the observation that the doors were shut is meant to compensate for the too human and familiar aspect of the appearance of the risen Christ; it is a sign which enables the visitor to be recognized. Is a sign intended here, for John at least, seeing that Peter does not in fact believe? And the Lucan tradition says simply that Peter 'wondered'. To appeal to a miraculous passing through the linen cloths is to place a value on these details which is not in the text.

On the other hand, the context of the fourth gospel enables us to descry a symbolic meaning in addition to any apologetic intention. For when Lazarus returned to life, he came out of the tomb 'his hands and feet bound with bandages, and his face wrapped with a cloth' (11:44). The contrast is deliberate. If it is true that here we have a tradition anterior to John, it is imaginable that the story of the resurrection of Lazarus establishes a contrast between this man, who was to die once again (he is still bound by the linen cloths) and him who would die no more, Jesus the Lord (who leaves the cloths behind). When the napkin is folded separately from the cloths 'in a place by itself', this may symbolize the unity and the order to which all things are from now on restored.

Finally, the scriptural theme must be noted: the scriptures cannot be understood without a personal intervention of the risen Christ. Moreover, for John too, it is impossible to believe simply on the basis of the empty tomb, even if the linen cloths are folded up in a surprising way. Is there here a criticism of those who attempt to make use of this fact to impose belief in the resurrection? This is not out of the question.

The Johannine revision   There are two significant details in the present text: the identification of the beloved disciple and the context for which the passage was written.

The other disciple (be it Mary or an unknown disciple) becomes 'the one whom Jesus loved'. He is presented in a favourable light, since although he runs faster than Peter, he respects his elder colleague, and also because he 'saw and believed', while nothing is said about the personal reaction of Peter.

By introducing this figure, John seems to be creating a contrast between him and Peter. It does not necessarily follow that John's purpose was to belittle Peter by implying that he had not believed. Rather, he meant to stress the fact that love gives a special faculty of intuition, both here in 20:8 and also in 21:4, 7, when the disciple whom Jesus loved immediately recognizes the unknown person walking on the beach as the Lord. The beloved disciple is the typical disciple who follows Jesus and knows him. What does his faith consist of? Some scholars think that by observing that the disciple believed, John is anticipating what he says in 20:29, 'Blessed are those who have not seen and yet believe.' But in that text, as we shall show below, there is no question of giving a privileged status to those who have not seen. Nor has John any intention of belittling the value of the appearances of Jesus.

There are nevertheless both Catholic and Protestant writers who have attempted to use this text to defend their theological position. Catholics have suggested that by waiting for Peter, the beloved disciple is demonstrating the superiority of Peter, that is, of the Pope. Anti-catholics have emphasized the importance placed on faith, and have used this to protest against the pretensions of 'Peter'. There are others again who consider that the passage reflects the rivalry of the original gentile community (the beloved disciple) with the original Jewish community (Peter). In fact the contrast between Peter and the beloved disciple is accidental. If the text is read closely, there is no aspect which is to the discredit of either. The value of each must be maintained. The primacy of Peter is affirmed in the earliest tradition and has no need to be reaffirmed polemically by John; but John wishes to show that there is also a primacy in the order of love (cf. John 21:7).

To the eyes of love, the folded and tidy linen cloths are the occasion of faith. And here we must say something about the meaning of the verb 'see'. It does not refer to an ordinary visual observation, but to a seeing which is of itself an understanding, a preamble to true faith.

Unlike Luke, who mentions the visit of the disciples after that by the women, John has deliberately woven it into his account of the visit by Mary. But in his own way he returns to the Lucan tradition, according to which the disciples did not believe the women (Luke 24:11), but nevertheless went to the tomb (24:24). John probably intends in this way to show that the tomb was first found empty by the disciples, and especially by the beloved disciple.

2 *Mary at the Tomb*

Scholars see a common tradition as the starting point of the present narrative, and we shall indicate some of its features. The scene takes place 'on the first day of the week' (Mark, Luke), 'very early' (Mark). So Mary goes to the tomb; seeing that the stone no longer blocks the entrance (cf. Mark 16:4; Luke 24:2) she goes back to tell Peter (cf. Luke 24:24). A few Johannine details are added to this common basis. 'It was still dark.' Perhaps this is a symbolic detail intended to enhance the splendour of the resurrection, although it is not emphasized. Perhaps it is equivalent to Matthew's statement 'after the sabbath', that is, as night fell (Matthew 28:1)? According to John, there is no angel to tell her that Jesus is no longer there; Mary deduces this directly from the fact that the stone has been removed, a modification made by the redactor in order to anticipate what Mary later says to the angel (20:13). The stone has not been 'rolled back' (a more descriptive term), but 'taken away' (a term to which a more profound significance can be given: 11:39, 41; cf. 1:29; 10:18). It perhaps means that every obstacle has been removed in the face of life triumphing over death.

In basis and structure the narrative of the appearance resembles that of Matthew 28:9-10. Just as the holy women held the feet of Jesus, Mary takes hold of Jesus, then receives a message for the disciples and carries out her mission. It is equally close to the summary given in the conclusion of Mark. In the view of C. H. Dodd and several other scholars,[7] the text of ps.-Mark 16:9-11 does not seem to derive from that of Mark or John, but from a tradition which is not preserved in the gospels. Thus John seems to have located at the tomb an ancient tradition of an appearance of Christ to the holy women. For this reason, in his account the angels do not interpret the event; by the question which they ask Mary, they prepare in advance her encounter with Christ.

The appearance to Mary Magdalene is related to that which the disciples had on the road to Emmaus; it is a recognition appearance, describing, with details peculiar to each evangelist, the awakening of faith. This description is made easier by the fact that John limits to Mary an appearance which in Matthew, and probably in the original tradition ('we do not know', v. 2; 'I do not know', v. 13) was vouchsafed to several women. John concentrates on showing Mary's progressive transformation; preoccupied at first by Jesus as he was before Easter, she sees herself invited to apprehend the new presence of him who is alive.

The Jesus of the past   Mary's threefold repetition, 'They have taken away my Lord, and I do not know where they have laid him,' (20:2, 13, 15) draws the attention of the reader to the thoughts of the distressed woman. To the disciples, to the angels and to the gardener Mary goes on repeating the same lament. The disciples on the way to Emmaus mourn the crucified liberator and their disappointed hopes; Mary laments the impossibility of finding the body of him whom she loved so much. A subtlety typical of John has her call Jesus 'Sir', which in Greek is the same word as 'Lord' (20:15); Mary is looking for the Lord without knowing it. She weeps, as Jesus had foretold shortly before his death: 'You will weep and lament' (16:20).

The disciples do not reply to her. The angels do no more than ask, 'Why are you weeping?' and this merely makes her repeat her refrain. Finally, the gardener adds, 'Whom do you seek?' The progression is deliberate. The angels do not state anything; sitting at the head and the feet of the place where Jesus's body had been, they form a guard of honour; they do not reveal anything to Mary, but question her about herself, making her say what is in her heart and is causing her tears. Nor does the gardener tell her anything, like the mysterious traveller who began by questioning the disheartened disciples. Mary does not recognize Jesus, any more than did the disciples, whose 'eyes were kept from recognizing him'; 'she did not know that it was Jesus' (20:14), any more than did the steward of the feast at Cana (2:9), the Samaritan woman (4:10) or the disciples (4:32). The question which Jesus asks echoes that which began his public life, when he said to the disciples of John the Baptist, 'What do you seek?' (1:38). Here the risen Christ suggests the answer by asking clearly, 'Whom do you seek?' When Mary has repeated her sorrowful utterance, Jesus calls her name, 'Mary'. Spoken by the Good Shepherd who knows his sheep and calls them to him one by one by name (cf. John 10:3, 14, 27) this name awakens the memory of the past in Mary's heart, and she cries, 'Rab-boni! (which means Teacher).' It is not only the prompt answer which is surprising; so too is the fact that, remarkable as it is, it does not go beyond what the disciples replied at the beginning of Jesus's public life: 'Rabbi (which means Teacher), where are you staying?' (1:38). Thus Mary does not achieve the faith of Thomas, who cries, 'My Lord and my God!' (20:28). Mary gets no further than the Jesus whom she knew on earth, and did not attain to faith in the Lord. Why not? Is it because the Spirit has not yet been given (7:39; 20:22)? This reply may seem premature, for after her encounter with Jesus, as Paul was to say later (I Cor 9:1), she declares to the disciples, 'I have seen the Lord' (20:18).

While the disciples at Emmaus recognize Christ at the moment when, having broken the bread, he disappears from their eyes, Mary is able to enter into a dialogue with Jesus. But everything she says shows that she gets no further than the figure of the past, and has not fully 'recognized' Jesus. For the moment, she has found the Jesus of the past alive again, the Jesus who said, 'So you have sorrow now, but I will see you again and your hearts will rejoice' (16:22).

Jesus alive If Mary is able to say that she has 'seen the Lord', the reason is that between her first recognition of the beloved rabbi and this declaration, the Lord has spoken to her. 'Do not hold me, for I have not yet ascended to the Father; but go to my brethren and say to them, I am ascending to my Father and your Father, to my

God and your God' (20:17). In this saying, two elements must be distinguished: the request not to hold Jesus, and the message to the disciples. We must examine these two points in more detail.

What does Jesus mean by 'ascend to the Father'? Does he mean the ascension, as is often supposed? In this case, Jesus would be saying to Mary that he is on the point of ascending to his Father; but then he would have to come back down again so that he could appear later to his disciples. This interpretation, which has the advantage of being closer to the Lucan presentation, cannot be attributed to the fourth evangelist. In fact the ascent to the Father is not thought of as an event, as Luke represented the ascension which, according to Acts 1:3 at least, took place forty days after the resurrection. For John, not only is the ascent of Jesus to the Father not 'visible' (cf. 6:62); above all, there is no question of an ascension, apart from the 'lifting up' which takes place on the cross (12:32-33). Thus if the lifting up or exaltation coincides with the crucifixion, then the resurrection is in exactly the same way the return to the Father. Jesus does not speak of 'resurrection' when he foretells the fate he is expecting: he is going to the Father (13:1; 14:12, 28; [16:5]; 16:10, 28; 17:13).

How, then, are we to interpret John's 'narrative'? John sets out in space and time the mystery which he affirms in a way which is not susceptible to division. In a way, we can say that for John crucifixion, exaltation, resurrection and return to the Father are a single mystery, that of the glorification of the Son by his Father (12:23, 28; 17:1, 5). This implies that John has no intention of telling us that 'events' followed the death and resurrection in a temporal succession. This is no more than a literary projection, intended to give a better account of the multiple aspects of the indivisible mystery of the glorification of the Son. Thus we must not look in John for information about what he has no intention of telling us, for example whether the ascension took place between the appearance to Mary and that to the disciples. This is a false problem and brings inextricable complications with it. In particular, how could Jesus have come back down from his Father to visit his disciples? Père Lagrange rightly said that here 'ascend' does not imply 'descend'. Jesus is not about to carry out a new act, but is demonstrating that his situation has changed, and that he has passed from the earthly state to that of glory.

We can turn now to the difficult problem raised by the text. Why does Jesus forbid Mary to 'hold' him? Let us note first that the original expression (*mē mou haptou*) must not be translated, 'Do not touch me,' for in Greek the present tense of the imperative does not mean that something must be done, but that an action which has begun should continue; preceded by a negative, it is not a prohibition of an action taking place, but of the continuation of an action already begun. Thus the correct translation is, 'Stop touching me.' Mary is already embracing Jesus's feet, a similar gesture to that of the holy women according to Matthew 28:9. Thus there is no contradiction between this text and the request which Jesus made to Thomas, to put his hand in his side (20:27). The term is not the same, and the verb is not in the same tense. Nor does Jesus intend to suggest to Mary that she can touch him later; 'not yet' does not imply 'later on'.

Most critics suppose that Mary was wrongly interpreting the true nature of Jesus's new presence. This meaning is of course present. But if we are to retain the classical translation, 'for I have not yet ascended', we have to explain how Mary could have understood however vaguely, the subtleties implied by Jesus's words at that moment; for she would have had to understand that the reason why she had to stop holding Jesus was that he had not yet ascended to his Father and that therefore the nature of his relations with his disciples would have to be modified. This is even more difficult, since, immediately afterwards, he declares that he is going to ascend to the Father.

For this reason we hold that a more correct reading of the Greek phrase is necessary. In the Hellenistic language which is known as the Koinē (the common language or the Greek of the empire), it is common for the real reason which is being put forward to be held back until the second half of the sentence, 'Do not hold me, for *of course* I have not yet ascended to the Father, *but* go to my brethren...'[8] Here the reason is the sending of Mary to the brethren. Jesus begins by anticipating the argument which Mary might present to him in order to retain him, 'You have not yet ascended to the Father'; no doubt she remembers that, in his farewell discourse, Jesus foretold that he would go away to the Father to prepare places for the disciples, and would then come back to look for them (14:1-3). She understands completely, in the same way as Jesus himself, that he must first ascend to the Father.

But she wrongly interprets the fact of her encounter with him, when she imagines that Jesus is to remain here below for a time to give himself in an earthly way as before. This is why Jesus corrects her.

And he corrects her not only by anticipating her possible objection, but also by entrusting a mission to her; and this is the main reason why she must not hold back. According to John's pattern of representation, Mary understands not only that she has not to remain at his feet even though he is still here below, but that the most important thing is to go to carry a message to the disciples.

These disciples are called 'my brethren'. The novelty of the expression is surprising, even though the beloved disciple had been given by Jesus to his mother to be 'her son' (19:26). Its meaning is given only by the subsequent statement about the Father. From now on the disciples have become 'brothers' of Jesus, for, he says, 'I am ascending to my Father and your Father, to my God and your God.' In these words Jesus crowns the whole of the previous revelation. The translation must give a proper rendering of the 'and', which is not an adversative 'and', as if Jesus was saying, 'my Father by nature' and 'your Father by adoption'; this interpretation may be read indirectly into the text, but it does not translate it exactly. It has rightly been said that the particle normally has a conjunctive and not a disjunctive value.[9] It is the same Father, for the brethren as for Jesus. One can be even more precise about the underlying sense of the expression. The same scholar has drawn attention to a text in Ruth (1:16). To Naomi, who suggests that she should return to Moab, Ruth replies, 'Where you go I will go, and where you lodge I will lodge; your people shall be my people, and your God my God.' Thus the meaning of Jesus's saying is, 'I am ascending to my Father *who is also* your Father, to my God *who is also* your God.' This gives a much more profound meaning: Jesus is affirming that now the God who was in constant contact with him has entered into a similar relationship with the disciples. And this is the purpose of Jesus's activity on earth: when he has been lifted up from the earth, he will lift all men up to him, will unceasingly bestow the spirit and will make the Father dwell among them. In this way the new covenant foretold by the prophets will come about (Hos 2:25; Jer 31:33; Ezek 36:28).

From now on there is a new kind of relationship between the

Father and the disciples, between God and the disciples. Jesus wants this unity to be perfect. Though he is ascending to the Father, this is not, according to this text, to 'prepare a place', but to crown the work which he has inaugurated upon earth. And he remains with the Father, where he lives as the ultimate 'advocate' (I John 2:1); he had promised, 'You will see me; because I live, you will live also' (John 14:19).

B. JESUS AND HIS DISCIPLES REUNITED (20:19-29)

The second part of the chapter seems to be attached to the first part in a very loose way. For these appearances have not been foretold by the Lord to Mary; on the contrary, Jesus's words to her did not even suggest that they were possible. Nor had they any connection with the faith of the beloved disciple, who is no longer mentioned here. It may be supposed, and to some extent is true, that having announced that he was ascending to the Father, Jesus had consummated his earthly work. That is why some scholars suppose that this 'coming' of Jesus to the disciples lies outside the Johannine structure. In fact the appearances described here belong much more to the Jerusalem type outlined in chapter 5 above. But it would be a futile expedient to consider these latter narratives as interpolated, since they are so full of Johannine theology. We must also remember that according to the farewell discourse, Jesus was to see the disciples again, give them peace, bring them joy and send the Paraclete, the Holy Spirit. In this sense, the two narratives are indispensable if Jesus is to complete his work upon earth.

The two scenes are dated and located. In accordance with the Jerusalem tradition, they take place on the first day of the week, and on the evening of that day (cf. Luke 24:33, 36; ps.-Mark 16:14). The appearance to Thomas takes place eight days later. These two dates must not be taken as firm chronological indications, but as liturgical allusions. The eucharist is celebrated on the first day of the week (Acts 20:7; I Cor 16:2), probably not on Sunday morning (Rev 1:10), but on Saturday evening, after the Jewish sabbath service. The origin of the choice of this day is complex; not only has it a connection with the sabbath, but also points to the eschatological day (Is 52:6), 'that day' of which Jesus spoke (John 14:20; cf. 16:23, 26).

Like Luke, John locates the scenes at Jerusalem, but in a place which is not specified. Tradition, no doubt with good reason, has identified the place with the upper room, where the disciples met before Pentecost (Acts 1 : 13) and where the eucharist was instituted (Luke 22 : 12). In fact the purpose here is only to emphasize that the disciples were all gathered in the same place, in order to demonstrate that the appearance was collective in nature and of significance to the church as such.

If there are two distinct scenes, this seems to be because John wished to separate the theme of lack of belief and that of the mission entrusted to the disciples; we shall make this clear with regard to each episode.

1　*Jesus Sends his Disciples*

[19]On the evening of that day, the first day of the week, the doors being shut where the disciples were, for fear of the Jews, Jesus came and stood among them

And said to them
'Peace to you!'

[20]When he had said this
he showed them
his hands and his side

Then the disciples were
glad when they saw the
Lord.

[21]Jesus said to them again,
'Peace to you!'
As the Father has sent me,
even so I send you!

[22]And when he had said this,
he breathed on them,
and said to them,
'Receive the Holy Spirit.
[23]If you forgive the sins of any,
they are forgiven; if you retain
the sins of any, they are retained.'

This narrative fits the classic pattern of an appearance which we studied in chapter 5. In two parallel descriptions (19-20 and 21-23) it includes a gesture meant to bring about recognition and a mission saying, both introduced by the same formula: 'When he had said this'. The initiative belongs to Jesus, and he enables the disciples to recognize him (joy) and entrusts a mission to them. But the manner is profoundly Johannine. When it is contrasted with the parallel narrative in Luke, the text appears to have been reduced to the minimum: there is no longer any apologetic (Luke 24: 41-42), and in particular the allusion to the doubt of the disciples is eliminated. Whether this very bleak pattern is thought to be ancient or more recent, John uses it to serve one of his basic purposes.

For Jesus to appear there when the doors are closed is not, as might be supposed by a simple reader, who in fact would be over-simplifying, meant to show that he can pass through solid objects. The text says nothing about that, but makes it clear that Jesus intends to rejoin his disciples who have shut themselves away for fear of the Jews (cf. 7:13; 19:38). This emphasizes the purpose of the meeting; when Jesus was taking his farewell, the disciples became afraid, but Jesus promised them peace (14:1, 17; 16:33). It is no use now the disciples locking themselves away for fear of the Master's enemies, for he has the power to return to them when he wishes. The theme of the 'subtle nature' of the body of Jesus can be deduced from the text, but it is not what the evangelist intends to teach. This nuance can be found again in the way in which, shortly afterwards, he recounts the way Jesus shows his hands and side. It seems that John is not directly interested in the question of the corporeality of the living Lord.

Thus Jesus comes to meet the 'disciples'. Scholars, and particularly denominational writers, have discussed endlessly whether by this Jesus meant the apostolic college, or all believers. It seems certain that in the pre-gospel traditions, the official appearance of Jesus was to the Eleven (I Cor 15:5; Matthew 28:16). Perhaps a fragment of this tradition may be recognized in the reference to Thomas, 'one of the Twelve' (20:24). But gradually a movement can be discerned to extend this to a greater number. Thus in Luke 24:33, we read of 'those who were with them', whom the disciples returning from Emmaus came to join.

Vv. 21 and 22 suggest that John wished to extend the mission and the gift of the Spirit to all believers. In fact he based the mission on the relationship with his Father, which holds for every believer (cf. 15:9) and the new creation suggested at the moment when the Spirit is given no doubt affects all Christians. Only v. 23, concerning the power over sin, is not subject to this extension, as we shall note below.

When he greets his disciples by his words 'Peace to you!', Jesus is not simply giving the ordinary greeting, the usual *shalōm* which is common amongst the Jews. Nor is he simply wishing them peace (here I disagree with translations which propose, 'Peace be with you'); he is giving them peace, in accordance with what he said during his farewell discourses (14:27-28). In giving peace, Jesus shows his feet and his side. It is important to realize the contrast here with the text of Luke. According to Luke, the gesture is meant to remove the apostles' doubts: 'they supposed that they saw a Spirit' (Luke 24:37). There is nothing like this in John. What, then, is the purpose of the gesture? Perhaps it is an anticipation of what will be said to Thomas in the scene where the disciple does not believe. But it is preferable to note the modification which is peculiar to John: Jesus does not show his hands and his feet, but his hands and his side. Jesus is presenting himself as the crucified Jesus from whose side flowed blood and water (19:34). With what follows in mind, we may give as our interpretation that Jesus is he from whose side flows the Spirit, the stream of living water destined to water the earth.

Once Jesus presents himself, the disciples, in a vision which is not simply human but which is already that of faith, see in him the Lord and are filled with joy, the eschatological joy which the farewell discourse had foretold (16:21-22; cf. Rev 19:7; 21:1-4), and which none can take away from those who have received it from the living Jesus. At once the disciples achieve fullness of faith, requiring no further confirmation, simply because Jesus who has come to meet them has enabled them to recognize him as him who was crucified and lifted up from the earth to draw all things to him.

The words that follow hardly resemble at all those which the risen Christ pronounces in the narratives of Luke or Matthew. The proposal for the mission is retained, but transformed. It is not connected with any scriptural proof, and is not directed towards all nations, except by way of those who are sent as intermediaries. Jesus does not merely promise but himself gives the Spirit who is the symbol of his new and efficacious presence. The formula of the missionary command is typically Johannine, but is rooted in a tradition to which there is ample witness. The power over sins corresponds to another tradition which seems equally reliable.

Jesus had asked Mary Magdalene to tell his brethren that he was ascending to the Father; in a way, Jesus now bestows upon the disciples the final outcome of this return to the Father. The mission he entrusts does not derive in substance from a saying of

Jesus; it is rooted in the utmost depths of the mystery of the relationship which unites Jesus to his Father. Jesus had already presented himself as the expression of the Father: 'He who sees me sees him who sent me' (12:45; cf. 13:20); the hour has now come when his are the very actions of the Father: 'As the Father has sent me, even so send I you' (20:21). This saying echoes his prayer, 'As thou didst send me into the world, so I have sent them into the world' (17:18).

This is why, from John's point of view, the moment has come to give the Spirit. This fulfils the prophecy which was made during the farewell discourse. When Jesus of Nazareth is no longer with the disciples, the Paraclete will come, 'the Holy Spirit, whom the Father will send in my name' (14:26), the same 'Spirit of truth' whom Jesus will 'send to you from the Father' (15:26). This is why Jesus has to go away (16:7). Jesus, lifted up above the earth, gives the Spirit of truth symbolically by 'breathing' on the disciples, recalling in this way the primordial gesture of the creation of man (the verb is the same as in Gen 2:7; Wis 15:11), and in accordance with the Johannine tradition which sets forth the Logos as creator and re-creator (cf. Ezek 37:3-5, 9; John 3:5). In this way, on the 'first day of the week', he inaugurates the paschal age.

Some theologians have asked if the gift of the Spirit by Jesus is identical with that of Pentecost. We recall the view, which was rejected, of Theodore of Mopsuestia, that the act of Jesus was purely figurative. Others, such as Chrysostom, attempted to make a distinction in the functions of the Spirit. In Luke, he thought, it was the power of working miracles, and in John the power to forgive sins. Or again, it has been thought that John is describing the gift to individuals and Luke that to the church. Others again believe that in John it is an impersonal gift (no article), but in Luke a gift which is personal. But it is impossible to harmonize Luke and John in this way. They agree at a much more profound level. It seems obvious that they are presenting the same event in two different ways, and a contradiction only exists if one goes no further than the date on which the gift is given. Thus the archimandrite Cassian thought it reasonable to abandon John's dating, in order to speak of a 'Johannine Pentecost';[10] but in so doing he goes beyond the text. Yet there is reason to believe that for practical purposes the episode is the same. For the variation is of no more importance than that of the topographical distinction between Galilee and

Jerusalem as the location of the appearances. If there is a difference, it is in their total perspective: according to Luke, the Spirit can only be promised and expected on the day of Pentecost; in John, he must be given on Easter day itself, so that the part played by Jesus is accomplished to the full.

By so doing, John sets forth an essential dimension of the Easter mystery which Luke has deliberately extended in time, thereby running the risk of separating the Spirit and Jesus. For in fact in the Lucan narrative the Spirit comes down on the disciples who have gathered together after Jesus has ascended into heaven. In John, Jesus in person, after referring to his relationship with the Father, sends the Spirit which will enable the disciples to remain faithful to the mission entrusted to them.

It is the same Spirit who sets up the church with the authority to forgive sins. We must first note that here John gives a version, more comprehensible to a Greek, of the saying of Jesus recorded by Matthew, 'I will give you the keys of the kingdom of heaven, and whatever you bind on earth shall be bound in heaven, and whatever you loose on earth shall be loosed in heaven' (Matthew 16:19; cf. 18:18). There has been lengthy discussion, especially between Protestants and Catholics, about the persons to whom this promise was given and the extent of their power. Does this power extend to sins committed after baptism? We shall not attempt to reply, since we feel that for our present purpose it is sufficient to establish the essential point, that in John the risen Christ bestows upon his church the role which it is to play with regard to the nations: Jesus, alive for ever, commissions his church to show the way to heaven, just as in Matthew, Jesus, living on earth, had entrusted to Peter the task of deciding who should enter the kingdom of heaven.

While a comparison of v. 23 with the Matthew tradition is not very enlightening, to compare it with Johannine ideas is much more so. V. 21, where Jesus sends the disciples as the Father sent him, reminds us that the function of Jesus was to exercise judgment amongst men to discern those who were coming to the light (9:39-41; 3:17-21), just as Paul said that for some he was a fragrance from death to death, and for others a fragrance from life to life (II Cor 2:15-16). V. 22 shows that by the Spirit Jesus has driven sin from the world (1:29) and we know that the blood of Jesus cleanses us from all sin (I John 1:7). Here John is reproducing a Jewish tradition, of which a trace can still be seen in the Qumran writings (I QS 3:7-8), according to which the Messiah will cleanse men from all sin.[11]

Of course it may seem that John has restricted the scope of the promise and the gift given by Jesus; it appears as though the disciples have no longer to go to the nations, and that word has no longer to go out to the ends of the earth. None of this is made clear. But although nothing is said about it, the reason is that what we have is an infinite openness, which precisely defines the place of the church in the world. It is not commensurable with the world in any respect; and the sin over which the church has power affects all men, without any distinction of race, place or time.

And there are no grounds for distinguishing between sins committed before baptism and sins committed after.[12] Thus the universality proclaimed in the other traditions is also fully present in the text of John.

2   *The Faith of Thomas*

[24]Now Thomas, one of the twelve, called the Twin, was not with them when Jesus came. [25]So the other disciples told him, 'We have seen the Lord.' But he said to them, 'Unless I see in his hands the print of the nails, and place my finger in the mark of the nails, and place my hand in his side, I will not believe.' [26]Eight days later, his disciples were again in the house, and Thomas was with them. The doors were shut, but Jesus came and stood amongst them, and said, 'Peace to you!' [27]Then he said to Thomas: 'Put your finger here, and see my hands; and put out your hand, and place it in my side; do not be faithless, but believing.' [28]Thomas answered him, 'My Lord and My God!' [29]Jesus said to him, 'Have you believed because you have seen me? Blessed are those who have not seen and yet believe.'

In the gospel tradition, the theme of doubt forms an integral part of the appearances; the disciples do not immediately recognize him who appears as Jesus in person. In the previous narrative, John has produced a highly schematic version of the encounter with the risen Christ, to the point that the traditional theme of doubt is entirely concentrated on the appearance to Thomas. Thomas is already a significant figure in the Gospel of John. He committed his companions to facing death with Jesus as he set out to raise Lazarus from the dead (11 : 16); he reproached Jesus for talking to the disciples of the place where he was going when they did not know the way (14 : 5). Nevertheless, it would be wrong to describe Thomas as a doubter; rather, he is the disciple who moves slowly towards authentic faith.

The narrative is constructed in strict parallel to the previous passage. Vv. 24-25 are transitional, v. 25 recalls v. 20; and v. 26 is a paraphrase of v. 19. The narrative is then recast by adding the three Johannine themes of vv. 27, 28 and 29. This reconstruction shows that John completely readapted to his purposes the material which he possessed.

At first sight, Thomas represents the opposite attitude to that of the other disciples. They saw the Lord and believed; Thomas requires a proof. In Luke, the disciples want to experience, and are still unable to believe. In John, Thomas wishes to verify what his companions say by assuring himself with his own eyes that he who is appearing is in fact the crucified Jesus. He rigorously applies the categories of Jewish thought concerning the resurrection of the dead. He requires a strict continuity between the two worlds, in order to be able to verify in a concrete way that he who is appearing is the same being as before. Philip had already expressed a desire to see the Father (14:8); now Thomas wishes to see, in the ordinary sense of the word, the glorified Son. He remains at an earthly level, just as Nicodemus did when he tried to understand how man could return into his mother's womb (3:4). Jesus seeks to convince Thomas by granting his wish. He does not of course proceed to a similar demonstration to that given by Luke when he describes Jesus eating in sight of his disciples; but the words he utters are such that Thomas is abashed even before he carries out Jesus's request. John's delicate touch can be observed here; in spite of what later authors, like Ignatius of Antioch,[13] were to say, Thomas does not carry out the request. He at once proclaims his faith. Jesus knows the innermost wishes of men; thus Nathanael was surprised to learn that Jesus knew that one day he had been beneath the fig tree (1:48-50). Here again, Jesus was the first to 'see' into Thomas's heart, and that is why Thomas in his turn saw Jesus.

His profession of faith, 'My Lord and my God', is not meant as Thomas utters it to express rigorous ideas such as that of the Council of Chalcedon about the divine nature of Christ, consubstantial with the Father. Where does this expression come from?[14] It forms a literal parallel to the acclamation by which the Emperor Domitian (A.D. 81-96) claimed to be worshipped: *Dominus et Deus noster*. The Book of Revelations in fact seems to have the pretensions of this emperor in mind, and the gospel was probably composed in part during his reign, but the context of the passage does not permit any possible comparison. Scholars tend to think, therefore, that here John has transposed an Old Testament usage: *YHWH— Elohay* (cf. Ps 35:23 'My Lord and My God'). However, it is to the Gospel of John itself that we should look for an explanation. There, the Son should be honoured as the Father is honoured (5:23); and we should also note the saying of Jesus, 'I am' (8:28). The full meaning of this proclamation becomes apparent when it is seen in a liturgical context similar to that portrayed in Revelations: 'Worthy are thou, our Lord and God, to receive glory and honour and power ...' (Rev 4:11). This last text refers of course to God, but did not Jesus say, 'I and the Father are one' (10:30)? Thus by emphasizing the words '*My* Lord and *my* God', Thomas makes explicit what Jesus said to Mary Magdalene when he spoke to her of the God of the covenant: he is saying 'Amen' to the covenant which God has now brought into being with men through Jesus.

Finally, Jesus recognizes that Thomas has achieved true and authentic faith, something which the disciples do not do in Luke. He congratulates him, though he is not prepared to link this faith with what Thomas has just seen. By stating that those who have not seen are blessed, Jesus is in no way disparaging those to whom the privilege of appearances has been vouchsafed.[15] In spite of what used to be thought, Christ is pronouncing equally blessed those to whom he has not shown himself but who nevertheless believe with all their heart. C. H. Dodd has compared this beatitude with that in the gospels, 'Blessed are your eyes, for they see, and your ears, for they hear ...' (Matthew 13:16), and even more with the beatitude found in I Peter: 'Without having seen him you love him; though you do not now see him you believe in him and rejoice with unutterable and exalted joy. As the outcome of your faith you obtain the salvation of your soul' (I Peter 1:8-9). John's purpose is certainly not to belittle the appearances, but to show that believers who live after this privileged time, long after the disappearance of the eye-witnesses of the glory of Jesus, possess the same joy.[16]

CONCLUSION

It is very difficult to sum up in a few lines the contribution of John to the Christian understanding of the Easter message. Let us do no more than point to a few lines of reflection.

John carries out a process of simplification and redaction. The apologetic arguments become blurred, for everything is illuminated by the understanding of love. Thus the empty tomb, which was apparently important of itself, is now given its true significance: it is a sign for whoever is a beloved disciple. The fact that it is empty can be the sign of the totality of the mystery; negative, but significant by that very fact.

John personalizes everything that the tradition records. Thus the mission is not simply a saying which is heard and commits the disciple to continue Jesus's work; it is a relationship which the believer understands and which unites him to Jesus, as Jesus is united to the Father. No one is in any danger of attributing anything in this activity to himself, for it consists of realizing here below what Jesus himself is doing.

More than any of the other evangelists, John bases everything that is seen upon the Word which brings the believer into contact with Jesus; there can be no proof of the resurrection, except the Word of Christ. Even the appearances lack the demonstrative value which one might have tended to attribute to them. They are replaced by the word of Jesus alone. Jesus shows his wounds, but this is not to prove his corporeality, but to demonstrate that his passion is the source of the peace which he has just given and the Spirit whom he is going to bestow.

Finally, the unity of this chapter is formed by the alliance established between the Father and the disciples, on the basis of the relationship with the Father which Jesus has restored. And this relationship is ultimately expressed by the gift of the Spirit, which, like Jesus becoming 'God with us' in Matthew, is an everlasting assurance of the new presence of the Lord amongst the disciples and on earth. Thanks to the disciples who have power over sin, the whole world can enter the covenant with God.

Hermeneutics

This brings us to the conclusion of our exegetical study of the New Testament texts which speak of the resurrection of Jesus. Thus we are not now setting out upon a fourth stage, following our three previous stages. We are now moving on to a reflection of a different kind, and in so doing, hope to reply to two kinds of concern which the reader has been asked to restrain, and which he will nevertheless feel to be urgent.

The first concern of a believer who reads this book, as of the author, is to know how to express and communicate the Easter message. This concern can be expressed on two levels. One may wish to *express one's faith to oneself* with the aid of appropriate language. But is it necessary simply to re-state the message in the language of the past? And of the languages which we have identified, which shall we choose? Again, which gospel should be followed in re-expressing it? At the more external level, that of communication, one may wish not only to express one's own faith to oneself, but to *utter it* in intelligible language. What principles of 'preaching' can be isolated from the numerous ways of presenting the message? What part can be accorded to the 'fact' itself? All these problems are included within the technical term 'hermeneutics'.

In addition to this noble desire to understand, translate, and give expression, the reader will have another urgent desire: that of basing his faith on firm historical foundations. In responding to this wish, care must be taken to avoid excess in two directions, and to remember the attitude of the church in the course of the centuries. In every age, the church has been wary of 'gnostics', that is, of those who propagate a doctrine which, while it may be inspired by the gospel, has cut itself off from its historic roots. At the same time, apologists have always gone to the opposite extreme, but have not been encouraged by the church any more than the gnostics. They have sought to prove their faith, either by demonstrating it in arguments which they regard as appropriate, or by pious inventions to fill the historical gaps in the gospels. By so doing, they tend to reduce the mystery to an event in this world. But Christian faith depends both upon history and upon doctrine.

The reader is right to ask whether he 'can' believe in the resurrection of Jesus; but must he go to the point of demanding historical proofs? Caught in the cross-fire of his conflicting desires—to be free of history and to demonstrate with the aid of history—the believer runs the risk of not knowing where to turn and therefore of giving up hope of any certainty at all on this central issue of faith. The chapter that follows will attempt to locate the problems and to open the way to a new understanding of the mystery and its communication.

CHAPTER ELEVEN

Hermeneutics

So far, using the methods of literary analysis, we have attempted to explain the texts. As far as possible we avoided passing judgment on the twofold distinction between the object that is affirmed and the subject who interprets. Sound method made this necessary. Now we have reached the conclusion of this investigation, the time has come to practise hermeneutics in a sense in which this word is nowadays accepted.[1] Hermeneutics is not content with *explaining* the texts, but also seeks to *understand* and *express* their meaning for me at the present day. This purpose makes the task singularly complicated, and we must define our understanding of it.

Again, the reader who has voluntarily suspended his thirst for historical knowledge must now be satisfied. Of course, he would say, the Easter message is full of meaning, but it relates to an event: God raised his Son. How do we know this event? Has it left any traces which can be affirmed historically by all men? The urgent questions are: Was the tomb empty? Of what exactly did the appearances of the risen Christ consist? These questions are pressing, but they can find a satisfactory answer only within genuine hermeneutics. Thus the reader is asked to consider some reflections on methodology before turning to a summary of our conclusions about the event and its interpretation.

The Knowledge of Faith and Historical Knowledge

We must take care not to confuse these two types of knowledge, especially with regard to the present subject.[2] When I say, 'Jesus died on the cross,' or 'Jesus declared himself to be the Son of God,' I am stating a proposition which is verifiable by the methods of historical science. These are facts which can be called 'historical'. Events of this kind really took place at a specific date and in a certain place, and these are details which in theory are accessible to historical science. In this sense the existence of Jesus of Nazareth is like that of the battle of Waterloo.

When I say, 'Jesus fulfils the Old Testament,' or 'Jesus died for our sins,' I am accepting a certain interpretation of historical facts which no longer depends upon universal knowledge, but on faith in the strict sense. Believers may testify to these events as facts which we can qualify as 'real'; for a believer, they are neither imaginary nor fictional; but that does not mean that, at least within the limits of the vocabulary which we use, they are 'historical'.

Let us apply these ideas to the resurrection of Jesus. When I say, 'Paul testifies that he has encountered the risen Christ,' or 'The women found the tomb empty,' I am making statements which are a matter of historical knowledge; thus we can say that they are historical facts. On the other hand, if I say, 'Jesus is risen,' I am stating a fact which is real to me because I am a believer; but as this fact is the mystery of an existence which never ends, it is a matter neither of science nor of historical knowledge. In so far as it is rising from the dead and lifting up to be with God, the resurrection is not a historical fact, even though the believer apprehends it as a real fact. To express this, we may coin a neologism and say that the resurrection as such is a *trans-historical* event,[3] so reserving the term historical to what can be known by science, and leaving history open to matters other than scientific facts. In fact, *reality* goes beyond *history*, and 'history' goes beyond the sphere laid down by 'historical science'. Given the increasing importance of historical science, we prefer to use the term *historical* in the restricted sense described above, and the term *real*, rather than 'trans-historical', which is artificial.

This terminology will help us to guard against the temptation of 'proving' the resurrection of Jesus; on the contrary, it enables us to authenticate the knowledge of the facts. We still have to decide in what sense these facts are an invitation to believe. This is the second point which we must now examine.

The Historian, Facts and Openness to Their Meaning

Apologetics is sometimes out of favour. For it is too often identified with the demonstration of truths which at some point go beyond reason. But if it restricts itself to faithfully setting out facts, without straying into the domain of faith, it becomes an invitation to look for the meaning concealed in the facts; and in the case of 'religion' it is an invitation to listen to God who reveals the meaning through the facts.

It may seem paradoxical, but nowadays the historian finds himself in a position very similar to that of the authentic apologist. The time is past when he could limit his work to looking for 'what exactly took place'. He has abandoned the illusion of possessing bare facts which are known independently of the subject who knows them. The latter leaves his mark upon the fact, which are not 'objects' existing prior to his activity as a historian: they become 'facts' by virtue of him who knows them and gives them their quality of 'historical fact'.[4] The historian no doubt concludes by stumbling upon something which his criticisms can reduce no further, something which simply happens to him, an event. This is something beyond the texts, something which we may call a 'focal point', without which there would be neither text nor interpretation. When face to face with this focal point, the historian can adopt two types of behaviour.

The fact as such does not amount to much. The testimonies of those who narrate events, or their assumptions, are so profoundly associated with the way they utter them that the historian often restricts himself to affirming the existence of a fact, even if he attempts to fit it into some pattern of meaning; but normally he cannot make clear in detail exactly how the fact took place.

Furthermore, the focal point, the fact, accounts for a certain number of interpretations already given; but above all, it provides an opening to the future. In fact, to the extent to which this focal point has a human significance, it imposes on the historian himself the duty of replying to the question which it asks of him. The historian feels himself challenged; to calm the disquiet which the fact raises in his mind, he must appeal to means of investigation other than those of historical science.

The Exegete and the Meaning

Like the historian, the exegete stumbles against the fact and is challenged by the question which it raises, and he too must remain open to all possible meanings, in addition to the meaning supplied by the texts.[5] But the exegete is not simply a historian; by his basic presupposition (that of the unity of holy scripture) and his ultimate aim (to make the word of God a present reality) he tends to become a 'theologian'. In what sense?

As the basis of his work, the exegete takes a choice which may derive from an act of faith or from a working hypothesis. The sphere of his investigation is limited by the books which are called 'canonical', that is by the writings included in the 'bible'. That is why, however interesting texts such as the *Book of Enoch* or the *Gospel of Peter* may be, they do not strictly contribute to the understanding which is sought. Indirectly, they illuminate the canonical books, and assist in understanding the mentality of the biblical period, but they do not form an integral part of the sphere entrusted to exegetical study. The 'canon' of scripture (whatever one includes in it) or the 'apostolic age' imposes a horizon which, while it restricts research, at the same time gives it a unique kind of penetration.

For by contrast to the historian, the exegete presupposes, as a first principle, that the unity of the bible is given by the living Christ towards whom everything tends. Thus it has a 'meaning'. Assuming that he acquires or holds the Christian conviction that Jesus is alive and will die no more, the exegete reaches forward to the conclusion of history and recognizes the fullness of meaning in the bible. Whereas interpretations of events can continue to be given until the end of time, the exegete regards the interpretations which he uncovers in the bible as privileged. The bible forms a totality full of meaning, not of a meaning which can be expressed in a sentence, or even in one of the works which compose it, even in a gospel, but with a meaning which is the point of reference of all the various kinds of significance put forward in the different books of the bible.

The situation of the exegete is made more complicated here by the fact that in order to show this 'meaning' in and through the various kinds of significance found in the texts, his knowledge has a further dimension at his disposal. The 'focal point' no longer consists simply of the 'fact' towards which he is working through all the testimonies, but also of 'that which gives meaning to the fact itself', the resurrection of Jesus. At the heart of all the facts there is this 'event', not a 'historical' but a 'real' event, that 'without which nothing would have any meaning'. Obviously, the exegete cannot seize hold of and control the resurrection, which is his ultimate 'focal point', any more than the historian can seize hold of and control the fact, which is his. But he keeps his sights on it, as the origin and condition of all interpretation. In the developments which follow, it is important to recognize the various meanings of the expression 'focal point'. According to the context, it may signify the Easter event (the act of God who raised his Son, the existence of Jesus after his death) or historical facts such as the testimonies concerning the appearances and the discovery of the empty tomb.

The task of the exegete is now becoming clear. He must first of all get a grip of the successive interpretations which the texts offer. This is what we have tried to do in the previous stages of this study. He must then attempt to identify the focal point, in the sense of the historical facts. That is what we are now going to outline in the development which follows. Nevertheless, the ultimate task of the exegete is not limited to carrying out these two tasks in turn, but consists in establishing their mutual relationship. Too often, depending upon his temperament, the exegete restricts himself to looking for the meaning either in the interpretations or in the event itself, which he believes he has isolated. In so doing, he misunderstands his own situation in two ways.

First of all, he imagines that it is possible to abolish the distance which separates the interpreter and the past (either a past interpretation, or the event). And so he falls into the illusion of positivism. Others have thought that they could remedy this situation by reading the future in the past, submitting the past to an existential interpretation. Much of this is worth retaining, particularly the discovery and the admission that the interpreting subject conditions knowledge. But when it is reduced to a system, this attitude ultimately does nothing more than dodge the issue.

Finally, if he is to be wholly faithful to his situation, the exegete must first of all, as a historian, establish the relationship which unites the various interpretations and the event that he is seeking, and at the same time he must try to demonstrate their meaning for his contemporaries, and in this way make the word of God a present reality. Only this meaning gives an openness to the future. Unlike the historian, we dare not state that the past has a meaning; the exegete considers that he knows, through the resurrection of Jesus, the totality of the meaning of what is past. A diagram may help to represent this working hypothesis. Let us call the event which is being sought X, and show the various interpretations which are given to it by converging lines. The task of the historian is to demonstrate the relationship which unites these interpretations with each other and with the focal point X. Then the exegete can draw a circle around the relationship between the interpretations and events, and locate his own position with regard to this totality; he himself becomes, in a fuller sense, an interpreting subject (Z). By so doing, he is challenged to define himself for the future.

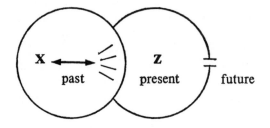

By demonstrating the meaning of the past for the present day, the exegete makes the word of God a present reality. He is a theologian.

The task is a worthy one, but it is difficult, and we do not believe that in the pages which follow we have succeeded in achieving it; but we would like at least to suggest certain lines of thought. We shall set out in succession what it is possible to look for in the focal point—in the event as far as it can be discerned with a sufficient degree of accuracy. Then, after showing how some interpreters, Paul, Luke and John, have tried to make into a present reality in the existence of the believer the presence of that event which is the resurrection of Jesus (what one might call the second degree of interpretation), we shall attempt in our turn to outline the unity of the mystery and its meaning for us at the present day.

A. THE FOCAL POINT

'What exactly happened?' This is the classical question of those who are disturbed by the interpretations of scholars. As we have said in the introduction to this chapter, in our search for the focal point we are not attempting to supply a 'support' for faith, nor to prove the reality of the resurrection. Nor do we wish to give the impression that the task of the exegete consists of nothing more than this search. In our view, aiming at the focal point can form, in exegetical study, only one factor in the search for meaning.

Nevertheless, we regard it as indispensable, and disagree with those who consider it vain and illusory, usually for philosophical or dogmatic reasons.[6] We have said elsewhere[7] that, in order to discover the meaning of the blessing of the poor in the gospel, it is not enough to ascertain the meaning given to it by Matthew and Luke; both interpretations must be related to what Jesus probably said himself. Only when it is related to Jesus, who first uttered it, does the meaning of the blessing of the poor become clear. The focal point (Jesus uttering the beatitude) must be placed in a dynamic relationship with the interpretations (Matthew and Luke). Here too, we have to identify the focal point (the witnesses, the appearances, and the discovery of the empty tomb) in order to relate it to the interpretations of it which we possess. Two basic literary categories are concerned with the Easter event: witness and narrative.

I. WITNESS

By a witness we mean here one who certifies to others the reality of a fact or of an experience. In principle, this testimony is verifiable, for since the experience is communicated to others, they can adopt a position in relation to it. In the case of the resurrection of Jesus, we are faced with a special case in which fact and mystery are united. Thus the witness will be a matter of faith as much as of reason. How can we unravel this complexity? We shall consider here only what is a matter of reason and historical knowledge.

1 *The List of Witnesses*

Following the creed which he hands on to the Corinthians,[8] Paul gives a list of people who have the right to say, 'The Lord appeared to me.' In this list, Paul no doubt included the witnesses who were fundamental, and those, who, since they were still alive, could be consulted.

[5]He appeared to Cephas, then to the twelve. [6]Then he appeared to more than five hundred brethren at one time, most of whom are still alive, though some have fallen asleep. [7]Then he appeared to James, then to all the apostles. [8]Last of all, as to one untimely born, he appeared also to me.... [11]Whether then it was I or they, so we preach and so you believe.... [14]If Christ has not been raised ... [15]We are even found to be misrepresenting God,

because we testified of God that he raised Christ. . . .
A historian will immediately ask whether this list is in chronological order. In fact the conjunction ('then': *eita, epeita*) may require this meaning. Thus shortly afterwards, in v. 24, Paul lists a certain number of events and concludes 'then comes the end' (cf. also I Tim 2:13; 3:10).[9] This hypothesis is strengthened by the way in which Paul introduces the appearance to himself: 'Last of all . . .' (15:8).

These comments are of course justified in respect of the first appearance, to Cephas, and the last, to Paul. As for the others, the same conjunctions are used to list various groups of words: 'Then workers of miracles, then healers' (I Cor 12:28), and it should be noted that in one of the texts quoted above 'then' (*eita*) is preceded by 'first' (*prōton*) (I Tim 3:10; cf. 2:13). Finally, there is a general argument which is not without value: the New Testament is rarely concerned with chronology. Thus it cannot be said that this list follows strict chronological order. This comment is not without interest for scholars of the history of Christian origins, such as Harnack, who chose to construct a course of events which in his view reflected the rivalry of the Cephas and James parties.

However, two series can be distinguished within the list:

Cephas and the Twelve (v. 5)

James and the apostles (v. 7)

It is not impossible that two parallel traditions, originally separate, derive from two different settings. But what matters to Paul, and to us here, is the large number of witnesses.

Between the two verses above occurs v. 6 (the appearance to the five hundred), which is isolated both in form and content. It is usually considered to be a comment by Paul added to the original list, and this is of course true of the remark that most of the five hundred are still alive. But it cannot be denied that the beginning of the verse is an ancient tradition: 'He showed himself to more than five hundred brethren at once.' The last two words translate *ephapax*, which usually means 'once for all': 'the death he died he died for sin, once for all' (Rom 6:10; cf. Heb 7:27; 9:12; 10:10). On the basis of this customary meaning, P. Seidensticker has attempted to reconstruct the history of the tradition.[10] Originally, he suggests, there was only this collective appearance, in Galilee. As for the appearances to Cephas (and to the Twelve) and to James (and to the apostles), they were the result of the growing awareness of the church, which wanted to attribute appearances to the important persons in the community. Finally, with the conjunctions 'then', 'next', the list took on the appearance of a historical sequence, and so increased the credibility of the message because of the large number of witnesses.

This hypothesis is very interesting. It emphasizes that v. 6 is very ancient, and stresses the need which the church has to supply witnesses. From the point of view of literary criticism, the independence of this tradition can be justified. But does this mean that we can conclude that it was earlier than the verses which surround it, and is of exclusive importance? This hypothesis runs up against a number of fundamental difficulties: the almost unanimous affirmation of the primordial fact that there was an appearance to Cephas, and the implication that it is impossible to accept a later appearance than that to the five hundred. Thus we cannot accept it.

2   *The Different Witnesses*

First of all there is *Cephas*, the Aramaic name which Jesus gave to Simon (Mark 3 : 16; Matthew 16 : 18). Most critics accept that Peter was the first to see the risen Christ.[11] This is what, in his own way, Luke suggests when the disciples, returning from Emmaus to tell the others that they have seen the Lord, are told by them: 'The Lord has risen indeed, and has appeared to Simon' (Luke 24 : 34), a formula inserted artificially into the context and no doubt deriving from an earlier tradition. It is interesting to note that, as in our list, the appearance to the Eleven is described immediately afterwards. Here the contact between the list and the gospel narratives is closer than anywhere else. There are other traces of a narrative of an appearance to Peter in a scene which takes place at the sea of Tiberias (John 21) and in fragments in the synoptic tradition: the narrative of Peter walking on the waters (Matthew 14 : 28-33), the confession of Peter at Caesarea (Matthew 16 : 16b-19), and the miraculous draft of fishes (Luke 5 : 1-11).[12]

The appearance that follows is to *the Twelve*, that is the apostolic college, from the official name which records the special circle of disciples gathered together by Jesus before his death (Mark 3 : 13-14; Luke 6 : 12-13). It seems likely that this appearance can be identified with the narratives of appearances to the group of disciples (Matthew 28 : 16-20; Luke 24 : 36-49; John 20 : 19-29; 21 : 2-14; Acts 1 : 4-13).

The *five hundred* brethren are believers who were alive at the time of Paul, perhaps including some women (cf. Acts 16:40). Though the Jews usually counted 'without women or children', this does not exclude them, except as official witnesses in isolation. The number five hundred is a round figure which must not be taken literally. Nor is any date or place given. Most critics refuse to identify this appearance with Pentecost, for in the Lucan narrative there is no trace of an appearance of the Lord, and the number there is 120. The problem should be re-examined on a broader basis, as a function of the Lucan theology of Pentecost. For the time being, it seems impossible to date the appearance to the five hundred. It simply exists.

James is the 'brother of the Lord' (and not the brother of John, the son of Zebedee) and it is him of whom Paul speaks in Gal 1:19 (cf. Acts 12:17; 15:13; 21:18). The appearance to him is mentioned in the *Gospel according to the Hebrews.*

The *apostles*, according to Pauline terminology, which differs from that of Luke, who restricts the expression to the Twelve,[13] form a wider circle than the traditional group of the Twelve. They are those who share the work of evangelization, such as Barnabas, Andronicus, Junias, and Epaphroditus. We may compare this with the remark of Luke concerning the official appearance: 'The Eleven ... and those who were with them' (Luke 24:33).

For the appearance to *Paul*, the reader may refer to chapters 2 and 4.

From the listing of these witnesses, the historian retains one most significant conviction: that those who received an appearance of the risen Christ were numerous. This is the essential point. But on secondary matters there is no certainty. These events can neither be located nor dated. There is firm evidence on only one point, that Peter was the first to encounter the risen Christ; but there is no guarantee that after Paul there were no further appearances. In spite of these uncertainties, the testimony of those who are named clearly refers to the same fact. What is this fact? It is to this which we must now turn.

3   The Fact Stated

When Paul states that Christ 'appeared' to him, as to Cephas,

James, the Twelve and the five hundred, it is his purpose to recall to the Corinthians the testimony of the primitive church, as we have indicated in chapter 1.

I might at first make a naive assumption, naive because it confuses two realities, that Paul and the other witnesses saw Jesus *in the process of* rising. If I do this, I am making the resurrection of Jesus an event of the same kind as that to which Paul bears witness when he states that he went to Arabia or met Peter in Jerusalem and in Antioch. But in none of the canonical writings is there any mention of a witness of the *resurrection as such*. Only the apocryphal *Gospel of Peter* dares to make the Roman guards witnesses of Jesus as he was rising from the tomb.[14] Before criticizing this 'miraculous' presentation, we must ask whether it may not represent the realization of an inner need of our own. Of course we have no wish, like the misguided apologists of the past, to convict unbelievers of deceit; but do we not, in order to bring within the bounds of reason a mystery the essence of which escapes us, seek to imagine ourselves in a very natural human relationship with the act by which God raised Jesus? Such a propensity must be resisted. For man cannot reach God in the secret of his activity; God alone comes to encounter man. This encounter is not a fact which impinges on the senses whatever the circumstances. The act by which God raised Jesus cannot be the object of historical knowledge, that is, of knowledge obtained exclusively with the aid of reason and on the basis of experience. By its nature, it is not a public fount which can be known by all. St Thomas said so long ago.[15]

To what then, do the apostles bear witness? To judge from St Paul, we cannot deduce that they are bearing witness to the discovery of the empty tomb. We show this in chapter 1. Using a term of ordinary experience, 'see, be seen', the apostles testify that 'he showed himself' to them.

Paul, like the others, bears witness to a personal experience. Is this experience nevertheless 'historical', like that which he had when he encountered Peter at Jerusalem or Antioch? In Paul's eyes, it is. In the eyes of the disciples, it is so too. Does it follow that today we can formulate a historical judgment, not only as to whether the testimony is well founded, but concerning the event to which it bears witness? Not in the ordinary sense of the term. *Our historical knowledge is direct knowledge not of Christ, returned from the*

*dead, but of the conviction of Paul who testifies that he has en-
countered him.*

Up to the present moment, remaining faithful to the choice we
have made, we have used the term 'historical' in its limited sense.
Thus the focal point which we can reach is Paul, testifying that
Christ is risen. But we have no right to restrict the work of the
historian to this conclusion, even though he is anticipating the
hermeneutic section of this chapter. The historian does not restrict
himself to establishing the existence of past facts, simply as events
of the past. He also considers the past as 'open' to the future, as a
'present' which concerns us at the present day. When the historian
affirms Paul's conviction, he comes up against a historical event
which provokes him. He is challenged by the personal testimony
of Paul and the apostles concerning their experience of an encounter. He must feel that this testimony touches him directly. If he
is content to relegate it to the past, he overlooks its present significance, for every person who reads this text finds himself called into
question by it. This is the result of historical enquiry carried to its
conclusion by hermeneutics: I am challenged by the apostolic
witness, for ever alive and present in the words of believers.

4   *The Mode of Encounter*

When we add to it the analyses carried out in the first chapters of
this work, does the testimony of Paul have any bearing on the way
in which the encounter with the risen Christ took place? We do not
think so, for the kinds of language used vary so much that we have
no right to treat one of them as privileged rather than the other.
Thus with regard to the appearance to Paul, which are we to
choose: the language of Luke or that of Paul? And Paul's own
presentation varies. These languages are necessary, but they interpret the original fact, so that the historian can retain only what
is common to them. The experience concerns the whole being of
man, and no distinction is possible between bodily and spiritual,
outward and inward. This already tells us much about the mode
of encounter.

When we study Paul's testimony, we find two major elements
that are characteristic of his experience: *the initiative comes from
the risen Christ, and the mission entrusted determines his future.*
These are the factors which, as far as historical knowledge is

concerned, are characteristic of Paul's experience in encountering the risen Christ.

Conclusion

Thus men whose existence and activities are known from elsewhere testify that they have encountered a man returned from the dead. No doubt our contemporaries would like more, so that they could judge the value of this testimony. But a testimony to an experience which is a matter of faith cannot be verified in itself. For the men of the bible, verification cannot relate to God, who does what he wants, but only to man, who may be mistaken. The men of antiquity thought in this way, and judged works from their results. They would never have demanded 'proofs' of God, for the quality of a tree is known by its fruit.

In different terms, modern men proceed in the same way when they evaluate the statements of 'visionaries'. Thus there is no proportion between the social behaviour of Bernadette of Lourdes and that of the hysterical visionaries of La Salpetrière. There is no proof of this, but there are indications which give us guidance concerning the truth of a testimony. A definitive reply is obtained from sources other than clinical facts.

By his acts and his words, Jesus posed a question to everyone: 'Who do you say that I am?'[16] By their testimony concerning the risen Christ, Paul and the apostles put a question to everyone: 'Are you too prepared to believe that Jesus rose from the dead?' This is the historical fact with which the enquirer is faced.

II. THE NARRATIVES

1 *The Discovery of the Empty Tomb*

The reader who is aware of the criticism that we made of this expression in chapter 6 will be surprised to find us using it once again. But we are now examining the documents, regardless of their own point of view, in order to get down to the bare fact, that is, was the tomb of Jesus found empty? Critics disagree strongly on this subject. For some the narrative bears witness to a historical fact, while for others it is a wholly legendary invention.

Let us mention first of all two difficulties. The literary facts do not lead directly to the conclusion that the fact was historical, and this in itself is surprising. But on this latter point, there is some possibility that certain critics read more into the text than it contains. More or less consciously, they interpret it as saying that the body was *withdrawn* from our universe. But the narratives do not say this; they say no more than that the women did not find the body of Jesus in the tomb. Of course in the later texts at least, they are concerned to show that the body was not stolen or carried off. But they do not propose any positive solution. It is at this point that various assumptions come into play in the reader's reaction. From the philosophical point of view, it is scarcely possible for him to admit that the reanimated body could be withdrawn from the world of phenomena, which would amount to its 'volatilization'; from a dogmatic point of view, he might be inclined to appeal to the divine omnipotence. It is very difficult to limit the study of the phenomenon to what the texts strictly say.

The fact itself is so slight that to be called 'historical' it must be placed in a wider context of thought. 'If the historian has not recognized the value of the gospel testimony to the appearances and the resurrection of Jesus and does not accept the mystery in faith, he is bound to have the utmost reserve with regard to the discovery of the empty tomb.... Historicity can only be attributed to an event on some scale and significant in itself.'[17] There must also be agreement about what 'resurrection' means, for this assumption often governs the interpretation of the narrative. For example anyone who follows Bultmann in identifying the resurrection with the present preaching of the church will have no hesitation in declaring all the narratives which 'materialize' faith to be legendary. Others, for various reasons in which the philosophical and dogmatic factor plays a large part, reach a similar conclusion.[18]

Some see this narrative as a *theologoumenon*, that is, a legend illustrating a conviction of faith. For W. Marxsen, H. W. Bartsch and others,[19] the only narrative of any historical significance is that of the appearances; the rest is a deduction on the part of believers. For critics like H. Grass or P. Althaus,[20] the narrative is a legend elaborated on the basis of a certain notion of 'bodily' resurrection: Jewish anthropology demanded that the body should no longer be in the tomb.

Finally, others have sought a natural explanation. At the present day, of course, no one tries to claim that Jesus only seemed to die, but the hypothesis of two burials, worked out by G. Baldensperger,[21] continues to be regarded as valid by some: the women went to the tomb in which Jesus had been placed after his death, but from which he had been removed by Joseph of Arimathea in order to be buried in a more honourable way.

Let us try ourselves to define the historical value of the narrative of the visit of the women to the tomb. First of all, in our view, we must give an answer to the problem which has been raised. Jesus was certainly buried, but in what way? According to rabbinic tradition, those who were executed could not be buried in the tombs of their fathers; they were buried in common tombs near the place of execution, in accordance with the provisions of the law (Deut 21:22-23). According to Roman custom, the bodies of those executed could be returned to their friends. But did this custom, which applied to Roman citizens, extend to others? Yet the texts are unanimous in speaking of a real burial. There are two traditions.

Burial by friends The four gospels mention the request of Joseph of Arimathea to Pilate to be given the body of Jesus. The behaviour of the women, who were certainly amongst those close to Jesus, shows that Joseph was not well known to them. But, as the tradition develops, he acquires Christian qualities which unquestionably he did not originally possess. But this 'christianization' of Joseph does not reduce the value of his gesture; on the contrary, it shows that in fact Jesus had been abandoned by his disciples. As for Nicodemus, who later on occurs in addition to Joseph, it is difficult to base any historical conclusion on him, even though the Jewish historian D. Flusser has succeeded in producing his genealogy on the basis of rabbinic sources. The testimony of John alone is not sufficient to include him among those who were present at the scene. On the other hand, scholars are generally agreed that the narrative concerning Joseph is of considerable historical value.

Official burial by 'the Jews' Another tradition has left traces in the New Testament. According to Paul's sermon at Pisidian Antioch (Acts 13:29), the Jews 'asked Pilate to have him killed. And when they had fulfilled all that was written of him, they took him down from the tree, and laid him in a tomb.' The evangelist John echoes this tradition when he says that 'the Jews asked Pilate that their legs might be broken, and that they might be taken away.' (John 19:31). Although John then goes on to record that Joseph 'asked Pilate that he might take away the body of Jesus' (19:38), he also bears witness to a different tradition. Of what value is it? It is difficult to attempt a harmonization, suggesting that Joseph took over from the Jews, particularly as it was the Romans who carried out the usual practice. On the other hand, Paul's address shows clear signs of anti-Jewish polemic. By attributing the burial to the Jews, Paul is setting out to show that the Jewish people gave definitive approval to his murder. But it is hard not to feel that this other tradition about the burial of Jesus is strange.

An attempted interpretation   M. Goguel believes that there was an evolution from 'ritual burial' (Deut 21:22-23) to 'honoured burial'.[22] J. Schmitt is less certain: probably the Jews carried out the burial as usual, but Joseph, who was also a Jew of some importance, took the matter in hand, so transforming the ritual burial into burial by a friend.[23] Our own opinion as a historian is that Joseph of Arimathea probably carried out the burial of Jesus. We cannot be totally certain, because the parallel tradition cannot be subordinated to that of burial by friends. In any case, this high degree of probability makes it possible to state that the disciples of Jesus could have known the place of his tomb.

After clarifying this essential preliminary issue, let us recall the conclusion permitted by our analysis of the narratives in chapter 6, and attempt to draw some historical conclusions from the internal criticism of the texts, and also from the facts provided by an external criticism.

All scholars should agree that the narrative of the visit of the women to the tomb is not, originally at least, apologetic in purpose. If it was, why should women have been chosen as witnesses, since according to Jewish custom, they were not qualified to give legal testimony? Moreover, why was the visit dated on the 'first day of the week', and not, according to the traditional phrase, on the 'third day'? Finally, why was the narrative never used in this way by primitive Christian preaching, and why does it not occur at all in the apostolic kerygma?

For those who believe that what we have is a record of the visit (H. von Campenhausen, P. Benoit, A. Vogtle),[24] the historical conclusion is obvious. But we cannot share this way of reading the texts.

For those who admit that the narrative has a cult or theological origin (G. Schille, J. Delorme, L. Schenke), it seems 'simpler to admit that the memory of a fact, the visit to the tomb by the women who did not find the body of Jesus, was illuminated by the faith derived from the appearances, and then given stylized form in a narrative suitable for preaching and meditation, at the tomb of Jesus, on the mystery of his resurrection.'[25]

Other arguments of more doubtful value can be introduced. It is possible to point to the difficulty of harmonizing the different recensions, the presence of semitisms in the narrative ('the first of the sabbaths'), and the historical value of the names of the women; it can also be pointed out that Christian preaching at Jerusalem could not have lasted long if the tomb had contained the body of Jesus, for Jewish anthropology required its disappearance. Finally, some consider that in their polemic concerning the theft of the body the Jews never called into question the fact that the tomb was empty.

We may conclude that *the women came to the tomb of Jesus and did not find his body there.*

Beyond this conclusion, there is historical uncertainty about the time of the visit (we tend to the view that it was at nightfall) and its motivation (mourning rather than anointing). The encounter with the angel derives not from historical fact, but from the literary category of the narrative, which sets out to give a meaning to the fact. The uncertainty about these details in no sense diminishes the very considerable probability, if not historical certainty, concerning the discovery of the absence of the body of Jesus in the tomb. A historian can go thus far.

We would have greater reservations about the other details. The tradition of the guards on the tomb is of real value, but the style is that of the epiphany, and can be attributed to a desire to transform a conviction of faith into a narrative. As for the tradition concerning the visit of the disciples to the tomb, it seems to us too dependent upon that of the women, too late and too apologetic in its tendency, to make historical conclusions possible.

Can the historian go a step further and state that the body of Jesus was taken out of the universe, or, within the perspective of faith, 'taken on' by the risen Christ? No, for a reply to this question is not his affair. The historical fact is that the body of Jesus was not there; nothing can be said about where it was, nor about its sudden 'disappearance'. Whatever hypothesis is envisaged to take account of the historical fact, the historian must stand back and deny any competence to state what became of the body; he can say neither that it was lifted up in to heaven, nor that it was to be found in the tomb. These two interpretations are an attempt to give, to questions left unanswered by historical study, answers based on philosophical or dogmatic assumptions, whereas at the present stage of our inquiry, we are attempting only to establish the reality of historical facts.

2 *The Gospel Narratives of Resurrection Appearances*

Unlike the story of the finding of the empty tomb, these narratives raise very few problems with regard to the fact of the appearances, particularly as there is evidence for them in the list of witnesses of which Paul reminds the Corinthians. Have they anything to tell the historian who is trying to identify the bare historical facts?

The total number of appearances If we combine the different gospel narratives, we find five official appearances: the universal mission (Matthew; ps.-Mark), the Eleven (Luke, ps.-Mark), the Ten (John 20), the Seven (John 21), the ascension (Acts); and three or four private appearances: Mary Magdalene (John, ps.-Mark) and the holy women (Matthew), Emmaus (Luke, ps.-Mark) and Thomas (John). The historian cannot reconcile these narratives with the appearances mentioned in Paul's list. We must conclude that the tradition was not fixed, and that the number of appearances was not necessarily limited to those mentioned there.

Location It is not possible either to locate or to date the different appearances, for the places and dates given by the evangelists are difficult to reconcile.

According to Matthew, there was only a single appearance, in Galilee. According to Luke, there were none except in Jerusalem. John records a series of two in Jerusalem and one in Galilee. The conflict cannot be resolved by a harmonization in which all these appearances take place one after the other, in Jerusalem on Easter Day (Luke, John) and the eighth day (John), then in Galilee (Matthew, John) and back in Jerusalem for the ascension (Luke). This harmonization is unacceptable, because it is contradicted by definite statements in the texts. According to Luke 24:49, the disciples are to stay in Jerusalem until the day of Pentecost, which excludes any appearance in Galilee. By contrast, Matthew and Mark state that the meeting place is to be Galilee. These different indications of place cannot be reconciled. Here we have a sign that the purpose behind them is not historical but derives from the writers' theological point of view. A historian cannot base his arguments on data of this kind.

Nor can he rely upon the chronology, which it seems impossible to establish. The 'forty days' mentioned in Acts 1:3 conflict with Luke 24:51, according to which the appearances seem to have ceased on the evening of Easter day. There is a further conflict between John 20:22, where the Spirit is given on Easter day, and Acts 1:4 or Luke 24:49, which promise it on the day of Pentecost. It is obvious that Luke 24 (appearances concentrated into a single day at Jerusalem) and John 20 (where the structure of the narrative is based on the pattern of a week) are examples of literary construction. The forty-day pattern is also artificial, so that the appearances cannot be limited to this period. We find ourselves back at what is implied by St Paul, as well as the list in I Cor 15: the appearance to the five hundred could have taken place long after the first appearance to Peter.

To conclude, it seems that the appearance to Peter was deliberately placed before the private appearance to the disciples at Emmaus, and the appearance to Mary Magdalene could have taken place at any time from the first day of the week on.

The nature of the appearances   What exactly took place? We find in the narratives what is absent from the list of witnesses, a particular way of looking at what took place. Are we then to suppose that we are watching a film of what happened? Alternatively, must we give up any attempt to ascertain details? Both tendencies are found amongst exegetes; but it is not impossible to avoid these extreme positions.

From the literary form as we have established it above, we can draw certain historical conclusions. The initiative is always attributed to the risen Christ; in other words, the disciples do not think that the appearances originated with them. They are called upon to identify the risen Christ with Jesus of Nazareth. They become aware that they have to continue the history of him whom they have recognized, but it is a history of a radically new kind by comparison with his former ministry. Finally, they understand that from that moment they are sent out as missionaries and that the church has really been founded. Here we have the historical experience of the first disciples.

We can even establish certain details. Two aspects are simultaneously emphasized. The risen Christ is set free from the normal conditions of earthly life; he appears and disappears as he wishes, like God in the Old Testament theophanies (Gen 18; Num 12:5; Josh 5:13, etc.). On the other hand, he is not a ghost, and consequently there is an emphasis upon tangible realities. Jesus shows his hands, his feet, his side, invites the disciples to touch his wounds, and even takes food. But these details cannot be isolated without risk of error from the other 'spiritual' aspect found in the narratives. These two aspects are an attempt to express what Paul states concerning the resurrection body: it is a *sōma pneumatikon*, a 'spiritual body' (I Cor 15:44-49) for it is a body, his body, which has been transformed by the Spirit. In order to encompass this mystery, which is beyond our conceptual grasp, Paul links together two apparently contradictory terms: body and spirit. The procedure in the gospels is the same: the risen Christ is a body and a spirit, or more precisely a spiritual body. We must be satisfied with apprehending this eschatological reality by means of representations which seem to be contradictory as long as the real contradictions in them are not resolved in the higher unity of the mystery.

As far as the words of the risen Christ are concerned, we cannot establish them as *ipsissima verba* of Jesus. These words unquestionably bear the mark of the theology of the primitive church. It is hopeless to try to pick out some words which are 'more' original than others. Through all of them, the church is acknowledging and recognizing her Lord.[26]

The context in which the appearances are described may recall the circumstances in which they were produced. During a walk, a liturgical gathering, a meal, a fishing expedition, the risen Christ suddenly manifests his presence. In so saying, we are certainly not stating that the gardener whom Mary met was a person belonging to this earth, a man like any other, or that Mary understood that from now on Christ was present in every man. Such a way of interpreting the texts has no connection with what we find in the gospels.

Conclusion

The material is scanty. Could it have been otherwise? The richer the meaning of an event, the more its interpretation tends to swamp the narratives which convey it to us, and the less it is possible to separate 'historically' the fact and its interpretation. However, neither scholarly method nor the apprehension of faith ask any more. In fact, as the historian pursues his search for the actual event, he approaches closer and closer to it but never actually reaches it, being well aware that the past as such always remains the past, and lies beyond the grasp of it which he now possesses. This is not to deny the existence of the actual event as something other than a product of human subjectivity, but it is a recognition that someone has intervened in the process by which it is constituted as a 'historical fact'. Thus the historian can say of this event, the resurrection, that it is bound to be the point at which all interpretations intersect, the focal point to which they all relate.

Nor can the believer ask for more, at least in the search for the bare fact. (We shall turn later to an examination of the terminology of the gospel as the vehicle of interpretation.) The decisive event with which he comes face to face, and which is always an open question for him until he responds to it through his faith, is not the resurrection itself, but the apostolic faith in God who has raised Jesus from the dead.

The historian, however, can say something about the nature of the appearances. For the disciples, the risen Christ was something they had experienced in the course of their own lives. In talking about this experience, two extremes must be avoided. The 'spiritualizing' extreme consists in reducing it to a purely subjective experience, deriving from a purely terrestrial source. The witness of Paul and the descriptions of the evangelists contradict this interpretation: the experience, one may say, was an 'objective' vision with regard to its source (someone other than myself) with a subjective effect (within myself). The 'literalist' extreme tends to assimilate the experience to an ordinary event, not an interior but an external event. Paul's expression 'spiritual body', and the freedom of movement of the risen Christ according to the evangelists, show that in fact the risen Christ cannot be called 'external' to the disciples in his new being. He becomes so in a terminology which makes a spiritual reality objective. But it is pointless to appeal to the distinction between 'interior' and 'external', between 'spiritual' and 'tangible', for this would be to restrict the risen Christ to the categories of space and time.

By way of a positive formulation, we venture to propose the following. *The spiritual experience of the disciples, not purely subjective, repeated, and shared by them, was communicated through the medium of contemporary terminology and their religious tradition, and in particular through the medium of their faith in the general resurrection at the end of the ages.* This attempt at a definition is and must always remain inadequate, if only because of what it attempts to do. Thus the historian will prefer to have recourse to the actual terminology of the gospels. The intention of that terminology is not to describe a thing, an object, but the presence of a subject which is not of this world. The risen Christ is present (initiative), he is linked with the past (recognition) and he gives a command for the future (mission).

Finally, the historian may attempt to retrace, with great caution, the course of events following Jesus's death on the cross. Here is the reconstruction proposed by a systematic historian whose concern throughout his work is to recover the bare facts.

'The risen Lord met Peter, and shortly afterwards the twelve in Galilee, where they had fled after the catastrophe. For them, this meeting was an invitation to return to Jerusalem and to preach the good news of the risen Christ. In the community which gradually formed, resurrection appearances were still often experienced, beginning with an appearance before a crowd of more than five hundred witnesses. Thus Jerusalem, the centre of the new movement, can claim the honour of being the principal location of the appearances. . . . We shall maintain the hypothesis according to which the return and the first arrival of the disciples at Jerusalem was for the feast of Pentecost. Just as the Master threw Jerusalem into turmoil shortly before the feast of the Passover, so too did the disciples at Pentecost, with their new, unheard of message.'[27]

This removes the need to justify the strange interval of seven weeks between the Passover and Pentecost, during which one would have to suppose the disciples spent their time at home, doing nothing.

Much of this reconstruction can be retained. We may perhaps hesitate on one point, that of the 'flight to Galilee' after the day of the crucifixion. There are many who have described this hypothesis as pure romance. But if we do not attempt to insist that it took place during the night between Friday and Saturday, so that the disciples' return home could have taken place after the end of the sabbath, it is easy to understand how the appearances in Galilee, which according to the statements in the gospels cannot be dispensed with, in fact took place. An exception may be made for Peter, who played a distinctive part during the Passion and who may have remained at Jerusalem. This would not exclude the possibility of a visit to the tomb by Peter. We are inclined to accept the rest of the reconstruction; in particular, for the disciples to have gone up to Jerusalem round about Pentecost would be in accordance with many of the statements in the New Testament.

B. INTERPRETATION

We set out to define as far as possible the outlines of the past event, within the limits of the early interpretations found in the New Testament. It would be naive, however, to suppose that from then on it is easy to describe its significance. This is a lengthy task, and must take into account the various kinds of terminology used to interpret the event. At the beginning of this book we established that the earliest terminology made use of two different patterns to represent the event: resurrection from amongst the dead, and exaltation into glory. We noted that the first pattern, that of resurrection, had a tendency to absorb the second, that of exaltation. We were able to find traces of the latter, especially in passages in a liturgical style, but we had to recognize that it was the terminology of resurrection, though influenced by that of exaltation, which eventually prevailed in the New Testament: Jesus rose from the dead.

This is the fundamental terminology which the believer has to use. It is not perfect, as we said in chapter 1. In itself, it says nothing more about Jesus than about Lazarus, who was also raised from the dead. The narratives of the appearances help us to comprehend the vastness of the mystery of Christ; but in spite of the precautions taken by the narrators, it is still possible for the reader to go on thinking of the risen Christ as a body come back to life. But Jesus did not simply 'survive'; he can no longer die, he lives for ever. Thus this language has to be complemented by the aspect of the exalted Christ: the resurrection leads to the exaltation.[28] In this way, the interpretations which we are now going to examine all bring to light riches which are concealed in the original formulation.

In spite of its imperfection, it is against this terminology that all interpretations must be measured: it is the *standard terminology*. In saying this, we are consciously limiting the field of rational investigation which is open to the scholar and the exegete. On what grounds, then, can such privileged status be conferred upon the terminology of a single period? Why should not this primitive formula (which some people nowadays consider to be incomprehensible) simply be replaced by another: 'Christ is alive'? The question is worth asking, because the reply that is given is too often simply a paraphrase, which there is no concern to justify methodologically.

Exegetes find themselves torn between two extreme solutions. For some, all that is necessary is to repeat what is said in the New Testament: 'Christ is risen'. For others, it is enough to be freely inspired by what is found in the scripture, for example by saying, 'Jesus is alive'. The former are slaves to the letter, while the latter have broken away from it. In fact both seem to have failed to recognize the true nature of revelation.

God has spoken in his son Jesus; that is to say, not through a unique personality who might be supposed to have expressed himself in isolation from his own age. In order to understand fully the mystery of the incarnation, we must see in Jesus a man who was conditioned by the language and the culture of his own time. Thus the word of God was itself uttered in a specific terminology. Just as a Christian turns to the redeeming act of Christ to receive his salvation from it, similarly he turns to the language of the New Testament in order to communicate the message of Christ. There is no need for a Christian to be enslaved to this terminology by repeating it just as it is, in a way which becomes inappropriate when our contemporaries fail to listen to it. But it is no better to break away from it in order to adapt one's language to the chance variations of a succession of subsequent civilizations. Of course the word of God must be uttered in a manner intelligible to modern man, but for this to be done it is necessary to maintain contact with a terminology dating from a certain period and characterized by a certain culture. This is the touchstone of our terminology.

We have asked: 'On what grounds should a privileged status be conferred upon the terminology of the bible?' Our reply is: 'In

the name of faith in God who spoke definitively in Jesus Christ.'
In our view, this terminology must be adopted by the believer who
considers that he possesses full revelation in the bible; and it can
be accepted as a provisional hypothesis by an unbeliever. In any
case, this is the point of view from which these pages are written.

The immediate purpose of the preceding stages has been not to
identify the focal point and to state its meaning, but to become
familiar with the standard terminology upon which all later interpretative discourse depends. That is why we have limited our study
to the formulas and gospel narratives through which the Easter
faith was uttered. We shall now look at three New Testament
writers who interpreted the Easter message. This will better equip
us to undertake our own interpretation of this message.

I. LUKE: CHRIST IS ALIVE

In his gospel, Luke does not convey the Easter faith solely by way
of the 'resurrection from the dead' pattern of thought. In his gospel,
the angel at the tomb was not content, as in Matthew or Mark, to
announce, 'He is not here; for he has risen.' He began by saying,
'Why do you seek the *living* amongst the dead?' (Luke 24:5). And
when he writes more freely, it is the word 'life' to which he constantly returns. At the central point of the Emmaus story, his narrative masterpiece, the disciples speak as follows: 'Some women
. . . came back saying that they had even seen a vision of angels,
who said that he was alive' (24:23; cf. Mark 16:11). In the second
part of his work, Luke sums up the events at Easter: 'He presented
himself *alive* after his passion by many proofs' (Acts 1:3). Again,
when the Roman procurator Festus is explaining Paul's case to
King Agrippa, he does not speak of resurrection, but says that the
accusers of Paul 'had certain points of dispute with him about their
own superstition [the disagreements between Pharisees and Sadducees: cf. Acts 23:7-10] and about one Jesus, who was dead, but
whom Paul asserted *to be alive*' (Acts 25:19).

This terminology is a novelty in the gospel tradition, and to
understand its significance, we must first of all turn to Jewish usage.
We have seen that there were two ways of expressing the triumph
of God over death: 'God makes alive' and 'God raises from the

dead'.[29] Luke, it seems, has restored to prominence one of these forms of expression, that which is concerned more directly with the reality of life than the way that reality is reached. Nevertheless a shift of emphasis has taken place. Whereas the Jews speak of the act of God who 'makes alive', Luke talks of the condition of Jesus who 'is alive'. He does not merely take over a Jewish usage, nor does he simply 'translate' it, but reinterprets it by using it of a present reality.

That is why, at the source of Luke's terminology, one may seek an experience of a different kind, that of a Greek popular setting. By emphasizing the rejection of Paul's preaching by the Areopagus at Athens (Acts 13:31), Luke raises the problem of the encounter of the Christian message, formulated in Semitic terms, with Greek civilization. He is concerned for the intelligibility of the Christian message. It may be suggested that Luke, aware of the ambiguity of the word 'resurrection' for the Greek imagination, may have preferred the equally biblical term 'life', using this word for the actual result of the action carried out by God in raising Jesus.

By doing so, did Luke create a genuinely new language to describe the Easter event? We do not think so. He did not attempt to substitute it for the former language, but simply placed the two side by side. He expressed the same reality, not in its actual occurrence (God raises, God makes alive), but in its result (Jesus is alive). In the final analysis, the two expressions are interchangeable. But the same Semitic meaning has to be read into it. Both terminologies are valid, but both are subject to criticism.

To appreciate their relative value, let us begin by assessing the errors of interpretation to which both can lead. When I say 'Jesus is alive', am I giving a sufficient description of the new life of Jesus? How does it differ from that of Mozart, who, for those who listen to his symphonies, is always alive? The great risk is that of failing to recognize that the statement affirms a reality; the life of Jesus could be reduced to the imaginary product of a love which is stronger than death, whereas it is the outcome of the action of God who makes alive. The condition that has been brought about must be related to the original act which alone provides its true meaning.

It is this initial act which is emphasized by the term 'resurrection'. Thus this standard terminology provides a measure of the risk inherent in the derived terminology, if it were to replace the older terminology, instead of being a predecessor and preparation for it.

Moreover, Luke does not replace the primitive terminology by a different language, but considers it necessary in certain cases to transpose it into the terminology of 'life'. By so doing, he also emphasizes that he who is alive is the same Jesus of Nazareth who died. Thus this language can provide an authentic interpretation of the mystery of Christ; but if its true meaning is to be retained, the earlier terminology must always be borne in mind when it is used.

II. PAUL: CHRIST LIVES IN ME

Whereas the evangelist Luke is attempting to give his readers a better account of the event of the resurrection, Paul, who is not an evangelist but a founder and leader of the church, does not offer the same kind of transposition concerning the existence of Jesus; he is attempting to tell those to whom he is writing how a believer should live as a function of the Easter message. When we read some texts from Paul in this light, we shall see that the presentation of the risen Christ acquires a new dimension by contrast to the letter of the gospel. We do not wish to give here a 'theology' of the resurrection according to Paul, but to give a modest account of some aspects of Paul's hermeneutic of the resurrection.[30]

When he refers to the event of the resurrection of Jesus, both in traditional formulas and in original terms, Paul does so in order to instruct or change the life of those to whom he is writing. This was of course necessary in a letter, but there are other more profound reasons, as we shall shortly make clear.

1 *The Resurrection of Christ and the Resurrection of the Dead*

The example that immediately comes to mind is that of the First Epistle to the Corinthians, chapter 15. Paul did not quote the catechetical formula (which we have already analysed) in order to teach it for its own sake, but to base upon it a faith in the resurrection of the dead: 'Now if Christ is preached as raised from the dead, how can some of you say that there is no resurrection of the dead?' (I Cor 15:12). The event derives its meaning by relation to men: 'Christ has been raised from the dead, the first fruits of those who have fallen asleep' (15:20). In this way Paul shows that the past event matters here only because Jesus is 'the last Adam' who 'became a life-giving spirit' (15:45). The meaning inherent in the fact is at once evident. Paul is interpreting: he is demonstrating the supra-temporal significance of the Easter event, which is valid until the end of time.

2   *The Death and Resurrection of Christ, the Pattern of the Believer's Life*

In other passages, it is not simply the fact of the resurrection which offers us hope, it is the complete sequence of death-burial-resurrection which becomes the prototype of the present existence of a believer. This issue is no longer a guarantee of the future, but the understanding of a new kind of existence.

> [3]Do you not know that all of us who have been baptized into Christ Jesus were baptized into his death? [4]We were buried therefore with him by baptism into death, so that as Christ was raised from the dead by the glory of the Father, we too might walk in newness of life. [5]For if we have been united with him in a death like his, we shall certainly be united with him in a resurrection like his.... [8]But if we have died with Christ, we believe that we shall also live with him. [9]For we know that Christ being raised from the dead will never die again; death no longer has dominion over him. [10]The death he died he died to sin, once for all, but the life he lives he lives to God. [11]So you also must consider yourselves dead to sin and alive to God in Christ Jesus (Rom 6:3-11; cf. Col 2:12).

This is not the place for a detailed exegesis of this hotly disputed passage. For our purpose, it supplies some new information about Paul's hermeneutic of the resurrection.

As before, the resurrection of Jesus is introduced in this text only in relation to our own transformation. What took place at a single moment has an effect which lasts for ever. Paul makes this quite clear elsewhere: 'He died for all, that those who live might live no longer for themselves but for him who for their sake died and was raised' (II Cor 5:15).

This act actually determines a new structure of being. For in this passage the event of the resurrection is related to death, not in so far as Jesus rose from the dead, but in that the death of Jesus is considered as such; like the resurrection, it plays a vital role in the existential life of the believer. The duality of death and resurrection is replaced by that of death and life, better adapted to the situation of the believer. When speaking of Christ, Paul normally uses the term 'resurrection', and the same is true when he is speaking of the resurrection to come. But for the believer here below, Paul speaks of 'life', at least before the period of the captivity epistles. Thus when he is explaining the ultimate purpose of baptism into death, Paul appeals to the resurrection of Christ, in order to say not that a baptized person will 'rise again', but that he must 'live' a new life: we have been baptized, he says, 'that as Christ was raised from the dead by the glory of the Father, we too might walk in newness of life' (Rom 6:4). The reader would probably expect a different conclusion, perhaps 'so we shall rise again' or 'so we have been raised'. Paul does not seem to be able to say that we have already been raised from the dead (cf. Col 3:1; Eph 2:5-6). This would have been too definite an image, and had to be reserved either for the initial act in Jesus Christ or for the final act in all men. Between the two, the effect of the resurrection of Jesus Christ is to introduce us to a 'new' life. There is a further consequence, and that is that the existence of the risen Jesus is a new life: 'The life he lives he lives to God' (6:10). And so Paul returns to the 'exaltation' terminology when he declares 'to this end Christ died and lived again, that he might be Lord both of the dead and of the living' (Rom 14:9).

3 The Risen Christ is the Life of the Believer

In the eyes of Paul, the Lord initiates and guarantees our future and provides the pattern of our existence. In addition, he is already present to us in two ways.

The glory of the Father is not only at the origin of the resurrection of Jesus (Rom 6:4) but also constitutes the body of Christ which is a 'body of glory'; and this glory is at work within the believer. Of what, then, does the expectation of the Lord Jesus consist, Paul asks in his letter to the Philippians? He 'will change our lowly body to be like his glorious body' (Phil 3:21). To grasp the meaning of this first statement, we must remember that the word 'body' (*sōma*) cannot simply signify the material body here; it signifies the expression of the human person (cf. I Cor 6:12-20). We may paraphrase as follows: 'Our person, which is wretched here below, will be transformed by being made like the glorious person of Christ.' Or again, in Paul's own words, 'Though our outer nature is wasting away, our inner nature is being renewed every day' (II Cor 4:16; cf. Rom 8:16; Eph 3:16). The glory of Christ, communicated by the Father, acts not only upon the outer man (that is, on what we would nowadays call the body in the sense of flesh and blood) but upon the inner man, on what Paul calls the body which is destined to be manifested later. There is a continuity between these two conditions, thanks to the glory of Christ, which, starting here below, penetrates this 'inner man'. The whole man is renewed at the very depth of his being, 'that what is mortal may be swallowed up by life' (II Cor 5:4). These ideas are drawn even closer together in a number of texts which show Christ himself living within us. Paul here is not giving a theoretical account; he identifies himself with those to whom he is speaking, and who, like him, identify themselves with the Christ whom he knows is alive and is the source of life:

> It is no longer I who live, but Christ who lives in me; and the life I now live in the flesh I live by faith in the Son of God, who loved me and gave himself for me (Gal 2:20).

These words are true of every believer. Faith does not simply consist of accepting truths, even the truth that Christ is risen; it is a relationship between two persons, and a relationship which develops into a communion, as is set out in the text quoted above. What Luke says of Jesus, Paul says of the believer: he does not state that he has risen, but that he is alive. In a certain sense, Paul is the living Christ. He knows and feels himself to be in a relationship with Christ as with someone other than him on whom he depends totally, without whom to live is no longer to live, and with whom everything becomes love.

But this love is crucified love. Paul never forgets this. Strictly speaking, he does not proclaim the resurrection, he proclaims the cross (I Cor 1:23). But in order to proclaim the cross as the event of salvation, it is necessary for the resurrection to have taken place and to reveal the meaning of the cross. Thus the mystery of the risen Christ is there, but it is always related to that of his death and his cross, whether it is a question of our future resurrection from the dead or of the present structure of our being and our everyday existence. The personality of Christ, crucified and alive, is henceforth expressed by way of the life of the believer.

III. JOHN: THEY SHALL LOOK UPON HIM WHOM THEY HAVE PIERCED

For John as for Paul, death on the cross is the worst possible humiliation. But for John, unlike Paul, the resurrection is not simply what gives meaning to the ultimate humiliation, it is already present at the very lowest point of descent upon earth. The cross *is* the beginning of the glorification: in this 'hour' Jesus is exalted, 'lifted up'. John is not simply an heir of the classical terminology which places the resurrection after the crucifixion; he also integrates with it the primitive terminology which speaks of the exaltation at the very moment of death. He is a legitimate heir of the tradition, but with the freedom of the son who takes over the legacy, he transforms the words themselves and the symbols.[31)]

Notice that John has no inclination to use the classical vocabulary which describes the resurrection as the act of God setting his Son free from death. Yet he is aware of the term. Does not Jesus himself state to the sister of Lazarus, 'I am the resurrection (and the life)' (John 11:25)? But he is talking here of the final resurrection. On one single occasion (two, if one includes 21:14) the evangelist adds a footnote to an episode which it would be difficult for the reader to interpret. The reply of Jesus, 'Destroy this temple, and in three days I will raise it up' (2:19), is explained: 'When therefore he was raised (*ēgerthē*) from the dead, his disciples remembered ...' (2:22). Similarly, after the entry of Jesus into Jerusalem, we read, 'When Jesus was glorified (*edoxasthē*), then they remembered ... (12:16). For John, the resurrection is identical to the glorification. Jesus is glorified in the 'hour of the Father' (12:23, 27; 17:1) which is 'his hour' (7:30; 8:20; 13:1). This is his rendering of the theme of the fulfilment of the divine will, expressed in the synoptic tradition by 'it is necessary'.

This glorification, foretold here for the hour of Jesus's death, was attributed in Paul and the synoptic gospels only to Christ lifted up to heaven. For John, it shines through into the earthly life of Jesus. From this point, the gospel narrative is penetrated and transformed by the glory which is always present. Of course the synoptic gospels too are composed in the light of the Easter mystery, but this light does not normally shine beyond the framework in which the evangelist recounts the events of Jesus's life. Thus the healing of the blind man of Jericho is presented simply as a mighty miracle; but the context in which it is narrated gives it a symbolical value which can only come from the redactor, who himself was enlightened by his Easter faith. The blind man calls Jesus the Son of

David, thereby anticipating the triumphal entry into Jerusalem; and when he is healed he follows Jesus. He has recovered his sight and we may say that he has become a disciple (Mark 10:46-52). In the Johannine miracle of the healing of the man born blind, the significance of the episode is quite different: it becomes a 'sign' which, by way of what is carried out, indicates the quality of him who is doing it. It directly signifies the glory of him who is the light of the world (John 9). Thus John can say: 'We have beheld his glory' (1:14).

John is not content with demonstrating the retroactive effect of the Easter glory. He finds several new symbols for expressing the act of the resurrection itself. Note that each time it is not God but Jesus himself who is the agent. The understanding of the relationship between Jesus and his Father is made clear: there is an identity of action between Jesus and his Father.

The first symbol is that which we met in the appearance to Mary Magdalene (20:17), that of 'ascending to the Father'. This says that the resurrection of Jesus is going to the Father (13:1), using the symbol of an ascent, which as we shall see is an extension of that of the 'lifting up' on the cross. We can nevertheless discern behind the Johannine presentation the pattern of descent from heaven and re-ascent to heaven (3:13), which may derive from a Hellenistic mentality. All the same, this symbol is firmly located within the direct line of the classical tradition of exaltation (cf. 6:62).

A second symbol is found in the Good Shepherd discourse:

[16]I have other sheep, that are not of this fold; I must bring them also, and they will heed my voice. So there shall be one flock, one shepherd. [17]For this reason the Father loves me, because I lay down my life, that I may take it again. [18]No one takes it from me, but I lay down of my own accord. I have power to lay it down, and I have power to take it again; this charge I have received from my Father (10:16-18).

To rise again here is like putting a garment back on (13:4, 12), 'taking up his life', the life which, according to the tradition of antiquity, was universally longed for after death. The inexorable 'it is necessary' of the synoptic tradition is personalized here in the Father's commandment, which itself should be understood as an expression of his love. There is also an indication of the fruit of Jesus's voluntary sacrifice, that is, the union of all men.

The third symbol is more closely linked with the resurrection as such, since this word itself is used, but in a sense which may be understood at a more or less profound level. To the Jews who protest against his clearing of the sellers and money changers from the temple, Jesus says, 'Destroy this temple, and in three days I will raise it up' (2:19), a statement which is at once ironically repeated by his enemies. The verb 'raise up' here translates *egeirein*, which as we know means 'raise' (from the dead). Thus John's explanation is natural: 'When therefore he was raised ...' (*egeirein*). This saying is pregnant with the Johannine theology of the temple, which does not signify the church (as in Paul) but Jesus Christ. From this temple rivers of living water shall flow (7:37-38) and water will in fact come out of his pierced side (19:34). The new temple is in fact the risen body of Jesus, a body from which rivers of living water flow abundantly and for ever (Rev 21:22ff.).

Is this the risen body or the crucified body? In Johannine theology the distinction is not clear. For in addition to the previous texts which are marked with the sign of glorification, John has tended to concentrate the attention of his reader on to the 'lifting up' of Christ upon the cross. The verb *hypsōthēnai*, usually found in the passive, clearly refers to the 'passion' which Jesus underwent by 'being lifted up' on the cross. But this cross is not a shame nor apparently a scandal. In the eyes of John it becomes a throne of glory, on which he who gives life is to be found: 'They shall look on him whom they have pierced' (19:37), as in the past the Hebrews lifted their gaze towards the serpent who was 'lifted up', so that they should receive life from it (Num 21:8). This 'token of de-liverance' (Wis 16:6) is now fulfilled: 'As Moses lifted up the serpent in the wilderness, so must the Son of Man be lifted up, that whoever believes in him may have eternal life' (John 3:14-15). 'When you have lifted up the Son of Man, then you will know that I am he' (8:28), for 'I, when I am lifted up from the earth, will draw all men to myself' (13:32). And John comments: 'He said this to show by what death he was to die' (12:33).

The cross is not strictly identical with the glorification, but is the beginning of a movement which concludes in the ascent to the Father. When we examined the two kinds of terminology, resurrec-tion and exaltation, we tried to show that, if they are rightly under-stood, the resurrection is the inauguration of the exaltation. John makes clear that the lifting up inaugurates the exaltation. But it must be noted that when the matter is expressed in this way, there is no interval of time between lifting up and glorification. John avoids the temporal pattern of the resurrection terminology, and makes contact with history in a different way.

By concentrating upon the lifting up upon the cross, John specifies the only point valid for faith at which his narrative makes contact with history (apart from the witness to the resurrection appearances). But there is a risk in this way of looking at the matter, that of 'docetism'. For it might be possible to suppose that at the death of Jesus his spirit or his divinity ascended to heaven, while his body remained on the cross. John guards against this risk by including the narratives of the empty tomb and the appearances; they make it clear to the reader that Jesus is alive in his entirety. As he says to Mary Magdalene, he is ascending to his Father, completing the movement which has begun on the cross. As he says again to Thomas, to correct the misunderstanding to which believers might be subject concerning the 'vision' vouchsafed to the disciples: 'Blessed are those who have not seen and yet believe.' Faith does not consist of seeing the risen Christ, but in contemplating Christ lifted up on the cross.

IV. THE PRESENT DAY

Anyone who listens to our fathers in the faith and is convinced of the focal point, can come to only one conclusion: it is not enough for him to contemplate this focal point in the residual state in which the historians have left it.

Even within the apostolic period, the New Testament gives evidence of a constantly renewed effort to 'translate', depending upon whether circumstances required an apologetic, theological, anti-gnostic or anti-Jewish presentation. And this is found not at the conclusion of the New Testament tradition, but at its very origins. All language is interpretation as the function of an experience, and all language is conditioned by a particular environment. Interpretation is not a luxury, but a duty which is still incumbent upon us today.

We do not have to choose from the various interpretations that which seems least remote from our own mentality. Why should we choose one rather than the other, and what right have we to reject those which reveal other depths? The duty of hermeneutics is to consider everything and to repeat nothing as it is, but by referring to a fundamental and standard terminology to translate the presence of the risen Christ into a language which is accessible to contemporary minds.

This is not an easy task, for the attempt to draw the numerous interpretations in the New Testament into a synthesis carries a great and no doubt fatal risk of giving a privileged status to one or other of them. The task must nevertheless be undertaken, in the assurance that other interpreters will bring different nuances or even different points of view. We shall set about the task by drawing on a necessary distinction in respect of the persons concerned (God, the disciples, Christ), a distinction which relates to the spheres of revelation which are recognized as fundamental: eschatology, ecclesiology and christology.[32)]

1   *The Act of God*

Behind the two original terminologies, those of resurrection and exaltation, we perceive a single agent: God raises Jesus, and God exalts him. The first kind of terminology links God to time; the second tends to abstract from time in order to contemplate the mystery directly. This freedom of usage is an indication that the act radically transcends our categories. In fact it remains absolutely hidden, and even the apocryphal gospels fail to bring it completely into the light. Deduced by believers from their experience of the living Jesus, it was either related to the final act of God in raising the dead, or was understood as an exaltation into glory at his side.

In one sense, the historian can place a date upon this act, on the basis of the change which he can identify in the disciples, and which they attributed to the intervention of God in his Son. But in another sense, no 'date' can be given to this act of God. There is no witness who gives any authority for locating it at a particular moment in history as it is known to us. The mention of the 'third day' indicates no more than a decisive turning point in the divine intervention. As for the 'first day of the week' this relates to a liturgical and not a chronological interest. In this sense, the event cannot be called 'historical'. Brought about in the 'eternal silence of God', it is not located in the course of the history which is accessible to human reason.

And yet there is firm testimony to it on the part of earthly human beings. Though it is not accessible to historical science, it dominates history and takes account of it. It shows that this new kind of existence belongs, in a new way, to history, though its true reality is not restricted by this. In the vocabulary of exegesis, this act is described as 'eschatological'. It is an 'end of time', attained by Jesus and recognized by the believer. This is the way in which Paul understood his encounter with the Lord on the Damascus road: the 'revelation' vouchsafed to him was not the unveiling of a truth hidden hitherto, but the proclamation of an unexpected event, something that had 'come about'. The 'God ... who gives life to the dead and calls into existence the things that do not exist' (Rom 4:17) 'raised from the dead Jesus our Lord' (4:24). A particular man has lived out what was foretold for the people of God at the end of time (Ezek 37). The breaking in of this divine act inaugurates a new world, not in order to replace the present world immediately, but in order to give history a new dimension, and to give it its meaning. This act also gives the believer the possibility of a new way of 'knowing', for he has been brought into contact with him who lives for ever.

Thus the act of God is not presented in itself, but only in its consequences. Is this 'negative' theology the last word that is said to us, and must we abandon all attempt to grasp the mystery? How can we pass from silence to words? Here the gospel narrative intervenes. Though we cannot attempt to tie down the act of God in thoughts and words, it is possible to place oneself immediately in front of it and before it, so that it can come and respond to the expectation that this sets up. The end of Jesus's life still belongs to history, and forms the threshold of meta-history. The texts do in fact tell of the visit which the holy women made to the tomb of Jesus, and the historian can accept that this fact is probable, together with the statement that the body of Jesus was not there. What does this fact signify for us?

Let us deal with two main interpretations. Some consider[33] that the tomb found empty on Easter morning is the trace left by the resurrection of Jesus in the world of phenomena. The absence of the body symbolizes the beginning of the lifting up of the universe into the new world of the resurrection. In this way the tomb, in which the body of Jesus is no longer to be found, takes on a theological meaning: God has begun the new creation.

Others prefer to follow Matthew in taking as the symbol of the act of God raising his Son not the empty tomb itself, but the open tomb or the stone rolled back from the tomb. Symbolizing the triumph of God over death, the open tomb states by way of the gap it leaves, by the sign of absence, the change that has come about in a world subject to death. If God has conquered death, this means that death is no longer meaningless. The sublime consequence of this is that life has a meaning. Note that this possibility becomes real to us not by way of words—resurrection or exaltation—which claim to explain everything, but in the symbol of the empty tomb, which is an 'opening' to meaning. The act of God is not an event which follows the death of Jesus, it is the manifestation of what took place therein.[34] In the death of Jesus, new, eschatological and definitive life is present. We do not mean by this that Christ rose at the very moment of his death. This would contradict the nature of the language that is used, which postulates a period of time between the different acts of death and resurrection.[35] But, remaining within the historical world of symbols, we may say that, as in certain Russian icons, Jesus dies with his eyes wide open, for he is entering eternal glory; he is raised into glory from the very moment of his death. With the holy women, in the full light of the risen sun on that first day of the week, we are able to set out, to begin, to search. This symbol manifests the explosive power of the original act which transcends the search for meaning.

2 *The Manifestation*

This meaning is presented to us in the historical manifestation of him who lives for ever, and who therefore gives the meaning of life. This manifestation took place when Jesus encountered his disciples, in what we call the 'appearances'. From the point of view of the disciples, they consisted of an experience which took over their whole being. There is no question of discussing whether it was an inward or outward experience, and whether it was spiritual or tangible. The appearances were no doubt firmly rooted in the community which the disciples formed in the name of Jesus before Easter, and which they must have spontaneously set up once again after Easter; but they were a radically new experience. An interpretation of this historical fact which sets out to give a meaning for us at the present day must be upon two levels. It must take into account the distance which separates us from the fact and also that of the archetypal presence which it forms within the being and existence of the believer.

The archetype   These appearances are the event which founded the church. Luke makes this quite clear by closing, with the symbolic number of forty days, these privileged encounters between the Lord and his disciples. In this sense, the appearances are exemplary, but unique. They are the historic roots for the starting point of Christian faith and of the church. In a historical experience, the witnesses saw the Lord. As we have seen, this took place during a community meal, a walk, and a fishing expedition. Suddenly, they were in contact with the living Christ. By enabling them to recognize Jesus, God gave them faith: the disciples saw and believed.

It is a different matter for believers who are not privileged witnesses. They have not seen *what* the disciples saw, but they know *that* they saw it. A believer knows the meaning of the appearances only through the proclamation made here and now by the church, the body of Christ. In this proclamation, through his word and his life, the risen Christ is manifested today.

The path towards faith   The gospels normally narrate the encounter between the Lord and his disciples according to a pattern which remains typical of every encounter. It does not consist in the revelation of some particular fact, but of the progressive recognition of a person. The pattern is in the first instance a passage from a tangible experience to a spiritual conviction. The first contact takes the form of touching or seeing, but is subordinate to the recognition of the identity of him who is present. We must in fact go further: the recognition takes place, as on the road to Emmaus, at the moment at which the Lord disappears, and the joy of the disciples is unmixed *after* the Lord has left them (Luke 24:52-53). The final outcome of the encounter is not a vision, but faith. This is one of the paths to faith, starting with the earthly Jesus and arriving at the risen Christ. Doubt itself forms part of this process. In other words, one does not encounter Christ as one encounters a person in the street, but rather as the adventure of love between two beings takes place. This brings us back to the Semitic conception of truth, dialogue and testing.

In the fourth gospel, the pattern is no longer that of a process leading from the tangible to the spiritual, but from hearing to indwelling. Mary Magdalene herself does not turn towards the Saviour because she has seen him, but because she has heard him utter her name. And if she testifies little after she has 'seen' the Lord, the reason is that the term 'seeing' has ceased to denote something tangible. The interpretation given by John is best seen in the discourse at the last supper, when Jesus promises his disciples that he will come again.

[18]I will not leave you desolate: I will come to you. [19]Yet a little while, and the world will see me no more. [20]In that day you will know that I am in my Father, and you in me, and I in you. [21]He who has my commandments and keeps them, he it is who loves me; and he who loves me will be loved by my Father, and I will love him and manifest myself to him. [22]Judas (not Iscariot) said to him, 'Lord, how is it that you will manifest yourself to us, and not to the world?' [23]Jesus answered him, 'If a man loves me, he will keep my word, and my Father will love him, and we will come to him and make our home with him. [24]He who does not love me does not keep my words; and the word which you hear is not mine but the Father's who sent me' (John 14:18-24).

As in the whole of the fourth gospel, it is the question, based on partial understanding, which indicates the purpose of the passage.[36] For Judas, Jesus likened the Easter appearances to a 'coming' and therefore to a 'parousia'; his error arises from a typically Jewish conviction, that the parousia must be a glorious manifestation, a definitive triumph over the enemies of God. Judas confuses the two 'parousias', that of Easter and that of the end of time. He therefore asks why the promised experience is reserved only for those who are privileged (cf. Acts 10:40-41: 'not to all the people'). He is unaware of the nature of the age of the church, and even of its necessity as a period of the secret manifestation of the Lord of glory. This brings with it another error. Judas prematurely regards the disciples and the world as on the same level, failing to recognize the true nature of the relations of Jesus with those who live on earth, which is one of love. The distinction which creates an abyss between the disciples and the world in the Johannine sense is the presence or absence of love, the basis of all authentic contact between the Lord and his own until the fullness of time. This is the sense in which the problem was posed and in which Jesus resolved it. If in the term 'manifestation' Jesus is alluding to the Easter appearances, his purpose is to show the spiritual nature of the 'coming', described by some as 'mystical', in contrast to the splendid triumph of the parousia. The pattern of an outward process, assumed by seeing and even by hearing, is replaced by that of 'making our home', of indwelling. All standing apart, all encounter is abolished; in the personal relationship of love, duality becomes unity.

If this is so, then the Johannine interpretation gives a reply to the problem raised by the appearance of the risen Christ to Saul on the Damascus road. When we compare Luke's narrative and Paul's mentions of the experience, we conclude that they broke down the Lucan framework of the forty days. The privileged period of appearances in the strict sense is not defined by this lapse of time, but by the apostolic age in the course of which the church was founded. It seems that John wanted to take this interpretation even further, by isolating the feature which runs throughout the manifestation of Jesus to his disciples. In the vocabulary he chooses, he wishes both to allude to the Easter appearances and to suggest the permanent significance of the promise made during the address after the last supper. This address was of course made in the first instance to the Twelve, but through them is meant for all who, without having seen, believe. For believers in the future, the Easter appearances become the authentic manifestation of the living Christ, or, to use the language of exaltation which takes no account of time, of the Lord exalted into glory.

The structure of faith   The gospels allow us to conceive in concrete terms of what the 'presence' of the Lord can be at the present day. It is not to be reduced simply to an encounter in an individual relationship: the Johannine individualism does not exclude but assumes the more 'ecclesial' presentation of the common tradition. As we have noted,[37] according to the Jerusalem tradition the appearance narratives are dominated by a typical structure of initiative, recognition and mission. Now this structure also governs the way in which the believer enters into and remains in contact with the Lord. For the believer as for the disciples, the initiative is always that of the Lord, but it becomes the presence of the risen Christ by way of the apostolic kerygma of the present-day church, for the proclamation of the church is the actual word of the Lord. The recognition of Jesus of Nazareth, which was essential for the disciples, becomes for the believer the knowledge of the historical experience of the first disciples. Finally, the mission entrusted to the disciples is still imparted today: there is a direct continuation of that mission. Thus the 'presence' of the risen Christ is realized not in a simple dialogue, but in a dynamic relationship which, within the present, unites the past and the future.

The initiative of the risen Christ guarantees the objectivity of the encounter. We shall say nothing more about this, because it belongs to the secret of the believer's existential life. On the other hand, we need to go more deeply into the two dimensions of recognition and mission.

Thanks to the apostolic testimony, the believer still can, and always must, turn towards Jesus of Nazareth. To authenticate his actions, he measures the situation in which he finds himself not directly against the risen Christ himself, but against Jesus of Nazareth who spoke and lived on earth. What part has the act of God, raising his Son, to play in this? It ratifies the existential life of Jesus, that is, his teaching and his life of sacrifice and love. I do not make contact with a glorious being from whom all traces of the crucifixion have vanished, but with him whose wounds are still visible, though they are glorious. This is how Jesus appeared to his disciples: 'See my hands and my feet.' Thus we encounter not a Christ from whom all personal identification has been removed, but him who laid down his life for his friends. Thus the necessary return to the past is a return to the gospel of love and death; it is an encounter with the 'lamb standing as though it had been slain' (Rev 5:6), with him who is called 'faithful and true' seated upon a white horse and 'clad in a robe dipped in blood' (19:11-13). Love is perfectly expressed in Jesus; in this sense, love is behind us.

It is also before us, for this horseman 'judges and makes war' in righteousness (19:11). For the appearances do not amount to the simple 'visual' recognition of him who was known in the past; by way of the aspect of 'hearing' they open the way to a relationship to the future, which from henceforth is to govern the existential life of the disciples. They have to develop the riches of the present which have been given to them by the risen Christ. The promise of the Holy Spirit, or the gift of the Spirit here and now, makes possible a mission which is not simply a continuation of the pre-paschal activity of the disciples, but is the assumption and trans-figuration of this work by the presence and activity of the Holy

Spirit. While the church was founded in principle by the appearances to the disciples, its life can continue only if it seeks from God the coming of the final kingdom. In this sense, God is ahead of us.

The authentic presence of the Lord assumes that these three dimensions are always there. By the initiative of the Lord who comes upon me I am charged; I am called to manifest in the world not only that death has been conquered in Jesus, but that the love which Jesus lived gives meaning to life. By the dialectic relationship which unites the past and the future, the believer is preserved both from the escapism of false contemplation and from earthly activism.

3 *Jesus Christ*

At the conclusion of the act of God and at the origin of the manifestation stands he whom we call Jesus Christ, both Jesus of Nazareth, a person who lived and died at the beginning of the present era, and Christ, a person acknowledged in faith who lives for ever. This double designation recapitulates what we have just said and raises a problem: what is the personality of Jesus Christ? A reply is not as easy as one might think at first. Bultmann refuses to recognize anything of Jesus Christ except the proclamation made by the church, for Christ is not the promulgation, more or less 'glorified', of Jesus of Nazareth, but one who is risen for us in the kerygma. Marxsen, on the other hand, is unwilling to bypass the problem of Christ; he considers that he who is present even today in apostolic work is Jesus of Nazareth. In our view these two views are excessive, and we consider it possible to follow the New Testament in saying something about Jesus Christ. This can be done not by repeating the numerous 'titles' which the primitive church accorded to Jesus (Son of God, Christ, Lord) but by interpreting the gospel narratives in the light of the theologies of Paul and John.

Jesus Christ and his body To profess faith in Jesus Christ is not simply a matter of recalling the earthly existence of Jesus of Nazareth, someone who lived as a being of flesh and bone. It is to declare that this man is still alive, today and for ever. How can Jesus of Nazareth, we stumble against the mystery of a personality which transcends our ordinary categories, and which, nevertheless, to assimilate it to the hearing of the kerygma or the memory of then we perceive and affirm such an existence? If we refuse simply we wish to affirm.

For various reasons, and particularly for fear of reducing the risen Christ to a kind of reanimated corpse, some scholars propose simply to talk no longer of 'resurrection' but only of 'life'. They consider that in this way they are following Luke, who in fact sometimes seems to be imposing this kind of interpretation, as we have already noted. But if we replace one term by the other, we are forsaking Luke, who unceasingly takes up the basic language of resurrection. To act in this way would be to close one's mind to the reading of the gospel narratives, which sooner or later require the terminology of resurrection. It would also be to bypass and not to face up to the problem raised by the 'body' of Jesus Christ. First, the expression 'He is alive' cannot be made either a panacea or a definitive formula. In order to be faithful to the New Testament, we still have to speak of the *bodily resurrection*. What do we mean by this? Basically we are declaring that the being of Jesus does not only live on the memory of men, but that he has been personally carried over in his entirety into the life which never ends; the object of the divine act of resurrection is the being of man, which is transformed in its totality. In other words, the risen Christ is the same as Jesus of Nazareth, but a Jesus who has been entirely fulfilled in glory. So far, so good. But something more is required: what about the body of Jesus Christ? Scholars agree that to speak of the bodily resurrection of Jesus is not to affirm that the resurrection body is in simple continuity with the earthly body. This would be to assimilate the resurrection of Jesus who lives for ever unduly to the 'resurrection' (which should strictly not be so termed) of Lazarus, who was to die again. To use Paul's term, it is a 'spiritual body'. At this level and at this degree of generality, every believer recognizes in this the common terminology of faith. But the divergencies appear as soon as one attempts to define what is meant by the adjective *bodily*. Here the scientific or philosophical assumptions which govern our view of the body intervene. Thus with courage and modesty we must attempt to show what is implied by the two traditional terminologies, that of the Hellenistic world which is the most familiar to us, and that of the Semitic world, which will assist us to give a better present day expression to faith.

In its simplicity and its complexity, the language of the gospels is the most appropriate for communicating the Easter message. That can be taken for granted. Nevertheless, a correct understanding of it assumes that the reader still approaches it with the simple eyes of a child, and this is unfortunately rare. What takes place when a reader reflects more or less consciously on the gospel accounts?

According to the most widespread anthropology, the immortal soul of Jesus took on his body once again after three days, with the one distinctive feature, that although appearing to survive in a form similar to that of earthly life, the body was endowed with properties which enabled it to escape from the material and mortal condition. But what is the connection between the *spiritual body* which appears and the *earthly body*, the remains of which were placed in the tomb?[38] As an extension of the previous way of envisaging the matter, and as an echo of the discovery of the absence of the body from the tomb, some have gone on to speak of a *reanimation of the body*, though with an immediate qualification: the bodily resurrection is not the *simple* reanimation of the body, although it is that as well. Others consider that the discussion can be raised to a higher level by talking of the *transcendent* reanimation of the body.

This terminology is coherent. But it runs up against considerable difficulties which we must now summarize by re-examining these last statements. The term *reanimation*, even when qualified by adjectives of little significance (except to admit the inability of the noun to say what it is intended to mean), has no right to supplant nor to qualify that of resurrection.[39] Furthermore, the representation of the risen Christ in the form of a surviving body effectively defines the individuality of Jesus and, as in the gospel narratives, counterbalances the human tendency to regard the appearances as an illusion;[40] but it tells us nothing about the total dimension of the body of Christ. As an attempt to describe this dimension we find the statement that in addition to the personal body of Jesus, there is also the body of Christ which is the church. This connection is indispensable but artificial, like the philosophy which attempts to think of the particular before the universal.

However firm its basis, the above terminology cannot claim to be the sole language of faith, excluding every other. In fact elements have intervened which do not derive from faith itself. Thus underlying this terminology there is a dualist anthropology, according to which the body is something material which, with the soul, forms a human being. Moreover, while it is true that the body of Jesus disappeared from the eyes of the women who came to the tomb, nothing is yet said about the disappearance itself. Thus to speak of a reanimated body is to superimpose upon a scriptural fact a representation which derives from a particular philosophy.

Thus it seems opportune to us to suggest another way of expressing the mystery, derived not solely from Semitic anthropology, but also from the recent conclusions of genetics. This admission of dependence must emphasize the hypothetical and provisional nature of the argument which follows.[41]

First of all, we must remember that the body is not something material which forms part of my nature as a human being, but the site of my expression and my communication with others. At the present day, this definition can be made more precise, for contemporary genetics calls into question the stable autonomy which was naively attributed to the human body by making it the exclusive property of an individual. It leads to the view that in the universe there circulates a total body of 'materials' which are the object of unceasing exchanges. For example, of the sixty million million cells which compose the human organism, five hundred million are renewed every day! The notion of a body determined by the absolute property of certain atoms gives place to that of *structure*;[42] by way of this structure, the living being, or, to use 'humanist' language, the liberty of man is expressed. *My body* is the universe received and made particular in this instant by myself. This definition makes clear the twofold dimension which is now included in the notion of a body. It is in direct relationship with the universe, and it is continuance. My *historical* body is constituted by the various relationships which I establish in the midst of the universe.

To talk of a bodily resurrection is to state that a being who is dead is called to everlasting life. It is no doubt concerned with the dead body, but what is a *dead body*? Is it still he who has just died? The reply is subtle, but clear. Yes, it does in a certain respect still symbolize my self to others; and when it has decomposed, the tomb, in some civilizations at least, remains the symbol which makes it possible to identify the person whose earthly life has ceased. But the reply to the above question must be negative, if it is meant to imply that the dead body has a *special* relationship with him who was alive; for it returns to the undifferentiated universe of matter. Throughout his earthly life, a particular man has left traces of his objectivization in the universe. His dead body is no more than the ultimate conclusion of this process. It is what from now on no longer exists except to others and does not express the particular individual in any special way.

Far from attempting to reduce the resurrection to the reanimation of a dead body, we must affirm that the whole of the historical body, including the corpse, has now been transformed into the Christ. This does not mean the dissolution of the personality into an undifferentiated world. The continuity which unites the risen Christ to the man who lived on earth is therefore not determined by the taking on of some chemical or organic particle of what was his body, but by two associated factors. First of all, and essentially, it is guaranteed by the same God who brought it into existence and brings it back to life; secondly it is maintained in being because the object of the divine action is not a 'spiritual soul' and a 'material body' in turn, but a being who was a living body, a person who was previously maintained in being throughout a continual transformation of the parts which composed him.

Let us try to apply these reflections upon resurrection in general in order to achieve a better understanding of the particular case of the resurrection of Jesus. One difference is immediately obvious, whether by reason of the person (Jesus), the time (the brief delay) or the observed fact (the absence of the body). But there is also a resemblance: Jesus shares the whole of the human condition, apart from sin, and his body is like ours. Thus we have the right to think of his bodily resurrection in similar categories. Jesus wholly escaped from death; he was glorified in his historical body, that is, in everything which throughout his existence was the site of his expression and his communication with others, and which was consecrated to death, even to his final death on the cross. That is, he was glorified in that by which he personally entered into a relationship with the universe of men and things. His corpse too forms part of this historical body, and as such it is taken on by the glorified Christ. The precise way in which it was taken up again is beyond our understanding, by virtue of the mystery which is the basis of this taking up, and which is wholly the object of faith. The essential lies elsewhere, for anyone who understands that the resurrection consists in reality of a change in the relationship between the natural body and the self which is expressed in it. Before his death, and during his carnal life, in the 'body of sin', Jesus was like any one of us (though by his own will), subject to spatio-temporal conditions which limited his human expressions and were an obstacle to him.

After the resurrection, this body of flesh was transformed wholly into a pure vehicle of action for his person, an action which was not limited by anything else any more, not by space nor time nor matter. On the contrary, the universe is from now on wholly at the service of his manifestation, as his appearances to the disciples bear witness. Thus in the special case of the resurrection of Jesus, which alone has taken place within our historic time, the body placed in the tomb does not simply return to the universe to which it belongs, but is wholly taken up by the living Christ who transforms the universe by integrating it to himself.

Some would go further and discuss in detail what happened to the body of Jesus. But scripture tells us only that the women came to the tomb and did not find the body of Jesus. This is the basis of the language in which the disciples were able to speak. To attempt to give more detail is to venture into the realm of hypothesis, and to forget that the resurrection is an object of faith and not of scientific knowledge.[43] The concerns of faith in the risen Christ lie elsewhere.

We must now ask what *the body of Jesus Christ is*. Our reply depends upon our understanding of the role played by Jesus of Nazareth. If it is true that Jesus is what he proclaimed, a man with a unique relationship to all men, his presence is coextensive with the universe. To use other words, which are not meant to blur the individuality of Jesus nor the continuity of his risen body with his historical body, the body of Jesus Christ is the universe drawn up and transfigured in him. In the words of St Paul, Christ is from now on expressed by his body which is the church. Thus the body of Jesus Christ must not be limited to his 'individual' body. In the same way, in the poems of Isaiah, the figure of the Servant of Yahweh points at the same time both to a person and to a collective, and so in fact to Jesus Christ: in him, the alternative between the individual and the collective has been transcended. Jesus Christ is both a person into whom the universe is drawn, and the universe made personal in him.

Jesus Christ and the universe In every kind of terminology, the New Testament states that from now on the dominion of the risen Christ extends to the whole universe. He has 'all authority in heaven and on earth' (Matthew); he went down into the underworld (I Peter 3:19); he ascended into heaven, so passing through the different levels of the universe (Paul, Luke). From the moment of the very earliest christology, the church was concerned to show how the Christ lifted up into heaven in glory remains in a close relationship with his church on earth.[44)] The Lord is Emmanuel, God with us (Matthew), he is he who sends the Spirit (Luke), he who re-establishes the covenant of believers with his Father (John). This active presence with regard to the universe is described by Paul in the Epistle to the Corinthians, at the precise point where faith in the resurrection of the dead is based upon faith in the resurrection of Christ. Now the resurrection of the dead is not the final act of history:

> [22]In Christ shall all be made alive. [23]But each in his own order: Christ as the first fruits, then at his coming those who belong to Christ. [24]Then comes the end, when he delivers the kingdom to God the Father after destroying every rule and every authority and power. [25]For he must reign until he has put all his enemies under his feet. [26]The last enemy to be destroyed is death. [27]'For God has put all things in subjection under his feet.' But when it says, 'All things are put in subjection under him,' it is plain that he who put all things under him is excluded. [28]When all things are subjected to him, then the Son himself will also be subjected to him who put all things under him, that God may be everything to everyone (I Cor 15:22-28).

The note that runs through this passage, as in Revelations, is that of a conflict of universal dimensions. Christ appears here as the Lord, whose task is to fight the good fight of faith, in the warrior style of Ps 110. Thus while it can be said that Jesus has attained the fullness of life, it must also be stated that he continues to struggle with and in believers, so that the kingdom of God may come. These overtones make it impossible to treat eschatology (the *eschaton*) as a present reality in an oversimplified way. Paul understood it like this, and was not satisfied with stating that in Christ he possessed all good things; but he travelled through the inhabited world to found and maintain the churches of Christ. Hope is a fundamental dimension, not only of the appearances of the risen Christ, but of Jesus Christ in person.

Jesus Christ is Lord of the universe. This statement can be understood, so long as the aspect of 'becoming', of the hope which is still characteristic of it, is not maintained. The question is simply that of expressing in spatio-temporal language a reality which no longer exists in time. The situation is similar to that of the 'resurrection' language: only at the end of time will Jesus be truly Lord of the universe. This language has a dynamic function: it calls upon the believer to manifest in the world the love which is the supreme value and reality.

Jesus Christ, my Lord   As Lord of the universe, Jesus Christ is none the less the Lord of each disciple. Jesus Christ said so when he was on earth, demanding from each in his own place an unconditional love. The church has affirmed this, by showing that now Jesus has been raised up to heaven, he does not remain inactive until the parousia comes.[45] Paul recognizes in him the principle of his existence ('It is no longer I who live, but Christ who lives in me') and the author of his coming glorification: 'The Lord Jesus Christ ... will change our lowly body to be like his glorious body, by the power which enables him even to subject all things to himself' (Phil 3:21). Thus Jesus Christ is in relationship not only with the universe in its present and future totality, but is also in personal relationship with each believer. But what can the presence to us of a being who is no longer of this world, and who nevertheless embraces every part of it, actually consist of? The exegete often runs the risk of giving undue weight to one of these two aspects, the individual and the collective, to the detriment of the other, either by objectivizing the idea of an individual Christ standing beside him, or by allowing his personality to be absorbed in some pan-christological essence. These statements will depend largely upon philosophical or dogmatic assumptions;[46] and the only question which we wish to raise here is that of the relationship with Christ, as between one person and another. When I speak to Jesus Christ, am I speaking to another person?

I begin by following St Paul, and making a personal profession which is inspired by his own words. I too know and feel myself in a relationship with the living Christ as with someone other than myself, on whom I depend entirely, without whom to live would no longer be to live, and with whom everything becomes love. And yet I believe I have dismissed the conception of the risen Christ as a Jesus who has survived. For Christ is no longer simply an individual, numerically distinct from others; he also has a particular and exclusive relationship with all men at all times. To admit this factual presence to universal humanity is to mutilate

Jesus Christ. The pre-Easter Jesus has become the Easter Christ for ever. Thus the problem consists of maintaining simultaneously the relationship to a unique person, and manifesting his presence to all time and to all beings. In describing this new condition of existence, the threefold dimension of the appearance narratives is full of significance.

Where is the individual, where is he whom I can encounter? By way of the element of *initiative*, I know that the Christ is other than myself (I do not say 'an' other); of course everything is already there, and yet this other remains someone unknown whose features I cannot descry; I can only confess his sovereign presence, by which I am touched and seized. The *recognition* which he calls upon me to make determines the location of his individuality; the history of his love took form and shape during his earthly life. There is no need to dream of some other configuration. Its 'historical' individual expression is to be found there. During his life, he concentrated the experience of the people of Israel, which itself symbolized humanity on its way towards God. This concentration formed his personal being for ever. But it had not yet displayed its explosive force, which is manifested in the entrusting of a *mission*. Here the risen Christ affirms his presence throughout the centuries. This is the way in which Jesus will be expressed from now on: his body is the community of disciples, the church. His person is still there, acting and recognizable through his body; but it calls upon us at once to turn back to the pre-Easter Jesus to know exactly what he wants to say at the present day.

In the whole breadth of the Easter message, it is the risen Christ speaking to us and living in us. At the level of profundity which St Paul reached, the perception of identity in difference is such that language is no longer capable of uttering the mystery of 'two in one'; the situation is similar to that of Master Eckhart, who found himself incapable of maintaining his own being before the sight of God and who called himself God in the creative act. But the Pauline 'mysticism' is more balanced, thanks to the variety of expressions in which it attempts to set out the mystery of the presence of Christ.

If I wish to hear and encounter Jesus Christ, I find him in the word and in the bread: the past fact of Jesus of Nazareth becomes a present reality for me, first of all in the preaching of the church which takes me back to the Word of Jesus of Nazareth, and then in the eucharist which makes the sacrifice of the cross and his glory a reality here and now. Through both, kerygma and eucharist, it is the same Jesus of Nazareth, whom God raised from the dead and who, in the form of the Word and in the form of the act, makes himself present here and now.

Finally, if I am to talk to Jesus Christ as an individual person, I must go back to Jesus of Nazareth. But my situation is not exactly the same as that of the disciples who accompanied him on the roads of Palestine. They were in the presence of a man who was coming to the end of a life, each moment of which was subject to change. We, like the evangelists, find ourselves face to face with a being who has achieved the end of his life, who has finally passed into glory, who at the supreme moment of his death recapitulated, and by his resurrection expressed the real meaning of his life and his existence. Every moment of his life takes on significance, because it is pregnant with the totality conferred upon it by the glory of the resurrection.

Finally, let us try to sum up the attitude of the believer. I aim at and pursue the establishment of the kingdom of the love of Jesus Christ in the entire universe; but I keep before my eyes the image of Jesus on the cross. The message which I preach is of course a proclamation of love (I dare not say, of glory); but it is a proclamation of crucified love which conquers still because of the confidence which I have in the righteousness of God. I recognize the face of Christ in that of my human brother, disinherited and persecuted by the unrighteousness of men. I struggle that he may be less disfigured in his body of flesh, and that he may discover the meaning of suffering. By looking on him whom they pierced, they will realize that God is capable of giving full life to what does not deserve to be called life. The act which God carried out in restoring life to his Son Jesus is still carried out here and now.

CONCLUSION

This work was conceived and composed in Christian faith, though in an attempt to remain faithful to contemporary scientific requirements. On the latter point, it is clear that my own views are not shared by all scholars; for example, with regard to the literary relationships between the gospels, or the possibility of working back to the pre-redactional state of the Pauline letters or the gospels. That is why the conclusions to which I come will not all be endorsed by scholars. But I have tried to make clear the points on which I have frankly left the beaten track, in the hope that my conclusions will be acceptable to them.

On the other hand, as far as the language of faith is concerned, it is possible that some readers, accustomed to the classical formulas of the catechism or of preaching, will find themselves disorientated, and perhaps even disturbed, as if my conclusions were not in accordance with traditional language. On the contrary, I consider that they are in the direct line of the tradition, though I know that they call into question a number of customary expressions. Thus the reader will be led to repudiate a number of ways of speaking which entail difficulties for the profound understanding and the communication of the Easter message. Let me give some examples. It is useless to look for 'proofs' of the resurrection or to use the fact of the empty tomb to demonstrate it. The resurrection should no longer be seen as a 'miracle', nor should the gospel narratives be read in naive fashion as 'biographies' of the risen Christ. One must avoid imagining the appearances as taking place in a 'marvellous' way. Finally, above all, the resurrection of Jesus must no longer be spoken of as a 'problem' which has to be resolved; the reader is not an 'observer', he is called upon to reply and to commit himself.

This book is not entitled, like so many other, *The Resurrection of Jesus*, but in a more complex way, *The Resurrection of Jesus and the Message of Easter*. In fact, as it was written, the expression (not the fact) 'resurrection of Jesus' has come to seem both full of significance and at the same time ambiguous. The title calls on the reader to place the formula and even the event in an existential context; we have fallen into the habit, either in the catechism or in theological reflection, of treating the mysteries of faith in isolation, as though when we approach them, we were cut off from their context and location; whereas we learn to know them as we encounter them. I do not myself, by my efforts of imagination and my scholarly ability, 'raise' Jesus by demonstrating his eternal features; the risen Christ himself comes to meet me. It is under these conditions that anyone enters into contact with the Good News, the human condition common to all, and the theological condition peculiar to the believer.

The paths which lead to Jesus Christ are varied. I have described elsewhere[1] how the church brings us into contact with Christ through three fundamental activities: the message of some one who is holy (a mother, a friend, a priest), the message of the Word (the catechism, theology), and the message of the text (holy scripture). The first is the ordinary path of faith, and the two latter are related to each other. The Word assumes the reference to scripture, for the scripture text remains the norm of Christian faith, while the text is a call to communicate. Thus our 'theological condition' is that of men who have set out on their course within a tradition, and are tied to a certain language. It is not a matter of repeating indefinitely the language of scripture; this must be interpreted. To interpret is to say in a new way what has been said already, that is, to feel oneself bound to the primordial and original terminology, which, as we saw above, is our 'standard terminology'. We cannot overemphasize this relationship, because it is the only defence against the haphazard 'gnostic' approach, which is a continual threat to anyone concerned to adapt his language to make it intelligible to his contemporaries. In this work, I have tried as an exegete to remain within my limits, and to restrict my ambition: not to usurp the place of the 'holy person' nor impose the terminology of exegesis as 'the word', but to travel from the 'text' to the mysterious point at which God comes to meet us.

This theological condition makes specific the common condition of man, which some people imagine they are escaping when they read the texts and draw conclusions from them. I would like to say, and this whole book shows, that man has no immediate access either to persons or to 'events', but that everything comes to him through the medium of language. This statement may seem banal, and yet it is not always the controlling assumption of the process of interpretation. We encounter a particular language, and the humility of the scholar consists in listening to it as best he can.

In fact, as we have just recalled, the language of the New Testament is manifold. Let us also recall the extent to which the terminology of the bible has become strange to us, as a result of a long and valid hellenization of Christian language. At the present day, we are conditioned by the Greek mentality, and we often reason as if the course on which we have set out is unique. But as was shown in chapter 1, biblical anthropology hardly corresponds at all to the body-soul dualism to which we are accustomed. Once this is realized, conceptions of 'personality' vary depending upon the anthropology accepted, and the 'body' does not play the same role, since it is not conceived in the same way. Finally let us recall that the conception of 'history' has considerably changed in the last fifty years; historical fact cannot be separated from the activity of the human being who knows it, and makes it what it is.[2]

These considerations lead us to a final problem: how are we to pass on to others the experience which we have received in the utmost depths of our being? The communication of the Easter message depends amongst other things of two factors: the results of exegesis and the disposition of our interlocutor.

An exegete will not be satisfied with supplying a simple statement of what exactly took place in the past. He also seeks to indicate the meaning which the texts have at the present day for his contemporaries. His procedure is similar to that of the evangelists themselves, for they were not concerned to record the reality of certain historical facts; they were announcing Good News, which was itself rooted in these events, and which then came to encounter the hearer. Similarly, at the present day, a Christian does not wait for the outcome of the subtle task of exegesis, or its results concerning bare facts, but for the meaning of the texts. Here the work of the preacher and the exegete is one and the same.

But there is a difference in the terminology in which the proclamation must be made. The texts are always the same, but the point of view from which they are considered changes. At the time of Melito of Sardes or Hippolytus of Rome, the mystagogic catechists presented the fruit that was there to be tasted in a Christian life which had already made considerable progress; they assumed that the hearers were convinced of the reality of the events which they recorded. Thirty years ago, what seemed important was to demonstrate this same reality, to strengthen faith against those who denied it.

At the present day, the proclamation of the Easter message by way of the gospel narratives requires something else again. For the most part, our contemporaries have heard a false apologetic which sets out to prove the resurrection of Jesus either by the empty tomb, or by the appearances. In this way, more or less consciously, the resurrection is assimilated to a simple reanimation of the body, and if they are taken literally, the gospel descriptions strengthen this unfortunate impression. Heaven is thought of as a place, and the texts which speak of ascent into heaven are taken literally, as are the forty days preceding the ascension. For this and other reasons, there is a tendency to reject the reality of the resurrection along with these illusory representations of it. Or at least no one dares to speak of it any more. Some fall back on the idea of the immortality of the soul, and so abandon any intrinsic relationship to the body. Others give up thinking anything, telling themselves that everything finishes with death. Faced with this, a believer has a right to make clear the exact meaning of the texts, struggling to lead his interlocutor forward without meeting him head on. Above all, he will not attempt at the present day to obtain a hearing for the word of God by *de-historicizing* the text in order to present some eternal truth, for that would be to relax into the liberalism which our forefathers already rejected. Nor will he *de-mythologize* the text in order to express the Good News in a more appropriate fashion; for the principle of this de-mythologization derives not from revelation, but from a philosophical anthropology which claims to become the norm of truth. Nor will he do so by *repeating* either the text or the interpretation given in the gospels or by those who comment upon them. He must *translate* the gospel message into contemporary language. One of the privileged methods available is to give due value to the symbolic dimension of the texts, and I have tried to show how this can be done by a few examples in the appendix to this work.

Finally, this task of translation must be undertaken in complete freedom, no doubt with the risk of betrayal, but the task must be carried out in order to set free the word of God.

The outcome of these pages should be a command calling for authentic freedom. Interpretation is the task not only of the exegete, nor only of the preacher; it is the task also of the Christian believer, in the first instance through his 'holiness', but also through his 'word'. Accepting the standard terminology from tradition, the believer undertakes in total freedom to pass on, to communicate his experience. Is it not then Christ who speaks through him? Let him always remember the origin of his message:

I AM THE FIRST AND THE LAST, AND THE LIVING ONE: I DIED, AND BEHOLD I AM ALIVE FOR EVERMORE, AND I HAVE THE KEYS OF DEATH AND HADES (Rev 1:17-18).

To Help Communication

Here, by way of example, are some suggestions about the way of approaching and presenting particular gospel narratives of the Easter events. I offer them as an exegete, with no claim that they say all that can be said, but with the aim of indicating what might be the wrong course and to suggest more appropriate considerations.[1]

A. THE VISIT BY THE WOMEN TO THE TOMB

1 *Three Dangers to Avoid*

a. Recording the bare facts for their own sake Describing the 'discovery of the empty tomb' in such a way that it tends to become a proof of the resurrection, or even a step towards faith. But according to the texts it provokes nothing but dismay, and is never the cause of faith (except in John 20:8, where the meaning of the verb 'he believed' is open to dispute). By contrast with what is sometimes printed in books and articles, the apostles never *stated* that the tomb was empty on Easter morning. To use such terms is to imagine that there was a proclamation by the apostles of the fact of the discovery, while in fact there is never any mention of it in their preaching.

To draw attention to the absence of the body of Jesus or to the folded linen cloth is to distract the attention of the hearer from the message and to reduce the gospel to a narrative of miscellaneous facts. The only valid presentation is to follow John in bringing out the symbolism hidden in this detail.

To go into the problems of the date of the visit, the women's motive, etc., is to become entangled in considerable and even insoluble difficulties, and to raise awkward historical problems with no real significance for the gospel, such as that of the burial of Jesus.

b. Decorating the narrative to make it more probable Insisting on details until they are no longer subordinated to the whole narrative; inventing imaginary narrative settings (the springtime, the route they followed, etc.) or psychological motives for the women's visit, other than to anoint the body or to 'see'.

c. To attempt to prove faith in the resurrection To reason as follows: 'He is risen, *because* he is not here.' The first Christians did not establish any intrinsic link between the empty tomb and faith in the living Christ; they reflected upon their faith and recalled that the tomb had been found empty. The empty tomb is not even a secondary basis for faith in the resurrection.

2 *Three Approaches*

Once a particular approach has been selected, the choice must then be made between the different versions, which must be followed strictly, and there must be no attempt to say anything or to confuse the different points of view.

The holy women Their behaviour may be used to unify the preaching. From the point of view of the evangelist Mark, the hearer is in fact invited to identify with them and follow their course. They set out because they are loyal to Jesus; but their loyalty is to someone who is dead. Seized with the idea of entering the tomb, they pay no attention to the stone which has been rolled back. When they are distracted from their plan by the unexpected presence of a young man, who reveals to them the absence of Jesus and entrusts a mission to them for the disciples, they are surprised, astonished, overcome. Mark brings his reader face to face with the mystery which is going to be brought about, but gives him no idea what it is. At no moment in the narrative do we learn that the women leaned forward to make sure that the tomb was empty. It is from the proclamation of the resurrection that it becomes clear that Jesus is not there. The reader is invited to follow continuously the course taken by the women; while it is right to look back to the past, this is in order to find a greater impetus towards the future, towards the Lord who is coming (cf. p. 134).

The message of the angel forms the focal point of the narrative and can also form a unifying point for a sermon. The link between the crucified and the risen Christ demonstrates the essential connection between past and present, which persists to the present day. 'He is not here' may form the main theme of the sermon. Where is Jesus? Can one say in advance where he is? Ought one not to say first of all simply that one does not know? Shall I look for Jesus Christ in the past, in the tomb? Am I ready to set off promptly towards the future where he will meet me?

How am I to meet him? Luke can be our guide. Though a superficial reading may suggest otherwise, Luke does not concentrate the attention upon the fact of the tomb. For him, the living Christ is he who spoke to us in the past and who is going to continue speaking to us. There must always be a return to this past which was recounted in the gospel, but which becomes present to us here and now through the risen Christ.

The stone rolled away plays an important role in all four narratives, but in *Matthew* it becomes the major symbol of the sermon.

For a Jew, the tomb is not simply the 'final dwelling place': it is Sheol, that is, the underworld, or the power of death, a beast whose gaping mouth is ready to devour men. When it is closed by the stone, this is a sign that death has triumphed over life. When it is open, because the stone has been set aside, it symbolizes the defeat of death. The stone rolled away, the open tomb, concentrates in a symbol the triumph of God over death.

This explains the sight the women see, probably in the middle of the night, as we said in chapter 8. By contrast with the darkness, here is the angel of the Lord, shining bright. As at the moment when Jesus died, the earth shakes before the face of the Lord. The stone is not the cause of unease to the women, nor the object of the observation that it has been rolled back. Its immediate function is not to allow the women to go in, but to symbolize the object of the conflict between man and God. By sitting on the stone, the angel of the Lord signifies the final triumph of God over death. The guards are left for dead; the enemy are conquered; the message can be given to the women. Man can examine himself in the face of death, the experience is always pressing upon him.

B. THE APPEARANCE TO THE DISCIPLES ON THE ROAD TO EMMAUS

The preacher's difficulty lies in the fact that this narrative is unified by both a dogmatic and a psychological factor. Consequently neither of these aspects can be sacrificed, and the delicacy of the description must be allowed to arise from its dogmatic richness. Thus it is right to go in depth into the analogy between the situation of the travellers to Emmaus and the contemporary hearer.

Here are disciples who, like us, have heard of the risen Christ, but have not 'seen' him. On the road on which they are walking they are led to encounter him in the Word and the bread. This route is ours at the present day, whatever the degree of religious experience we have achieved, for it is a long way from hearing him to experiencing him, and the gap has always to be filled. Let us follow the three steps in this encounter.

a. Without hope The disciples know that Jesus, a great prophet in the sight of God, died on the cross and is therefore finished; yet the women, who found his tomb empty, declared that he is alive. In spite of this knowledge, they are sad, crushed by the death which has slain the righteous one. To know is not to see. How much knowledge there is in our own days! But how much less certainty and therefore how little hope.

b. The encounter with the risen Christ takes place progressively, and the gradual opening of their eyes is worth a description. But we shall mention here only the two means of communication by which Jesus makes himself recognized.

The encounter takes place in the *Word* which the unknown traveller addresses to them, and not in some sublime theophany which would satisfy a longing for the extraordinary, nor by any invitation to consider the miraculous and human vestiges which he left behind on earth. Jesus leaves them to understand what has taken place by an appeal to holy scripture. What God wants is not the brilliance of success, but the acceptance of suffering, according to a mysterious plan prefigured by the fate of the servant of God in the song of the prophet Isaiah. Accordingly, the cross is not a catastrophe, but a necessary turning point in existential life. All this is realized only by listening to the Word.

But they do not realize that they have understood, they do not notice that their hearts were burning within them until the moment of *the breaking of bread*, and more precisely at the moment of separation. The guest who was invited to spend the evening with them becomes the host who feeds them. In this way the eyes of the disciples are opened. But they are opened not to see, as eyes of flesh, but to understand and apprehend the presence of Jesus at the moment when he vanishes. The relationship which is established with the risen Christ is not one of the senses, of seeing or touching, but of hearing the Word and of sacramental eating.

c. The disciples become witnesses in the sense that they go to communicate to their brethren the discovery that they have just made. They have left, they have set out, probably leaving their brethren behind them; they now return to the community. There is no reason to suppose that when they heard that the risen Christ had appeared to Simon, the disciples were disappointed. That would be to imagine a purely human psychological development, as though the disciples had wanted to remain the first to make the discovery. On the contrary, Luke's purpose is to show that Christ has appeared to all, and that all can rejoice.

There is a unifying symbol in Luke's familiar theme, that of a journey and an encounter. The risen Christ comes to us in the steps we take, in the moves we make, perhaps in our 'flights', and is always ready to be recognized.

C. THE APPEARANCE TO THE DISCIPLES GATHERED TOGETHER
   (John 20: 19-29)

Above all, the preacher must make clear the way in which the appearance concerns the church; it is the founding of the church to which we belong.

a. Situation   Jesus appears on 'the first day of the week' or 'eight days later', that is, on 'Sunday', the time of the liturgical assembly. The evangelists wanted to make clear the meaning of Sunday from its very beginning. What takes place on this day? We are not far out if we speak of a 'commemoration' of the Easter event; so it is necessary to know exactly what we mean by this. Too often, it is a remembering of a past event, which took place a thousand years ago, and by which God raised his Son, and Jesus showed himself to the disciples. But this past is of no interest if it does not have a significance for the present time in which we live. To commemorate means to make a presence into a reality here and now; this of course assumes a past, but a past which belongs to today. Every Sunday, the assembly of the Christian people must make the living presence of him without whom it does not exist a reality here and now.

b. The encounter with the Lord The theme of *initiative* makes it possible not to place too much emphasis on the phenomenon of Jesus passing through closed doors. Jesus does not want to localize the body of Christ by implying the belief that it is spatially distant from his disciples and endowed with some kind of magic powers. Christ lifted up into heaven in his glory can, if he wants, be present in spite of the obstacles set up by men, and above all in spite of their fear. Symbolically Christ is present in spite of the barriers behind which men shut themselves off.

By saying 'Peace to you!' Jesus positively demonstrates the initiative he is taking. This is not a wish, equivalent, to those who hear it, to a possibility which may come about; it is a gift, conferred at that moment in the way in which the proclamation of the Good News takes place in prophecy or in the gospel (Is 40:9; Mark 1:15). This peace is not sentiment which derives from man, but a gift given by God himself (cf. John 14:27). It is important to demonstrate the richness of this term in biblical thought: good health, salvation, righteousness and reconciliation. All this is linked no longer with the earthly presence of Jesus, but with his victory over the world (16:33).

When Jesus shows his hands and his side, it is he who is alive seeking to be recognized as he who was crucified. The preacher should not stress that the wounds of the risen Christ were material wounds; he may even make clear that the evangelist does not say that the disciples touched the Lord. Above all, he must show the symbolic significance of the gesture. It expresses the necessity for the believer always to look back to the history that took place in the past. Except by an abstraction which is deceptive, the original event cannot be abolished. We must constantly return to it, not to rest there, but to make clear the routes of our present encounter with the Lord.

Finally, the disciples are filled with *joy*. This joy must not be confused with a completely human emotion, but signifies the flowering of a unique and definitive experience: 'No one will take your joy from you' (16:22); it is 'full' (15:11). The church lives in joy, and is 'saved'; nothing more can overcome it. It must always make the encounter with its Lord a present reality in its gatherings.

c.   The mission stops the church from sinking back, as it always can, into the illusory satisfaction of 'possessing' its Lord. For the Lord has conquered the sin which takes peace and joy away from the whole world. He therefore sends his disciples. The new revelation is that this mission, by way of the mission of Jesus himself, is the mission of the Father. There is only one mission (John 17:18) and this gives confidence, for the mission of Jesus completely succeeded by way of his being lifted up on the cross.

Jesus does not reveal only the origin of his mission, but in fact gives the agent which alone can bring it to a successful conclusion. The creative breath (cf. Gen 2:7) makes the disciple a new creature, born again (John 3:3-5), capable of bearing witness to the truth, and also capable of making into a present reality the judgment which Jesus inaugurated during his earthly life. The trial that takes place on that one day takes place for ever, and in it the spirit bears witness in the heart of believers that the cause of Jesus is just (16:8-11). The power to remit sins is best placed in this context. It should not be limited to the 'sacrament of penance'; the promise should be extended to the dimension of the conflict between Jesus and the sin of the world.

d.   The appearance to Thomas is in fact an appearance to the whole group of disciples. Here again, the scope of the scene must not be limited to psychological considerations which tend to mean that the essential is lost.

The *setting* is the same as that of the previous scene, but eight days later, that is, on the following Sunday. But the scene is introduced by the reflections of Thomas and is concluded by the saying of Jesus: 'Blessed are those who have not seen and yet believe.' Thus this narrative must be read as one specially addressed to all who, like Thomas, like the readers of the gospel at the end of the first century, have not 'seen' and will not see the risen Christ, unlike the privileged disciples. Is it, then, possible to believe, if one has not seen? What can be the basis of faith? The question is a real one today, and corresponds to our problems concerning the relationship between reason and faith. The preacher may therefore outline the similarity between our situation and that of Thomas, so long as he first points out that we are all 'unbelievers', even within our faith.

Thomas will not have faith on the testimony of the other disciples, but wishes like them to experience the presence of the risen Christ, in a 'seeing' which becomes actual touching. Jesus grants him what he asks, but adds a call to believe; he does not refuse him the tangible experience, but calls for true faith, leaving in ambiguity the act of faith which he is going to make. Now Thomas immediately confesses his faith, and we do not hear that he touched the wounds. The very word of Jesus aroused faith in him, and Thomas 'saw' the risen Christ. In a sense, Thomas passed the test of faith, because he replied by a magnificent proclamation based solely on the word of him who showed himself in this way. In another sense, he deserves a certain reproach, and it is important to make quite clear what this is.

'Blessed are those who have not seen and yet believe,' declared Jesus. This does not refer to seeing and touching, the evidence of the senses, but to the direct experience of the risen Christ. Thomas did not accept the testimony given by the disciples; but believers today and in times to come have to believe through the testimony of the church, which hands on the tradition of the first disciples. Jesus does not criticize the 'appearances' recounted in the gospels; he pronounces his blessing upon believers in ages to come. This is the lesson given by the risen Christ concerning the 'tradition' in which we are born in faith, and it is also a lesson on the impossibility of asking for personal demonstrations from him; we have all set out together on the ship which is the church.

D.   THE APPEARANCE TO THE ELEVEN (Luke 24:36-49)

This narrative is more descriptive than the former, and there is a risk of becoming involved in inordinately long discussions of some particular element of the narrative, to the detriment of the total effect (cf. chapter 9). The main difficulty lies in the passages which tend to make the scene more 'realistic'. They should not be passed over; but they should be noticed in such a way that they are not presented for their own sake, but are always balanced by the more 'spiritualizing' passages, such as the initiative of Jesus.

One approach, it seems, can be followed without risk: that of demonstrating how everything is concentrated upon the affirmation of Jesus: 'It is I myself.' Here we find a concern for the tradition that emphasizes the identity between the risen Christ and Jesus of Nazareth (the theme of recognition).

In the same direction, the longer passage concerning the interpretation of the scriptures takes up what was said on the Emmaus road: the law of existence according to the plan of God.

The passage on the entrusted mission takes up the idea of a plan of God and makes it a constituent element in the church. There should be reference here to the linear conception of history: the church is to be founded at Pentecost and must await the return of Jesus at the end of time.

Finally, there is an opportunity to set the scene at a eucharistic meal. To do so, it is necessary to bring out what the meal signified at that period (cf. Acts 10:41); it is the principal expression of the community of life.

E.   THE APPEARANCE TO MARY MAGDALENE (John 20:11-18)

We will not discuss this narrative at length. To a certain extent, it presents the same interest and the same difficulty as the Emmaus narrative. Yet in a way it is more complete, because it very clearly presents the threefold aspect of the classical appearance narratives: initiative, recognition, mission.

The theme of recognition is developed with particular care. Mary's mind is fixed upon the past; she must be turned away from this past, and from her own past. She must discover a new way of entering into contact with the living Christ, and of apprehending how there can be presence through absence. The mission plays an essential part in this. By going to the brethren, Mary is to leave her past and to discover a new way in which her Lord is present.

The preacher may if he wishes emphasize certain psychological aspects of the scene, such as Mary's tears, but only on condition that, by way of the discourse after the last supper, he gives them a theological dimension. 'Because I have said these things to you, sorrow has filled your hearts. Nevertheless I tell you the truth: it is to your advantage that I go away, for if I do not go away, the Counsellor will not come to you' (16:6-7). 'You will weep and lament ... you will be sorrowful, but your sorrow will turn into joy' (16:20).

F. THE ASCENSION

The most important thing is to choose one of the three texts (Mark 16:14-20; Luke 24:50-51; Acts 1:3-11), but without losing sight of any of the theological points mentioned in chapter 2 of this work. Let us briefly recall some of the risks which the preacher runs in setting forth this mystery. The first risk is that of attempting to describe the scene, perhaps by reading between the lines in order to 'make it more lively'. There are even those who do not hesitate to say that Jesus made a short detour to Bethany in order to say good-bye to his friends Lazarus, Martha and Mary. Some take the opportunity of showing off their archaeological knowledge, which is a sure way of diverting attention from what really matters. Other preachers have imagined Jesus, as he ascended, seeing the places where he lived: Bethlehem, the streets of Jerusalem, Golgotha ... and imagined what passed through his mind about them. In short, it is dangerous to lay any emphasis on the chronology of the forty days, on the location (right hand of God), and on anything that suggests 'going up in a balloon', the mist of the cloud, and the bright sky.

In addition to the dangers that arise from too visual a description, there can also be a false theological emphasis. The theme of separation, departure, and the preparation by Jesus of a place for us can sometimes lead to emphasizing that the earth is 'this vale of tears', a wretched place of pilgrimage, and that believers should have a melancholy longing for eternity. This is but a poor caricature of hope.

Given this, it must be admitted that one cannot present the mystery without adopting for the sake of argument a certain *cosmology*. Our contemporaries may smile if we try to make them think objectively of ascending into heaven. They are wrong to imagine that it is possible to speak without any symbolic language. It is therefore indispensable to invite the hearers to become poets, or at least children. To this end, one may recall that psychologists unanimously recognize the symbolical value of height and depth, and that heaven is not a place to which one goes, but a person whom one encounters. They will be less tempted to imagine the ascension as an ascent into the stratosphere and to imagine, like the astronaut Gagarin, that if you went up to a higher heaven you would meet God. Once this is accepted, the cosmology of the ancient world must be recalled. The earth was thought of as a kind of plateau, beneath which lay Sheol, and above which the various heavens were ranged. To signify that Jesus has become Lord, he is represented as passing through the heavens and the levels of the underworld; but this is only a means used by faith to express the ultimate triumph of Jesus the Christ. Thus the preacher must recall in a straightforward fashion this way of thinking of the universe, in order to show that he is not taken in by the images and symbols used to express the mystery.

1. *The basic affirmation* (Mark 16:19) The essential can be summed up in the festival of Christ, king and Lord of the universe (cf. Ps 110:1), as is clearly indicated by the tradition of Christ exalted into heaven (chapter 2). Thus it is important to apprehend the symbolic meaning of the 'lifting up into heaven'.

It does not in the least signify that from now on there is a gap between heaven and earth. On the contrary, it means that the risen Christ, who has become the Lord, is present at every point in the universe.

It symbolizes exaltation, in the form of lifting up: 'I am ascending to my Father and your Father' (John 20:17). By contrast, the cloud has only a secondary function, and forms part of the apparatus of theophanies: it both conceals and reveals the divine being which it accompanies or bears.

Two lines of development can be followed:
The *separation* from the disciples (Luke 24:50-51), which is the cessation of a certain kind of relationship between Christ and the disciples. This separation brings with it the *awaiting* of his return and of the parousia. But at the same time, their hearts are filled not with the sadness which normally accompanies any separation, but with joy because of the promise of the Holy Spirit. The disciples attain a new kind of presence, through absence.
The *lifting up* through all the heavens signifies a continual *presence*

(cf. Matthew 28:20). In following this line of development, there should not be a description of the 'ascent', but an emphasis upon the ultimate situation on high, from which the earth is governed as a whole. This brings a new conception of the relationship between earth and heaven, from which is derived Paul's development in the Epistle to the Ephesians: we are seated with Christ in heaven.

2. *The mission* Perfectly comprehensible as coming from the Lord who governs the whole world, the mission can be described in detail along the lines of the different versions. It is perhaps preferable not to emphasize the 'signs' described in ps.-Mark, but to draw attention to the *triumphant universalism*.

From another point of view, the preacher might explain the relationship which from now on exists between *mission and contemplation*. A Christian must not remain with his gaze fixed upon heaven, but remembering the words of the angel, 'He is not here', make the new presence a reality through the mission to all nations.

This mission is the culmination of the threefold dimension of the resurrection appearances. Since the disciples recognized Jesus in the risen Christ, they must not remain gazing up into heaven, where he has gone, but must carry out the mission entrusted to them by Jesus and made possible by the Spirit.

G. THEMES

Changing his point of view once again, the preacher may fill out his development by taking up the hints given in the chapters in this book. We shall do no more than list one or two. The *triple* aspect of the appearance narratives may be used to describe the existential life of the disciples. The *theme of the meal* taken in common, and with the risen Christ, indicates the significance of the liturgical celebration in the course of which Christ gives his presence. The fact that the church is rooted in this privileged period makes it easier to stop the church community becoming a purely natural society. Finally, the *dominion over the universe* inaugurated by Jesus remains an inexhaustible source of hope.

Texts

Matthew's Narrative

27 55There were also many women there, looking on from afar, who had followed Jesus from Galilee, ministering to him; among whom were Mary Magdalene, and Mary the mother of James and Joseph, and the mother of the sons of Zebedee. 57When it was evening, there came a rich man from Arimathea, named Joseph, who also was a disciple of Jesus. 58He went to Pilate and asked for the body of Jesus. Then Pilate ordered it to be given to him. 59And Joseph took the body, and wrapped it in a clean linen shroud, 60and laid it in his own new tomb, which he had hewn in the rock; and he rolled a great stone to the door of the tomb, and departed. 61Mary Magdalene and the other Mary were there, sitting opposite the sepulchre. 62Next day, that is, after the day of Preparation, the chief priests and the Pharisees gathered before Pilate 63and said, 'Sir, we remember how that impostor said, while he was still alive, "After three days I will rise again." 64Therefore order the sepulchre to be made secure until the third day, lest his disciples go and steal him away, and tell the people, "He has risen from the dead," and the last fraud will be worse than the first.' 65Pilate said to them, 'You have a guard of soldiers; go, make it as secure as you

can.' ⁶⁶So they went and made the sepulchre secure by sealing the stone and setting a guard.

28 ¹Now after the sabbath, towards the dawn of the first day of the week, Mary Magdalene and the other Mary went to see the sepulchre. ²And behold, there was a great earthquake; for an angel of the Lord descended from heaven and came and rolled back the stone, and sat upon it. ³His appearance was like lightning, and his raiment white as snow. ⁴And for fear of him the guards trembled and became like dead men. ⁵But the angel said to the women, 'Do not be afraid; for I know that you seek Jesus who was crucified. ⁶He is not here; for he has arisen, as he said. Come, see the place where he lay. ⁷Then go quickly and tell his disciples that he has risen from the dead, and behold, he is going before you to Galilee; there you will see him. Lo, I have told you.' ⁸So they departed quickly from the tomb with fear and great joy, and ran to tell his disciples. ⁹And behold, Jesus met them and said, 'Hail!' And they came up and took hold of his feet and worshiped him. ¹⁰Then Jesus said to them, 'Do not be afraid; go and tell my brethren to go to Galilee, and there they will see me.' ¹¹While they were going, behold, some of the guard went into the city and told the chief priests all that had taken place. ¹²And when they had assembled with the elders and taken counsel, they gave a sum of money to the soldiers ¹³and said, 'Tell people, "His disciples came by night and stole him away while we were asleep," ¹⁴And if this comes to the governor's ears, we will satisfy him and keep you out of trouble.' ¹⁵So they took the money and did as they were directed; and this story has been spread among the Jews to this day. ¹⁶Now the eleven disciples went to Galilee, to the mountain to which Jesus had directed them. ¹⁷And when they saw him they worshiped him; but some doubted. ¹⁸And Jesus came and said to them, 'All authority in heaven and on earth has been given to me. ¹⁹Go therefore and make disciples of all nations, baptizing them in the name of the Father and of the Son and of the Holy Spirit, ²⁰teaching them to observe all that I have commanded you; and lo, I am with you always, to the close of the age.'

Mark's Narrative

15 ⁴⁰There were also women looking on from afar, among whom were Mary Magdalene, and Mary the mother of James the younger and of Joses, and Salome, ⁴¹who, when he was in Galilee, followed

him, and ministered to him and also many other women who came up with him to Jerusalem. ⁴²And when evening had come, since it was the day of Preparation, that is, the day before sabbath, ⁴³Joseph of Arimathea, a respected member of the council, who was also himself looking for the kingdom of God, took courage and went to Pilate, and asked for the body of Jesus. ⁴⁴And Pilate wondered if he were already dead; and summoning the centurion, he asked him whether he was already dead. ⁴⁵And when he learned from the centurion that he was dead, he granted the body to Joseph. ⁴⁶And he bought a linen shroud, and taking him down, wrapped him in the linen shroud, and laid him in a tomb which had been hewn out of the rock; and he rolled a stone against the door of the tomb. ⁴⁷Mary Magdalene and Mary the mother of Joses saw where he was laid.

16 ¹And when the sabbath was past, Mary Magdalene, and Mary the mother of James, and Salome, bought spices, so that they might go and anoint him. ²And very early on the first day of the week they went to the tomb when the sun had risen. ³And they were saying to one another, 'Who will roll away the stone for us from the door of the tomb?' ⁴And looking up, they saw that the stone was rolled back; for it was very large. ⁵And entering the tomb, they saw a young man sitting on the right side, dressed in a white robe; and they were amazed. ⁶And he said to them, 'Do not be amazed; you seek Jesus of Nazareth, who was crucified. He has risen, he is not here; see the place where they laid him. ⁷But go, tell his disciples and Peter that he is going before you to Galilee; there you will see him, as he told you.' ⁸And they went out and fled from the tomb; for trembling and astonishment had come upon them; and they said nothing to any one, for they were afraid.

Luke's Narrative

23 ⁵⁰Now there was a man named Joseph from the Jewish town of Arimathea. He was a member of the council, a good and righteous man, ⁵¹who had not consented to their purpose and deed, and he was looking for the kingdom of God. ⁵²This man went to Pilate and asked for the body of Jesus. ⁵³Then he took it down and wrapped it in a linen shroud and laid him in a rock-hewn tomb, where no one had ever yet been laid. ⁵⁴It was the day of Preparation, and the sabbath was beginning. ⁵⁵The women who had come with him from Galilee followed, and saw the tomb, and how his body was

laid. [56]Then they returned, and prepared spices and ointments. On the sabbath they rested according to the commandment.

24 [1]But on the first day of the week, at early dawn, they went to the tomb, taking the spices which they had prepared. [2]And they found the stone rolled away from the tomb, [3]but when they went in they did not find the body. [4]While they were perplexed about this, behold, two men stood by them in dazzling apparel; [5]and as they were frightened and bowed their faces to the ground, the men said to them, 'Why do you seek the living among the dead? [6]Remember how he told you, while he was still in Galilee, [7]that the Son of man must be delivered into the hands of sinful men, and be crucified, and on the third day rise.' [8]And they remembered his words, [9]and returning from the tomb they told all this to the eleven and to all the rest. [10]Now it was Mary Magdalene and Joanna and Mary the mother of James and the other women with them who told this to the apostles; [11]but these words seemed to them an idle tale, and they did not believe them. [13]That very day two of them were going to a village named Emmaus, about seven miles from Jerusalem, [14]and talking with each other about all these things that had happened. [15]While they were talking and discussing together, Jesus himself drew near and went with them. [16]But their eyes were kept from recognizing him. [17]And he said to them, 'What is this conversation which you are holding with each other as you walk?' And they stood still, looking sad. [18]Then one of them, named Cleopas, answered him, 'Are you the only visitor to Jerusalem who does not know the things that have happened here in these days?' [19]And he said to them, 'What things?' And they said to him, 'Concerning Jesus of Nazareth, who was a prophet mighty in deed and word before God and all the people, [20]and how our chief priests and rulers delivered him up to be condemned to death, and crucified him. [21]But we had hoped that he was the one to redeem Israel. Yes, and besides all this, it is now the third day since this happened. [22]Moreover, some women of our company amazed us. They were at the tomb early in the morning [23]and did not find his body; and they came back saying that they had even seen a vision of angels, who said that he was alive. [24]Some of those who were with us went to the tomb, and found it just as the women had said; but him they did not see.' [25]And he said to them, 'O foolish men, and slow of heart to believe all that the prophets have spoken! [26]Was it not necessary that the Christ should suffer these things and enter into

his glory?' ²⁷And beginning with Moses and all the prophets, he interpreted to them in all the scriptures the things concerning himself. ²⁸So they drew near to the village to which they were going, ²⁹but they constrained him, saying, 'Stay with us, for it is toward evening and the day is now far spent.' So he went in to stay with them. ³⁰When he was at table with them, he took the bread and blessed and broke it, and gave it to them. ³¹And their eyes were opened and they recognized him; and he vanished out of their sight. ³²They said to each other, 'Did not our hearts burn within us while he talked to us on the road, while he opened to us the scriptures?' ³³And they rose that same hour and returned to Jerusalem; and they found the eleven gathered together and those who were with them, ³⁴who said: 'The Lord has risen indeed, and has appeared to Simon!' ³⁵Then they told what had happened on the road, and how he was known to them in the breaking of the bread. ³⁶As they were saying this, Jesus himself stood among them. ³⁷But they were startled and frightened, and supposed that they saw a spirit. ³⁸And he said to them, 'Why are you troubled, and why do questionings rise in your hearts? ³⁹See my hands and my feet, that it is I myself; handle me, and see; for a spirit has not flesh and bones as you see that I have.' ⁴¹And while they still disbelieved for joy, and wondered, he said to them, 'Have you anything here to eat?' ⁴²They gave him a piece of broiled fish, ⁴³and he took it and ate before them. ⁴⁴Then he said to them, 'These are my words which I spoke to you, while I was still with you, that everything written about me in the law of Moses and the prophets and the psalms must be fulfilled.' ⁴⁵Then he opened their minds to understand the scriptures, ⁴⁶and said to them, 'Thus it is written, that the Christ should suffer and on the third day rise from the dead, ⁴⁷and that repentance and forgiveness of sins should be preached in his name to all nations, beginning from Jerusalem. ⁴⁸You are witnesses of these things. ⁴⁹And behold, I send the promise of my Father upon you; but stay in the city, until you are clothed with power from on high.' ⁵⁰Then he led them out as far as Bethany, and lifting up his hands he blessed them. ⁵¹While he blessed them, he parted from them. ⁵²And they returned to Jerusalem with great joy, ⁵³and were continually in the temple blessing God.

John's Narrative

19 ³⁸After this Joseph of Arimathea, who was a disciple of Jesus,

but secretly, for fear of the Jews, asked Pilate that he might take away the body of Jesus, and Pilate gave him leave. So he came and took away his body. [39]Nicodemus also, who had at first come to him by night, came bringing a mixture of myrrh and aloes, about a hundred pounds' weight. [40]They took the body of Jesus, and bound it in linen cloths with the spices, as is the burial custom of the Jews. [41]Now in the place where he was crucified there was a garden, and in the garden a new tomb where no one had ever been laid. [42]So because of the Jewish day of Preparation, as the tomb was close at hand, they laid Jesus there.

20 [1]Now on the first day of the week Mary Magdalene came to the tomb early, while it was still dark, and saw that the stone had been taken away from the tomb. [2]So she ran, and went to Simon Peter and the other disciple, the one whom Jesus loved, and said to them: 'They have taken the Lord out of the tomb, and we do not know where they have laid him.' [3]Peter then came out with the other disciple, and they went towards the tomb. [4]They both ran, but the other disciple outran Peter and reached the tomb first; [5]and stooping to look in, he saw the linen cloths lying there, but he did not go on. [6]Then Simon Peter came, following him, and he went into the tomb; he saw the linen cloths lying, [7]and the napkin, which had been on his head, not lying up in a place by itself. [8]Then the other disciple, who reached the tomb first, also went in, and he saw and believed; [9]for as yet they did not know the scripture, that he must rise from the dead. [10]Then the disciples went back to their homes. [11]But Mary stood weeping outside the tomb, and as she wept she stooped to look into the tomb; [12]and she saw two angels in white, sitting where the body of Jesus had lain, one at the head and one at the feet. [13]They said to her, 'Woman, why are you weeping?' She said to them, 'Because they have taken away my Lord, and I do not know where they have laid him.' [14]Saying this, she turned round and saw Jesus standing, but she did not know that it was Jesus. [15]Jesus said to her, 'Woman, why are you weeping? Whom do you seek?' Supposing him to be the gardener, she said to him, 'Sir, if you have carried him away, tell me where you have laid him, and I will take him away.' [16]Jesus said to her, 'Mary.' She turned and said to him in Hebrew, 'Rab-boni!' (which means Teacher). [17]Jesus said to her, 'Do not hold me, for I have not yet ascended to the Father; but go to my brethren and say to them, I am ascending to my Father and your Father, to my God and your

God.' ¹⁸Mary Magdalene went and said to the disciples, 'I have seen the Lord'; and she told them that he had said these things to her.

¹⁹On the evening of that day, the first day of the week, the doors being shut where the disciples were, for fear of the Jews, Jesus came and stood among them and said to them, 'Peace be with you.' ²⁰When he had said this, he showed them his hands and his side. Then the disciples were glad when they saw the Lord. ²¹Jesus said to them again, 'Peace be with you. As the Father has sent me, even so I send you.' ²²And when he had said this, be breathed on them, and said to them, 'Receive the Holy Spirit. ²³If you forgive the sins of any, they are forgiven; if you retain the sins of any, they are retained.'

²⁴Now Thomas, one of the twelve, called the Twin, was not with them when Jesus came. ²⁵So the other disciples told him, 'We have seen the Lord.' But he said to them, 'Unless I see in his hands the print of the nails, and place my finger in the mark of the nails, and place my hand in his side, I will not believe.' ²⁶Eight days later, his disciples were again in the house, and Thomas was with them. The doors were shut, but Jesus came and stood among them, and said, 'Peace be with you.' ²⁷Then he said to Thomas, 'Put your finger here, and see my hands; and put out your hand, and place it in my side; do not be faithless, but believing.' ²⁸Thomas answered him, 'My Lord and my God!' ²⁹Jesus said to him, 'Have you believed because you have seen me? Blessed are those who have not seen and yet believe.'

Another Narrative—John

21 ¹After this Jesus revealed himself again to the disciples by the Sea of Tiberias; and he revealed himself in this way. ²Simon Peter, Thomas called the Twin, Nathanael of Cana in Galilee, the sons of Zebedee, and two others of his disciples were together. ³Simon Peter said to them, 'I am going fishing.' They said to him, 'We will go with you.' They went out and got into the boat; but that night they caught nothing. ⁴Just as day was breaking, Jesus stood on the beach; yet the disciples did not know that it was Jesus. ⁵Jesus said to them, 'Children, have you any fish?' They answered him, 'No.' ⁶He said to them, 'Cast the net on the right side of the boat, and you will find some.' So they cast it, and now they were not able to haul it in, for the quantity of fish. ⁷That disciple whom Jesus loved said to Peter, 'It is the Lord!' When Simon Peter heard that it was

the Lord, he put on his clothes, for he was stripped for work, and sprang into the sea. [8]But the other disciples came in the boat, dragging the net full of fish, for they were not far from the land, but about a hundred yards off. [9]When they got out on land, they saw a charcoal fire there, with fish lying on it, and bread. [10]Jesus said to them, 'Bring some of the fish that you have just caught.' [11]So Simon Peter went aboard and hauled the net ashore, full of large fish, a hundred and fifty-three of them; and although there were so many, the net was not torn. [12]Jesus said to them, 'Come and have breakfast.' Now none of the disciples dared ask him, 'Who are you?' They knew it was the Lord. [13]Jesus came and took the bread and gave it to them, and so with the fish. [14]This was now the third time that Jesus was revealed to the disciples after he was raised from the dead. [15]When they had finished breakfast, Jesus said to Simon Peter, 'Simon, son of John, do you love me more than these?' He said to him, 'Yes, Lord; you know that I love you.' He said to him, 'Feed my lambs.' [16]A second time he said to him, 'Simon, son of John, do you love me?' He said to him, 'Yes, Lord; you know that I love you.' He said to him, 'Tend my sheep.' [17]He said to him the third time, 'Simon, son of John, do you love me?' Peter was grieved because he said to him the third time, 'Do you love me?' And he said to him, 'Lord, you know everything; you know that I love you.' Jesus said to him, 'Feed my sheep. [18]Truly, truly, I say to you, when you were young, you girded yourself and walked where you would; but when you are old, you will stretch out your hands, and another will gird you and carry you where you do not wish to go.' [19](This he said to show by what death he was to glorify God.) And after this he said to him, 'Follow me.' [20]Peter turned and saw following them the disciple whom Jesus loved, who had lain close to his breast at the supper and had said, 'Lord, who is it that is going to betray you?' [21]When Peter saw him, he said to Jesus, 'Lord, what about this man?' [22]Jesus said to him, 'If it is my will that he remain until I come, what is that to you? Follow me.' [23]The saying spread abroad among the brethren that this disciple was not to die; yet Jesus did not say to him that he was not to die, but, 'If it is my will that he remain until I come, what is that to you?'

The Conclusion of Mark

16 [9]Now when he rose early on the first day of the week, he appeared first to Mary Magdalene, from whom he had cast out

seven demons. ¹⁰She went and told those who had been with him, as they mourned and wept. ¹¹But when they heard that he was alive and had been seen by her, they would not believe it. ¹²After this he appeared in another form to two of them, as they were walking into the country. ¹³And they went back and told the rest, but they did not believe them. ¹⁴Afterward he appeared to the eleven themselves as they sat at table; and he upbraided them for their unbelief and hardness of heart, because they had not believed those who saw him after he had risen. ¹⁵And he said to them, 'Go into all the world and preach the gospel to the whole creation. ¹⁶He who believes and is baptized will be saved; but he who does not believe will be condemned. ¹⁷And these signs will accompany those who believe: in my name they will cast out demons, they will speak in new tongues; ¹⁸they will pick up serpents, and if they drink any deadly thing, it will not hurt them; they will lay their hands on the sick; and they will recover.' ¹⁹So then the Lord Jesus, after he had spoken to them, was taken up into heaven, and sat down at the right hand of God. ²⁰And they went forth and preached everywhere, while the Lord worked with them and confirmed the message by the signs that attended it.

The Narrative of Pseudo-Peter (Gospel of Peter)

²⁸But the scribes and Pharisees and elders gathered one with another, for they had heard that all the people were murmuring and beating their breasts, saying: If these very great signs have come to pass at his death, behold how righteous he was. ²⁹And the elders were afraid and came unto Pilate, entreating him and saying: ³⁰Give us soldiers that we may watch his sepulchre for three days lest his disciples come and steal him away and the people suppose that he is risen from the dead, and do us hurt. ³¹And Pilate gave them Petronius the centurion with soldiers to watch the sepulchre; and the elders and scribes came with them unto the tomb, ³²and when they had rolled a great stone to keep out the centurion and the soldiers, then all that were there together set it upon the door of the tomb; ³³and plastered thereon seven seals; and they pitched a tent there and kept watch. ³⁴And early in the morning as the sabbath dawned there came a multitude from Jerusalem and the region round about to see the sepulchre that had been sealed. ³⁵Now in the night whereon the Lord's day dawned, as the soldiers were keeping guard two by two in every watch there came a great sound

in the heaven, [36]and they saw the heavens opened and two men descend thence, shining with a great light, and drawing near unto the sepulchre. [37]And that stone which had been set on the door rolled away of itself and went back to the side, and the sepulchre was opened and both of the young men entered in. [38]When therefore those soldiers saw that, they waked up the centurion and the elders (for they also were there keeping watch); [39]and while they were yet telling them the things which they had seen, they saw again three men come out of the sepulchre, and two of them sustaining the other and a cross following after them. [40]And of the two they saw that their heads reached unto heaven, but of him that was led by them that it overpassed the heavens. [41]And they heard a voice out of the heavens saying: [42]Hast thou preached unto them that sleep? And an answer was heard from the cross, saying: Yea. [43]Those men therefore took counsel one with another to go and report these things unto Pilate. [44]And while they yet thought thereabout, again the heavens were opened and a man descended and entered into the tomb. [45]And the centurion and they that were with him, when they saw that, hasted to go by night unto Pilate and left the sepulchre whereon they were keeping watch, and told all that they had seen, and were in great agony, saying: Of a truth he was the son of God. [46]Pilate answered and said: I am clear from the blood of the son of God, but thus it seemed good unto you. [47]Then all they came and besought him and exhorted him to charge the centurion and the soldiers to tell nothing of that they had seen: [48]For, said they, it is expedient for us to incur the greatest sin before God, rather than to fall into the hands of the people of the Jews and to be stoned. [49]Pilate therefore charged the centurion and the soldiers that they should say nothing. [50]Now early on the Lord's day Mary Magdalene, a disciple of the Lord—which, being afraid because of the Jews, for they were inflamed with anger, had not performed at the sepulchre of the Lord those things which women are accustomed to do unto them that die and are beloved of them—[51]took with her the women her friends and came unto the tomb where he was laid. [52]And they feared lest the Jews should see them, and said: Even if we were not able to weep and lament him on that day whereon he was crucified, yet let us now do so at his tomb. [53]But who will roll away for us the stone also that is set upon the door of the tomb, that we may enter in and sit beside him and perform that which is due? [54]for the stone was

great, and we fear lest any man see us. And if we cannot do so, yet
let us cast down at the door these things which we bring for a
memorial of him, and we will weep and lament until we come unto
our house. [55]And they went and found the sepulchre open: and
they drew near and looked in there, and saw there a young man
sitting in the midst of the sepulchre, of a fair countenance and
clad in very bright raiment, which said unto them: [56]Wherefore
are ye come? whom seek ye? not him that was crucified? He is
risen and is departed; but if ye believe it not, look in and see the
place where he lay, that he is not here: for he is risen and is departed thither whence he was sent. [57]Then the women were
affrighted and fled. [58]Now it was the last day of unleavened bread,
and many were coming forth of the city and returning unto their
own homes because the feast was at an end. [59]But we, the twelve
disciples of the Lord, were weeping and were in sorrow, and each
one being grieved for that which had befallen departed unto his own
house. [60]But I, Simon Peter, and Andrew my brother, took our nets
and went unto the sea: and there was with us Levi the son of
Alphaeus, whom the Lord. . . .

The Narrative of the Visionary Baruch (II Baruch 49:1 – 51:10)

49 [1]'Nevertheless, I will again ask from Thee, O Mighty One, yea,
I will ask mercy from Him who made all things. [2]In what shape
will those live who live in Thy day? Or how will the splendour of
those who [are] after that time continue? [3]Will they then resume
this form of the present, and put on these entrammelling members,
which are now involved in evils, and in which evils are consummated, or wilt Thou perchance change these things which have
been in the world as also the world?'

50 [1]And he answered and said unto me: 'Hear, Baruch, this
word, and write in the remembrance of thy heart all that thou shalt
learn. [2]For the earth shall then assuredly restore the dead, which it
now receives in order to preserve them. It shall make no change in
their form, but as it has received, so shall it restore them, and as
I delivered them unto it, so also shall it raise them. [3]For then it will
be necessary to show to the living that the dead have come to life
come to pass, when they have severally recognized those whom
they now know, then judgement shall grow strong, and those things
again, and that those who had departed have returned. [4]And it shall
which before were spoken of shall come.

51 [1]And it shall come to pass, when that appointed day has gone by, that then shall the aspect of those who are condemned be afterwards changed, and the glory of those who are justified. [2]For the aspect of those who now act wickedly shall become worse than it is, as they shall suffer torment. [3]Also, the glory of those who have now been justified in my law, who have had understanding in their life, and who have planted in their heart the root of wisdom —their splendour shall be glorified in changes, and the form of their face shall be turned into the light of their beauty, that they may be able to acquire and receive the world which does not die, which is then promised to them. [4]For over this above shall those who come then lament, that they rejected my law, and stopped their ears that they might not hear wisdom or receive understanding. [5]When therefore they see those, over whom they are now exalted, but who shall then be exalted and glorified more than they, they shall respectively be transformed, the latter into the splendour of angels, and the former shall yet more waste away in wonder at the visions and in the beholding of the forms. [6]For they shall first behold and afterwards depart to be tormented. [7]But those who have been saved by their works, and to whom the law has been now a hope, and understanding an expectation, and wisdom a confidence, shall wonders appear in their time. [8]For they shall behold the world which is now invisible to them, and they shall behold the time which is now hidden from them; [9]and time shall no longer age them. [10]For in the heights of that world shall they dwell, and they shall be made like unto the angels, and be made equal to the stars, and they shall be changed into every form they desire, from beauty into loveliness, and from light into the splendour of glory.

A Second Century Narrative: The Epistle of the Apostles

The *Epistle of the Apostles* (or *Testament in Galilee of Our Lord Jesus Christ*, according to the title given it by L. Guerrier in the *Patrologie Orientale*, IX, 1913) seems to date from the beginning of the second century. It is interesting to see how the sobriety of the gospel rapidly gave way to psychological or apologetic developments.

[8]Therefore have we not shrunk from writing unto you concerning the testimony of Christ our Saviour, of what he did, when we followed with him, how he enlightened our understanding.... [9]Concerning whom we testify that the Lord is he who was crucified

by Pontius Pilate and Archelaus between the two thieves and with them he was taken down from the tree of the cross, and was buried in a place which is called the place of a skull (*Kranion*). And thither went three women, Sarrha, Martha, and Mary and took ointments to pour upon the body, weeping and mourning over that which was come to pass. And when they drew near to the sepulchre, they looked in and found not the body, they found the stone rolled away and opened the entrance. [10]And as they mourned and wept, the Lord showed himself unto them and said to them: For whom weep ye? Weep no more, I am he whom ye seek. But let one of you go to your brethren and say: Come ye, the Master is risen from the dead. Mary came and told us. We said unto her: What have we to do with thee, woman? He that is dead and buried, is it possible that he should live? And we believed her not that the Saviour was risen from the dead. Then she returned unto the Lord and said unto him: None of them hath believed me, that thou livest. He said: Let another of you go unto them and tell them again. Sarrha came and told us again, and we believed her not: and she returned unto the Lord and she also told him.

[11]Then said the Lord unto Mary and her sisters, Let us go unto them. And he came and found us within sitting veiled and called us out; but we thought that it was a phantom and believed not that it was the Lord. Then said he unto us: Come, fear ye not. I am your master, even he, O Peter, whom thou didst deny thrice; and dost thou now deny again? And we came unto him, doubting in our hearts whether it were he. Then said he unto us: Wherefore doubt ye still, and are unbelieving? I am he that spake unto you of my flesh and my resurrection. But that ye may know that I am he, do thou, Peter, put thy finger into the print of the nails in mine hands, and thou also, Thomas, put thy finger into the wound of the spear in my side; but thou, Andrew, look on my feet and see whether they press the earth; for it is written in the prophet: A phantom of a devil maketh no footprint on the earth.

[12]And we touched him, that we might learn of a truth whether he were risen in the flesh; and we fell on our faces and worshipped him confessing our sin, that we had been unbelieving. Then said our Lord and Saviour unto us: Rise up, and I will reveal unto you that which is above the heaven and in the heaven and your rest which is in the kingdom of heaven. For my Father hath sent me to take you up thither, and them also that believe on me.

Bibliography

GENERAL WORKS

W. Bauer, *Griechisch-Deutsches Wörterbuch zu den Schriften des Neuen Testaments und der übrigen urchristlichen Literatur*. Töpelmann, Berlin, 1958 (=Wörterbuch); trans. Arndt and Gingrich, *A Greek-English Lexicon of the New Testament, etc.*, Cambridge, 1957.

M. Black, *An Aramaic Approach to the Gospels and Acts*, Oxford, 1954, 1967 (=*Aramaic Approach*).

R. E. Brown, *The Gospel according to John*, Doubleday, Anchor Bible no. 29, New York, 1970 (=*John*).

L. Cerfaux, *Le Christ dans la théologie de saint Paul*, Cerf, coll. 'Lectio divina' no. 6, Paris, 1951 (=Le Christ); trans. *Christ in the Theology of St Paul*, New York, Edinburgh and London, 1959.

La Théologie de l'Église suivant saint Paul, Cerf, coll. 'Unam Sanctam', no. 10, Paris, 1942 (no. 54, Paris, 1965) (=*L'Église*); trans. *The Church in the Theology of St Paul*, New York, Edinburgh and London, 1959.

Recueil Lucien Cerfaux, Études d'Exégèse et d'Histoire Religieuse, J. Duculot, Gembloux, I-II 1954, III 1962.

C. H. Dodd, *According to the Scriptures*, J. Nisbet, London, 1952.

The Apostolic Preaching and its Developments, Hodder and Stoughton, London, 1944.

J. Dupont, *Études sur les Actes des Apôtres*, Cerf, coll. 'Lectio divina' no. 45, Paris, 1967 (=*Études*).

Introduction à la Bible, ed. A. Robert et A. Feuillet, Desclée, Tournai and Paris, II, 1959 (=*Intr Bibl*).

X. Léon-Dufour, *Études d'Évangile*, Seuil, coll. 'Parole de Dieu', Paris, 1965 (=*Études*).

Les Évangiles et l'histoire de Jésus, Seuil, coll. 'Parole de Dieu', Paris, 1963 (=*Les Évangiles*).

J. Pedersen, *Israel: its life and its culture,* Oxford, 1926.

R. Schnackenburg, *Das Johannesvangelium,* I, Einleitung und Kommentar zu Kap. 1-4, Herders Theol. Kommentar zum NT IV/I, Herder, Fribourg-en-Br., 1965.

E. Schweizer, *Neotestamentica,* Deutsche und Englische Aufsätze 1951-63, Zwingli, Zurich and Stuttgart, 1963.

G. Stemberger, *La symbolique du bien et du mal selon saint Jean,* Seuil, coll. 'Parole de Dieu', Paris, 1970.

L. Strack and P. Billerbeck, *Kommentar zum Neuen Testament aus Talmud und Midrasch,* 6 volumes, Beek, Munich, 1922-61, (=Strack-Billerbeck).

Theologisches Wörterbuch zum Neuen Testament, ed. G. Kittel and G. Friedrich. Kohlhammer, Stuttgart, 1933-71 (=*TWNT*); trans. *Theological Dictionary of the New Testament,* Grand Rapids and London, 1964 (=*TDNT*).

Vocabulaire de théologie biblique, ed. X. Léon-Dufour, J. Duplacy, A. George, P. Grelot, J. Guillet, M. F. Lacan, Cerf, Paris, 1970 (= *VTB*).

L. Vaganay, *L'Évangile de Pierre,* Gabalda, Études bibliques, Paris, 1930.

WORKS ON THE RESURRECTION

This bibliography gives only books or articles used in this work or recently published. More technical details are given in the bulletin we published in *RSR* 57 (1969), p. 585; an exhaustive bibliography by G. Ghiberti appeared in the *Actes du Symposium,* Rome, Easter, 1970.

Assemblées du Seigneur. St André, Bruges, 1961-9, N. S. Cerf, 1969. On Matthew 28 : 16-20, W. Trilling, no. 28; on Mark 16 : 1-8, J. Delorme, no. 21; on Luke 24, G. Gaide, nos. 21 and 24; on John 20, D. Mollat, nos. 21 and 30; on John 21, B. Schwank, no. 24.

Die Bedeutung der Auferstehungsbotschaft für den Glauben an Jesus Christus, by W. Marxsen, U. Wilckens, G. Delling, H. G. Geyer, G. Mohn, Gütersloh, 1966; trans. *The Significance of the Message of the Resurrection for Faith in Jesus Christ,* Studies in Biblical Theology, 2nd series, London, 1968.

P. Benoit, 'Marie-Madeleine et les disciples au tombeau vide selon

John 20:1-8', in *Judentum, Urchristentum, Kirche*, Mélanges J. Jeremias, Töpelmann, Berlin, 1964, pp. 141-52 (=P. Benoit, *Exégèse et théologie*, III, Cerf, Paris, 1968, pp. 271-82).
Passion et résurrection du Seigneur, Cerf, coll. 'Lire la Bible' no. 6, Paris, 1966.
'L'Ascension', *RB* 56 (1949), pp. 161-203.
'Résurrection à la fin des temps ou dès la mort?', *Concilium* 60, (1970), pp. 91-100.
J. Blank, 'Die Auferstehung Jesu als Offenbarungsereignis', in *Paulus und Jesus. Eine theologische Grundlegung*, Kösel, Studien zum A u NT no. 18, Munich, 1969, pp. 133-83.
'Die Berufung des Paulus als offenbarungshafter Grund seines Christusverhältnisses, seines Apostolats und seiner Theologie', ibid., pp. 184-249.
J. Blinzler, *Der Prozess Jesu*, Pustet, Regensburg, 1969.
E. L. Bode, *The First Easter Morning. The Gospel Accounts of the Women's Visit to the Tomb of Jesus*, Biblical Institute, Anal Bibl no. 45, Rome, 1970.
G. Bouwmann, 'Die Erhöhung Jesu in der lukanischen Theologie', *BZ* 14 (1970), pp. 257-63.
M. Brändle, 'Musste das Grab Jesu leer sein?', *Orientierung* 31 (1967), pp. 108-12.
F. M. Braun, 'La sépulture de Jesus', *RB* 45 (1936), pp. 184-200, 346-63.
R. Bultmann, 'Neues Testament und Mythologie', conference 4 June 1941, first published *Offenbarung und Heilsgeschehen*, Munich, 1941, pp. 27-61; trans. 'New Testament and Mythology', in *Kerygma and Myth*, London, 1948.
'Zu J. Schniewinds Thesen das Problem der Entmythologisierung, betreffend', in *Kerygma und Mythos*, ed. H. W. Bartsch and H. Reich, Hamburg, 1948, I, pp. 122-38; trans. 'A reply to the Theses of J. Schniewind', in *Kerygma and Myth*, pp. 102-23.
Das Verhältnis der urchristlichen Botschaft zum historischen Jesus, C. Winter, Heidelberg, 1960.
H. von Campenhausen, *Der Ablauf der Osterereignisse und das leere Grab*, C. Winter, Heidelberg, 1966.
M. Carrez, 'Avec quel corps les morts ressuscitent-ils?', *Concilium* 60 (1970), pp. 81-9.
'L'herméneutique paulinienne de la Résurrection', dans *La résurrection du Christ et l'exégèse moderne* (1969), pp. 53-73.

F. M. Catherinet, 'Note sur un verset de l'Évangile selon saint Jean (XX, 17)', dans *Memorial J. Chaine*, Lyon, 1950, pp. 51-9.

N. Clark, *Interpreting the Resurrection*, SCM, London, 1967.

O. Cullmann, *Immortalité de l'âme ou Résurrection des morts?* Delachaux, Neuchâtel, 1956.

Les premières confessions de foi chrétiennes, Paris, 1943 (=*La foi et le culte dans l'Église primitive*, Delachaux, Neuchâtel, 1963, pp. 47-87).

J. Daniélou, *La résurrection*, Seuil, Paris, 1969.

G. Dautzenberg, *Sein Leben bewahren*. Psychē *in den Herrenworten der Evangelien*, Kösel, Studien zum A u NT no. 14, Munich, 1966.

R. Deichgräber, *Gotteshymnus und Christushymnus in der frühen Christenheit. Untersuchungen zu Form, Sprache und Stil der frühchristlichen Hymnen*. Vandenhoeck, Studien zur Umwelt des NT no. 5, Göttingen, 1967.

J. Delorme, 'Résurrection et tombeau de Jésus', dans *La résurrection du Christ et l'exégèse moderne* (1969), pp. 105-51.

'La resurrection de Jésus dans le langage du Nouveau Testament', to appear in *Actes du IIIᵉ Congrès de l'ACFEB*, Cerf, Paris.

A. Descamps, 'La structure des récits évangéliques de la Résurrection', *Bib* 40 (1959), pp. 726-41.

Diskussion um Kreuz und Auferstehung, Zur gegenwärtigen Auseinandersetzung in Theologie und Gemeinde, ed. B. Klappert, Aussaat, Wuppertal, 1968.

C. H. Dodd, 'The Appearances of the Risen Christ: An Essay in Form-Criticism of the Gospels', in *Studies in the Gospels*, Mem. R. H. Lightfoot, Oxford, 1957, pp. 9-35.

J. Dupont, 'La conversion de Paul et son influence sur la conception du salut par la foi', dans *Foi et salut selon saint Paul*, Biblical Institute Anal Bibl no. 42, Rome, 1970, pp. 67-80.

'Les pèlerins d'Emmaüs (Luc XXIV, 13-35)', *Miscellanea Biblica*, B. Ubach, Montserrat, 1953, pp. 349-74.

'Le repas d'Emmaüs', *LV* 31 (1957), pp. 77-92.

'Ressuscité "le troisième jour"', *Bib* 40 (1959), pp. 742-61 (=*Études*, pp. 321-36).

F. X. Durwell, *La résurrection de Jesus, mystère du Salut*, Mappus, Le Puy, 1963.

R. H. Fuller, *The Foundations of New Testament Christology*, Lutterworth, London, 1965.

The Formation of the Resurrection Narratives, Macmillan, New York, 1971.

A. George, 'Les récits d'apparitions aux Onze à partir de Lc 24 : 36-53', dans *La résurrection du Christ et l'exégèse moderne* (1969), pp. 75-104.

F. Gils, 'Pierre et la foi au Christ ressuscité', *ETL* 38 (1962), pp. 5-42.

J. Gnilka, 'La résurrection du corps dans la moderne discussion exégétique', *Concilium* 60 (1970), pp. 115-25.

J. M. Gonzalez-Ruiz, 'Vers une demythologisation de "l'âme separée"', *Concilium* 41 (1969), pp. 73-84.

M. Goguel, *La foi à la résurrection de Jesus dans le christianisme primitif. Étude d'histoire et de psychologie religieuses*, E. Leroux, Paris, 1933.

A. Grabner-Haider, 'Resurrection et Glorification', *Concilium* 41 (1969), pp. 59-71.

H. Grass, *Ostergeschehen und Osterberichte*, Vandenhoeck, Göttingen, 1956, 1962.

P. Grelot, 'L'eschatologie de la Sagesse et les apocalypses juives', in *Mémorial A. Gelin*, Mappus, Le Puy, 1961, pp. 165-79.

De la mort à la vie éternelle, Études de théologie biblique, Cerf, coll. 'Lectio divina' no. 67, Paris, 1971.

'La résurrection de Jésus et son arrière-plan biblique et juif', dans *La résurrection du Christ et l'exégèse modern* (1969), pp. 17-53.

G. Greshake, *Die Auferstehung der Toten. Ein Beitrag zur gegenwärtigen theologischen Diskussion über die Zukunft der Geschichte*, Ludgerus, coll. 'Koinonia' no. 10, Essen, 1969.

J. Guitton, *Le problème de Jesus, Divinité et Résurrection*, Aubier, Paris, 1953.

E. Gutwenger, 'Auferstehung und Auferstehungsleib Jesu', *ZKT* 91 (1969), pp. 32-58.

'Zur Geschichtlichkeit der Auferstehung Jesu', *ZKT* 88 (1966), pp. 257-82.

F. Hahn, *Christologische Hoheitstitel. Ihre Geschichte im frühen Christentum*, Vandenhoeck, coll. FRLANT no. 83, Göttingen, 1963.

P. De Haes, *La résurrection de Jésus dans l'apologétique des cinquante dernières années*, Gregorian Univ., Rome, 1953.

G. Hartmann, 'Die Vorlage der Osterberichte in Joh 20', *ZNW* 55 (1964), pp. 197-220.

P. Hoffman, *Die Toten in Christus. Eine religionsgeschichtliche und exegetische Untersuchung zur paulinischen Eschatologie*, Aschendorff, NT Abhandlungen, NF, no. 2, Münster, 1966.

H. Hooke, *The Resurrection of Christ as History and Experience*, Darton-Longman and Todd, London, 1967.

B. van Iersel, 'La résurrection de Jésus: information ou interpretation?' *Concilium* 60 (1970), pp. 51-62.

B. A. Johnson, *Empty Tomb Tradition in the Gospel of Peter*, Th. D. Harvard Univ., June 1965.

F. Kamphaus, *Von der Exegese zur Predigt. Uber die Problematik einer schriftgemässen Verkündigung de Oster- Wunder- und Kindheitsgeschichten*, Mathias-Grünewald, Mainz, 1960.

M. Kehl, 'Eucharistie und Auferstehung. Zur Deutung de Ostererscheinungen beim Mahl', *Geist und Leben* 24 (1970), pp. 90-125.

G. Koch, *Die Auferstehung Jesu Christi*, Mohr, Tübingen, 1959, 1965.

W. Kramer, *Christos, Kyrios, Gottessohn. Untersuchungen zu Gebrauch und Bedeutung der christologischen Bezeichnungen bei Paulus und den vorpaulinischen Gemeinden*, Zwingli, Abh. zum Theol. A u NT no. 44, Zurich, 1963.

J. Kremer, *Das älteste Zeugnis von der Auferstehung Christi. Eine bibeltheologische Studie zur Aussage und Bedeutung von I Kor 15:1-11*. Katholisches Bibelwerk, coll. SBS no. 17, Stuttgart, 1966.

Die Osterbotschaft der vier Evangelien Katholisches Bibelwerk. Stuttgart, 1968.

'La resurrection de Jésus, principe et modèle de notre résurrection d'après saint Paul', *Concilium* 60 (1970), pp. 71-80.

G. W. H. Lampe et M. MacKinnon, *The Resurrection. A Dialogue Arising from Broadcasts,* Mowbray, London, 1966.

K. Lehmann, *Auferweckt am dritten Tag nach der Schrift. Exegetische und fundamentaltheologische Studien zu I Kor 15:3-5,* Herder, Freiburg, 1968.

X. Léon-Dufour, 'Apparitions du Réssuscité et herméneutique', in *La résurrection du Christ et l'exégèse moderne* (1969), pp. 153-73.

'L'exégète et l'évènement historique', *RSR* 58 (1970), pp. 555-9.

'Sur la résurrection de Jesus', Bulletin d'exégèse du NT, *RSR* 57 (1969), pp. 583-622.

E. Le Roy, 'Résurrection de Jesus' in *Dogme et critique*, Bloud, Paris, 1907, pp. 155-257.

J. Lindblom, *Gesichte und Offenbarungen. Vorstellungen von gött-*

lichen Weisungen und übernaturlichen Erscheinungen im ältesten Christentum, Gleerup, Lund, 1968.

G. Lohfink, 'Eine alttestamentliche Darstellungsform für Gotteserscheinungen in den Damaskusberichten' *BZ* 9 (1965), pp. 246-57.

'Der historische Ansatz der Himmelfahrt Christi', *Catholica* 17 (1963), pp. 44-94.

Paulus vor Damaskus. Katholisches Bibelwerk, coll. SBS no. 4, Stuttgart, 1966.

D. Lys, *La chair dans l'Ancien Testament. 'Basar'*, Ed. univ., Paris, 1967.

NÈPHÈSH, *Histoire de l'âme dans la révélation d'Israel au sein des religions proche-orientales*, PUF, Paris, 1959.

R. Martin-Achard, *De la mort à la résurrection. L'origine et le développement d'une croyance dans le cadre de l'Ancien Testament*, Neuchâtel, 1956.

C. Martini, *Il Problema storico della Risurrezione negli studi recenti. Lo stato attuale della questione del problema storico-critico della Risurrezione di Cristo alla luce degli studi e dei metodi esegetici recenti.* Gregorian Univ., Rome, 1959.

W. Marxsen, *Die Auferstehung Jesu als historisches und als theologisches Problem*, G. Mohn, Gütersloh, 1968 (=*Auferstehung I*); trans. *The Significance of the Message of the Resurrection*, London 1968, pp. 15-50 (=*Message*).

Die Auferstehung Jesu von Nazareth, G. Mohn, Gütersloh, 1968 (=*Auferstehung II*); trans. *The Resurrection of Jesus of Nazareth*, London, 1970 (=*Resurrection*).

C. Masson, 'Le tombeau vide (Marc 16 : 1-8)', *Revue de Théologie et de Philosophie* (1944), pp. 161-74.

Le problème historique de la résurrection de Jésus', ibid., 1950, pp. 178-86.

J. Molitor, 'Auferstehung Jesu und sein Gesehenwerden', in *Grundbegriffe der Jesusüberlieferung im Lichte ihrer orientalischer Sprachgeschichte*, Düsseldorf, 1968.

F. Mussner, *Die Auferstehung Jesu*, Kösel, Handbibliotek no. 7, Munich, 1969.

V. H. Neufeld, *The Earliest Christian Confessions*, Leyden, 1963.

F. Neyrinck, 'Les femmes au tombeau: étude de la rédaction matthéenne (Matt. 28:1-10)', *NTS* 15 (1968-9), pp. 168-90.

F. Nötscher, *Altorientalischer und alttestamentlicher Auferstehungsglauben*, Würzburg, 1926; new ed. Darmstadt, 1970, by J. Scharbert with an important bibliographical appendix.

E. Pax, *Epiphaneia. Ein religionsgeschichtlicher Beitrag zur biblischen Theologie*, K. Zink, coll. Münchener Th. St. I no. 10, Munich, 1955.

A. Pelletier, 'Les apparitions du Ressuscité en termes de la Septante', *Bib* 51 (1970), pp. 76-9.

E. Pfaff, *Die Bekehrung des hl.Paulus in der Exegese des 20. Jahrhunderts*, Gregorian Univ., Rome, 1942.

E. Pousset, 'La résurrection', *NRT* 91 (1969), pp. 1009-44.

K. Rahner, 'Dogmatische Fragen zur Osterfrömmigkeit' (1959), *Schriften zur Theologie*, vol. IV, Einsiedeln, 1960, p. 166.

F. Refoulé, 'Immortalité de l'âme et résurrection de la chair', *RHR* 163 (1963), pp. 11-52.

K. Rengstorf, *Die Auferstehung Jesu. Form, Art und Sinn der urchristlichen Botschaft*, Luther-V., Witten, 1954, 1967.

La résurrection du Christ et l'exégèse moderne, by P. de Surgy, P. Grelot, M. Carrez, A. George, J. Delorme, X. Léon-Defour, Cerf, coll. 'Lectio divina' no. 50, Paris, 1969.

J. A. T. Robinson, *The Body*, SCM, London, 1952.

E. Ruckstuhl and J. Pfammater, *Die Auferstehung Jesu Christi. Heilsgeschichtliche Tatsache und Brennpunkt des Glaubens*, Rex, Lucerne and Munich, 1968.

L. Schenke, *Auferstehungsverkündigung und leeres Grab. Eine traditionsgeschichtliche Untersuchung von Mark 16:1-8*. Katholisches Bilbelwerk, coll. SBS no. 33, Stuttgart, 1969.

G. Schille, 'Das Leiden des Herrn. Die evangelische Passionstradition und ihr Sitz im Leben', *ZTK* 52 (1955), pp. 161-205.

H. Schlier, 'L'Ascension de Jésus d'aprés les écrits de Saint Luc' (1961), in *Essais sur le Nouveau Testament*, Cerf, coll. 'Lectio divina' no. 46, Paris, 1968, pp. 263-78.

Über die Auferstehung Jesu Christi, Johannes, Einsiedeln, 1968.

J. Schmitt, *Jesus ressuscité dans la prédication apostolique. Étude de théologie biblique*, Gabalda, Paris, 1949.

'La résurrection de Jesus: Des formules kérygmatiques aux récits évangeliques', *Mélanges J. J. Weber*, Paris, 1962, pp. 93-105.

'Le récit de la résurrection dans l'évangile de Luc: étude de critique littéraire', *RevSR* 25 (1951), pp. 119-37, 219-43.

'Simples remarques sur le fragment Jo XX, 22-23', *Mélanges M. Andrieu*, Strasburg, 1956, pp. 415-23.

R. Schnackenburg, 'Zur Aussageweise "Jesus ist (von den Toten) auferstanden" ', *BZ* 13 (1969), pp. 1-17.

K. Schubert, 'Die Entwicklung der Auferstehungslehre von der nachexilischen bis zur frührabbinischen Zeit', *BZ* 6 (1962), pp. 177-214.

P. Schubert, 'The Structure and Significance of Luke 24', *Neut. Studien f. R. Bultmann*, Töpelmann, Berlin, 1954, pp. 165-88.

E. Schweizer, *Erniedrigung und Erhöhung bei Jesus und seinen Nachfolgern*, Zwingli, Abh. z. Th. A u NT no. 28, Zurich, 1962.

Jesus Christus im vielfältigen Zeugnis des Neuen Testaments, Siebenstern, Munich and Hamburg, 1968.

'Two New Testament Credo compared, I Corinthians 15:3-5 and I Timothy 3, 16', *Current Issues in N.T. Interpretation* (for O. A. Piper), New York, 1962, pp. 166-77, 291-3 (=*Neotestamentica*, pp. 122-35).

Ph. Seidensticker, 'Das Antiochenische Glaubensbekenntnis I Kor 15, 3-7 im Lichte seiner Traditionsgeschichte', *Theologie und Glaube* 57 (1967), pp. 286-323.

Die Auferstehung Jesu in der Botschaft der Evangelisten. Ein traditionsgeschichtlicher Versuch zum Problem der Sicherung der Osterbotschaft in der apostolischen Zeit, Katholisches Bibelwerk, coll. SBS no. 26, Stuttgart, 1967.

Zeitgenössische Texte zur Osterbotschaft der Evangelien, Katholishes Bibelwerk, coll. SBS no 27, Stuttgart, 1967.

G. Stemberger, *Le corps de la resurrection dans le monde juif*, published in Anal Bibl, Biblical Institute, Rome.

P. A. van Stempvoort, 'The Interpretation of the Ascension in Luke and Acts', *NTS* 5 (1958), pp. 30-42.

W. Thüsing, 'Erhöhungsvorstellung und Parusieerwartung in der ältesten nachösterlichen Christologie', *BZ* 11 (1967), pp. 95-108, 205-22, and *BZ* 12 (1968), pp. 223-40; repr. Katholisches Bibelwerk, coll. SBS no. 42, Stuttgart, 1970.

Die Erhöhung und Verherrlichung Jesu im Johannesvangelium, Aschendorff, Nt Abh XXI/1-2, Münster, 1960.

W. Trilling, 'Les traits essentiels de l'Église du Christ', *Assemblée du Seigneur,* 1st series (1964), no. 53, pp. 21-23.

J. Villette, *La résurrection du Christ dans l'art chrétien du IIe au VIIe siècle*, H. Laurens, Paris, 1957.

A. Vögtle, 'Ekklesiologische Aufragsworte des Auferstandenen', *Sacra Pagina* II, Paris and Gembloux, 1959, pp. 280-94.

G. Wagner, *La résurrection, signe du monde nouveau*, Cerf, coll. 'Avenirs' no. 13, Paris, 1970.

U. Wilckens, *Auferstehung. Das biblische Auferstehungszeugnis historisch untersucht und erklärt*, Kreuz, coll. 'Themen der Theologie' no. 4, Stuttgart and Berlin, 1970.

'Die Bekehrung des Paulus als religionsgeschichtliches Problem', *ZTK* 56 (1959), pp. 273-93.

'Die Perikope vom leeren Grab Jesu in der nachmarkinischen Traditionsgeschichte', *Mélanges F. Smend*, Berlin, 1963, pp. 30-41.

'Die Überlieferungsgeschichte der Auferstehung Jesu', in *Die Bedeutung der Auferstehungsbotschaft* (1966), pp. 41-63.

'Der Ursprung der Uberlieferung der Erscheinungen des Auferstandenen', in *Dogma und Denkstrukturen* (for E. Schlink), Göttingen, 1963, pp. 53-95.

Abbreviations
(PERIODICALS AND SERIES)

Anal Bib	Analecta Biblica, Biblical Institute (Rome, 1952–).
Ass.S	*Assemblées du Seigneur* (Bruges, 1961–).
Bib.	*Biblica* (Rome, 1920–).
BZ	*Biblische Zeitschrift* (Paderborn, N.F. 1957–).
Cahiers Laennec	*Cahiers Laennec*. Revue médicale de technique et de doctrine (Paris, 1934–).
Catholica	*Catholica, Vierteljahresschrift für Kontroverstheologie* (Münster, 1932–).
Concilium	*Concilium*, International Review of Theology, English ed., Search Press.
ETL	*Ephemerides Theologicae Lovanienses* (Bruges, 1924–).
Ev. T	*Evangelische Theologie* (Munich, 1934–).
GL	*Geist und Leben. Zeitschrift fur Aszese und Mystik* (Würzburg, 1947–).
Greg.	*Gregorianum.*
Intr.Bib.	*Introduction à la Bible*, ed. A. Robert and A. Feuillet (Paris and Tournai, I 1959; II 1959).
JTS	*The Journal of Theological Studies* (London, 1899–).
LTK	*Lexikon für Theologie und Kirche* (Frieburg, 1957–).
LV	*Lumière et Vie* (Saint-Alban-Leysse and Lyon, 1950–).
NTD	*Neues Testament Deutsch.*
NRT	*Nouvelle Revue Théologique* (Tournai and Louvain, 1879–).
NTS	*New Testament Studies* (Cambridge, 1954–).
RB	*Revue Biblique* (Paris, 1892–).

RevSR   *Revue de Sciences religieuses* (Strasburg, 1921–).
RHPR   *Revue d'Histoire et de Philosophie religieuses*
                (Strasburg, 1921–).
RHR   *Revue de l'Histoire de Religions* (Paris, 1880–).
RSR   *Recherches de Science religieuse* (Paris, 1910–).
SBS   Stuttgarter Bibel Studien (Stuttgart, 1965–).
SDB   *Supplément au Dictionnaire de la Bible* (Paris,
                1928–).
TDNT   See TWNT
TLZ   *Theologische Literaturzeitung* (Leipzig, 1842–).
TWNT   *Theologisches Wörterbuch zum Neuen Testa-*
                ment (Stuttgart, 1933–); *ET, Theological Dic-*
                tionary of the New Testament (Grand Rapids
                and London, 1964–).
VTB   *Vocabulaire de théologie biblique*, ed. X. Léon-
                Dufour, J. Duplacy, A. George, P. Grelot, J.
                Guillet, M. F. Lacan (Paris, 1970).
ZKT   *Zeitschrift für katholische Theologie* (Innbruck,
                1877–).
ZNW   *Zeitschrift für die neutestamentliche Wissen-*
                schaft und die Kunde der alteren Kirche (Gies-
                sen and Berlin, 1900–).
ZTK   *Zeitschrift für Theologie und Kirche* (Tübin-
                gen, 1891–).

Abbreviations

(BIBLICAL BOOKS)

Acts	Acts of the Apostles
Bar	Baruch
I and II Chron	Chronicles
I and II Cor	Corinthians
Col	Colossians
Dan	Daniel
Deut	Deuteronomy
Eccles	Ecclesiastes
Ecclus	Ecclesiasticus
Eph	Ephesians
Est	Esther
Exod	Exodus
Ezek	Ezekiel
Ezra	Ezra
Gal	Galatians
Gen	Genesis
Hab	Habakkuk
Heb	Hebrews
Hosea	Hosea
Is	Isaiah
Jer	Jeremiah
Judg	Judges
Job	Job
Joel	Joel
John	Gospel of John
I, II and III John	Epistles of John
Jonah	Jonah
Josh	Joshua
I and II Kings	Kings
Luke	Gospel of Luke

Lev	Leviticus
I and II Macc	Maccabees
Mark	Gospel of Mark
Matthew	Gospel of Matthew
Neh	Nehemiah
Num	Numbers
I Peter	I Peter
Phil	Philippians
Prov	Proverbs
Ps	Psalm
Rev	Revelation of John
Rom	Romans
Ruth	Ruth
I and II Sam	Samuel
S of S	Song of Songs
I and II Thess	Thessalonians
I Tim	I Timothy
Tit	Titus
Tob	Tobit
Wis	Wisdom of Solomon
Zech	Zechariah

NON-BIBLICAL BOOKS

Apoc Bar	Apocalypse of Baruch
Apoc Mos	Apocalypse of Moses
Asc Is	Ascension of Isaiah
Ber	Berakoth (Talmud treatise)
IV Esd	IV Esdras (II Esdras)
Gen r.	Midrash Rabbah on Genesis
Eth Enoch	Book of Enoch (Ethiopian version).
II Enoch	Book of the Secrets of Enoch (Slavonic Enoch)
Lev r.	Midrash Rabbah on Leviticus
I QS	Rule of Discipline (*sēder*) of the Qumran sect
Sanh	Sanhedrin (Talmud treatise)
Or Sib	Sibylline Oracles

Glossary

This glossary includes only terms which present some technical difficulty. Further explanations can be found in such reference works as the *Oxford Dictionary of the Christian Church* ed. F. L. Cross, 1966; the published and forthcoming volumes of *The Catholic Dictionary of Theology*, ed. E. F. Davis, A. Williams, I. Thomas and J. Crehan, 1962–; *A Dictionary of Theology*, ed. A. Richardson, 1969. There are discussions also in our previous works, *Les Évangiles et l'Histoire de Jésus* (EHJ) and *Études d'Évangile* (EE).

Aorist   A tense of the Greek verb which, in the indicative mood, indicates a completed past action.

Apocalyptic   From the Greek *apokalypsis*, the action of discovering or unveiling; and hence, 'that which concerns a revelation'. It signifies a literary category, the typical representatives of which, in addition to the revelation or Apocalypse of John, are the Book of Enoch and the Fourth Book of Esdras.

   The term *synoptic apocalypse* refers to the group of eschatological sayings of Jesus which are found in Matthew 24=Mark 13=Luke 21.

Apocrypha   From a Greek word which means 'hidden things'. Writings resembling the canonical books, but not found in the canon of scripture (EHJ pp. 51-53).

Apocryphon of James (Apocryphal Letter of James)   One of the five writings in the 'Jung Codex', discovered about 1945 in upper Egypt near Nag Hammadi. A Coptic text, translated from the Greek, dating from the second century A.D. Esoteric communications by the risen Christ to James, brother of the Lord. Its thought is connected with that of gnosticism, but not with Valentinian gnosticism. Text edited as *Epistula Iacobi Apocrypha* by Michel Malinin, etc., with English, French, and German translations, Rascher Verlag, Zurich and Stuttgart, 1968.

Apostolic age   The period covered by the authority of the apostles.

Aramaic   The Semitic language spoken in the time of Christ by the people of Palestine and Syria.

Authentic   Deriving from the speaker or author to whom it is attributed (a saying of Jesus, a narrative by Luke) or forming a true part of a particular book (verses of Matthew).

That of which the truth or authority cannot be contested.

Aeon   from the Greek *Aion*, signifying world, century, long duration (Hebrew: *olam*). Late Jewish apocalyptic distinguishes two aeons: 'this aeon' which is to pass and is subject to sorrow, and 'that aeon', which is to come and which will be the kingdom of justice and peace.

Baruch (Apocalypse of)   =Apoc Bar. An Old Testament apocryphal book. Composed towards the end of the first century A.D., originally in Hebrew, but preserved only in Syriac. Close to rabbinical theology. Seeks a response to the question why Jerusalem has been destroyed, and to the problem of sin in relation to eschatological judgment. (English translation in R. H. Charles, *Apocrypha and Pseudepigrapha of the Old Testament*, vol. II, reprinted 1963).

Canon of Scripture   From the Greek *ƙanōn*: rule (hence, 'rule of faith').

List of the books of the Old Testament and the New Testament officially recognized by the church as inspired by God.

Category (literary)   Way of expressing oneself in a fixed form. This implies the working out in a personal vision of a certain stable and common way of living, acting, thinking and writing (EHJ p. 30).

In addition to the categories into which the sayings of Jesus fall (logia, community rules, parables, etc.), the gospels present the actions of Jesus in the form of miracle stories, apothegemata (brief epigrammatic sentences in a setting), dialogues, narratives concerning Jesus, summaries, etc. (EHJ pp. 237-41).

The determination of literary category is a matter of literary criticism and does not immediately imply a judgment from the point of view of historical criticism.

Chiasma   From the Greek *chiasma*: a crossing. Distribution of the words of a phrase of the elements of a passage in such a way that they correspond one to the other around a central point which is not always explicit:

A B C D X D' C' B' A'

Example: Whoever would save his life (A)
will *lose it* (B).
Whoever *loses his life* for my sake (B')
will find it (A')
(Matthew 16:25; EHJ p. 159).

Confessions of faith A literary category in which the primitive church proclaimed its belief in brief stereotyped formulas.

Context (in life) see *Sitz im Leben*.

Criticism (historical) A scientific study which seeks to determine the historicity of the narrative of an event, or the authenticity of a saying: this took place; this was said by a certain person (EHJ pp. 32-4).

Criticism (literary) A scientific study which attempts to establish the history and meaning of a text (EHJ pp. 20-5).

Criticism (textual) A scientific study which attempts to establish the original text on the basis of variants in manuscript versions.

Docetists Heretical Christians who regarded Jesus as a God who had no more than the appearance of a man.

Economy From the Greek: art of administering (*nomos*: law) a house (*oikos*).

Describes the organization of a totality, a study, or the organic distribution of a life.

The 'economy of salvation' is a term for the history of salvation.

Enoch A compilation of exaltations, parables and prophecies attributed to Enoch. The different parts of the book were composed between 170 B.C. and A.D. 100; there are also some later interpolations.

The Slavonic Enoch (II Enoch) dates from the first century B.C. It is even more influenced by Hellenism.

Epiphany From a Greek word meaning 'appearance'. The term may signify the manifestation of God (theophany), of Christ (christophany) or of the angels.

Eschatology From the Greek *eschata*: 'the last things'.

That which concerns the final age, or the end of the world.

For a Christian, the final age is inaugurated by the coming of Jesus and will conclude with his return at the parousia.

Esdras (Fourth Book of Esdras: IV Esd) An Old Testament apocryphal book, composed towards the end of the first century A.D. It is apocalyptic in nature. (It appeared in the *Apocrypha* of Protestant bibles as II Esdras.)

Exegesis A scientific study which attempts to establish the meaning of a text or a literary work.

Gnostics The adherents of gnosticism (from the Greek *gnosis*: knowledge), a pre-Christian movement which tended to identify salvation with nothing more than the knowledge of divine secrets and to despise earthly values.

Gospel of Peter An apocryphal gospel, of which a fragment was discovered in 1886. Sixty verses recount the last moments of Jesus and his resurrection. It dates from the end of the first century A.D. (between 70 and 130). It echoes ancient traditions.

Hellenism The period between Alexander the Great (died 323 B.C.) and Augustus (died 14 B.C).

The term also refers to the diffusion of Greek culture which was made possible by the conquest of Alexander, and the mixture of this culture and the world of oriental thought.

Hermeneutics From the Greek *hermēneuein*: to explain, interpret. It was first limited to the theory of explanation, but nowadays tends to refer to the actual interpretation which, presenting itself as a 'translation' or 'transposition', attempts to understand and express the text at the present day.

Hillel The great Hillel was a contemporary of Herod the Great, and lived from 30 B.C. to A.D. 10. He was a Pharisee teacher who put forward a broad interpretation of the texts of the Lord.

Hymns Texts of liturgical origin in which Jesus was acclaimed as the Lord glorified by God (cf. pp. 25-6).

Ignatius of Antioch One of the first Apostolic Fathers, by whom we possess several letters written towards A.D. 110 (to the churches of Ephesus, Magnesia, Philadelphia, Rome, Smyrna, Tralles, and to Polycarp).

Encapsulation The procedure by which a literary unit is enclosed between two similar words or phrases.

Isaiah (Ascension of) A Christian compilation of the Jewish legend concerning the martyrdom of the prophet Isaiah. The Jewish parts date from the first century B.C., while some of the Christian passages date from A.D. 80-100, and others from A.D. 100-150.

Josephus Born at Jerusalem in A.D. 37, died at Rome about A.D. 98.

Experienced the Jewish war, the history of which he wrote (75-79); also composed the *Antiquities of the Jews* (about 93) and *Contra Apionem* (about 96).

Judaism   Later Judaism signifies the religion of post-exilic Israel.
The development of Old Testament thought, especially under the influence of Hellenism.

Kenōsis   From the Greek word signifying the action by which one empties oneself of something. In biblical theology, signifies the humiliation of Christ in his incarnation (cf. pp. 26-8).

Kerygma   From the Greek word *kerygma*: proclamation, preaching. The proclamation of Jesus, who has become Christ, Lord and Saviour through his resurrection.
In the broader sense, includes catechesis; the response echoing the experience by the church of the living Lord (EHJ p. 256; p. 303).

Koinē   A Greek adjective signifying 'common'. Refers to the language commonly spoken in the Roman Empire at the time of Christ (EHJ pp. 90-91).

Liber Antiquitatum Biblicarum (LAB)   An edifying book on the *Biblical Antiquities*, which we possess in Latin, a free translation of the Greek, which itself derives from a Hebrew original. There are no Christian interpolations. It probably dates from before A.D. 70. The work has been falsely attributed to Philo (Pseudo-Philo).

Life of Adam and Eve   A Judaeo-Christian apocryphal work which has come down to us in the Latin tradition of a Greek writing, which itself derives from a Jewish work written in Hebrew (between 20 B.C. and A.D. 70).

Matthean, Marcan, Lucan, Johannine   Characteristic of the redactional work of Matthew, Mark, Luke and John. These characteristics are largely based upon the statistics of the use of terms or expressions.

Midrash   From a Hebrew word signifying 'seek out'.
In this literary category, which was practised in Judaism, the author attempts to explain a passage of scripture in relation to the present time. It must not be regarded as identical with fables, nor the creation of legends (cf. Stemberger, *Symbolique*, p. 254).

Moses   *The Assumption of Moses* dates from a short time after A.D. 4.
The Apocalypse of Moses, corresponding to the *Life of Adam and Eve*, dates from 20 B.C. to A.D. 50.

Parousia   A Greek word: coming, presence.

A specialist word to signify the return of Christ at the end of time.

Pattern   A term of literary criticism referring to that which under-lies the structure of a passage.

Pericope   A passage which can be cut away (*peri-koptō*) from a larger totality, such as the healing of the leper, Mark 1:40-44 (EHJ p. 237).

Philo of Alexandria   A Jewish philosopher (20 B.C. – A.D. 50).

Positivism (historical)   The tendency of historical science to regard as valid only the knowledge of bare facts, independently of the interpretations given to them (EE pp. 21-24).

Pre-   This prefix is used to refer to a period or a stage preceding the word which follows: pre-gospel, pre-literary, pre-paschal, pre-redactional, pre-synoptic.

Primitive   A term for the oldest tradition, text or setting, closest to the events.

Qumrân   The dwelling place of the Jewish sect on the shores of the Dead Sea (inhabited from the second century B.C. until A.D. 68). Beginning in 1947, what are known as the Qumrân manuscripts have been found there: copies and translations of the bible and of apocryphal works, together with the special writings of the sect.

Quotation   Passages of scripture included in a text in order to explain it.

Recension   A literary criticism, the putting of a tradition into writing.
In textual criticism, refers to a particular manuscript.

Redactional   Refers to a passage, the style of which has been re-edited by an author for a certain purpose.

Rule of the Community   Sérék, 'rule'. Also known as the *rule of discipline*. Quoted by the sign I QS, contains rules, theological instructions and poetic meditations. Probably composed by the founder or reorganizer of the Qumrân sect.

Sanhedrin   In Rabbinic literature, refers to a section of the treatise *Mezikin*, 'damages' in the *Mishnah*. It describes the constitution and procedure of the courts of justice, and particularly judicial procedure.

Semitisms   Certain passages of the New Testament betray the influence of Semitic thought and Aramaic style. These should not be confused with Hebraisms, due to a servile imitation of the Septuagint.

Septuagint (LXX)   Greek translation of the Old Testament. It was composed, according to legend, by seventy (Septuaginta) Jewish scholars, but as a matter of historical fact, by numerous writers between 250 and 150 B.C.

Sibylline Oracles A compilation of traditions of Jewish origin, with Christian interpolations, dating from the fifth and sixth centuries.

Sitz im Leben A German term of literary criticism, referring to the context or situation in life in which a literary tradition is 'formed'. For example, we distinguish between the Sitz im Leben of liturgy, catechesis, and missionary work according to their characteristic activities and between the Easter setting and the pre-paschal setting according to their content of faith.

The term should not be confused with the time and place of the events. Determining these is a matter of historical criticism.

Structure From a Latin word signifying construction, building. A large totality composed of small literary units.

This term refers to their gathering together, architecture, and purpose: the parts gathered together are consciously organized in relation to a whole.

The harmonization of the relationships which remain, even if what was ultimately related has disappeared.

Symbol 'In a general sense, symbols are materials by which a convention of language, a social fact, or a sign of mutual recognition between liberties are composed' (Ortigues).

A meaningful reality, setting forth to the world the values which it expresses and to which it belongs.

The concept is not to be identified

with allegory, since in a symbol the reality is prior to the idea,

with form or structure, for content and expression are inseparable;

with sign, for a symbol forms part of what it represents.

A distinction must be made between

a conventional symbol, produced by society;

a traditional symbol, which is a constituent element of society.

Symbolism According to the philosophical outlook of the person using this term, it may or may not imply that the fact to which it refers is a reality. For us, to say that a miracle is symbolical describes it, but does not deny its historical reality.

Synoptic Etymologically, making it possible to view several elements at a single glance (*syn*: with; *optikos*: relating to sight).

The three first gospels are called 'Synoptic', because in a common framework they present numerous differences and resemblances.
Term referring to matters set out in a table (EHJ pp. 225-36).

Talmud   'Teaching', and hence a gathering of explanations of the juridical and haggadic texts of the Torah, based on the Mishnah.
Consists of the Gemara and the Baraitoth. It is the Torah in the wider sense.
The Jerusalem or Palestinian Talmud (JerT) was complete by the end of the fourth century, and the Babylonian Talmud (TB) at the end of the fifth century. The latter is four times longer that the Palestinian. They are usually quoted by treatise and folio.
The *talmīdīm* are the disciples of the rabbis.

Targum (Tg)   A term of Hittite origin, signifying 'announce, explain, translate'.
An Aramaic paraphrase of the Old Testament. Amongst others, the Targum Onkelos (Babylonian, with official authority), the Targum of Pseudo-Jonathan (Palestinian) and the Targum Neofiti should be noted.

Tradition (historical)   The recollection handed down of an event. The transmission of the recollection of an event.

Tradition (literary)   The chain of writings concerning a single subject, starting with the original manuscript to the present text (EHJ pp. 226-8).

Tradition (theological)   The transmission of revelation. Everything that the apostles handed down for the life and faith of the people of God, which the church has maintained throughout the centuries.

Notes

INTRODUCTION

1. B. Bultmann, 'Neues Testament und Mythologie' (1941), pp. 44-6; trans. in *Kerygma and Myth* (1948), pp. 38-43.

2. R. Bultmann, *Verhältnis* (1960), p. 27.

3. Cf. G. Koch, *Auferstehung* (1959), p. 4.

4. G. Bornkamm, *Jesus von Nazareth*, Stuttgart, 1957, p. 168; trans. *Jesus of Nazareth*, London, 1960, p. 184.

5. W. Marxsen, *Die Auferstehung Jesu als historisches und als theologisches Problem* (1964); trans. *The Significance of the Message of the Resurrection* (1968); *Die Auferstehung Jesu von Nazareth* (1968); trans. *The Resurrection of Jesus of Nazareth* (1970). See my review in *RSR* 57 (1969), pp. 588-94.

6. W. Marxsen, *Auferstehung II* (1968), p. 151; *Resurrection* (1970).

7. W. Marxsen, *Auferstehung II* (1968), pp. 153-8; *Resurrection* (1970).

8. This is the objective of H. von Campenhausen, *Ablauf* (1966) and H. Grass, *Ostergeschehen* (1956, 1964).

9. In my *Études* (1965), pp. 20-29.

10. The principal texts concerning the resurrection of Jesus can be found in the appendix.

STAGE I

1. The New Testament consists of the four gospels, the Acts of the Apostles, the thirteen letters attributed to Paul, the Epistle to the Hebrews, the 'catholic' epistles (James, Peter, John and Jude) and Revelations. These writings are placed not in chronological order, but according to category (gospels, 'Acts', epistles, apocalypse) or by length (St Paul's epistles). They can be dated only approximately; the authentic

letters of Paul fall between the years 50 and 65, the Gospel of Mark dates from the years 65-70, those of Matthew and Luke from 70-80, and that of John from the year 100. With regard to the other writings, scholars do not agree, except in dating most of them within the first century.

2. Recently, for example, in a work which was nevertheless highly critical: P. Seidensticker, *Auferstehung* (1967), pp. 11-16.

3. Acts 2:14-36; 3:12-26; 4:8-12; 5:29-32; 10:34-43; 13:16-41. We exclude here the address by Stephen (7:1-53) and that of Paul on the Areopagus (17:22-31).

4. The account given by C. H. Dodd, *The Apostolic Preaching* (1944) has been disputed by U. Wilckens, *Die Missionsreden der Apostelgeschichte*, Neukirchen (1961). Against the latter, J. Dupont has suggested a tenable interpretation: 'Les discours missionaires des Actes des Apôtres d'après un livre récent', *RB* 69 (1962), pp. 37-60 (= *Études*, pp. 134-55).

5. Twelve criteria have been suggested by E. Stauffer, *Die Theologie des Neuen Testaments*, Stuttgart, 1949, pp. 322-4; trans. *New Testament Theology*, London, 1955, pp. 338f. They have been applied in close detail by P. E. Langevin, *Jésus Seigneur et l'eschatologie*, DDB, coll. 'Studia' no. 21, Montreal, 1967.

6. 'If you confess with your lips ... and believe ...' (Rom 10:9). 'I deliver to you ... what I also received' (I Cor 15:3).

7. I Tim 3:16 proclaims a 'mystery of religion' (*mystērion* is a neuter word) which in fact concerns Jesus Christ, who himself is introduced by a masculine relative.

8. In Rev 1:4, grace and peace are asked for 'from him who is and who was and who is to come'; but while the preposition 'from' (in Greek, *apo*) requires the genitive, we find in fact the nominative. This shows that the formula 'he who is, etc.' is stereotyped.

9. I Cor 16:22; Phil 2:6.

10. I Thess 1:10; I Cor 6:14; 15:3-4; Gal 1:1; II Cor 4:14; Rom 4:24; 8:12; 10:9.

11. Col 1:15-16; I Tim 3:16; Acts 4:10.

12. I Thess 4:3-5; Rom 2:3-4.

13. In spite of the attempt of W. Kramer, *Christos, Kyrios, Gottessohn* (1963).

CHAPTER I

1. O. Cullman, *Les premières confessions de foi chrétiennes* (1943); V. H. Neufeld, *The Earliest Christian Confessions* (1963); W. Kramer,

Christos, Kyrios, Gottessohn (1963); R. Deichgraber, *Gotteshymnus und Christushymnus* (1967), pp. 107-17.

2. Col 2:6, 7; II John 7-9.

3. Heb 4:15; 10:23.

4. Phil 2:5-11; I Cor 12:3; Acts 8:37 (Vg); cf. Rom 10:9; I Tim 6:12; II Tim 2:2; I Peter 3:18-22; I John 4:2.

5. John 1:34; I John 4:15; Matthew 16:16; Mark 14:61; John 11:27; 20:31.

6. Gal 3:20; I Cor 8:6; Mark 10:18; 12:29; Rom 3:30; Eph 4:6; I Tim 2:5; Rom 16:27; cf. Deut 6:4.

7. See below, chapter 9.

8. In addition to commentaries on the epistles to the Corinthians and works on the resurrection of Jesus, there are also numerous monographs on the passage. One of the most recent and the easiest to read is that by J. Kremer, *Älteste Zeugnis* (1966).

9. According to R. Bultmann, 'Zu J. Schniewinds Thesen' (1948), p. 130; trans. 'Reply to the Theses of J. Schniewind' in *Kerygma and Myth*, p. 112, Paul is trying to prove the credibility of the kerygma. Here Bultmann misunderstands the nature of Paul's argument in I Cor 15.

10. J. Molitor, 'Auferstehung Jesu' (1968), pp. 43-94; J. Jeremias, in *Actes du Symposium sur la Résurrection de Jésus*, Rome, 1970 (to be published in 1972).

11. I Cor 15:12, 13, 14-16, 17, 20.

12. E.g. H. von Campenhausen, *Ablauf* (1966), pp. 12 and 51. See chapter 6 below.

13. F. Hahn, *Christologische Hoheitstitel. Ihre Geschichte im frühen Christentum* (1963), p. 205.

14. J. Dupont, 'Ressuscité "le troisième jour"' (I Cor 15:4; Acts 10:40)', *Bib* 40 (1959), pp. 742-61 (=*Études*, pp. 321-36).

15. 'In three days': *Matthew 26:61 para.*; *27:40 para.*; John 2: 19-20. 'After three days': *Matthew 27:63*; Mark 8:31; 9:31; 10:34. 'On the third day': Matthew 16:21; 17:23; 20:19; Luke 9:22; 18:33; 27:7, 46; *Acts 10:40*. (Italics where the formula is not spoken by Jesus.)

16. K. Lehmann, *Auferweckt* (1968), especially pp. 262-90.

17. Very soon: Josh 1:11; II Sam 20:4; II Kings 20:8; Mark 14:58; 15:29. After some delay: II Chron 20:25; II Macc 5:14; Jonah 3:3; Luke 2:46.

18. Strack-Billerbeck, I, p. 747. In ancient Jewish texts, there is sometimes a mention of the seven days which are to precede the final resurrection (IV Esd 7:30-31), on the pattern of the seven days of the original creation.

19. See also Gen 42:18; Exod 19:11, 16; I Kings 12:12; II Chron 10:12; Est 5:1-8 and especially Luke 13:31-33.

20. Let us recall the hypothesis that the soul of a dead person remained by the body until the morning of the third day. This period has been explained by the time which passes until decomposition begins (cf. John 11:39). This hypothesis was maintained by M. Goguel, *Foi à la résurrection* (1933), pp. 167-9 and by J. Schmitt, *Jésus ressuscité* (1949), p. 171, but rejected by J. Dupont, 'L'utilisation apologétique de l'A.T. dans les discours des Actes' (1953), in *Études*, p. 256, no. 17. But it is not impossible that this popular conception, in connection with the theological interpretation which sees death as a power corrupting the body, may have influenced the working out of the formula.

21. See C. H. Dodd, *According to the Scriptures*, London, 1952.

22. Cf. J. Schmitt, *Jésus ressuscité* (1949), pp. 121-30; J. Kremer, *Älteste Zeugnis* (1966), pp. 38-39.

23. Cf. Gen 25:8-9; 35:8; II Chron 24:15-16; Judg 8:32; I Kings 2:10; 11:43; Deut 10:6; Luke 16:22; Acts 2:29.

24. J. Jeremias, *Die Heiligengräber in Jesu Umwelt*, Vandenhoeck, Göttingen, 1958.

25. I Thess 4:14 (*anestē*); Rom 8:34 (*egertheis*); 14:9 (*ezēsen*), all in the aorist.

26. Cf. Rom 8:32; Gal 1:4; 2:20; Eph 5:2, 25; I Tim 2:6; Tit 2:14. Following R. Deichgräber, *Gotteshymnus* (1967), p. 112, and in disagreement with W. Kramer, *Christos, Kyrios, Gottessohn* (1963), pp. 28-9, we believe that it cannot be shown that the formula 'for us' (*hyper hēmōn*) is older than the simple formula. Cf. W. Popkes, *Christus traditus. Eine Untersuchung zum Begriff der Dahingabe im Neuen Testament*, Zwingli, Zurich, 1967, pp. 201-3. So too K. Lehmann, *Auferweckt* (1968), pp. 120-31.

27. 'God, who makes the dead live!' was the prayer of the Jew in the second of the Eighteen Benedictions. This invocation has been said to date from the first century B.C. (L. Finkelstein, 'The Development of the Amidah', *Jewish Quarterly Review* 16 (1925-6), p. 23. For God to be designated in this way as the author of resurrection is something frequently found in the liturgical tradition and in later Rabbinic tradition (Ber 60a; Sanh 90a, etc.), but rarely in the apocalyptic texts of ancient Judaism (II Macc 7:9, 14; *Life of Adam* 28; 41; Or Sib II, 221-2, 238; IV, 179-83) where it is usually earth or Sheol which gives back the dead and which makes them rise (Apoc Bar 50:2-4; cf. the text in the appendix, p. 272).

28. See the references given in n. 11.

29. Cf. L. Cerfaux, *Le Christ* (1951); trans. *Christ in the Theology of St Paul* (1959).

30. P. Hoffmann, *Die Toten* (1966), pp. 180-5; F. Nötscher, *Altorientalischer und alttestamentlicher Auferstehungsglauben* (1926); second

ed., Darmstadt, 1970, by J. Scharbert, with an important bibliographical appendix.

31. A. Vögtle, 'Ekklesiologische Auftagsworte des Auferstandenen' (1959), pp. 280-94; W. Trilling, 'Les traits essentiels de l'Église du Christ' (1964), pp. 20-32.

32. P. Grelot, 'La résurrection de Jésus' (1969), pp. 21-22.

33. See the excursus by L. de Grandmaison, *Jesus Christ*, Paris, 1929, vol. II, pp. 522-4; T. Leipoldt, 'Zu den Auferstehungs-Geschichten', *TLZ* 73 (1948), pp. 737-42; P. Grelot, art. cit., pp. 18-23.

34. Here we might quote every 'Theology of the Old Testament', as well as the numerous monographs on this subject. Let us mention only: R. Martin-Achard, *De la mort à la résurrection* (1956); K. Schubert, 'Die Entwicklung' (1962), pp. 177-214; P. Hoffmann, *Die Toten* (1966), pp. 58-174; P. Grelot, 'La résurrection de Jésus' (1969), pp. 17-53.

35. The distinction between these two periods and these two areas of thought has been clearly established by M. Hengel, *Judentum und Hellenismus. Studien zu ihrer Begegnung unter Berucksichtigung Palästinas bis zur Mitte des 2. Jh. v. Chr.*, Tübingen, 1969, p. 193.

36. We have drawn here on the work of P. Hoffmann, op cit., and that of G. Stemberger, *Le corps de la résurrection dans le monde juif*, which is shortly to be published in *Anal Bib*, Rome.

37. J. Pedersen, *Israel* (1926). See in *VTB* the articles 'âme', 'chair', 'corps', 'esprit', 'homme' (soul, flesh, body, spirit, man).

38. H. W. Robinson, 'Hebrew Psychology' in *The People and the Book* (ed. Peake), 1925, p. 363; *Inspiration and Revelation in the Old Testament*, Oxford, 1946, p. 70.

39. J. Pedersen, op. cit. II, p. 153. Cf. P. Grelot, 'L'homme devant la mort' (1966), dans *De la mort à la vie éternelle* (1971), pp. 51-102.

40. Wis 44:16; 48:9; I Macc 2:58; Heb 11:5 and the apocryphal *Enoch*; cf. p. 68.

41. P. Grelot, 'La résurrection de Jésus' (1969), p. 27.

42. Ibid. p. 34.

43. 'We have a tendency to attach the label "Platonist" to doctrines as different as those of Plato, middle Platonism, Hermeticism, gnosticism, Judaism and Christianity, on the sole basis that these philosophies or religions profess the immortality of the soul, without regard to the context in which this belief is found and the principles which guide it. Similarly, we describe as Semitic the opposite conception, even if it is deduced from Aristotelian or Stoic principles. This leads to false oppositions, alternatives which are not alternatives at all, and which make it difficult to understand the novelty of Christian faith and its true originality. Too often, Protestant theologians, even O. Cullmann in his fascinating essay, *Immortalité de l'âme ou résurrection des morts* (1956),

have a tendency to present 'immortality and resurrection', 'Greek anthropology and Semitic anthropology' as the two horns of a perfect dilemma.... [On the contrary, Christian theologians have attempted to] overcome the supposed dilemmas and [to] create an anthropology which respects the specific nature of Christian faith' (F. Refoulé, 'Immortalité' (1963), p. 52). This is very true, and one cannot say that 'orthodoxy, from the metaphysical point of view, is Hebrew thought'. But are we right to criticize the latter because erroneous views such as that of the 'mortality of the soul' have been deduced from it? Thus we consider that for expressing the original Christian message, Semitic thought is more congenial than Hellenistic thought, but always needs to be interpreted. In this sense, the enterprise of C. Tresmontant, in his *Idées maîtresses de la métaphysique chrétienne*, Seuil, Paris, 1962, is to be encouraged.

44. According to Plato, the body (*sōma*) is a prison (*sēma*), from which the soul is set free (*Gorgias*, 400); death is the separation of 'soul and body' (*chōrismos psychēs apo sōmatos*), *Phaedo* 67d. On the whole question, see M. P. Nilsson, *History of Greek Religion*, Oxford, 1925; see also the comments by G. Dautzenberg, *Sein Leben bewahren* (1966), pp. 13-48, and C. Tresmontant, *Le problème de l'âme* (1971), pp. 22-8 (on Aristotle, pp. 28-50).

45. Cf. G. Dautzenberg, op. cit., p. 42 on the particular texts of Wis 1:4; 8:19-20; 9:15. According to P. Grelot, 'L'eschatologie de la Sagesse' (1961), p. 176, the author of the book used a Hellenistic terminology, but was faithful to Semitic eschatology: 'In short, souls are what survives of the living person when the bones rest in the ground', to the point at which one could talk of the 'resurrection of souls'.

46. *Liber Antiquitatum Biblicarum* (=LAB) 44:10; IV Esd 7:100; cf. IV Esd 5:14 (syr); 7:15 (ar); 7:78 (arm eth). According to G. Stemberger, only a single Jewish text seems to speak of the body as 'entrammelling members' (*Apoc Bar* 49:3). Normally the body is called the creation of God (IV Esd 3:5).

47. *promptuaria* (IV Esd 7:32; *Apoc Bar* 21:23-4).

48. 'I shall make the dead live, I shall raise from the earth those who sleep. And Sheol will give up what it owes and the abyss will render forth its contents' (LAB 3:10; cf. *Enoch 51:1*; Rev 20:13). For the liturgical texts, cf. n. 27.

49. Apoc Bar 49:2-51:3 (see the context in the appendix, p. 272).

50. P. Grelot, 'La résurrection de Jésus' (1969), p. 36.

CHAPTER II

1. See the references to the study given in n. 1, chapter 1.

2. Thus, amongst many others, R. Schnackenburg, 'Zur Aussageweise "Jesus ist (von den Toten) auferstanden" ', *BZ* 13 (1969), pp. 1-17.

3. Cf. P. Seidensticker, *Auferstehung* (1967), pp. 146-7.

4. The hypothesis is tenable, even though it must be recognized that the language of the kerygma reflects a Palestinian setting (probably older) and the terminology of the hymns a Hellenistic setting (later).

5. The authentic passages are important in that they show a traditional language: i.e.: Phil 2:6-11; I Tim 3:16. We shall not take into account the following texts: Eph 1:20-23; 2:14-18; Col 1:16-20; 2:9-15; Heb 1:3, 5:5-10; 7:1-3.

6. The translation here is varied somewhat from the RSV. Cf. J. Murphy-O'Connor, 'Philippiens (Épitre aux)', *SDB* 7 (1965), col. 1223-32 with bibliography. See also the study by R. P. Martin, 'Carmen Christi: Philippians 2:5-11', in *Recent Interpretation and the Setting of Early Christian Worship*, Cambridge, 1967. Cf. L. Cerfaux, 'L'hymne au Christ-Serviteur de Dieu', dans *Misc. historica A. De Meyer*, 1946, I pp. 117-30 (=*Recueil L. Cerfaux* vol. II (1954), pp. 425-37); P. Lamarche, *Christ vivant*, Cerf, 'Lectio divina' no. 43, Paris, 1966, pp. 25-43.

7. *Harpagmon hēgeisthai, morphēn labōn, hypēkoos, theou patros, schēmati.*

8. Among commentaries on the First Epistle to Timothy, that of J. Jeremias, *NTD* 9, Göttingen, 1949 is one of the most significant. See also E. Schweizer, *Erniedrigung und Erhöhung* (1962), pp. 104-8, and 'Two New Testament Credo Compared' (1962); R. Deichgräber, *Gotteshymnus und Christushymnus* (1967), pp. 133-7.

9. Thus we sometimes find explanations of this kind: ' "Justify in the Spirit": the righteousness and divinity of Christ were attested particularly by the fact of his glorious resurrection, cf. Rom 1:4. "Taken up in glory": at the ascension. But does the present text present the resurrection or the ascension as historical facts?

10. Cf. J. Jeremias, *NTD* 9 (1949), p. 21.

11. 'He who ...': Is 42:1; 52:13; Matthew 3:17; 12:18; Mark 9:7; John 1:29, 36. 'Preached among the nations': Is 52:7. Welcomed by the whole world, he is 'taken up in glory', which is surely a reference to his sitting at the right hand of the Father (Ps 110:1; Mark 16:19; Acts 2:33-34).

12. On the descent into the underworld, see for example, H. Vorgrimler, 'Questions relatives à la descente du Christ aux enfers', *Concilium* II (1966), pp. 129-39); C. Perrot, 'La descente du Christ aux enfers dans le Nouveau Testament', *LV* 87 (1968), pp. 5-29. The underworld here is not hell, where the damned go, but Sheol, the dwelling place of the

dead according to the Old Testament (cf. the excellent article by J. Guillet, in *VTB* (1970), pp. 352-6.

13. S. Lyonnet, 'Saint Paul et l'exégèse juive de son temps. À propos de Rom 10:6-8', *Mélanges A. Robert*, Paris, 1957, pp. 494-506. A longer and later article which mentions the Codex Neofiti is that of M. McNamara, *The New Testament and the Palestinian Targum to the Pentateuch*, Anal Bibl no. 27, Rome, 1966, pp. 70-81.

14. C. Spicq quotes the classic view: 'How could Christ ... not have taken advantage of his *Triduum sacrum* to go and show his compassion for the 'separated souls' like his own ... and to bring them their lost chance of salvation?' (*Les épitres de saint Pierre*, Paris, 1966, p. 137). C. Perrot, to whom we owe this reference, clearly refutes this interpretation (loc. cit., pp. 21-5). See also the detailed study by W. J. Dalton, *Christ's Proclamation to the Spirits*, Anal Bibl no. 23, Rome, 1965.

15. See the lengthy discussion by P. Benoit, 'L'Ascension' (1949), and 'Ascension', *VTB* (1970), pp. 87-92; G. Lohfink, 'Der historische Ansatz' (1963).

16. 545 days according to the *Ascension of Isaiah* 9:16 (ca. A.D. 100), 550 days according to the apocryphal letter of James 2:19 (second century), eighteen months according to the Valentians (Irenaeus, *Adv Haer* 1:3, 2) and according to the Ophites (ibid., 1:30, 14). On the figure 40, cf. H. Balz, *'tesserakonta'*, *TWNT* 8 (1966), pp. 134-9; P. Grelot, 'nombre', *VTB* (1970), pp. 833-4.

17. A. Oepke, 'nephelē', *TWNT* 4 (1942), pp. 904-12; trans. *TDNT* 4, pp. 902-10; X. Léon-Dufour, 'nuée', *VTB* (1970), pp. 845-8.

18. Cf. W. Michaelis, *'leukos'*, *TWNT* 4 (1942), pp. 247-56; G. Becquet, 'blanc', *VTB* (1970), pp. 135-6.

19. Cf. J. Goetz, 'Les religions des Primitifs', in F. M. Bergounioux and J. Goetz, *Les religions des Préhistoriques et des Primitifs*, Paris, 1958, p. 95.

20. Cf. G. Stemberger, *La symbolique* (1970), pp. 87-90, with the bibliography.

21. M. Eliade, *Traité d'histoire des religions*, Paris, 1949, p. 48; trans. *Patterns in Comparative Religion*, London, 1958, p. 39.

22. *Enoch* 70:1; 71:1; Josephus, *Antiquities* 4:8, 48 (= §326); *Apoc Moses* 37; *Life of Adam and Eve* 25-28 (which differs from 45-49).

23. M. McNamara, *N.T. and Palestinian Targum* (1966), pp. 145-9.

24. G. Kittel, 'izd^eqēf = hypsōthēnai = to be crucified', *ZNW* 35 (1936) pp. 282-5.

25. Cf. P. Grelot, *De la mort à la vie éternelle* (1971), pp. 78-9.

26. Strack-Billerbeck, I, 774.

27. E. Schweizer, 'Two N.T. Credo compared' (1962) and R. H. Fuller, *The Foundations* (1965), pp. 216-18.

28. Following E. Schweizer, *Jesus Christus* (1970), pp. 69-70.

29. H. Schlier, *Auferstehung* (1968), p. 23.

30. See the excellent study by W. Thüsing, *Erhöhungsvorstellung* (1967).

31. E. Schweizer, 'Two N.T. Credo compared' (1962), p. 126.

32. F. Hahn, *Christologische Hoheitstitel* (1963), and following him, R. H. Fuller, *The Foundations* (1965).

33. See the criticism of F. Hahn's thesis by P. Vielhauer, 'Ein Weg zur neutestamentlichen Christologie? Prüfung der Thesen Ferdinand Hahns', *EvT*, 25 (1965), pp. 24-72 (= *Aufsätze zum N.T.*, Munich, pp. 141-98).

34. Also used in Luke 24:34 and Acts 13:31 of Christ, and in Acts 9:17 and 26:16 for the appearance to Paul.

35. 'Objective', H. Grass, *Ostergeschehen* (1956), p. 248; W. Bulst, *Lexikon f.Theol u. Kirche*, I (1957), p. 1038; 'pneumatic', H. D. Wendland, *An die Korinther*, Göttingen, 1954, p. 122; J. Kremer, *Älteste Zeugnis* (1966), p. 63.

36. J. Blank, 'Auferstehung' (1969), p. 162, who agrees with J. Mouroux, *L'expérience chrétienne*, Aubier, Paris, 1952.

37. *De Abrahamo*, 8. In his commentary on this passage, A. Pelletier, 'Les apparitions du Ressuscité en termes de Septante', *Bib* 51 (1970), p. 77, skilfully distinguishes between the two classical usages: 'With the passive aorist, subject and object are directly reversed, and this has no connection with the middle voice, where the indirect object is not the agent.... The hebraism exploits an intransitive sense of *ōpthē* which is found in the Greek.'

38. Exod 23:15-17; 34:20, 23; Deut 16:16; I Sam 1:22; Is 1:12.

39. Gen 17:1; 18:1; 26:2; 35:1, 9; 48:3; Exod 3:2, 16; 4:1, 5; 6:3.

40. Not only because one cannot see God without dying (Exod 19:21; 33:20), but because in numerous cases the term introduces not a 'vision' but a 'revelation' (Gen 12:7; 26:2, 24 etc.).

41. 'We have *seen* the Lord' say Mary Magdalene (John 20:18) or the disciples (John 20:25; cf. Matthew 28:17; John 20:20). Or again, they are told 'You will *see* him' (Mark 16:7; Matthew 28:10). On the other hand, 'they did not *see*' (Luke 24:24; John 20:29; cf. ps.-Mark 16:14). We also find: *revealed himself* (John 21:1, 14; ps.-Mark 16:9, 12), *made him manifest* (Acts 10:40), *presented himself* (Acts 1:3), *stood among them* (John 20:19, 26), *came* (Matthew 28:18), *met* (Matthew 28:9), *ate and drank with* (Acts 1:4; 10:41).

42. Cf. W. Thüsing, *Erhöhung und Verherrlichung Jesu* (1960).

1. We need not discuss the often debated question, to whom the Epistle to the Galatians was addressed. In our view Paul's opponents were not gnostics (W. Schmithals, 'Die Häretiker in Galatien', *ZNW* 47 (1956), pp. 25-67), nor in all probability gentile Christians (J. Munck, *Paulus und die Heilsgeschichte*, Copenhagen, 1954, pp. 79-126) but Judaeo-Christians (cf. W. G. Kümmel, *Einleitung in das N.T.*, Heidelberg, 1963, p. 195) who in fact practised not a mitigated Judaism (Cornely, Loisy), but a judaized Christianity (Jerome, Augustine, Lagrange).

2. The translations 'in me' or 'to me' (RSV has 'to me') are both possible. But the 'outward' and non-subjective nature of the revelation must not be excluded.

3. See the detailed account of different views in E. Pfaff, *Bekehrung* (1942), pp. 3-97.

4. H. Schlier, *Der Brief an die Galater*, Vandenhoeck, Meyer's Kommentar, Göttingen, 1949, pp. 51-2.

5. That is, not the universal church, but the church of Jerusalem, following L. Cerfaux, *L'Église* (1965), p. 93 and J. Blank, 'Die Berufung' (1968), pp. 241-3.

6. U. Wilckens, 'Die Bekehrung des Paulus als religionsgeschichtliches Problem', *ZTK* 56 (1959), pp. 273-93. Cf. D. Rossler, *Gesetz und Geschichte*, Neukirchen, 1962. See also the recent contribution by J. Dupont, 'La conversion de Paul' (1970), pp. 67-88.

7. L. Cerfaux, 'Saint Paul et le "serviteur de Dieu" d'Isaïe', *Miscellenea Biblica et Orientalia A. Miller*, Rome, 1951, pp. 351-65 (= *Recueil L. Cerfaux*, II, 1954, pp. 439-54); T. Holtz, 'Zum Selbstverständnis des Apostels Paulus', *TLZ* 91 (1966), pp. 321-30; J. Blank, 'Die Berufung' (1969), pp. 226-9.

8. L. Cerfaux, 'Saint Paul et le "serviteur de Dieu"' (1951), p. 359 (= *Recueil*, p. 447).

9. J. Jeremias, *'pais theou'*, *TWNT* 5 (1954), p. 682; trans. *TDNT* 5, p. 684.

10. The prophecy of the suffering servant (Is 53) does not seem to have had any direct influence on Paul's thought; cf. J. Blank, 'Die Berufung' (1969), p. 227.

11. We refer to our article 'Une lecture chrétienne de l'Ancien Testament: Ga 3:6-4:20' in *Mélanges F. J. Leenhardt*, Labor et Fides, Geneva, 1968, pp. 109-15.

12. In Gal 1:15-16 'revelation' signifies 'an objective, eschatological (*weltenwendendes*) event, which, by the sovereign act of God, has inaugurated a new era and which is proclaimed in the gospel' (G.

Bornkamm, *Paulus*, Stuttgart, 1969, p. 44). Cf. A. M. Denis, 'L'élection et la vocation de Paul, faveurs célestes', *Revue thomiste* 57 (1957), pp. 405-28. Cf. also, by the same author, 'L'investiture de la fonction apostolique par "apocalypse" ', *RB* 64 (1957), pp. 359-62. On the other hand it does not seem right to draw a comparison with Matthew 11 : 25-26; 16 : 17-18 (ibid., pp. 422-515).

13. Following a number of scholars (cf. J. Murphy-O'Connor, 'Philippiens (l'épitre aux)', in *SDB* 7 (1965), col. 1211-20).

14. Cf. J. Dupont, *Gnosis. La connaissance religieuse dans les épitres de saint Paul*, Nauwelaerts, Louvain-Paris, 1949, pp. 51-104.

15. J. Gnilka, *Der Philipperbrief*, Herders Theologischer Kommentar, no. 10-3, Freiburg, 1968, p. 193 n. 48, follows W. Bauer, *Wörterbuch*, p. 325 (trans. Arndt and Gingrich, *Lexicon*, p. 163) in quoting an inscription which would give the word the meaning of a personal relationship with the emperors: *hē tōn Sebastōn gnōsis*.

16. A. Deissmann, *Paulus*, Tübingen, 1911, 1925, pp. 90-124; J. Lebreton, 'La contemplation dans la vie de saint Paul', *RSR* 30 (1940), p. 83; L. Cerfaux, 'L'Apôtre en présence de Dieu', *Recueil L. Cerfaux*, II (1954), pp. 472-3. [The English version does not follow the RSV here.]

17. Notwithstanding the disputed issue of the unity of the epistle, it is possible that 9 : 1-18 may form a passage which was originally independent; it is also possible to link chapters 8-10 by the common term *exousia*.

18. W. Marxsen, *Auferstehung* I (1965), p. 13; trans. *Message* (1968).

19. L. Cerfaux, *Le Christ* (1951), p. 350. More recently, J. Blank, 'Die Berufung' (1969), p. 205. Paul likes to describe himself as the 'servant of Jesus Christ' (Rom 1 : 1; II Cor 4 : 5; Gal 1 : 10; Phil 1 : 1) and plays on the antithesis between 'servant' and 'Lord' (I Cor 7 : 22-24).

20. Cf. Ps 110. W. Foerster, art. *'Kyrios'* in *TWNT* 3 (1938), p. 1088; trans. *TDNT* 3, p. 1089.

21. There is an absolute nuance in Paul's appeal which is reflected in the use of the superlative: Paul is 'the least'. In Eph 3 : 8, Paul uses only the comparative, describing himself as 'less than all the saints' (cf. I Tim 1 : 15).

22. The matter is still made a subject of controversy by those who are afraid to exaggerate or to minimize Paul's role. Following J. Blank, 'Die Berufung' (1969), p. 186, we consider that J. Geiselmann, *Jesus der Christus. Die Urform des apostolischen Kerygmas als Norm unserer Verkündigung und Theologie von Jesus Christus*, Stuttgart, 1951, p. 45, has no right to distinguish between Paul's witness concerning the appearance to him, and the witness of the Twelve concerning a datable historical event.

23. K. Wegenast, *Das Verständnis der Tradition bei Paulus und den Deuteropaulinen*, Neukirchen, 1962, sought to show this, without realizing that this is the view of Catholic tradition when properly understood (cf. *RSR* 51 (1963), pp. 601-3).

CHAPTER IV

1. The reader will find it very useful to refer to the excellent short work by G. Lohfink, *Paulus vor Damaskus* (1966), which also exists in a French translation, *La conversion de saint Paul* (1967). We have drawn very considerably from this.
2. Cf. G. Lohfink, *Paulus vor Damaskus* (1966), pp. 28-40 (French trans. pp. 39-57).
3. E. Meyer, *Die Apostelgeschichte und die Anfange des Christentums. Ursprung und Anfänge des Christentums*, Stuttgart and Berlin, III, 1923, p. 341.
4. F. J. Foakes-Jackson, *The Acts of the Apostles*, London, 1931, p. 80. See, in E. Pfaff, *Bekehrung* (1942), pp. 108-20, the desperate efforts of commentators to harmonize the texts.
5. E.g. E. Hirsch, 'Die drei Berichte der Apostelgeschichte uber die Bekehrung des Paulus', *ZNW* 28 (1929), pp. 305-12, and for a somewhat similar view, E. Trocme, *Le 'Livre des Actes' et l'histoire*, PUF, Paris, 1957, pp. 174-9.
6. M. Dibelius, 'Die Reden der Apostelgeschichte und die antike Geschichtsschreibung' (1944), in *Aufsätze zur Apostelgeschichte*, Göttingen, 1961, pp. 120-62; trans. 'The Speeches in Acts and Ancient Historiography' in *Studies in the Acts of the Apostles*, London, 1956, pp. 138-85; E. Haenchen, *Die Apostelgeschichte*, Meyer's Kommentar, Göttingen, 1961, pp. 274-5; trans. *The Acts of the Apostles*, Oxford, 1971, pp. 325-8.
7. Following E. Haenchen, *Apostelgeschichte*, pp. 274-5; trans. *Acts*, pp. 327-8.
8. These examples are gathered in G. Lohfink, *Paulus vor Damaskus* (1966), pp. 43-4 (Fr. trans. pp. 61-3). Cf. M. Dibelius, 'Die Reden', *Aufsätze*, p. 121; trans. *Speeches*, p. 139. Josephus *Antiquities*, preface 3; I: 228-31 (=XIII 2-3). The inscription is reproduced in the *Corpus Inscriptionum Latinarum* XIII: 1668. H. I. Marrou has drawn to our notice the article by J. Carcopino, *Journal des Savants* 1930 (=*Points de vue sur l'impérialisme romain*, 1934), pp. 159-99.
9. G. Lohfink, op. cit., pp. 81-2 (Fr. trans. pp. 116-18).
10. A. Wikenhauser, 'Doppelträume', *Bib* 29 (1948), pp. 100-11.
11. J. Dupont, 'Le salut des gentils et la signification théologique du

Livre des Actes', *NTS* 6 (1959-60), pp. 132-55 (= *Études*, pp. 393-419).

12. In these two passages, the use of the term does not derive from Luke (cf. Luke 11 : 49; II Cor 8 : 23; Phil 2 : 25). Cf. J. Dupont, 'Le nom d'apôtres a-t-il été donné aux Douze par Jésus?' (1962), in *L'Orient Syrien*, I (1956), pp. 267-90, 425-44.

13. See chapter 5, pp. 86-8. Cf. G. Lohfink, 'Eine alttestamenliche Darstellungsform für Gotteserscheinungen in den Damaskusberichten', *BZ* 9 (1965), pp. 246-57.

14. In the narrative of Peter and Cornelius, an identical process is found leading up to the appearance (9 : 10-16 and 10 : 10-16) : cf. 9 : 3 and 10 : 3; 9 : 17-19 and 10 : 24-27.

15. See, for example, our work *Les Évangiles* (1963), pp. 345-7.

16. Such a conviction would have made it easier for Paul to exhort the Corinthians to maintain unity by means of different individual charismas. In any case, Paul does no more than establish a comparison between the Christian community and the human body : just as the body unites the variety of limbs which compose it, so Christ is the source of the unity of the body. If the Corinthians form a body, it is because they are unified by Christ in person (I Cor 12 : 12-27); the reasoning is similar to that given a little later in Rom 12 : 4-5 : all of us, however numerous and various we may be, are 'one body in Christ' (cf. Gal 3 : 28-29). We share the opinion of L. Cerfaux, *Le Christ* (1951), p. 253; trans. *Christ in the Theology of St Paul* (1959).

CHAPTER V

1. The abbreviation ps.-Mark signifies the end of Mark, i.e. vv. 16 : 9-20. These verses have sufficient manuscript support to be declared canonical. There are however many literary indications that they should not be attributed to the author of the gospel but to a disciple of the Lord whose authority was recognized (see further details, pp. 129-30).

2. We do not however share E. Lohmeyer's hypothesis in *Galiläa und Jerusalem*, Göttingen, 1936.

3. Many studies deal with the relationship between Luke and John's accounts. Some of the most helpful are J. Schniewind, *Die Parallelperikopen bei Lukas und Johannes*, Hildesheim, 1958 (= 1914), pp. 92-6; J. Schmitt, 'Le récit de Luc' (1951), p. 231; J. A. Bailey, *The Traditions common to the Gospels of Luke and John*, Leyden, 1963; C. H. Dodd, *Historical Tradition in the Fourth Gospel*, Cambridge, 1963, p. 149.

4. See the text, given in synopsis, p. 182.

5. See A. George, 'Les récits d'apparitions aux Onze' (1969), p. 79.

6. See R. E. Brown, *John* (1970), p. 1094; cf. p. 316, n. 1.

7. This may be seen as an interpolation. For although the mention of peace is common in Luke (20 times, against 6 in John, 4 in Matthew and once in Mark), the formula 'peace to you' is specifically Johannine (20:19, 21, 26). Moreover, by contrast with John's presentation, according to Luke the gift of peace is without effect.

8. Although there is excellent manuscript evidence (even in P. 45), this verse is nevertheless typically Johannine: *touto eipōn* (John 18:1, 38; 20:14, 20:22; 21:19), *deiknȳnai*. As the whole passage is specifically Lucan, we are inclined to suppose there was an addition from the copyist who was very familiar with the gospel of John; moreover, this verse corresponds only incompletely to Jesus's command.

9. The verb *estē* is characteristic of Luke, indicating not a description but an action (cf. Matthew 12:46ff.; John 1:35; 7:37), usually a sudden appearance; it is found in narratives of visions (Luke 1:11; Acts 10:30; 16:19) but also elsewhere (Luke 5:1; 6:8; 8:44; 13:25; 24:36). In John, the expression is found only in the Easter traditions (20:14; 21:4); here it is preceded by the verb: 'he came' 20:19, 26).

10. The expression 'in the midst of', *en (tō) mesō* is also typically Lucan: Matthew (4 times), Mark (2), Luke (7), John (twice in the pericope of the woman taken in adultery), Paul (5), Rev (7). For *eis (to) meson:* 0/2/3/2/0. This too is a Lucanism.

11. We do not mention the two passages which seemed to be an interpolation: 'It is I, fear not' (24:36b; cf. Matthew 14:27 = Mark 6:50 = John 6:20), and in 24:37, the reading 'ghost' (Matthew 14:26 = Mark 6:49) instead of 'spirit'.

12. Cf. E. Pax, *Epiphaneia* (1955).

13. According to the most probable translation of the term: 'share the salt'. Cf. W. Bauer, *Wörterbuch* (1958), col. 1552; trans. Arndt and Gingrich, *Lexicon* (1957).

14. See the very interesting article by M. Kehl, 'Eucharistie und Auferstehung. Zur Deutung der Ostererscheinungen beim Mahl', *GL* (1970), pp. 90-125.

15. See my article, 'Le mystère du Pain de vie (Jean VI)', *RSR* 46 (1958), pp. 481-523.

16. *Epistle of the Apostles*, 12.

17. Ignatius of Antioch, *Smyrnians*, 3:2.

18. Thus, according to the Epistle to the Hebrews, the risen Christ gives the cloth to the servant of the high priest, and then appears to James and says to him, 'My brother, eat your bread, since the Son of man has awoken from amongst those who sleep' (Jerome, *De viris ill*, 2).

19. In spite of Jerome and M. J. Lagrange, for this aorist is close to another aorist.

20. In any case, this hypothesis cannot be attributed to Matthew.

21. As in certain theophanies (Gen 18:12; Judg 6:11-24; 13:8-20); cf. E. Lohmeyer, *Das Matthäusevangelium*, Göttingen, 1956, p. 415.

22. A. George, 'Les recits d'apparition aux Onze' (1969), p. 89.

23. A. George, 'Les recits d'apparition aux Onze' (1969), p. 93.

24. Ph. Seidensticker, *Auferstehung* (1969), pp. 67-75.

25. W. Thüsing, 'Erhöhungsvorstellung' (1967).

CHAPTER VI

1. We have recently explained our view on this subject at the Pittsburgh Festival on the Gospel, *Jesus and Man's Hope*, Pittsburgh, 1970, 'Redaktionsgeschichte of Matthew and Literary Criticism', pp. 9-35, emphasizing the value of the hypothesis of A. Gaboury, *La structure des synoptiques*, E. J. Brill, Leyden, 1970. The *Recherches de Science religieuse* propose to publish a special issue on the subject in 1972.

2. The *Gospel of Peter* was discovered in 1886. This fragment, which dates from the end of the first century, at least between the years 70 and 130, certainly echoes ancient traditions. The part of the text which concerns the events at Easter is reproduced in the appendix, p. 270-2.

3. This is the qualified opinion of L. Vaganay, *L'Évangile de Pierre* (1930), p. 81. This remains a fundamental study.

4. We disagree here with L. Vaganay, who takes the same view as T. Zahn, but we agree with G. Gardner-Smith (*JTS* 27 (1926), pp. 255-271; 401-7), and especially the excellent unpublished thesis by B. A. Johnson, *Empty Tomb Tradition in the Gospel of Peter* (1965). But it is clear that only a detailed study of this apocryphal gospel will make a final judgment possible.

5. This, however, is the method followed by most scholars who have studied the subject. See for example L. Schenke, *Tombeau vide* (1968); J. Delorme, 'Résurrection et tombeau de Jésus' (1969), pp. 105-51.

6. See for example the recent summary by E. L. Bode, *First Easter Morning* (1970), pp. 35-7. See also J. Delorme, 'Résurrection et tombeau de Jésus' (1969), pp. 113-15.

7. Cf. W. Rordorf, *Der Sonntag. Geschichte des Ruhe- und Gottesdiensttages im ältesten Christentum*, Zurich, 1962, pp. 175-87; his hypotheses are rightly criticized by E. L. Bode, op. cit., pp. 132-47, but Bode's suggestions have little more foundation.

8. J. Jeremias, *Die Abendmahlsworte Jesu, Vandenhoeck*, Göttingen, 1960, pp. 11-12 (trans. *The Eucharistic Words of Jesus*, Oxford, 1955, p. 3) refers to Mark 1:32, 35; 4:35; 10:30; 13:24; 14:12; 14:30; 14:43; 15:43.

9. M. Black, *An Aramaic Approach to the Gospels* (1954), pp. 99-100 = (1967), pp. 137-8.

10. Thus in a context where no doubt is possible, Luke writes, 'It was the day of Preparation and the sabbath was beginning (*epephōsken*)' (Luke 23:54).

11. Cf. L. Schenke, *Tombeau vide* (1968), pp. 20-30 (= p. 19-29).

12. Cf. L. Schenke, op. cit., p. 32, n. 5 (= p. 31, n. 5); J. Delorme, 'Résurrection et tombeau de Jesus' (1969), p. 132.

13. Cf. L. Schenke, op. cit., pp. 33-6 (= 31-7). We cannot accept the reasoning of F. Neyrinck, 'The Women at the Tomb' (1969), p. 175: 'Matthew, after the setting of the guard, should have omitted the theme of the anointing', for this is to assume gratuitously that Matthew had the text of Mark before him.

14. 'The "Ur"-grave we might call Sheol ... Where there is grave, there is Sheol, and where there is Sheol, there is grave' (J. Pedersen, *Israel* (1926), vol. I, p. 462).

15. Following G. Schille, 'Das Leiden des Herrn' (1955), pp. 161-205 (cf. X. Léon-Dufour, art. 'Passion [récits de la]', *SDB* 6 (1960), pp. 1426, 1437), J. Delorme, 'Résurrection et tombeau de Jesus' (1969), pp. 126-33 and L. Schenke, *Tombeau vide* (1968), pp. 86-113 (= pp. 87-116) have put forward the hypothesis that the narrative of Mark 16:1-8 took shape in the course of an annual Easter celebration in the form of a pilgrimage to the tomb of Jesus. So, recently, B. van Iersel, in *Concilium* 60 (1970), p. 58. In the view of several scholars, there is no firm support for this hypothesis (cf. E. L. Bode, *First Easter Morning* (1970), pp. 130-2).

16. A. Vögtle, 'Literarische Gattungen und Formen. Die Evangelien', in *Anzeiger für die kath. Geistlichkeit* 74 (1965), pp. 2-3. We learnt of this article from L. Schenke, *Tombeau vide* (1969), pp. 65-71 (= pp. 67-73). In the present work, the reader may refer to the synopsis on pp. 130-1.

17. P. Benoit, 'Marie-Madeleine' (1964). The reader will find the text of John in this work, pp. 169-70.

18. J. Delorme, 'Résurrection et tombeau de Jésus' (1969), p. 138.

19. Luke 24:12 is usually considered to be older than Luke 24:24 and John 20:3-10. We should return to the question in chapter 10 in relation to the point of view of John's gospel. See R. E. Brown, *John* (1970), p. 1004.

20. At the present time most scholars regard Luke 24:12 as authentic. Not only is it attested by the best manuscripts, including p. 75, but it is easier to understand why it should have been omitted than added. Cf. A. Nisin, *Histoire de Jésus*, Paris 1961, pp. 33-7, and R. E. Brown, *John* (1970), p. 969.

21. See pp. 171-5.

22. Especially F. Neyrinck, 'Les femmes au tombeau' (1969), who in addition to his judicious remarks, has carried the two-source theory to the utmost degree.

23. We owe these comments to the thesis by B. A. Johnson, *Empty Tomb Tradition* (1965).

24. The text is given in the appendix, pp. 270-2.

25. J. Dupont, 'L'interpretation des psaumes dans les Actes des Apôtres' (1962), in *Études*, p. 289. See also '*Ta Hosia ta pista* (Actes 13 : 34 = Isaie 55 : 3)', (1961), in *Études*, pp. 337-59. Our interpretation is valid, even if the Hebrew term *shaḥat* means corruption (cf. R. E. Murphy, *Bib* 39 (1958), pp. 61-6).

26. See the judicious comments by E. Pousset, 'La Résurrection', *NRT* 91 (1969), p. 1017.

CHAPTER VII

1. Of various studies, we draw attention in particular to J. Delorme, 'Résurrection et tombeau de Jésus' (1969); L. Schenke, *Tombeau vide* (1968). A detailed summary of recent opinions and a personal point of view can be found in E. L. Bode, *First Easter Morning* (1970).

2. E.g. the crowd at the healing of the man with the unclean spirit (Mark 1 : 27) or Peter on the occasion of the miraculous draft of fishes (Luke 5 : 9).

3. Cf. J. Delorme, 'Résurrection et tombeau de Jésus' (1969), p. 109, who quotes C. F. D. Moule, 'St. Mark 16 : 8 once more', *NTS* 2 (1955-6), pp. 58-9.

4. W. G. Kümmel, *Introduction to the New Testament*, London, 1966, quoted by E. L. Bode, *First Easter Morning* (1970), p. 47.

5. L. Schenke, *Tombeau vide* (1968), pp. 49-52, n. 71 (= pp. 50-3, n. 71).

CHAPTER VIII

1. Typical of this view is F. Neyrinck, 'Les femmes au tombeau' (1968-1969).

2. Noted, but not worked out by P. Gaechter, *Das Matthäus—Evangelium*, Innsbruck, 1963, p. 945.

3. See my *Etudes d'Évangile* (1965), pp. 49-63.

4. Cf. Gen 16 : 7; 22 : 11; Exod 3 : 2; see p. 314, n. 7.

5. J. Villett, *La résurrection du Christ dans l'art chrétien du IIe an VIIe siècle* (1957), p. 16. It is not without interest to mention, without necessarily sharing, the author's regrets:

'The rising from the tomb, which for us forms the very substance of the resurrection of Christ, so that we can scarcely imagine that it could ever have been represented otherwise, is something which Christians do not seem to have thought of portraying in a picture before the 9th-10th centuries in the East and the 11th century in the West.... The portrait of the Saviour coming out of the tomb never appears in the art of the generations which were still close to the birth of Christianity. There can be no doubt that the possibility of such a portrait never entered their minds. Yet no subject would have been a better response to the anguish at death which was so powerful in the generations of the imperial age...' (pp. 16-17).

And these lines were written only fifteen years ago! But the author carried out his study precisely in order to show that 'from the first half of the 3rd century the dogma of the resurrection of Christ gave rise to a number of images' (p. 18) which have nothing to do with Christ coming out of the tomb, a banner in his hand, the terrified guards protecting their eyes against the intolerable light of the mystery.

6. *Syriac Didascalia*, XXI: 'In the night when the Sunday began, he appeared...'; 'You are particularly recommended to fast on Friday and Saturday ... and also to wait and hope for the resurrection of our Lord Jesus Christ, until the third hour of the night which follows the Saturday,' that is, until nine o'clock in the evening. Similarly, Aphraates, *Hom*, XII, 6, and the addition which the *Codex Bobbiensis* makes to Mark 16:4: *subito autem ad tertiam horam tenebrae diei factae sunt per totum orbem.*

7. Several Old Testament texts 'do not distinguish clearly between the angel and Yahweh, and see the former not as a messenger but as a sort of manifestation of Yahweh himself, appearing to men in human form. In this context, the narrators—mainly Gen 22:11 ff. and Jg 6:17 ff.—talk of Yahweh in one sentence and of his angel in the next.' (G. von Rad, *Théologie de l'Ancien Testament*, t.1, Genève 1963, p. 251). See Gen 22:11; Exod 3:2; compare Exod 23:20-30; Josh 5:13; Judg 2:1; 6:12-14.

8. W. Trilling, 'Les traits essentiels' (1964), p. 30.

CHAPTER IX

1. P. Schubert, 'The Structure and Significance of Luke 24' (1954), pp. 165-88; A. R. C. Leaney, 'The Resurrection Narrative in Luke 24:12-53', *NTS* 2 (1955-6), pp. 110-14); J. Schmitt, 'Les récits des apparitions aux Onze' (1969), pp. 75-104.

2. See my extended comment on Luke's narrative form in *Intr Bibl*

(1959), II, p. 237, and in *Les Évangiles* (1963), pp. 199-200.

3. On the authenticity of Luke 24:12, see p. 312, n. 20.

4. The only other mention of witnesses are those put in the mouth of Paul: 22:15; 26:16 (Paul), 22:20 (Stephen). See p. 73 and also *Les Évangiles* (1963), pp. 244-56, with bibliographical notes.

5. See my book, *Les Évangiles* (1963), pp. 260-5.

6. See *Les Évangiles* (1963), pp. 198-203; *Intr Bibl* (1959), pp. 238-40.

7. With John 20:12, Luke is alone in calling Jesus's corpse 'body' (*sōma*): (Luke 24:3, 23).

8. See *Intr Bibl*, II (1959), p. 235.

9. According to Philo, *De op. mundi*, 105, quoted by Ph. Seidensticker, *Auferstehung Jesu* (1967), p. 94; cf. Dan 10:5.

10. Cf. Deut 17:6; 19:15; Matthew 18:16; Acts 1:10; II Cor 13:1; I Tim 5:19; Heb 10:28.

11. A. Loisy, *L'Évangile selon Luc*, Ceffonds, 1924, p. 584.

12. Following P. Schubert, 'The Structure and Significance of Luke 24' (1954), p. 174, rather than J. Schmitt, 'Le récit ... de Luc' (1961), p. 235, who believes that Luke 'drew on various sources', particularly for vv. 13-15, 18, 28-31, 33.

13. E. Lohmeyer, *Das Evanelium des Markus*, Göttingen, 1951, p. 362; E. Schweizer, *Das Evangelium nach Markus*, Göttingen, 1967, p. 217.

14. J. Dupont, 'Les pèlerins d'Emmaüs' (1953), p. 365.

15. A. Puech, *Histoire de la littérature grècque chrétienne*, vol. I, Paris, 1928, p. 115, quoted by L. Cerfaux, *La voix vivante de l'Évangile*, Tournai, 1956, pp. 97-9, who himself is referred to by J. Dupont, art. cit., p. 371, n. 63.

16. My attention was drawn to this lay-out by an unpublished study by G. Stemberger.

17. Cf. J. Dupont, 'Les pèlerins d'Emmaüs' (1953), p. 361.

18. Cf. J. Dupont, 'Les pèlerins d'Emmaüs' (1953), p. 364, n. 43; 'Le repas d'Emmaüs' (1957), p. 89. See above, chapter 5, pp. 92-3.

19. We owe a great deal to the study by G. Stemberger (cf. n. 16).

20. Cf. for example, Luke 4:6 with Matthew 4:9; Luke 4:20-22 with Matthew 13:54; Luke 5:26 with Matthew 9:8; Luke 6:11 with Matthew 12:14.

21. *Psēlaphaō* is found only in Acts 17:27; Heb 12:18; I John 1:1. *Sarx* is found only once elsewhere in Luke, in a quotation from Isaiah, Luke 3:6. *Ostea* is found only once in Matthew, Luke and John.

22. E. Sjöberg, art, 'pneuma', *TWNT* 6 (1957), p. 374; trans. *TDNT* 6, p. 376.

23. Cf. II Sam 19:13; Gen 29:14; Judg 9:2; II Sam 5:1; I Chron 11:1. In Job 2:5 there is a similar interpretation (cf. the reading of some manuscripts which in Eph 5:30 add to the word body (*sōma*) the words 'of his flesh and of his bones').

24. E. Schweizer, art, *'sarx'*, *TWNT* 7 (1960), p. 124; trans. *TDNT* 7.

25. E. Schweizer, art, *'pneuma'*, *TWNT* 6 (1957), p. 413; trans. *TDNT* 6, p. 412.

26. E. Schweizer, art, *'sarx'*, p. 99.

27. Lucian of Somosata (ca. A.D. 120-80), *Verae historiae,* II, 12 (ed. G. Dindorf, Paris, 1867, p. 290), quoted by E. Schweizer, art, *'sarx'*, p. 124, n. 211.

28. See chapter 11, p. 214.

29. See the indications in *Intr Bibl*, II, pp. 243-4, and in *Les Évangiles* (1963), p. 203-5.

30. P. A. van Stempvoort, 'The Interpretation of the Ascension' (1958), pp. 30-42.

31. See *Intr Bibl*, II (1959), pp. 244-5.

CHAPTER X

1. Here, however, are a few indications. The material of the narrative falls into two parts. In vv. 1-14, Jesus manifests himself to his disciples by Lake Tiberias, and in vv. 15-23, he entrusts to Peter the task of feeding his sheep; and then he reveals what Peter's lot will be, as well as that of the beloved disciple. The tripartite structure can be recognized. There is the initiative of the risen Christ (4-5), the gradual recognition by the disciples (6-13) and the entrusting of the mission (15-23). The redaction of the appearance narrative is based on a very ancient tradition, perhaps the oldest we possess. There is an echo of it in the *Gospel of Peter* (58-60):

> Now it was the last day of unleavened bread, and many were coming forth and returning unto their own homes because the feast was at an end. But we, the Twelve disciples of the Lord, were weeping and were in sorrow, and each one being grieved for that which had befallen departed unto his own house. But I, Simon Peter, and Andrew my brother, took our nets and went unto the sea: and there was with us....

According to this apocryphal gospel, the appearance on the side of the lake preceded every other appearance. Similarly, in John 21, the disciples have taken up their profession of fishermen once again: 'I am going fishing,' says Simon Peter (3), an attitude which is difficult to understand if it follows the appearance narrated in John 20. This is why the redactor tries to harmonize the two by saying that this was 'the third time' that Jesus had revealed himself (14). Johannine symbolism is clearly in evidence. The seven disciples probably represent the church in its totality (cf. the seven churches of Revelations); the hundred and fifty-three large fish correspond to the arithmetical sum of the first seventeen numbers (formula $\frac{n+1}{2}$), which formed the triangular figure of which the ancient world was so fond (each side of the triangle represents the same number of points, and each line is one unit greater, beginning at the top, and so forming a pyramid, the base of which in this case is 17. This represents the fullness of the human race for which Simon Peter and the church are going to fish. The fact that Simon Peter is naked recalls his awareness of being a sinner (cf. 5:8). We must in any case note the numerous similarities between this narrative and that of the miraculous draft of fishes in Luke 5:1-11, which is evidence for a tradition concerning an appearance meant specially for Peter. (Cf. R. E. Brown, *John* (1970), pp. 1085-1092). Finally, let us not forget the theme of the meal.

2. R. Bultmann, *Das Evangelium des Johannes*, Göttingen, 1959; trans. *The Gospel of John: A Commentary*, Oxford, 1971.

3. G. Hartmann, 'Die Vorlage der Osterberichte in Jo 20' (1964), pp. 197-220.

4. P. Benoit, 'Marie-Madeleine' (1960). See p. 114.

5. R. E. Brown, *John* (1970), pp. 998-1004.

6. Chrysostom, in Jo 85:4=PG 59,465.

7. Cf. C. H. Dodd, 'The Appearances' (1957), p. 33.

8. I have discussed this in detail in *Mélanges A. Robert* (1957), p. 393-394, and in my *Études* (1965), pp. 73-5.

9. F. M. Catherinet, 'Note sur un verset' (1950), p. 55.

10. Cassian (Serge Besobrasoff), *La Pentecôte johannique: John 20: 19-23*, Valence, 1939.

11. Cf. J. Schmitt, 'Simples remarques sur le fragment Jo XX, 22-23' (1956), pp. 415-23.

12. Cf. E. C. Hoskyns, C. K. Barrett, C. H. Dodd, R. E. Brown.

13. Ignatius, *To the Smyrnians*, 3:2; *Epistle of the Apostles*, 12 (see the text in the appendix, p. 273).

14. Cf. R. E. Brown, *John* (1970), p. 1047.

15. R. Bultmann's interpretation is rejected by most scholars.

16. Cf. *Apocryphon of James*, 3:13-24.

CHAPTER XI

1. See G. Ebeling, in *Die Religion in Geschichte und Gegenwart*, Tübingen, 1959, III, col. 242-62; R. Marle, *Le problème théologique de l'herméneutique*, Paris, 1968; R. Marle, *Herméneutique et catéchèse*, Paris, 1970; P. Ricoeur, *Le conflit des interprétations. Essais d'hermén-*

eutique, Paris, 1969; *Exégèse et herméneutique* (Proceedings of the 2nd congress of the ACFEB), Seuil, Paris, 1971.

2. Cf. J. Moingt, 'Certitude historique et foi', *RSR* 58 (1970), pp. 561-574.

3. J. Moingt notes that several theologians talk of 'meta-historical facts' (loc. cit., p. 571). I have myself made various suggestions in *RSR* 57 (1969), p. 618 and in the review *Études* (1970), pp. 610-11.

4. Cf. M. de Certeau, 'Faire de l'histoire', *RSR* 58 (1970), pp. 481-520.

5. This is why in 'L'exégète et l'évènement historique', *RSR* 58 (1970), p. 552, I criticize dogmatic theologians and popularizers who accuse exegetical scholars of lacking 'the theological courage' to 'take a step further' than the letter of the text in order to say 'what really took place', for example at the transfiguration of Jesus or in the appearances of the risen Christ.

6. So particularly R. Bultmann, who refuses to place the basis of his faith in any historical fact: 'The historical problem is scarcely relevant to Christian belief in the resurrection,' 'Neues Testament und Myth-ologie' (1941), pp. 46-7; trans. 'New Testament and Mythology' in *Kerygma and Myth* (1953), p. 42.

7. E.g. in 'L'exégète et l'évènement historique', *RSR* 58 (1970), pp. 555-9.

8. See chapter 1, pp. 6-12.

9. The same remark could be made in other cases, such as I Cor 15 : 23; Gal 1 : 18, 21; I Thess 4 : 17.

10. Ph. Seidensticker, 'Das antiochenische Glaubensbekenntnis' (1967); *Auferstehung Jesu* (1967), pp. 24-30.

11. So, amongst others, H. Grass, *Ostergeschehen* (1962), pp. 38-9, 74-85, 126; F. Gils, 'Pierre et la foi au Christ ressuscité' (1962); J. Kremer, *Älteste Zeugnis* (1966), pp. 67-70; W. Marxsen, *Auferstehung* II (1968), pp. 85-94 (i.e. the faith of Peter); trans. *Resurrection* (1970).

12. R. E. Brown, *John* (1970), pp. 1085-92.

13. See p. 73.

14. See the text of this narrative in the appendix, p. 270.

15. *Summa Th* III. 55.5, 'the resurrection . . . transcends human reason . . . Christ did not prove the resurrection to his disciples by "reasons" but by what were visible "signs" meant to demonstrate some truth.'

16. This is the conclusion of my study of the gospels, *Les Évangiles* (1963), pp. 372-450.

17. E. Pousset, 'La Résurrection', *NRT* 91 (1969), p. 1017.

18. See the summary of opinions in E. L. Bode, *First Easter Morning* (1970), pp. 151-75.

19. W. Marxsen, *Die Auferstehung* II (1968), pp. 85-94; trans. *Resurrection* (1970); H. W. Bartsch, *Das Auferstehungszeugnis, sein histor-isches und theologisches Problem*, Hamburg, 1965, p. 22.

20. H. Grass, *Ostergeschehen* (1962), pp. 183-4; P. Althaus, *Die Wahrheit des christlichen Osterglaubens*, Gütersloh, 1940, pp. 26-7.

21. G. Baldensperger, 'Le tombeau vide', *RHPR* 12 (1932), pp. 413-43; *RHPR* 13 (1933), pp. 105-44; *RHPR* 14 (1934), pp. 97-125. For the problem of the burial of Jesus, see the well documented arguments by J. Blinzler, *Der Prozess Jesu* (1969).

22. M. Goguel, *La Foi à la Résurrection* (1933), pp. 130-71.

23. J. Schmitt, 'Jesus ressuscité' (1949), pp. 117-18.

24. H. von Campenhausen, *Ablauf* (1966); P. Benoit, 'Marie-Madeleine' (1964); A. Vögtle (cf. chapter 6, n. 16), p. 160. My view is found pp. 114-16.

25. J. Delorme, 'Résurrection et tombeau de Jésus' (1969), p. 143.

26. W. Trilling, 'Les traits essentiels' (1964), pp. 21-3.

27. H. Grass, *Ostergeschehen* (1962), pp. 126-7.

28. Cf. H. Schlier, *Auferstehung* (1968), p. 23 (=p. 26).

29. See chapter 1, pp. 18-19.

30. See, e.g., M. Carrez, 'L'herméneutique paulinienne de la Résurrection' (1969), pp. 55-65.

31. See especially W. Thüsing, *Erhöhung* (1960).

32. Elsewhere I have described the message of Jesus from the point of view of eschatology, theology and christology (*Les Évangiles* (1963), pp. 377-450). Here eschatology rejoins theology, and christology is a stage which follows ecclesiology.

33. I have already argued this view myself, *Les Évangiles* (1963), p. 449.

34. The resurrection of Jesus 'is not another event *after* his passion and his death, but the manifestation (*Erscheinung*) of what took place in the death of Christ.... Good Friday and Easter can be seen as two interlinked aspects of what is strictly one and the same event in the being of Christ' (K. Rahner, 'Dogmatische Fragen zur Osterfrömmigkeit' (1959), p. 166).

35. That is why we cannot retain certain expressions which have become popular at the present day. Are we to suppose that the 'resurrection took place at the end of time or at the moment of death?' asks P. Benoit, in *Concilium* 60 (1970), pp. 91-8. And L. Boros replies firmly: 'The resurrection is realized at once in the death' (ibid., p. 17). Many necessary qualifications are included, but they are insufficient, because the term resurrection is firmly tied to a particular spatio-temporal pattern and to the destiny of the whole of humanity. The mystery of what took place after death can be envisaged only with the help of the two primitive forms of terminology by which the Easter faith is expressed: Christ is risen, and Christ is exalted in glory. With due modification, this is true of other men. Thus we should say that what took place at death was

not the resurrection, but the *glorification*, which derives from the terminology of *exaltation*.

36. For the Johannine dialogues, see my brief comments in *Les Évangiles* (1963), pp. 116-24. See the recent work by H. Leroy, *Rätsel und Missverständnis. Ein Beitrag des Johannesevangeliums*, Bonn, 1968.

37. See chapter 5, pp. 86-7.

38. Catholic tradition does not lay down any view about the link between the risen body and its earthly body. While there are those who have maintained the necessity of a material link with the corpse (Scheeben, Lépicier, d'Alès, Piolanti, de Broglie), others, following Durand de Saint-Pourçain, believe that in order to ensure the continuity of the resurrected person with him who was alive, the identity of the substantial form, i.e. the soul, is sufficient. Cf. L. Ciappi, 'La risurrezione dei morti secondo la dottrina cattolica', *Gregorianum* 39 (1958), p. 216-20. See also E. Gutwenger, 'Auferstehung und Auferstehungsleib Jesu', *ZKT* 91 (1969), pp. 42-9. Finally, the reader may compare what I have said with the excellent study by K. Rahner, 'Pour une théologie de la mort, in *Écrits théologiques*, t.III, Paris 1963, pp. 113-21, on 'Death, separation of body and spirit'.

39. The recent word 'reanimation' belongs to medical vocabulary: 'an action which consists in restoring the movements of the part of the respiratory apparatus which have just ceased' (Garnier, quoted in the *Dictionnaire Petit Robert*). If this word is used, it is no doubt because of its association with the idea of a dead body. This brings us back once again to the 'resurrection of Lazarus'. To adopt this term would be to make the communication of the mystery even harder, by identifying the resurrection with a medical act. It is enough to restore the body of the traditional word 'resurrection'.

40. The reason why the tradition so much stressed the material aspect of the resurrection body was that it was reacting against gnostic attempts to deny the resurrection of the 'flesh' at the end of time, or to 'spiritualize' the resurrected body to the extent of a radical breach with what was the historic body. It was necessary to maintain, throughout the total transformation due to the resurrection, the reality of the body and the value of matter. There was of course a long tradition which authorized such a representation: the magnificent vision of Ezekiel (chapter 37) of the dry bones being covered with flesh while waiting for the spirit to bring them back to life, the gospel narratives of the resurrection appearances, and Jewish traditions such as that which maintained that there existed in man's spinal column an almond-shaped bone, unbreakable and even incorruptible until the last judgment (according to Joshua ben Hananiah, *Gen r* on 6:7, ed. Freedman, Soncino, London, 1961, p. 224; *Lev r* 15, ed. Slotki, Soncino, London, 1961, p. 225; cf. J. Bonsirven, *Le Judaïsme Palestinien au temps de*

Jésus-Christ, Beauchesne, Paris, 1935, vol. I, p. 484; P. Volz, *Die Eschatologie der jüdischen Gemeinde im nt.chen Zeitalter*, Tübingen, 1934, pp. 250-1); and also numerous church fathers who described life after death on the pattern of earthly life, for example by saying that we will rise again with bones, nerves and veins (cf. G. Greshake, *Die Auferstehung der Toten* (1969), p. 362 n. 10). For a long time, and even sometimes at the present day, there have been theologians who considered that the resurrection body would have a particular link with the dead body, even though the latter had been decomposed for centuries; but in spite of their appeal to the axiom that nothing is impossible to God, their opinion never carried the day (cf. above, n. 38).

41. Our concern is not of course to *harmonize* the statements of faith with scientific discoveries, but to *express* faith in a language which is more comprehensible at the present day.

42. 'It is in the persistence of structure ... that we see the concrete basis of the individuality of each living being' (E. Cahane, *La vie n'existe pas!*, Union rationaliste, Paris, 1962, p. 172), quoted by C. Tresmontant, *Le probleme de l'âme*, Seuil, Paris, 1971, p. 156. The same writer records the opinion of a number of geneticists, holding different philosophical opinions, either Marxist, rationalist or spiritualist. What is transmitted from one generation to another is 'a certain characteristic structure of coded macromolecules' (J. Lejeune, preface to the book by J. de Crouchy, *Le Message héréditaire*, Paris, 1965, p. ix). C. Tresmontant concludes: 'For a century biologists have not only rediscovered the Aristotelian analysis that can be found in the *De anima*, but have discovered something more ... that the information principle, the structural principle, subsists in spite of the continued renewal of matter.... This structure is relatively independent of the material elements integrated into it, because it subsists when they have been changed' (op. cit., p. 161). In short, what Aristotle calls the (animal) *soul*, geneticists call *structure*. So long as they are not understood within a dualist anthropology, these propositions can indicate what the outcome of the divine action consists of: it raises a man whose structure, received at his conception and modified by his freedom in the course of his life until his death, can be restored once again. And from this point of view, there is no longer any question of the natural immortality of the soul, but only of the gift of life after death.

43. Numerous contemporaries are concerned to know what happened to the body of Jesus, whereas for the disciples there was no problem: they could suppose that he had been transferred and glorified in another place. For the Hebrews, the 'world' is not a static reality, but an event which is gradually unfurled, something which manifests itself to man in a constantly new aspect, which appears in the most diverse forms, and, as such, is far more difficult to grasp as an abstract concept, at least by

reduction to a principle. Israel did not consider the world to be a structured organism resting on itself' (G. von Rad, *Theology of the Old Testament*, vol. I). Unity of the world comes from God alone. Following the Hebrews, Christians have no difficulty in imagining a plurality of worlds, one of them being reserved as the heavenly dwelling of the blessed, as shown in the map of Peter Appianus, dated in 1539 (A. Koyre, *Du monde clos a l'univers infini*, PUF, Paris, 1962, p. 31). Only in recent years have theologians given up making heaven and hell 'places' existing in parallel to our own world.

It is a long way from a cosmology of this kind to our own, and there is still a great temptation to imagine what happened to the body of Jesus as a function of the way we ourselves represent cosmology or anthropology. Let us clearly repeat that the wise course is to abstain from all curiosity, since the gospel narratives do not offer any possible solution. If one persists in seeking an explanation, it must be realized that one is at the mercy of an ingenuity which has no basis in scripture. There is even the risk of confusing separate terminologies. To ask what happened to the dead body of Christ is to imagine that his remains still belong to the natural and historical order in which we live as mortal and sinful human beings, even though it is affirmed at the same time, in the name of faith, that Christ in his total person has triumphed over death and sin.

Yet there are many who turn their minds to ingenious solutions of the question raised by the fact of the discovery of the empty tomb, from which the body had disappeared. From the time of the first Christians there were those who imagined that the body had been stolen. At the present day, there are those who think that the body must have been moved elsewhere, that the women went to the wrong tomb, and so forth. All agree in appealing to some kind of rational evidence to take account of a fact, the interpretation of which is intrinsically linked to the mystery of the resurrection, which is a mystery of faith.

Let us add a final point, concerning the language used. We often read statements like the following: 'Even if the skeleton of Jesus had been found in his tomb, this would make no difference to the fact of his resurrection.' We refuse to use this kind of expression, because it contradicts the meaning of the New Testament. It moves to an improper extent from the question of terminology (the statement that the body was absent) to that of fact (what happened to the body). Even if, because of present-day anthropology or cosmology, our contemporaries suppose that they still believe in the resurrection of Jesus although they think that Jesus's skeleton remained in the tomb, this was not so at all for the disciples at the time of Jesus: if they had found the body in the tomb, they could not have accepted the resurrection nor proclaimed it to their contemporaries. Thus the hypothesis of the skeleton found in the tomb lacks historical foundation, contradicts the statement in the text and makes it impossible to read. Before daring to declare that things must have taken place in one way or another, we must therefore make clear the issue of the terminology in which they are recorded.

44. This has been clearly shown by W. Thüsing, *Erhöhungsvorstellung und Parusieerwartung* (1969), arguing against F. Hahn, *Christologische Hoheitstitel* (1963), and implicitly in disagreement with an admirer of the latter, R. H. Fuller, *The Foundations* (1965).

45. In addition to the excellent book by W. Thüsing, mentioned in the previous note, see also the contribution of J. Dupont, published in the *Actes du symposium sur la Résurrection du Christ*, Rome, Easter, 1970.

46. An attempt at a systematic presentation has been made by R. Slenczka, *Geschichtlichkeit und Personsein Jesu Christi. Studien zur christologischen Problematik der historischen Jesusfrage*, Vandenhoeck, Göttingen, 1967. See also A. Stock, *Einheit des Neuen Testaments. Erörterung hermeneutischer Grundpositionen der heutigen Theologie*, Benzinger, Einsiedeln, 1969.

CONCLUSION

1. 'Qu'attendre d'un exégète?', *Études*, October 1967, pp. 318-22.
2. Cf. M. de Certeau, 'Faire de l'histoire', *RSR* 58 (1970), pp. 481-520.

APPENDIX

1. An excellent study has recently appeared: F. Kamphaus, *Von der Exegese zur Predigt* (1968). H. Grass, *Ostergeschehen* (1962), pp. 281-7 previously tried to supply some examples of how the resurrection can be preached. So too has J. Kremer, *Älteste Zeugnis* (1966), pp. 131-44, though he restricts himself more to basic principles.

Index

Point of view: the message, *139-49*; the triple dimension, 94-8, 146-7; the Lordship of Christ, 97-8, 99, 103, 147-9; appearance at the tomb, 146.

Preaching: 250-2.

METHOD OF THE WORK: ix, *xx-xxii*, 3-4, 5, 62, 80-1, 105-6, 127, 150, 193-4, 200, 219, 229, 245-8.

ORIGINAL SETTING: *92-4*, 161-7.

PAUL
Appearance: described by, *46-59*; narrated by Luke, 63-79; vocation, 48-50, 51-3, 69; recognizing of Jesus, 58-9, 78; and appearances to the Twelve, 69, 73, 74, 77; and other visions, 51, 57, 58-9; Paul's language, 48-51, 56-7, 58-9, 78-9, 214; and the empty tomb, 122.
Hermeneutic of the Resurrection: 221-4, 244.

PEACE (GIFT OF): 84, 89, *183-4*, 255.

RESURRECTION OF JESUS
Terminology: 7-15, 36-7, 42-4, 225.
Language: problem, x-xii, xvi-xx, origin, 15-22; patterns of thought, 4, 38-42; underlying symbolism, 16-17; limits, 22-4, 103, 217-18; standard terminology, 218-19, 248-9.
Relation to: exaltation, 38-42; life, 153-4, 219-21, 223-4; death of Christ, 10-14, 231; 22-3, 51, 229-30, 231; history, 229-30.
The event: prophesied, 11, 15, 153-5; produced, 7-8, 12-14, 229-30; date, 8, 137, 229; attested, 9-15, 111-13, 155-7, 204-6; known, xx-xxi, 196-7, 205, 207, 229-30; symbolized, 230-1; actual, 10, 14, 99-100; interpreted, 198, 217-45; communicated, 247-8; badly related, 245-6.
Iconography: 143-4.
See Appearances, Sunday, Exaltation, Third Day, Life.

RESURRECTION OF THE DEAD: Jewish beliefs, 17-19; and resurrection of Jesus, 7, 221-2; and bodies of the risen, 21, 122, 236-8; moment, 319[35]; and glorification, 319[35]; language, 19-20, 22.
See Soul, Anthropology, Body, Lifting up to Heaven of the Righteous Man, Immortality, Sheol.

SHEOL: 11, 14, 18, 30, 36-7, 100; defeat of, 110, 124, 141, 252; Jesus descends to, 30-1, 113; and representation of the universe, 260. *See* Anthropology, Death, Resurrection of the Dead.

SOUL: 18, 20, 321[42]. *See* Body, Immortality.